GENDER AND EQUALITY IN MUSLIM FAMILY LAW

GENDER AND EQUALITY IN MUSLIM FAMILY LAW

Justice and Ethics in the Islamic Legal Tradition

Edited by
Ziba Mir-Hosseini, Kari Vogt,
Lena Larsen and Christian Moe

I.B. TAURIS
LONDON · NEW YORK

Paperback edition first published in 2017
by I.B.Tauris & Co. Ltd
London • New York
www.ibtauris.com

First published in hardback in 2013 by
I.B.Tauris & Co. Ltd

ISBN: 978 1 78453 740 1
eISBN: 978 0 85773 352 8

A full CIP record for this book is available from the British Library
A full CIP record is available from the Library of Congress

Library of Congress Catalog Card Number: available

Printed and bound by CPI Group (UK) Ltd, Croydon, CR0 4YY

MIX
Paper from
responsible sources
FSC® C013604

TABLE OF CONTENTS

ACKNOWLEDGEMENTS

Besides the authors of the following chapters, we would like to thank the many other scholars who made notable contributions to the discussions in our workshops: the Grand Mufti of Egypt, 'Ali Jum'a; the President of the Mohammedia League of Moroccan *'Ulamā'*, Ahmed Abbadi; and Mohammad Hashim Kamali (Malaysia), Syed Tahir Mahmood (India), Mohammed Khamlichi (Morocco), Abdelkarim Khamlichi (Morocco), Amira Sonbol (Qatar), Heba Raouf Ezzat (Egypt), Fikret Karčić (Bosnia-Herzegovina), Mohammed Fadel (Canada), Arzoo Osanloo (USA), Usama Hasan (UK), Hania El Sholkamy (Egypt), Mohamed Ahmed Serag (Egypt), Tahar Mahdi (France), Maleiha Malik (UK), Ali Mabrouk (Egypt), Azza Soliman (Egypt), Homa Hoodfar (Canada) and Ibodullo Kalonov (Tajikistan).

A warm thanks also to Aïcha El Hajjami, for helping to organise the Marrakech workshop; and to Gunilla Soliman and Mulki Al-Sharmani at the American University in Cairo, and the staff of the Norwegian Embassy in Cairo, for assistance with the two workshops there.

We wish to thank the Norwegian Ministry of Foreign Affairs for supporting this project.

The Editors

A NOTE ON TRANSLITERATION AND OTHER CONVENTIONS

Transliteration of Arabic words in this book follows the example of the *International Journal of Middle East Studies*. We distinguish between technical terms, on the one hand, and names, on the other. Only italicised technical terms are fully transliterated, with diacritics indicating long vowels (*ā*, *ī*, *ū*) and emphatic consonants (*ḍ*, *ḥ*, *ṣ*, *ṭ*, *ẓ*). The *tā' marbūṭa* and initial *hamza* are not transliterated, and *ā* is used both with *alif* and *alif maqṣūra*. Names are capitalised; diacritics are not used, but *'ayn* (') and *hamza* (') are marked. Some terms are also considered to have entered the English language. Accordingly, we write Qur'an, Shi'i, Sunni and Shari'a, as well as hadith, fatwa, mufti, jihad and hajj. A simplified Persian transliteration is sometimes used alongside the Arabic. Other local spellings are used for official names (e.g. Syariah Court in Indonesia).

All dates are Common Era; Hijri dates (whether Shamsi or Qamari) are only given in a few references to publications that use them. Qur'anic verses are cited as, for example, '4:34'.

INTRODUCTION

Muslim Family Law and the Question of Equality

Ziba Mir-Hosseini, Kari Vogt, Lena Larsen and Christian Moe

Gender equality is a modern ideal, which has only recently, with the expansion of human rights and feminist discourses, become inherent to generally accepted conceptions of justice. In Islam, as in other religious traditions, the idea of equality between men and women was neither relevant to notions of justice nor part of the juristic landscape. To use an idiom from Islamic juristic tradition, gender equality is among the 'newly created issues' (*masā'il mustaḥdatha*), that is, one of those issues for which there is no previous ruling. It is an issue that Muslim jurists have not had to address until the twentieth century. In the second half of the century, with the adoption of the United Nations Convention on the Elimination of all forms of Discrimination against Women (CEDAW), gender equality acquired a clear international mandate. Since it came into force in 1981, CEDAW has been ratified by all Muslim states except three (Iran, Somalia and Sudan); in most cases, however, ratification has been subject to 'Islamic reservations', which speak of unresolved tensions.

This book explores the political and hermeneutical challenges that the idea of gender equality poses to Islamic legal tradition, the problems faced by those who advocate such an idea, and their prospects of success. There are two related contexts.

The first is that of twentieth-century shifts, both globally and locally, in the politics of religion, with a particular focus on changed relations between Islamic legal tradition, states and social practices. The second is that of the encounter between two radically opposed value systems, one rooted in pre-modern conceptions of justice, gender and rights, as found in Islamic legal discourses that sanction discrimination on the basis of gender, the other shaped by the contemporary ideals of human rights, equality and personal autonomy, based on international human rights standards and documents, and advocated by feminism. The book firmly locates the issue of gender equality and Islamic legal tradition within these two contexts, and identifies several approaches that resolve and transcend what is still regarded by many as an irreconcilable conflict of ideas.

The first chapter sets the stage by sketching twentieth-century developments in the politics of religion, law and gender in Muslim contexts, focusing on two key reform texts and their implications for current debates. The following four chapters investigate current practical efforts at legal reform in the context of women's lived social reality: in Egypt, Morocco and the global Musawah movement. The next five chapters deal with fundamental questions of how gender equality before the law can be supported from within the Islamic tradition, addressing the purposes of Islamic law, the hermeneutics of the Qur'an and hadith (Prophetic traditions), and the role of reason and religious ethics. In lieu of a conclusion, the final chapter observes that equality must be negotiated and realised through broad social and political change.

The arguments in this book all deal, in their various ways, with institutes of Islamic law known by their technical Arabic terms as *qiwāma* and *wilāya*, both of which, in this context, denote forms of guardianship – traditionally, male guardianship over women, by the husband as provider, and by the father or other male relative as legal guardian arranging the marriage of his ward, respectively. These notions serve as a point of entry to tackling a broad range of problems relating to gender equality before the law. Another recurring concept is *maqāṣid al-sharīʿa*, the objectives of Islamic law. The idea that all Islamic legal norms pursue a set of general aims, connected with the common good and available to human reason, has a distinguished intellectual pedigree in classical thought and has inspired modern reform thinkers.

This approach, framing the problem in terms of guardianship and exploring *maqāṣid* theory as a means to finding solutions, was forged through three workshops held in Marrakech (2008) and Cairo (2009 and 2010), which involved participants from all over the world. Although organised by the Oslo Coalition on Freedom of Religion or Belief, this was not an inter-religious dialogue, but a Muslim project, bringing together Muslim experts – religious scholars, experts in the social, human and legal sciences from secular academia, and non-governmental organisation (NGO) activists – who share a commitment to engage with the Islamic tradition in order to bring about reform consonant with modern human rights ideals. This has two important implications. First, the framework has enabled us to have remarkably open, frank and constructive discussions, without the reciprocal accusations and apologetics that often impede constructive dialogue on Islam and gender equality in other settings. Second, the point of departure is a Muslim framework of religious, legal and ethical thought.

The Oslo Coalition, which has defined its own role as only facilitating the process, is an international network of experts and representatives from religious and other life-stance communities, academia, NGOs, international organisations and civil society, based at the University of Oslo and funded by the Norwegian government. It carries out a number of projects to promote freedom of religion or belief worldwide. The 'New Directions in Islamic Thought' project, a series of workshops with Muslim thinkers in 2004–7, resulted in a book exploring a broad range of topics in Islamic reform,[1] and in an initiative to continue the process with a narrower focus on gender equality and family law, resulting in the present volume.

Dilemmas and divergent approaches to reform

What family law reforms should Muslim women and their advocates aspire to, and how can the Islamic case for these reforms be argued? As the discussions made clear, there is no single, cut-and-dried answer; there are policy dilemmas to be negotiated, and multiple theoretical approaches.

The gap between modern and pre-modern notions of justice, already alluded to, raises the strategical question of whether a theory of gender equality before the law can be formulated somehow within the traditional framework, or whether this project requires radical new departures in Islamic knowledge. This tension runs through all the theoretical issues discussed: how to understand revealed scriptures and their hermeneutics? How can reformers deal with hadith? What are the roles of reason and the moral convictions of modern Muslims? Can and should change be sought through the dominant legal discipline (*fiqh*), or must the solution lie in a new emphasis on ethics?

Different contributors differ over the merits of the *maqāṣid* approach, over the foundations for 'objectives' of Shariʿa, over how these objectives are to be interpreted and over what role they can play in reform.

When discussions turned to practical legal reform, particularly in the context of ongoing developments in Morocco and Egypt, where we held our workshops, dilemmas soon arose. A fundamental question, for women's groups in the Muslim world as elsewhere, is how to deal with *difference* and still respect *equality*. In formulating their demands, these groups are aware that, because Islamic law accords different rights to men and women, equality before the law would do away not only with male privilege, but with certain female privileges that women may be loath to give up, such as the unilateral right to a bride-gift (*mahr*) and maintenance (*nafaqa*).

Another fundamental question concerns the use of Islamic references along with references to international human rights in advocacy. It is fraught with issues of religious legitimacy, internal divides between 'secular' and 'religious' activists, effective communication with the masses, and reluctance to press claims seen to go 'against the Qur'an', whether for reasons of personal piety or fear of societal reactions.

As noted above, many Muslim states have justified reservations against core articles of CEDAW with reference to the Islamic Shari'a. CEDAW is framed as being in conflict with the religion of Islam, which is presented as the monolithic and unchangeable religion of the collectivity of Muslims. This raises the problem of the right of individuals to have a different understanding of Islam from that of the state; for example, an understanding of Islam that supports gender equality as a matter of belief. Gender equality is, therefore, also an issue of freedom of religion or belief.

Convergent conclusions

Across these differences, it appears that a diverse group of Muslim reform thinkers can converge on a set of shared conclusions. First, and obviously, the participants generally agreed that there is an acute need to work for greater gender equality before the law. Second, they are concerned with bridging the gap between the secular and religious camps in women's issues – a stark social and organisational divide in some countries.

Third, they see a need to work within a triple reference frame: the religion of Islam, its sacred texts and normative tradition; human rights, as formulated in CEDAW and other instruments of international law; and the social reality of Muslim women's lives 'on the ground', which may confound the expectations and solutions offered both by classical *fiqh* and by reformists and human rights advocates. The project of reform is thus inherently inter-disciplinary, and requires experts and efforts in the social and human sciences as well as in law and in Islamic sciences. The extent to which 'reality' and research findings are being taken into account to formulate novel solutions in fields such as bioethics or Islamic finance makes it all the less comprehensible why only classical jurists' texts should matter where women's interests are at stake.

Fourth, they emphasise the relationship between the religious text and the social context. In particular, they insist that Islamic jurisprudence and positive law (*fiqh*) is a historical development, socially constructed and embedded in diverse social contexts, and not a sacred, revealed and unchangeable part of religion. This allows them to argue that *fiqh* must change with the times and be updated to take into account vast social changes, including the expansion of women's education and employment outside the home, and profound changes in the concept and structure of the family. For some, *fiqh* needs first to be thoroughly deconstructed and desacralised for meaningful discussion and reform to take place. Many thinkers find it useful to draw a sharp distinction between Shariʿa as the eternal law of God, and *fiqh* as the fallible and mutable human *understanding* of this law.

Perspectives and prospects

In Muslim countries, as in the West, gender equality is not a technical problem with a solution. Rather, it is a historical process that is still unfolding, and a moving target that is constantly negotiated.

The gender issue and advocacy for women's rights already have a long history in Islam, and much has changed since the pioneering efforts of Rifaʿa al-Tahtawi (1801–1873) for women's education. Other prominent male Muslim intellectuals took up the cause in the nineteenth and twentieth centuries, such as Qasim Amin (Egypt, d. 1908), al-Tahir al-Haddad (Tunisia, d. 1935) and ʿAllal al-Fasi (Morocco, d. 1974), and some of them are discussed in this book.

In more recent times, unfortunately, one thing has not changed since al-Haddad was denounced and ostracised in the 1930s: scholars and advocates dealing with gender equality, or with other sensitive issues of Islamic reform, sometimes pay a very high price. Among the contributors to this book, the late Nasr Abu-Zayd (1943–2010) found himself driven into exile after a court declared him an apostate and annulled his marriage. Mohsen Kadivar and Hasan Yusefi Eshkevari, too, have had to leave their country, where they had been imprisoned and the latter defrocked; their difficult situation did not allow them to join our workshops.

Other things *have* changed. Two significant changes must be highlighted. First, women have themselves entered the arena as a whole new group of social actors: as advocates, researchers, policy-makers, jurists and – controversially – producers of religious knowledge. To be sure, not all of them call for gender equality before the law; of those who do, not all would consider themselves 'feminists', Islamic or otherwise. But their participation has changed the terms of the debate, with profound and far-reaching implications.

A second massive social and political change is the Arab Spring, starting in December 2010, which could have significant impact on family law reform. Public expectations were raised as political and social change were seen to be possible. To the extent that these developments lead to democratisation, they could open up new avenues for advocacy and legislative change, as well as alter the terms of access to knowledge. Women have played key roles in the Arab Spring movement, but it remains uncertain whether their contributions will translate into permanent gains for women's political participation. The opposite outcome – a religious and political backlash against gender equality – seems all too possible. At this precarious moment, Islamic arguments in favour of equality before the law are particularly important.

Notes

1 Vogt, Kari, Lena Larsen and Christian Moe (eds), *New Directions in Islamic Thought: Exploring Reform and Muslim Tradition* (London: I.B.Tauris, 2009).

1

JUSTICE, EQUALITY AND MUSLIM FAMILY LAWS

New Ideas, New Prospects[1]

Ziba Mir-Hosseini

Contemporary notions of justice, informed by the ideals of human rights, equality and personal freedom, depart substantially from those that underpin rulings in classical *fiqh* (Islamic jurisprudence) and established understandings of the Shariʿa. This disjunction is a central problem that permeates debates and struggles for an egalitarian family law in Muslim contexts.

For instance, take the following two statements:

> The fundamentals of the Shariʿa are rooted in wisdom and promotion of the welfare of human beings in this life and the Hereafter. Shariʿa embraces Justice, Kindness, the Common Good and Wisdom. Any rule that departs from justice to injustice, from kindness to harshness, from the common good to harm, or from rationality to absurdity cannot be part of Shariʿa.[2]

> The wife is her husband's prisoner, a prisoner being akin to a slave. The Prophet directed men to support their wives by feeding them with their own food and clothing them with their own clothes; he said the same about maintaining a slave.[3]

Both statements are by Ibn Qayyim al-Jawziyya (1292–1350), a fourteenth-century jurist and one of the great reformers of his time.[4] The first statement speaks to all contemporary Muslims, and both advocates of gender equality and their opponents often use it as an epigraph.[5] But the second statement, which reflects classical *fiqh* conceptions of marriage, goes against the very grain of what many contemporary Muslims consider to be 'Justice, Kindness, the Common Good and Wisdom'. Consequently, Muslim legal tradition and its textual sources have come to appear hypocritical or, at best, contradictory. This presents those who struggle to reform Muslim family laws with a quandary and a host of questions: what is the notion of justice in Islam's sacred texts? Does it include the notion of equality for women before the law? If so, how are we to understand those elements of the primary sources of the Shariʿa (Qurʾan and hadith) that appear not to treat men and women as equals? Can gender equality and Shariʿa-based laws go together?

These questions are central to the ongoing struggle for an egalitarian construction of family laws in Muslim contexts and have been vigorously debated among Muslims since the late nineteenth century.[6] Some consider religion to be inherently patriarchal and any engagement with it to be a futile and incorrect strategy;[7] others argue that, given the linkage between the religious and political dimensions of identity in Muslim contexts, the path to legal equality for women in those contexts necessarily passes through religion.[8] This chapter aims to explore these questions and address what often remains neglected in this debate: how Muslim women's struggle for equality is embedded in the intimate links between theology and politics. My central argument has two elements. First, the struggle is at once theological and political, and it is hard and sometimes futile to decide when theology ends and politics begin. Secondly, in the last two decades of the twentieth century a growing confrontation between political Islam and feminism has made the intimate links between theology, law and politics more transparent. New voices and forms of activism have emerged that no longer shy away from engagement with religion. A new discourse, which came to be known as 'Islamic feminism', started to challenge the patriarchal interpretations of the Shariʿa from within.

After a brief examination of the notion of gender justice in classical *fiqh* texts, I sketch twentieth-century developments in the politics of religion, law and gender in Muslim contexts. This is followed by a discussion of two reform texts that negotiate and bridge the chasm – the dissonance – between contemporary notions of justice and gender rights and those informed by classical *fiqh* rulings, and that lay the groundwork for an egalitarian family law. These are the book *Women in the Shariʿa and in Our Society* (1930) by Tunisian religious reform thinker al-Tahir al-Haddad, and the article 'The status of women in Islam: a modernist interpretation' (1982) by Pakistani reform thinker Fazlur Rahman. I have chosen to focus on these two texts because they belong to two key moments in the Muslim debate and struggle to define the scope of women's rights in the twentieth century. Al-Haddad's book appeared in the context of early twentieth-century debates and the early phase of the codification of Muslim family law; Fazlur Rahman's article was published when political Islam was at its zenith and Islamists, trumpeting the slogan 'return to Shari'a', were dismantling some earlier reforms. Both thinkers met with a great deal of opposition from the clerical establishments in their own countries at the time, but their ideas, which conservative clerics declared to be heretical, proved to be instrumental in shaping later discourses and developments. Al-Tahir al-Haddad's ideas informed Tunisian family law, which was codified in 1956, and to this day remains the only Muslim code that bans polygamy. Fazlur Rahman developed a methodology and framework that, by the end of the century, facilitated the emergence of feminist scholarship in Islam. I conclude by considering the implication of this scholarship with regard to changing the terms of reference of the debates over Muslim family law reforms.

1. Men's authority over women: *qiwāma* as a legal postulate

At the heart of the unequal construction of gender rights in Muslim legal tradition lies the idea that men have guardianship or *qiwāma* over women. Verse 4:34 (from which the idea is derived) is commonly understood as mandating men's authority over women, and is frequently invoked as the main textual evidence in its support. This verse is often the only verse that ordinary Muslims know in relation to family law. It reads:

> Men are ***qawwāmūn*** (protectors/maintainers) in relation to women, according to what God has favored some over others and according to what they spend from their wealth. Righteous women are ***qānitāt*** (obedient) guarding the unseen according to what God has guarded. Those [women] whose ***nushūz*** you fear, admonish them, and abandon them in bed, and ***aḍribuhunna*** (strike them). If they obey you, do not pursue a strategy against them. Indeed, God is Exalted, Great.[9]

Since the early twentieth century, this verse has been the focus of intense contestation and debate among Muslims, centring on the four terms I have highlighted. There is now a substantial body of literature that attempts to contest and reconstruct the meanings and connotations of these terms as understood and turned into legal rulings by classical jurists.[10] Recent contributions have been most concerned with the last part of the verse, and the issue of domestic violence.[11] Neither this concern nor the contestation over the meanings of these terms is new; they occupied the minds of classical Muslim jurists when they inferred from the verse legal rulings regarding the rights and duties of spouses in marriage.[12] But the nature and the tone of the debates are new. Juristic disagreements were not, as now, about the legitimacy or legality of a husband's right to beat his wife if she defies his authority; they were about the extent and harshness of the beating he should administer. In classical *fiqh* texts, the validity and inviolability of men's superiority and authority over women was a given; the verse was understood in this light, and the four key terms were used to define relations between spouses in marriage, and notions of gender justice and equity. As we shall see, all revolved around the first part of the verse and the notion that men are women's *qawwāmūn*, protectors and providers.

Let us call this the *qiwāma* postulate,[13] which I shall argue is the lynchpin of the whole edifice of the patriarchal model of family in classical *fiqh*. We see the working of this postulate in all areas of Muslim law relating to gender rights, but its impact is most evident, as I have argued elsewhere, in the laws that classical jurists devised for the regulation of marriage.[14] They defined marriage as a contract (*nikāḥ*), and patterned it after the contract of sale (*bay'*). The contract renders sexual relations licit between a man and woman, and establishes a set of default rights and obligations for each party, some supported by legal force, others by moral sanction. Those with legal force revolve around the twin themes of sexual access and compensation, and are embodied in two central legal concepts: *tamkīn* (submission) and *nafaqa* (maintenance).[15] *Tamkīn*, obedience or submission, specifically with regard to sexual access, is the husband's right and thus the wife's duty; whereas *nafaqa*, maintenance, specifically shelter, food and clothing, is the wife's right and the husband's duty. The wife loses her claim to maintenance if she is in a state of *nushūz* (disobedience). The husband has the unilateral and extra-judicial right to terminate the contract by *ṭalāq* or repudiation; a wife cannot terminate the contract without her husband's consent or the permission of the Islamic judge upon producing a valid reason. There are numerous moral injunctions that could have limited men's power to terminate marriage; for instance, there are sayings from the Prophet to the effect that *ṭalāq* is among the most detested of permitted acts, and that when a man pronounces it, God's throne shakes. Yet classical *fiqh* made no attempt to restrict a man's right to *ṭalāq*. He needs neither grounds nor the consent of his wife.

There were, of course, differences between and within the classical schools over what constituted and what defined the three interrelated concepts – *nafaqa*, *tamkīn* and *nushūz* – but they all shared the same conception of marriage, and the large majority linked a woman's right to maintenance to her obedience to her husband. The reason for their disagreement, Ibn Rushd tells us, was 'whether maintenance is a counter-value for (sexual) utilization, or compensation for the fact that she is confined because of her husband, as the case of one absent or sick'.[16] And it was within the parameters of this logic – men provide and women obey – that notions of gender rights and justice acquired their meanings. Cognizant of the inherent tension in such a construction of marriage, and seeking to contain the potential abuse of a husband's authority, classical jurists narrowed the scope of this authority to the unhampered right to sexual relations with the wife, which in turn limited the scope of her duty to obey to being sexually available, and even here only when it did not interfere with her religious duties (for example, when fasting during

Ramadan, or when bleeding during menses or after childbirth). Legally speaking, if we take the *fiqh* texts at face value, according to some a wife had no obligation to do housework or to care for the children, even to suckle her babies; for these, she was entitled to wages. Likewise, a man's right to discipline a wife who was in the state of *nushūz* was severely restricted; he could discipline her, but not inflict harm. For this reason, some jurists recommended that he should 'beat' his wife only with a handkerchief or a *miswāk*, a twig used for cleaning teeth.[17]

Whether these rulings corresponded to actual practices of marriage and gender relations is another area of inquiry, one that recent scholarship in Islam has only just started to uncover.[18] What is important to note here is that the *qiwāma* postulate served as a rationale for other legal disparities – such as men's rights to polygamy and unilateral repudiation, women's lesser share in inheritance, or the ban on women being judges or political leaders. That is to say, women cannot occupy positions that entail the exercise of authority in society because they are under their husband's authority – and are thus not free agents and not able to deliver impartial justice. Similarly, since men provide for their wives, justice requires that they be entitled to a greater share in inheritance. These inequalities in rights were also rationalised and justified by other arguments, based on assumptions about innate, natural differences between the sexes: women are by nature weaker and more emotional, qualities inappropriate in a leader; they are created for childbearing, a function that confines them to the home, which means that men must protect and provide for them.[19]

2. The reform and codification of classical *fiqh* provisions of family law[20]

In the course of the twentieth century, as nation-states emerged among Muslim populations, classical *fiqh* conceptions of marriage and family were partially reformed, codified and grafted onto modern legal systems in many Muslim-majority countries.[21] The best-known exceptions were Turkey and Muslim populations that came under communist rule, which abandoned *fiqh* in all areas of law, and Saudi Arabia, which preserved classical *fiqh* as fundamental law and attempted to apply it in all spheres of law. In countries where classical *fiqh* remained the main source of family law, the impetus and extent of family law reform varied, but, with the exception of Tunisia, which banned polygamy, on the whole the classical *fiqh* construction of the marital relationship was retained more or less intact. Reforms were introduced from within the framework of Muslim legal tradition, by mixing principles and rulings from different *fiqh* schools and by procedural devices, without directly challenging the patriarchal construction of marriage in *fiqh*.[22] They centred on increasing the age of marriage, expanding women's access to judicial divorce and restricting men's right to polygamy. This involved requiring the state registration of marriage and divorce, or the creation of new courts to deal with marital disputes. The state now had the power to deny legal support to those marriages that were not in compliance with official state-sanctioned procedures.

All these changes transformed relations between Muslim legal tradition, state and social practice. Codes and statute books took the place of *fiqh* manuals; family law was no longer solely a matter for private scholars – the *fuqahā'* – operating within a particular *fiqh* school, rather it became the concern of the legislative assembly of a particular nation-state. Confined to the ivory tower of the seminaries, the practitioners of *fiqh* became increasingly scholastic, defensive and detached from realities on the ground. Patriarchal interpretations of the Shari'a acquired a different force; they could now be imposed through the machinery of the modern nation-state, which had neither the religious legitimacy nor the inclination to challenge them.

With the rise of Islam as both a spiritual and a political force in the latter part of the twentieth century, Islamist political movements became closely identified with patriarchal notions of gender drawn from classical *fiqh*. Political Islam had its biggest triumph in 1979, in the popular revolution that brought clerics into power in Iran. This year also saw the dismantling of some of the reforms introduced earlier in the century by the modernist governments – for instance, in Iran and Egypt – and the introduction of the Hudood Ordinances in Pakistan, which extended the ambit of *fiqh* to certain aspects of criminal law. Yet this was the year when the UN General Assembly adopted CEDAW, which gave gender equality a clear international legal mandate.

The decades that followed saw the concomitant expansion, globally and locally, of two powerful but seemingly opposed frames of reference. On the one hand, the human rights framework and instruments such as CEDAW gave women's rights activists what they needed most: a point of reference and a language with which to resist and challenge patriarchy. The 1980s saw the expansion of the international women's movement, and the emergence of NGOs with international funds and transnational links that gave women a voice in policy-making and public debate over the law. On the other hand, Islamist forces – whether in power or in opposition – started to invoke 'Shari'a' in order to dismantle earlier efforts at reforming and/or secularising laws and legal systems. Tapping into popular demands for social justice, they presented this dismantling as 'Islamisation', and as the first step in bringing about their vision of a moral and just society.

In other words, the twentieth century witnessed the widening of the chasm between notions of justice and gender rights found in Muslim legal tradition and those that were being adopted internationally. This chasm, this dissonance, was, as we shall see, as much political as epistemological. I now turn to the texts of al-Tahir al-Haddad and Fazlur Rahman, which try to negotiate and bridge the chasm. They appeared at two critical moments in the twentieth-century politics of modernism: the struggle against colonial powers and the challenges posed by political Islam. At both moments, the issue of gender rights and Muslim legal tradition became part of an ideological battle between different forces and factions.

3. Al-Tahir al-Haddad (1899–1935): a lonely reformer

Al-Tahir al-Haddad's book *Our Women in the Shari'a and Society* is part of a considerable nationalist and reformist literature dating to the early twentieth century and the fierce debate on the 'status of women in Islam' ignited by the encounter with Western colonial powers.[23] Two genres of texts emerged. The authors of the first more or less reiterated the classical *fiqh* positions, and confined themselves to enumerating the rights that Islam conferred on women. Texts of the second genre, the most influential of which was Qasim Amin's *The Liberation of Women* (1899), offered a critique of *fiqh* rulings and proposed reforms to realise women's rights. They called for women's education, for their participation in society and for unveiling. One subtext in these works was the refutation of the colonial premise that 'Islam' was inherently a 'backward' religion and denied women their rights; another was the quest for modernisation and the reform of laws and legal systems as part of the project of nation-building. Without women's education and their participation in society, the modern, independent and prosperous state for which they were struggling could not be achieved.[24]

Al-Haddad's book belongs to the second genre, and is not free of the ambivalence that permeated the nationalist/modernist texts of the time, which have rightly been criticised for their patriarchal undertones.[25] But it differs from the rest in two respects. First, in his proposals for reform al-Haddad went much further than other twentieth-century reformers, even arguing for equality in inheritance, an issue that became a priority for Muslim women's movements only in the next century.[26] Secondly, al-Haddad provided a framework for rethinking *fiqh* legal concepts, and offered a definition of marriage that was premised on mutual affection and responsibility. In that sense, it is indeed a feminist text.

Al-Haddad received only a traditional education, first at Qur'anic school and later at the Great Mosque of Zaytouna, where he studied Islamic sciences.[27] He obtained accreditation as a notary in 1920, but opted for journalism instead of a seminary life. As a journalist he became involved in the movement for independence from France, and joined the Dustur Party, which promoted a vision of a socially just, democratic and modern Tunisia. Critical of its policies, however, al-Haddad left the party after a short time to become active in labour movements, helping to launch the country's first independent trade union. These activities sensitised al-Haddad and made him deeply concerned about the situation of workers and women, and the injustices to which they were subjected, for which he held erroneous interpretations of Islam's sacred texts accountable. In 1927, he published a book on labour law, and three years later his second book, *Our Women in the*

Shari'a and Society, which contains his critique of how women are treated in Tunisian society. The book caused immediate outrage: al-Haddad was denounced and declared an apostate, and Zaytouna revoked his degree and notary licence. Many of his modernist and nationalist friends deserted him; they were in a politically difficult situation at the time, and an easy way out was to compromise on an issue that was sensitive and was already triggering the anger of the religious establishment and conservative forces.[28] Al-Haddad died in 1936 in poverty and isolation.

4. Al-Haddad's framework and proposals for reform

What was it in al-Haddad's book that provoked such a reaction from his seminary teachers and colleagues? The book has two parts. The first, 'Legislative section: women in Islam', contains al-Haddad's critique of *fiqh* rulings and his proposals for reform. In the final chapter of this part, he poses a set of questions to the scholars and jurists, including his teachers at Zaytouna, who included eminent scholars of the time such as al-Tahir ibn 'Ashur,[29] a former judge and a leading scholar of Maliki law. He did this 'in the hope of getting answers from them that would elucidate our position and where we stand in our reform of the judiciary which is necessary for the benefit of justice and progress for women' (p. 81).[30] This chapter – fascinating to read – reveals the distance between al-Haddad's vision of Shari'a and that of the *'ulamā'* of his time. It also gives us a glimpse of why al-Haddad caused such outrage.

The second part, 'Social section: how to educate girls to be wives and mothers', is his critique of the current situation and his proposals for socio-cultural change. I confine my discussion to the first part, which contains al-Haddad's framework for redressing gender inequalities in Muslim legal tradition. Al-Haddad is neither apologetic nor defensive. 'I am not oblivious to the fact that Shari'a accorded lower status to women than men in certain situations,' and that the sacred texts 'make us believe that in essence [Islam] favoured men over women.' But he goes on to argue the need to go beyond the literal meanings of the two main sources of the Shari'a, the Qur'an and the Prophet's Sunna: 'if we look into their aims, we realize that they want to make woman equal to man in every aspect of life' (p. 104).

There are two related elements in al-Haddad's approach to Islam's textual sources. The first is the distinction between laws that are essential to Islam as a religion, and those that are contingent and time- and context-bound; in his words:

> [W]e should take into consideration the great difference between what Islam brought and its aims, which will remain immortal in eternity, such as belief in monotheism, moral behaviour, and the establishment of justice, dignity and equality among people. Furthermore, we have to consider the social situation and the deep-rooted mindset that existed in Arab society in the pre-Islamic era when Islam

> first emerged. The prescriptions for confirming or amending previous customs remained in force as long as these practices existed. Their disappearance, however, did not harm Islam as practices such as slavery, polygamy, etc. cannot be considered inherent to Islam. (p. 36)

The second element in his perspective is what he calls the 'policy of gradualism' (*siyāsa tadrījiyya*), which he argues governs the process of legislation in the Qur'an and Sunna. In Islam the 'highest aim is equality among all God's creatures', but it was not possible to achieve this aim in the seventh century and during the lifetime of the Prophet; 'the general conditions in the Arabian Peninsula forced the legal texts to be laid down gradually, especially those concerning women' (p. 104). 'Islam is the religion of freedom,' but it tolerated 'the selling and buying of human beings as goods, and their exploitation as animals for the duration of their lives' (p. 48). This toleration was a concession to the socio-economic imperatives of the time. It was not then possible to do away with slavery all together, but the Qur'an and the Prophet encouraged the freeing of slaves, and made it crystal clear that the principle is freedom. For exactly the same reason, gender hierarchy was tolerated then, but the principle in Islam remains equality.

> Although Islam highlights a number of differences between man and woman in several verses in the Qur'an, this does not in any way affect the principle of social equality between them when the necessary conditions were [to become] present over time since Islam in essence aims for complete justice and fairness. It introduced its laws and gradually adapted them according to the capacity of people to obey them. There is no reason to believe that the gradual changes that took place in the life of the Prophet should stop after the passing away of the Prophet. The gradual changes in the Shari'a law took place at a pace that could be sustained by society and there are clear examples to testify to that. (p. 48)

The Qur'an's gradual ban on drinking wine, al-Haddad argues, is a clear example of the 'policy of gradualism' in the formulation of legislation that unfolded during the lifetime of the Prophet. At first, drinking was tolerated; then later verses abrogated the earlier one and the ban was introduced. But he maintains that other issues, such as slavery, polygamy, men's authority over women and unilateral divorce were to be resolved later. Slavery was eventually abolished, when societies evolved and humans realised its evil; abolition took place first in the West, Muslim countries followed suit, and Shari'a-based laws relating to slavery all became obsolete. Now, he argues, the time has come to honour 'Islam's love for equality' and to abolish unjust and discriminatory laws that have kept women backward and denied them their rights. To do so we must, first, discover the principle and the objective behind Qur'anic laws, and, secondly, understand that they were the means to an end;

they were not meant to be eternal or rigid in form, they are just shells and can be changed when they no longer serve the social objectives of Islam – freedom, justice and equality. These laws were revealed to the Prophet so that he could reform and change the unjust values and practices of his time.

With respect to family law, there are, again, two important elements in al-Haddad's approach. First, he rejects the argument that women are unfit for certain activities and that their primary role is motherhood. Islam does not assign fixed roles to men and women. 'Islam truly is a religion that is rooted in reality and evolves as it changes over time; herein lies the secret of its immortality. Nowhere in the Qur'an can one find any reference to any activity – no matter how elevated it may be – whether in government or society, that is forbidden to woman' (p. 39). Yes, men and women are different; women give birth and are physically and emotionally suited to care for children, but this in no way means that Islam wanted them to be confined to the home and to domestic roles. He argues for the creation of institutions to liberate women. As human societies progress and evolve, new institutions emerge to liberate women, such as crèches and nurseries, as in France and other nations that have advanced (p. 60). The problem is not with Islam but with patriarchy, with reducing women to sex objects; it is 'primarily due to the fact that we [men] regard them [women] as vessels for our penises'.[31]

Secondly, he breaks away from the transactional logic of marriage in *fiqh*, and places mutual affection and cooperation at the centre of the marital relationship.

> Marriage involves affection, duties, intercourse and procreation. Islam regards affection as the foundation of marriage since it is the driving force, as witnessed by the following verse:
>
> And among His signs is this, that He created for you mates from among yourselves, that you may dwell in tranquillity with them, and He has put love and mercy between your (hearts): Verily in that are signs for those who reflect.[32]
>
> As for duty, this refers to the fact that husband and wife have to work together to build a life. In this sense, duty both preserves and enhances the emotional ties that exist between them and which enable them to carry out their duty wilfully. (p. 57)

Having shifted the focus from verse 4:34 to verse 30:21, his starting point for discussing marriage becomes freedom of choice (*ḥurriyyat al-ikhtiyār*). Love and compassion cannot develop in a relationship that is imposed; women, like men, must have the freedom to choose their spouses and to be able to leave an unwanted marriage, and this is what Islam mandates. He then goes on to break the link between maintenance and obedience as constructed in classical *fiqh* texts.

> If we look at the origin of the Shariʿa in order to understand the meaning of duty in matrimony, we would find that it is incumbent upon the man to support his wife

> and children financially, on the grounds that they are not able to do so themselves. With the exception of this, no duty is specified, for either the husband or the wife, to dictate how they behave within the marriage or toward each other. Whatever duties the man has towards his wife, they are equal to the duties she has towards him. This is illustrated in the following verse 'Women have such honourable rights as obligations.' (p. 59)

The verse to which al-Haddad refers here (2:228) goes on to say 'but men have a degree (of advantage) over them';[33] this part of the verse is often invoked in conjunction with 4:34 as textual evidence of men's superiority in order to justify their authority over women. But his reading of these two verses is different from that of the classical jurists. He argues that both verses must be read in the context of the marriage and divorce practices of the time, and the privileges that men enjoyed before Islam: both verses aim to restrain these privileges. This becomes clear when we read these verses in their entirety and in conjunction with those that precede and follow them. In verse 4:34, a husband is required to provide for his wife, so that 'the continued growth of the world' (p. 59) can be ensured; he was given the right to 'correct' his wife's behaviour in order to prevent a greater ill, divorce. According to al-Haddad, this verse is not speaking about the rights and duties of spouses, but about the course of action to be taken when there is marital discord, and it offers ways to resolve it. This becomes clear in the verse that follows, which reads 'if you have reason to fear that a breach might occur between a couple, appoint an arbiter from among his people and an arbiter from among her people; if they both want to set things aright, God may bring their reconciliation' (4:35). Men are addressed because they are the ones who, then as now, have the power to terminate marriage, and the objective was to restrain this power and give the marriage a chance. Likewise, with respect to verse 2:228, which the jurists quote to argue for men's superiority, al-Haddad maintains that it must be read in its entirety and in connection with the preceding and following verses,[34] which are all related to marital separation and the protection of women. The final part of the verse speaks of men's power to divorce, and this is what 'men having a degree over women' is about: divorce was in their hands.

After a lengthy discussion of various forms of divorce in *fiqh* and the injustices and suffering that they entail for women, al-Haddad concludes that men's right to *ṭalāq* (i.e. unilateral and extrajudicial divorce) must be abolished:

> [T]here is no other way of dealing with matters relating to marriage and divorce cases, except through the courts so that everything is done in conformity with the spirit and the letter of the Shari'a. (p. 72)

Asserting that 'the Qur'anic text generally sets forth means of achieving justice between man and woman' (p. 79), al-Haddad also argues for the abolition of polygamy, which he contends 'has no basis in Islam; rather, it is one of the evils of the pre-Islamic era which Islam challenged through its gradualistic method' (p. 63). Polygamy is unjust, inimical to the very foundation of marriage, which is based on affection and harmony between the couple. It was one of those practices that Islam wanted to eradicate but had to tolerate and could only modify. The Qur'an limited the number of wives a man could have to four, and stipulated conditions of just equality among the wives; but made it clear that such justice is impossible to establish, however hard a man tries. Here al-Haddad quotes verse 4:3, which says 'Marry such women as seem good to you, two, three, four; but if you fear you will not be equitable, then only one.' He also rejects the conventional argument that the Prophet himself was polygamous, and thus his practice should be followed:

> The fact that the Prophet had many wives does not mean that he legislated for this practice or wanted the Muslim community to follow this path. Indeed he had taken these wives before the limitation had been imposed. It is worth bearing in mind that the Prophet was also a human being, and as such was subject to human tendencies as regards issues that had not been sent down to him as revelation from the heavens. (p. 64)

In short, al-Haddad argues for legal equality for women in all areas, including in inheritance. According to him, the Qur'an's assignment of a lesser share of inheritance to women was due to the conditions of the time; it was a concession to the social order. But here again equality is the principle and when we look closely, we find that,

> Islam did not allocate a lesser share in the woman's inheritance compared to that of man as a principle applicable to all cases. It gave her the same share in the case of parents inheriting from their dead son when there is a male child and if it involves inheritance among blood siblings ... (p. 47)

In other instances where women were allocated lesser shares, it had to do with the context; the Arabs then would not have accepted equal shares for women, which they would have seen as unjust, as women did not participate in warfare and were under men's protection. But 'there is no reason why such a position should remain fixed in time without change'.

Al-Haddad's ideas and proposals for reform were indeed radical for the time, which to a large extent explains the harsh reaction of the clerical establishment towards his book. A year later (1931), one of the officials of Zaytouna, Saleh ibn Murad, published a book in response, entitled *Mourning over al-Haddad's Woman or Warning off Errors, Apostasy and Innovation*. But, in 1956, in a changed political context, when the nationalists/modernists had prevailed and Tunisia was an independent nation-state, many of al-Haddad's proposals for reform were adopted. Under the leadership of Habib Bourguiba, the modernists embarked on the reform of the judiciary, and among their first acts was the codification of family law. The new code made polygamy illegal and gave women equal access to divorce and child custody, though the inheritance laws remained unchanged. All these reforms were, of course, introduced from above, as women were still not vocal participants in the debate.[35]

5. Fazlur Rahman (1919–1988): reforming Islamic intellectual tradition

Fazlur Rahman was another daring twentieth-century reformer whose ideas met with a great deal of opposition in his own country, Pakistan, though his situation and background were different from those of al-Haddad. More of a scholar than an activist, Fazlur Rahman's intellectual genealogy is through reform thinkers in the Indian subcontinent.[36] Furthermore, unlike al-Haddad, the formation of his ideas belongs to the tail end of Western colonialism in Muslim contexts, when processes of nation-building, modernisation and reform of the judiciary, and codification of family law were well under way.[37]

Born in pre-partition India, Fazlur Rahman was instructed in traditional Islamic sciences by his father,[38] and went on to study Arabic and Islamic studies at Punjab University in Lahore, and Islamic philosophy at the University of Oxford. After graduation in 1958, he taught at universities in the United Kingdom and Canada until 1961, when he was invited by General Ayub Khan to help with the reform of religious education in Pakistan. He became director of the Islamic Research Institute, which had been recently created to provide intellectual backing for Ayub Khan's modernisation project and to steer the path of reform in ways that would not offend the religious establishment.[39] He became entangled with the politics of modernisation and reform in Pakistan, and his reformist ideas and approach to Islamic tradition from a critical perspective made him a target for Ayub Khan's influential religious and political opponents. The fiercest opposition came from religious conservatives, and was centred on the question of women's rights and the reform of family law. Rahman began to receive death threats, and eventually decided to return to academic life in the West. In 1968 he was appointed professor of Islamic thought at the University of Chicago, where he remained until his death in 1988, leaving behind an impressive body of scholarship. His work, in turn, has been the subject of scholarship, and played an important role in the USA in the development of Islamic studies.[40] But his vast output, all in English, remains almost unknown in the Arab world and in traditional religious circles, and his influence in his own country, Pakistan, is limited.

Unlike al-Haddad, Rahman did not write a book about women's rights, nor did he offer specific proposals for reforming Muslim family law. But his writings are permeated by a critique of patriarchal readings of Islam's sacred texts, and his framework for interpreting the ethico-legal content of the Qur'an has been crucial to feminist scholarship in Islam.[41] He considered the reform of Muslim family laws to be, on the whole, moving in the right direction, and he saw the weight of conservatism in Muslim contexts as the main obstacle to bringing about radical reform. In 'A survey of modernization of Muslim family law', an article published in the 1980s, Rahman opens the discussion by pointing to the fate of al-Haddad, and the harsh reaction his book and proposals for family law reform received from the very clerics who had not been perturbed by his earlier quasi-Marxist book on the rise of trade unionism and the interpretation of history.[42]

In his approach to Islam's sacred texts, Rahman shares al-Haddad's historicism and gradualism in revelation and legislation. According to him, the Qur'an 'is the divine response, through the Prophet's mind, to the moral–social situation of the Prophet's Arabia, particularly to the problems of commercial Meccan society of the day'. Not all these solutions are relevant or applicable to all times and all contexts. What is immutable and valid are the moral principles behind these solutions. These moral principles, the Shari'a, show us how to establish a society on earth where all humans can be treated as equals as they are equal in the eyes of God. This is at once 'the challenge and the purpose of human existence, the trust – *amāna* – that humanity accepted at creation'.[43]

But Muslims betrayed this trust as, in the course of the historical development of Islam, the moral principles behind Qur'anic laws were distorted. This distortion has its roots in political developments after the Prophet's death and in the subsequent decay and stagnation of Islamic intellectualism, which predates Islam's encounter with Western colonial powers. Muslims failed to create a viable system of Qur'an-based ethics, and from the outset jurisprudence has overshadowed the science of ethics in Islam; in developing the latter, Muslim scholars relied more on Persian and Greek sources than on the Qur'an itself. The link between theology, ethics and law will remain tenuous as long as Muslims fail to make the crucial distinctions in the Qur'an and the Prophet's Sunna, between essentials and accidentals, and between prescription and description. They mistakenly view the Qur'an as a book of law, and take its legal and quasi-legal passages to be relevant to all times and places.

To revive the élan of the Qur'an, Rahman argues, Muslims need two things. The first is a fresh engagement with the Qur'an and a critical reassessment of the entire Islamic intellectual tradition: theology, ethics, philosophy and jurisprudence. The second is a realistic assessment and understanding of the contemporary socio-political context. It is only then that Muslims can overcome centuries of decadence and backwardness and meet the challenges of modernity. The interpretative process that Rahman proposes for this revival is a 'double movement', that is, a movement 'from the present situation to Qur'anic times, then back to the present'. In the first movement 'general principles, values and long-range objectives' of the Qur'an are elicited and separated from the socio-historical context of the revelation. In the second, these principles are applied to issues at hand, taking into consideration the current context and its imperatives.[44] In his words, this:

> requires the careful study of the present situation and the analysis of its various component elements so we can assess the current situation and change the present to whatever extent necessary, and so we can determine priorities afresh in order to implement the Qur'anic values afresh. To the extent that we achieve both moments of this double movement successfully, the Qur'an's imperatives will become alive and effective once again. While the first task is primarily the work of the historian, in the performance of the second the instrumentality of the social scientist is obviously indispensable, but the actual 'effective orientation' and 'ethical engineering' are the work of the ethicist.[45]

In 'The status of women in Islam: a modernist interpretation',[46] Rahman suggests what 'effective orientation' and 'ethical engineering' entail when it comes to the issue of gender equality and family law. This is the only place where Rahman focuses his attention on this issue (apart from his 1980 article on family law reforms, already cited); elsewhere he mentions it only in passing. Published in 1982, the same year as his last major work (*Islam and Modernity*), this article can be seen as the application of his 'double movement' theory in the area of gender rights and family law reform. Rahman begins by identifying himself as a 'Muslim modernist', one who pursues social reform through a new interpretation of Islamic sources and 'in contradistinction to the stance taken on most social issues by Muslim conservative–traditionalist leaders'. Islamic modernism, Rahman argues, 'developed under the impetus of modern Western liberalism but contains within it tangible differences on sexual issues, but is to be sharply distinguished from secularism'.[47] He is equally critical of social reform without reference to Islam, which he calls 'secularism (à la Mustafa Kemal Ataturk)', and the 'apologetic aspect' of Islamic modernism that rationalises and justifies gender inequality (p. 285).[48]

The legislation in the Qur'an on the subject of women, Rahman contends, is part of the effort to strengthen the position of the weaker segments of the community, which in pre-Islamic Arabia were the poor, orphans, women, slaves and those chronically in debt. Through reforming existing laws and practices and introducing new ones, the Qur'an aimed to put an end to their abuse and to open the way for their empowerment. Departing from the apologetic refrain on the position of women in pre-Islamic times, Rahman argues that the position of women was not altogether low, 'for even a slave woman could earn and own wealth, like a slave male, let alone a free woman. Khadija, the first wife of the Prophet, owned a considerable business which the Prophet managed for her sometime before their marriage, and after their marriage she helped him financially' (p. 286). But women could also be treated as property, as 'a son inherited his stepmother as part of his father's legacy and could force her to marry him or could debar her from marrying anyone else through her life, coveting her property' (p. 288). Women were also 'the central focus of the "honour" (*'irḍ*) of a man whose "manliness" (*muruwwa*) demanded that her honour remain inviolate' (p. 287). This, according to Rahman, was the distorted logic behind the practice of female infanticide, which was a way of preventing the eventual infringement of a man's honour.

What the Qur'anic reforms achieved was 'the removal of certain abuses to which women were subjected': female infanticide and widow-inheritance were banned; laws of marriage, divorce and inheritance were reformed. As with slavery, however, these reforms did not go as far as abolishing patriarchy. But they did expand women's rights and brought tangible improvements in their position – albeit not social equality. Women retained the rights they had to property, but they were no longer treated as property; they could not be forced into marriage against their will, and they received the marriage gift (*mahr*); they also acquired better access to divorce and were allocated shares in inheritance.

The essential equality between the sexes is clearly implied in the Qur'an; both men and women are mentioned separately 'as being absolutely equal in virtue and piety with such unflinching regularity that it would be superfluous to give particular documentation' (p. 291). Those sayings attributed to the Prophet that speak of women's inferiority and require them to obey and worship their husbands, Rahman argues, are clearly 'a twisting of whatever the Qur'an has to say in matters of piety and religious merit' (p. 292) and marriage.

> The Qur'an speaks of the husband and wife relationship as that of 'love and mercy' adding that the wife is a moral support for the husband (30:21). It describes their support for each other by saying, 'they (i.e. your wives) are garments unto you and you are garments unto them' (2:187). The term 'garment' here means that which soothes and covers up one's weakness. (p. 293)

Such sayings also contradict what we know of the Prophet's own conduct, thus must be rejected.

> The Prophet's wives, far from worshiping him – with all his religious authority – wanted from him the good things of life, so that the Qur'an had to say, 'O Messenger! Say to your wives: "If you want to pursue this-worldly life and its good things, then I will give you wealth, but let you go in gentleness (i.e. divorce you)"' (33:[29]). What the Qur'an required from a woman was to be a good wife, adding, 'Good women are those who are faithful and who guard what is their husband's in his absence as God wants them to guard' (4:34). (p. 293)

The Qur'an does speak of inequality between sexes. But when it does, it gives the rationale, which has to do with socio-economic factors.

> In 2:228 we are told, 'For them (i.e. women) there are rights (against them), but men are one degree higher than women.' That is to say, in the social (as opposed to religious) sphere, while the rights and obligations of both spouses towards each other are exactly commensurate, men are, nevertheless, a degree higher. The rationale is not given in this verse which simply adds 'And God is Mighty and Wise'. The rationale is given later, in verse 4:34. (p. 294)

This verse, Rahman continues, begins by saying that men are 'managers over (i.e., are superior to) women because some of humankind excel others (in some respects) and because men expend of their wealth (for women)', and then goes on to give them the authority to discipline their wives when they do not obey them. Thus the two rationales that this gives for male superiority in socio-economic affairs are: '(1) that man is "more excellent", and (2) that man is charged entirely with household expenditure', but not any inherent inequality between sexes (p. 294).

> What the Qur'an appears to say, therefore, is that since men are the primary socially operative factors and bread-winners, they have been wholly charged with the responsibility of defraying household expenditure and upkeep of their womenfolk. For this reason man, because by his struggle he has gained more life-experience and practical wisdom, has become entitled to 'manage women's affairs', and, in case of their recalcitrance, admonish them, leave them alone in their beds and, lastly, to beat them without causing injury. (pp. 294–5)

Having given his interpretation of verse 4:34 and the rationale behind the gender inequality in the Qur'an, Rahman then poses two questions: are these socio-economic roles on which gender inequality is based immutable, even if women want to change them? If they are changeable, how far can they be changed? His answer to the first question is a definite no, these inequalities are not inherent in the nature of the sexes: they are the product of historical socio-economic developments. Once women acquire education and participate in society and economy, the 'degree' [of privilege] that the Qur'an says men have over women also disappears. But the answer to the second question, Rahman contends, is not that simple, and he is hesitant regarding whether 'women should ask or be allowed to do any and all jobs that men do' – although he admits that 'if women insist on and persist in this, they can and eventually will do so' (p. 295).

However, he has no doubt that law reforms must give women equality in all other spheres; classical *fiqh* rulings in marriage, divorce and inheritance can and must be reformed because 'it is the most fundamental and urgent requirement of the Qur'an in the social sector that abuses and injustices be removed' (p. 295). These inequalities are now the cause of suffering and oppression and go against the Qur'anic spirit, which is that of the equality of all human beings.

He then goes on to discuss in detail the laws of polygamy, divorce, inheritance and hijab, and reiterates the gist of his framework:

> One must completely accept our general contention that the specific legal rules of the Qur'an are conditioned by the socio-historical background of their enactment and what is eternal therein is the social objectives or moral principles explicitly stated or strongly implied in that legislation. This would, then, clear the way for further legislation in the light of those social objectives or moral principles. This argument remains only elliptically hinted at by the Modernist, who has used it in an *ad hoc* manner only for the issue of polygamy, and has not clearly formulated it as a general principle. (p. 301)

Rahman ends by stressing that legal reform can only be effective in changing the status of women in Muslim contexts when there is an adequate basis for social change. It is only then that the Qur'anic objective of social justice in general, and for women in particular, can be fulfilled; otherwise its success will be limited, transitory and confined to certain social groups (p. 308).

6. Where we are now: new contexts and new questions

Appearing at two different junctures in the twentieth century, these pioneering texts by al-Tahir al-Haddad and Fazlur Rahman laid the ground for an egalitarian construction of family law within an Islamic framework. The issues that they raise are still with us, and still relevant to current debates and struggles to reshape and redefine Muslim family laws, but two developments towards the end of the last century changed the context and tone of these debates.

The first was the ways in which the successes of political Islam and the ideological use of Shariʿa transformed relations between religion, law and politics for Muslims. The slogan 'return to Shariʿa' amounted, in practice, to nothing more than an attempt to translate classical *fiqh* rulings on gender relations and family and some areas of penal law into state policy. In late colonial times and the immediately post-colonial middle decades of the century, activist women in Muslim contexts had increasingly come to identify Islam with patriarchy, and to fear that the removal of the latter could not be achieved under a polity and a legal regime dominated by Islam. Now, wherever Islamists gained power or influence – as in Iran, Sudan, Pakistan and Malaysia – their policies proved the validity of the activists' fears. Arguing for patriarchal rulings as 'God's Law', as the authentic 'Islamic' way of life, they tried to reverse some of the legal gains that women had acquired earlier in the century; they dismantled elements of earlier family law reforms and introduced morality laws, such as gender segregation and dress codes.

But these Islamist measures had some unintended consequences: the most important was that, in several countries, they brought classical *fiqh* texts out of the closet, and exposed them to unprecedented critical scrutiny and public debate. Muslim women now found ways to sustain a critique – from within – of patriarchal readings of the Shariʿa and of the gender biases of *fiqh* texts in ways that were previously impossible. At the same time, a new wave of Muslim reform thinkers started to respond to the Islamist challenge and to take Islamic legal thought onto new ground. Building on the efforts of previous reformers, and using the conceptual tools and theories of other branches of knowledge, they have developed further interpretive–epistemological theories. Their conceptual tools, such as the distinctions between religion (*dīn*) and religious knowledge (*maʿrifat-e dini*), between Shariʿa and *fiqh*, or between essentials and accidentals in the Qur'an, have stretched the limits of traditional interpretations of Islam's sacred texts. Revisiting the old theological debates, they have revived the rationalist approach that was eclipsed when legalism took over as the dominant mode and gave precedence to the form of the law over the substance and spirit.[49]

The second development was the expansion of transnational feminism and women's groups, and the emergence of NGOs, which led to the opening of a new phase in the politics of gender and law reform in Muslim contexts. In the first part of the twentieth century women were largely absent from the process of the reform and codification of family law and the debates that surrounded it. But by the end of the century, Muslim women were refusing to be merely objects of the law, but rather claiming the right to speak and to be active participants in the debates and in the process of law-making. The changed status of women in Muslim societies, and other socio-economic imperatives, meant that many more women than before were educated and in employment. Women's rights were, by now, part of human rights discourse, and human rights treaties and documents, in particular CEDAW, gave women a new language in which to frame their demands.

The confluence of these two developments opened new space for activism and debate. Both recognised religious authorities (*fuqahā'*), and those with other interpretations and agendas – not least women scholars and laypeople – started engaging in debate and in criticism of the interpretations, old and new, of key concepts such as *qiwāma*. There were always Muslim reformers and women who argued for an egalitarian interpretation of the Shariʿa, but it was not until the 1980s that critical feminist voices and scholarship emerged from within the Muslim legal tradition, in the form of a new literature that deserves the label 'feminist', in that it is sustained and informed by an analysis that inserts gender as a category of thought into religious knowledge. Pioneering authors of such literature included Azizah Al-Hibri, Riffat Hassan, Amina Wadud and Fatima Mernissi;[50] they are now being followed by others who are breaking new ground.[51] A new consciousness emerged, a gender discourse that came to be labelled 'Islamic feminism'.[52] This discourse, energised by new feminist scholarship in Islam, was further facilitated by the rapid spread of new technologies, notably the internet, and these new technologies have regularly shown their potential for the mobilisation of campaigns for change.

By engaging with the tradition from within, these new feminist voices and scholars in Islam have begun to insert women's concerns and voices into the processes of the production of religious knowledge and legal reform. In so doing, they can bridge two gaps in the Muslim family law debates and in the Muslim legal tradition. First, a majority of Muslim religious scholars are gender blind, being largely ignorant of feminist theories and unaware of the importance of gender as a category of thought. Secondly, in line with mainstream feminism, many women's rights activists and campaigners in Muslim contexts have long considered working within a religious framework to be counter-productive; choosing to work only within a human rights framework, they have avoided any religion-based arguments. They have tended to ignore that there is also an epistemological side to feminism, in the sense of examining how we know what we know about women in all branches of knowledge and in religious tradition. This knowledge not only sheds light on laws and practices that take their legitimacy from religion but enables a challenge, from within, to the patriarchy that is institutionalised in Muslim legal tradition.

Before considering, finally, the implication of feminist scholarship for twenty-first century debates over Muslim family laws, let me bring together the two elements that run through my narrative and argument in this chapter. First, the idea of gender equality, which became inherent to global conceptions of justice in the course of the twentieth century, has presented Muslim legal tradition with an 'epistemological crisis'[53] with varying degrees of success. Secondly, the breakthrough came in the last two decades of the century with the emergence of feminist voices and scholarship in Islam, which, as I have argued elsewhere, is the 'unwanted child' of political Islam. The Islamists' attempt to turn patriarchal interpretations of the Shari'a into policy made the intimate links between theology, law and politics more and more transparent. It led to new forms of activism among Muslims and the emergence of new discourses, which eventually opened the way for a constructive and meaningful dialogue between Muslim legal tradition and feminism.

By bringing the insights of feminist theory and gender studies into Islamic studies, feminist scholarship in Islam can enable us to ask new questions. For example, the *maqāṣid* approach has captured the imagination of many Muslim reformist thinkers:[54] what does it have to offer to those seeking gender equality? Does the concept of *qiwāma* have positive elements that should be retained? Should the link affirmed by classical *fiqh* between maintenance (*nafaqa*) and obedience (*tamkīn*) be redefined or severed? One of the basic necessities that the Shari'a aims to protect is *nasl*: progeny, family; so far, this has been done in a patriarchal form. What kind of family do Shariʿa-based laws aim to protect? What do equality and justice mean for women and the family? Do they entail identical rights and duties in marriage? In other words, is legal equality good for women and the family?

These questions are at the centre of debates in feminist scholarship. There is a shift from 'formal' models of equality to 'substantive' models that take into account the differing needs of different women and the direct and indirect discrimination that they face.[55] A formal model of equality, which often simply requires a reversibility and comparison between the sexes, does not necessarily enable women to enjoy their rights on the same basis as men. Feminist legal theorist Catherine MacKinnon tells us why such a model of equality rests on a false premise: neither the starting point nor the playing field are the same for both sexes.[56] Not only do women not have the same access as men to socio-economic resources and political opportunities, but women are not a homogeneous group; they do not experience legal inequality and discrimination in the same way; and class, age, race and socio-economic situation are all important factors. In short, what kind of laws and legal reforms are needed so that equality of opportunity and result can be ensured? CEDAW, for instance, does not define equality; rather, its provisions are directed at eliminating discrimination, and here it rightly adopts an abolitionist language. How useful is such a language in Muslim contexts, given the primacy of law in Islamic discourses and the intimate links between *fiqh* and cultural models of the family? Is this the best way of approaching the tension between 'protection' and 'domination' that is inherent in the very concept of *qiwāma*, however we define it? In Islamist and traditionalist discourses, *qiwāma* is presented as a manifestation of 'protection', not of discrimination; such an approach could draw attention to the 'domination' side of *qiwāma* and counter apologetic arguments that are based on ideologies and hypothetical cases rather than on lived realities and women's experience.

The search for answers to these questions takes us to realms outside Islamic legal tradition, to human rights law, feminist legal theory and experiences of family law reform in other legal traditions. If, in the twentieth century, scholars like al-Tahir al-Haddad and Fazlur Rahman bridged the gap between classical *fiqh* and modern notions of justice by providing a framework for an egalitarian interpretation of Islamic sacred texts, in the twenty-first century the new feminist voices and scholarship in Islam have opened up a dialogue with Muslim legal tradition. But a meaningful and constructive dialogue can only take place when the two parties can treat each other as equals and with respect, when they are ready to listen to each other's arguments, and to change position if necessary. This takes us once again to the realm of power relations; the theological is also necessarily – and intensely – political, in ways similar to the feminist understanding that the personal is political.

Notes

1 I would like thank Cassandra Balchin for her extensive and perceptive comments; and Richard Tapper, as always, for help with thinking through the argument and with editing. Any remaining faults are mine.

2 Al-Jawziyya, Ibn Qayyim, *I'lām al-Muwaqqi'īn 'an Rabb al-'Ālamīn* (Beirut: Dar al-Fikr al-'Arabi, 1955), Vol. 3, p. 1.

3 Quoted in Rapoport, Yossef, *Marriage, Money and Divorce in Medieval Islamic Society* (Cambridge: Cambridge University Press, 2005), p. 52.

4 He is also an inspiration for Islamist movements in Sunni contexts. For his thought and scholarship, see Bori, Caterina and Livant Holtzman (eds), *A Scholar in the Shadow: Essays on the Legal and Theological Thought of Ibn Qayyim al-Ǧawziyyah*, thematic issue of *Oriente Moderno* 90/1 (Rome: Herder, 2010).

5 For example, by Masud, Muhammad Khalid, *Shatibi's Philosophy of Islamic Law* (New Delhi: Kitab Bhavan, 1997); the statement also features on the Musawah website (www.musawah.org), as well as on those of many conservative and reactionary Muslim organisations.

6 In recent years this debate has come to centre on the notion of 'Islamic feminism', to which I return later. For recent contributions to this debate, see Badran, Margot, 'From Islamic feminism to a Muslim holistic feminism', *Institute of Development Studies Bulletin* 42/1 (2011), pp. 78–87; Mir-Hosseini, Ziba, 'Muslim women's quest for equality: between Islamic law and feminism', *Critical Inquiry* 32/1 (2006), pp. 629–45, and *idem*, 'Beyond "Islam" vs "Feminism"', *Institute of Development Studies Bulletin* 42/1 (2011), pp. 67–77.

7 For instance, see Moghissi, Haideh, *Feminism and Islamic Fundamentalism: The Limits of Post-Modern Analysis* (London: Zed Press, 1999).

8 For instance, see Mir-Hosseini, 'Muslim women's quest'.

9 The translation is by Ali, Kecia, 'Muslim sexual ethics: understanding a difficult verse, Qur'an 4:34', available at http://www.brandeis.edu/projects/fse/muslim/diff-verse.html (accessed 15 September 2012); transliteration added. Ali leaves the italicised words untranslated, pointing out that any translation is, in the end, an interpretation; she also provides links to three other translations of the verse and to additional interpretations: available at http://www.brandeis.edu/projects/fse/muslim/translation.html (accessed 15 September 2012).

10 See, for instance, AbuSulayman, AbdulHamid A., *Marital Discord: Recapturing the Full Islamic Spirit of Human Dignity*, Occasional Paper Series 11 (London and Washington: The International Institute of Islamic Thought, 2003); Al-Hibri, Aziza, 'An Islamic perspective on domestic violence', *Fordham Law Journal* 27 (2003–4), pp. 195–224; Wadud, Amina, *Qur'an and Woman: Rereading the Sacred Text from a Woman's Perspective* (Oxford and New York: Oxford University Press, 1999), pp. 70–9; *idem*, *Inside the Gender Jihad: Women's Reform in Islam* (Oxford: Oneworld, 2006), pp. 198–202; Guardi, Jolana, 'Women reading the Qur'an: religious discourse

in Islam', *Hawwa: Journal of Women in the Middle East and the Islamic World* 2/3 (2004), pp. 301–15; Dunn, Shannon and Rosemary B. Kellison, 'At the intersection of scripture and law: Qur'an 4:34 and violence against women', *Journal of Feminist Studies in Religion* 26/2 (Fall 2010), pp. 11–36; Marín, Manuela, 'Disciplining wives: a historical reading of Qur'ān 4:34', *Studia Islamica* 97 (2003), pp. 5–40; Shaikh, Sa'diyya, 'Exegetical violence: *Nushūz* in Qur'ānic gender ideology', *Journal for Islamic Studies* 17 (1997), pp. 49–73; Mubarak, Hadia, 'Breaking the interpretive monopoly: a re-examination of verse 4:34', *Hawwa* 2/3 (2004), pp. 261–89; Mahmoud, Mohamed A., 'To beat or not to beat: on the exegetical dilemmas over Qur'ān, 4:34', *Journal of American Oriental Society* 126/4 (2006), pp. 537–50.

11 For instance, a panel at the 2006 meeting of the American Academy of Religion was devoted to discussion of the verse; the papers were published in the *Comparative Islamic Studies* 2/2 (2006), see editorial; see also Al-Hibri, 'An Islamic perspective on domestic violence', pp. 195–224; Elsaidi, Murad H., 'Human rights and Islamic law: a legal analysis challenging the husband's authority to punish "rebellious" wives', *Muslim World Journal of Human Rights* 7/2 (2011), article 4, pp. 1–25.

12 They remained at the level of ethical recommendations without legal force. For discussion of al-Shafi'i's treatment of this verse and its contradiction with the Prophet's Sunna, see Ali, Kecia, *Sexual Ethics and Islam: Feminist Reflections on Qur'an, Hadith and Jurisprudence* (Oxford: Oneworld, 2006); *idem*, 'The best of you will not strike', *Comparative Islamic Studies* 2/2 (2006), pp. 143–55.

13 I take the concept of a 'legal postulate' from Chiba, who defines it as a norm, a value system that simply exists in its own right, as an element of a specific cultural context, which is connected with a particular 'official' or 'unofficial law'. For his tripartite model of legal systems ('official law', 'unofficial law' and 'legal postulates'), see Chiba, Masaji (ed.), *Asian Indigenous Law in Interaction with Received Law* (London and New York: KPI, 1986).

14 Mir-Hosseini, Ziba, 'The construction of gender in Islamic legal thought and strategies for reform', *Hawwa* 1/1 (2003), pp. 1–28; *idem*, 'Towards gender equality: Muslim family law and the Shari'a', in Zainah Anwar (ed.), *Wanted: Equality and Justice in Muslim Family Law* (Kuala Lumpur: Sisters in Islam, 2009), available at http://www.musawah.org/wanted-equality-and-justice-muslim-family (accessed 10 September 2012).

15 For discussions of how early jurists conceptualised marriage, see Ali, Kecia, *Marriage and Slavery in Early Islam* (Cambridge, MA: Harvard University Press, 2010); Rapoport: *Marriage, Money and Divorce*.

16 Ibn Rushd, *The Distinguished Jurist's Primer: Bidāyat al-Mujtahid wa Nihāyat al-Muqtaṣid*, trans. Imran Ahsan Khan Nyazee (Reading: Garnet Publishing, 1996), Vol. 2, p. 63.

17 See Mahmoud, 'To beat or not to beat', n. 35.

18 See, for instance, Rapoport: *Marriage, Money and Divorce*; Sonbol, Amira El Azhary (ed.), *Women, the Family, and Divorce Laws in Islamic History* (Syracuse: Syracuse University Press, 1996); Tucker, Judith, *In the House of Law: Gender and Islamic Law in Ottoman Syria and Palestine* (Berkeley: University of California Press, 2000).

19 For the ways in which these arguments shape legal rulings, see in particular Ali, *Marriage and Slavery*; 'Abd Al 'Ati, Hammudah, *The Family Structure in Islam* (Indianapolis: American Trust Publications, 1997); Mahmoud, 'To beat or not to beat'.

20 This section repeats an argument I have published in other places, but which I feel is essential background to what follows; see 'Criminalizing sexuality: *Zina* laws as violence against women in Muslim contexts' (Women Living Under Muslim Laws, 2010), available at http://www.stop-stoning.org/node/882 (accessed 15 September 2012).

21 For the codification, see Anderson, James Norman, *Law Reforms in the Muslim World* (London: Athlone, 1976); Mahmood, Tahir, *Family Law Reform in the Muslim World* (Bombay: N. M. Tripathi, 1972).

22 These were established *fiqh* procedures: eclectic choice (*takhayyur*) and mixing (*talfiq*) of legal opinions and rulings from different schools; the exercise of *ijtihād* remained limited. For a discussion, see Rahman, Fazlur, 'A survey of modernization of Muslim family law', *International Journal of Middle East Studies* 11 (1980), pp. 451–65.

23 The book was translated into English in 2007; Husni, Ronak and Daniel Newman, *Muslim Women in Law and Society: Annotated Translation of al-Ṭāhir al-Ḥaddād's* Imra'tunā fi 'l-sharī'a wa 'l-mujtama', *with an introduction* (London: Routledge, 2007).

24 For the intellectual genealogy of al-Haddad's text, see Husni and Newman: *Muslim Women*, pp. 1–25; for accounts of the intellectual and social change that made women's issues central to politics, see Ahmed, Leila, *Women and Gender in Islam: Historical Roots of a Modern Debate* (New Haven: Yale University Press, 1992), pp. 127–43; for the experience of different countries, see Keddie, Nikki, *Women in the Middle East: Past and Present* (Princeton: Princeton University Press, 2007), pp. 60–101.

25 These reformist texts – as others have noted – often tended to reinforce patriarchal notions of women's traditional roles as wives, mothers and guardians of Islamic tradition; Zayzafoon makes this criticism of al-Haddad's text. Zayzafoon, Lamia Ben Youssef, *The Production of the Muslim Woman: Negotiating Text, History, and Ideology* (New York: Lexington Books, 2005), chapter 4. For another critique of Qasim Amin, see Ahmed, *Women and Gender*, chapter 8.

26 A joint campaign by Moroccan and Tunisian women's organisations went public in 2006, with a two-volume publication, *Egalité dans l'héritage: Pour une citoyenneté pleine et entière* (Tunis: Association des Femmes tunisiennes pour la Recherche et le Développement).

27 For this biographical account, I have largely relied on Husni and Newman's 'Introduction', *Muslim Women*, pp. 19–25.

28 For a discussion of the political context, reactions to al-Haddad's book and the politics of family law in Tunisia, see Salem, Norma, 'Islam and the status of women in Tunisia', in Freda Hussain (ed.), *Muslim Women* (London: Croom Helm, 1984), pp. 141–68; Boulby, Marion, 'The Islamic challenge: Tunisia since independence', *Third World Quarterly* 10/2 (1988), pp. 590–614; Charrad, Mounira, *States and Women's Rights: The Making of Postcolonial Tunisia, Algeria and Morocco* (Berkeley and Los Angeles: University of California Press, 2001).

29 Husni and Newman, *Muslim Women*, n. 58 p. 174. Ibn 'Ashur's treatise on *maqāṣid al-sharīʿa* is now available in English: Ibn 'Ashur, Muhammad al-Tahir, *Treatise on Maqāṣid al-Sharīʿah*, trans. and annotated by Mohamed El-Tahir El-Mesawi (London and Washington: The International Institute of Islamic Thought, 2006).

30 Quotations and references are from Husni and Newman, *Muslim Women*.

31 This phrase appears towards the end of al-Haddad's preface to the book; here I did not use Husni and Newman's translation, which renders the phrase as 'we regard them as an object to satisfy our desires' (p. 31).

32 Qur'an 30:21, the translation is by Yusuf Ali, p. 1012; interestingly, Yusuf Ali finds it necessary to include a footnote comment to the effect that tranquillity, love and mercy are found in the normal relations of a father and mother, and love and mercy between men and women, excluding any possible alternative reading of the text.

33 This is from Yusuf Ali's translation, p. 92; see below for Asad's translation, which is rather different and, I find, clearer.

34 Asad's translation of the whole verse is: 'And the divorced woman shall undergo without marrying, a waiting period of three monthly courses: for it is not lawful for them to conceal what God may have created in their wombs, if they believe in God and the Last Day. And during this period their husbands are fully entitled to take them back, if they desire reconciliation; but, in accordance with justice, the rights of the wives [with regard to their husbands] are equal to [husbands'] rights with regard to them, although men have precedence over them [in this respect]. And God is almighty, wise.' Asad, Muhammad, *The Message of the Qur'an* (Bristol: Foundation Books, 2003), p. 61.

35 For an overview and analysis of these reforms, see Kelly, Patricia, 'Finding common ground: Islamic values and gender equity in Tunisia's reformed personal status

code', in *Shifting Boundaries in Marriage and Divorce in Muslim Communities*, Special Dossier 1 (Women Living Under Muslim Laws, Autumn 1996), pp. 74–105.

36 Prominent among them were Syed Ahmad Khan (1817–1898) and Muhammad Iqbal (1877–1938). Iqbal delivered his reform agenda in a series of six lectures published in Lahore in 1930: Iqbal, Muhammad, *Reconstruction of Religious Thought in Islam* (London: Oxford University Press, 1934). These lectures, which did not receive much attention at the time, later became central to the formation of Muslim reform thought. For an illuminating exposition of Iqbal's lecture on the notion of *ijtihād*, see Masud, Khalid, *Iqbal's Reconstruction of Ijtihad* (2nd edn, Lahore: Saadat Art Press, 2003).

37 For an analysis of their impact on the rethinking of notions of gender rights in Muslim legal tradition, see Moosa, Ebrahim, 'The poetics and politics of law after empire: reading women's rights in the contestations of law', *UCLA Journal of Islamic and Near Eastern Law* 1/1 (Fall/Winter 2001–2), pp. 1–46.

38 His father, Mawlana Shibat al-Din, was a graduate of the Deoband Seminary in India.

39 Major family law reforms in the subcontinent took place before Rahman's directorship, such as the 1939 Dissolution of Marriages Act and the 1961 Muslim Family Laws Ordinance. Women's groups were instrumental in pushing for these reforms.

40 For studies on Fazlur Rahman's work, see Sonn, Tamara, 'Fazlur Rahman's Islamic methodology', *The Muslim World* 81/3–4 (1991), pp. 212–30; Ebrahim Moosa's introduction to Rahman's *Revival and Reform in Islam* (Oxford: Oneworld, 2000); Saeed, Abdullah, 'Fazlur Rahman: a framework for interpreting the ethico-legal content of the Qur'an', in Suha Taji-Farouki (ed.), *Modern Muslim Intellectuals and the Qur'an* (Oxford: Oxford University Press, 2004), pp. 37–66. For his impact on American Islamic discourse, see Waugh, Earle H. and Frederic M. Denny (eds), *The Shaping of An American Islamic Discourse: A Memorial to Fazlur Rahman* (Atlanta: Scholars Press, 1998).

41 For his views on gender rights and his impact on the development of a new Islamic feminism, see Part III of Waugh and Denny: *The Shaping*, in particular the chapter by Tamara Sonn, 'Fazlur Rahman and Islamic feminism', pp. 123–46.

42 Rahman, 'A survey of modernization', p. 451.

43 Sonn, 'Fazlur Rahman and Islamic feminism', p. 128.

44 Rahman, Fazlur, *Islam and Modernity: Transformation of an Intellectual Tradition* (Chicago and London: University of Chicago Press, 1982), p. 5.

45 Rahman, *Islam and Modernity*, p. 7.

46 Rahman, Fazlur, 'The status of women in Islam: a modernist interpretation', in Hanna Papanek and Gail Minault (eds), *Separate Worlds: Studies of Purdah in South Asia* (Delhi: Chanakya Publications, 1982), pp. 285–310. The article also appeared in a revised and shortened version in a later collection on women's

rights in Islam: Nashat, Guity (ed.), *Women and Revolution in Iran* (Boulder, CO: Westview Press, 1983), pp. 37–54.

47 Rahman does not spell out the differences here, but in a later article he gives us a clue as to what he means when he states the position of a Muslim modernist: 'While he espouses the cause of the emancipation of women, for example, he is not blind to the havoc produced in the West by its new sex ethics, not least in the dilapidation of the family institution.' Rahman, Fazlur, 'Islam and political action: politics in the service of religion', in Nigel Biggar, Jamie Scot and William Schweiker (eds), *Cities of Gods: Faith, Politics and Pluralism in Judaism, Christianity and Islam* (New York: Greenwood Press, 1986), p. 160.

48 References are to Rahman, 'Status of women', in Papanek and Minault.

49 In this respect, the works of the new wave of Muslim thinkers such as Mohammad Arkoun, Khaled Abou El Fadl, Nasr Hamid Abu-Zayd, Mohammad Mojtahed Shabestari and Abdolkarim Soroush are of immense importance and relevance. For Arkoun, see Gunther, Ursula, 'Mohammad Arkoun: towards a radical rethinking of Islamic thought', in Taji-Farouki: *Modern Muslim Intellectuals*, pp. 125–67; for Abou El Fadl, see his *Speaking in God's Name: Islamic Law, Authority and Women* (Oxford: Oneworld, 2001); for Abu-Zayd, see Kermani, Navid, 'From revelation to interpretation: Nasr Hamid Abu-Zayd and the literary study of the Qur'an', in Taji-Farouki: *Modern Muslim Intellectuals*, pp. 169–92; for Soroush, see his *Reason, Freedom, and Democracy in Islam: Essential Writings of 'Abdolkarim Sorush*, trans. and ed. with a critical introduction by Mahmoud Sadri and Ahmed Sadri (Oxford: Oxford University Press, 2000) and the articles available on his website (http://www.drsoroush.com/English.htm), and for his ideas on gender, see Mir-Hosseini, Ziba, *Islam and Gender: The Religious Debate in Contemporary Iran* (Princeton: Princeton University Press, 1999), chapter 7; for Shabestari, see Vahdat, Farzin, 'Post-revolutionary modernity in Iran: the subjective hermeneutics of Mohamad Mojtahed Shabestari', in Taji-Farouki, *Modern Muslim Intellectuals*, pp. 193–224, and articles and interviews at *Qantara.de* (http://qantara.de/webcom/show_article.php/_c-575/i.html).

50 Their early works are: Al-Hibri, Aziza, 'A study of Islamic herstory: how did we get into this mess?' in *Islam and Women*, special issue of *Women's Studies International Forum* 5/2 (1982), pp. 201–19; Hassan, Riffat, 'Feminism in Islam' in Arvind Sharma and Katherine Young (eds), *Feminism and World Religions* (New York: State University of New York Press, 1999), pp. 248–78; Mernissi, Fatima, *Women and Islam: An Historical and Theological Enquiry*, trans. Mary Jo Lakeland (Oxford: Blackwell, 1991); Wadud, *Qur'an and Woman*.

51 See, for instance, Ali, Kecia, 'Progressive Muslims and Islamic jurisprudence: the necessity for critical engagement with marriage and divorce law', in Omid Safi (ed.), *Progressive Muslims* (Oxford: Oneworld, 2003), pp. 163–89; Barlas, Asma,

'Believing Women' in Islam: Unreading Patriarchal Interpretations of the Qur'an (Austin: University of Texas Press, 2002); Shaikh, 'Exegetical violence'; Engineer, Asghar Ali, *The Rights of Women in Islam* (London: Hurst, 1992); Jawad, Haifaa, *The Rights of Women in Islam: An Authentic Approach* (London: Macmillan, 1998); Mir-Hosseini: 'Construction of gender'; Sonbol, Amira El-Azhary, 'Rethinking women and Islam', in Yvonne Haddad and John Esposito (eds), *Daughters of Abraham: Feminist Thought in Judaism, Christianity, and Islam* (Gainesville: University of Florida Press, 2000); Anwar, *Wanted.*

52 I was among the first to use the term 'Islamic feminism', to refer to the new gender consciousness emerging in Iran a decade after the 1979 Revolution. Mir-Hosseini, Ziba, 'Stretching the limits: a feminist reading of the Shari'a in post-revolutionary Iran', in Mai Yamani (ed.), *Islam and Feminism: Legal and Literary Perspectives* (London: Ithaca, 1996), pp. 285–319. However, more recently I have questioned its usefulness as an analytical or descriptive tool, given the heavy political and rhetorical baggage it has since acquired. *Idem*, 'Beyond "Islam" vs "Feminism"', pp. 67–77.

53 I borrow this concept from the philosopher Alasdair MacIntyre, who argues that every rational inquiry is embedded in a tradition of learning, and that tradition reaches an epistemological crisis when, by its own standards of rational justification, disagreements can no longer be resolved rationally. This gives rise to an internal critique that will eventually transform the tradition, if it is to survive. It is then that thinkers and producers in that tradition of inquiry gradually start to respond and assimilate the idea that is alien to the tradition. See MacIntyre, Alasdair, *Whose Justice? Which Rationality?* (Notre Dame, IN: University of Notre Dame Press, 1988), pp. 350–2; *idem*, 'The rationality of traditions', in Christopher W. Gowans (ed.), *Moral Disagreements: Classic and Contemporary Readings* (London, Routledge, 2000), pp. 204–16. For a critique of MacIntyre's theory of justice and his neglect of gender, see Okin, Susan Moller, 'Whose traditions? Which understanding?' in *idem, Justice, Gender and the Family* (Princeton: Princeton University Press, 1987), chapter 3.

54 'Objectives of Shari'a'; for an explanation and discussion, see Khalid Masud's chapter, this volume.

55 For instance, see Scott, Joan, 'Deconstructing equality-versus-difference: or, the uses of poststructuralist theory for feminism', *Feminist Studies* 14/1 (1998), pp. 33–50; Fredman, Sandra, 'Providing equality: substantive equality and the positive duty to provide', *South African Journal of Human Rights* 21 (2005), pp. 163–90.

56 MacKinnon, Catherine, *Towards a Feminist Theory of the State* (Boston: Harvard University Press, 1989).

Part I
Perspectives on Reality

2

QIWĀMA IN EGYPTIAN FAMILY LAWS

'Wifely Obedience' between Legal Texts, Courtroom Practices and Realities of Marriages

Mulki Al-Sharmani

Egyptian Muslim family laws (known as personal status laws) were codified in 1920.[1] Personal Status Law No. 25 of 1920 and its amendments (i.e. Law No. 25 of 1929 and Law No. 100 of 1985) were largely drawn from the doctrines of classical Islamic jurisprudence (*fiqh*) through a process of selection, modification and patching together of different legal opinions of classical jurists. Some well-known historians, who have studied this process and the earlier, pre-codification legal system of Shari'a Courts, argue that codification has, for the most part, worked against Egyptian women.[2] These scholars contend that although the old legal system of *fiqh* manuals and Shari'a Courts – presided over by religiously trained judges from different schools of Islamic law – espoused a patriarchal model of marriage, its legal pluralism, fluidity and decentralised judicial process still enabled women to have choices, to exercise agency and to enjoy protection from the abuses of the doctrinally sanctioned patriarchy.

Thus, Egyptian women's rights activists, from the 1920s until the present day, have engaged in various efforts to reform the codified personal status laws. Some of the main problem areas in the existing personal status laws for present-day activists seeking gender justice are unequal parenting rights and men's right to unilateral repudiation and polygamy, both of which men can exercise without resorting to the court. While men have almost unconditional divorce rights, women have restricted access to limited types of divorce that can only be obtained through court.

According to current family laws, a wife can file for fault-based judicial divorce on six grounds, namely non-maintenance, absence, defect, harm, the husband's polygamy and imprisonment. In fault-based judicial divorce, a female litigant has to provide to the court proof of spousal fault and often undergoes a long and costly legal process. Moreover, even when women win such cases, court judgments can be appealed by husbands. In 2000, women were granted the right to no-fault divorce known as *khulʿ*. Yet women still have to seek *khulʿ* through a lawsuit, undergo court-ordered arbitration and forfeit their post-divorce financial dues.

Another contentious area in the current family code is that it stipulates and upholds men's right to wifely obedience, which is linked to the notion of the husband's *qiwāma* (i.e. guardianship) over his spouse. In this chapter, I will examine how *qiwāma* (men's obligation to protect, provide and guard their family) is constructed in Egyptian substantive family codes,[3] and how this legal construction is implemented in courtroom practices. My goal is to explore the ways in which this legal concept shapes women's rights in marriage and how it impacts women's claims and strategies in the courtroom.[4] I wish to shed light on the ways in which existing laws on *qiwāma* are implicated in the hierarchical and discriminatory model of marriage that Egyptian reformers are seeking to change.[5] *Qiwāma* will be examined through the laws regulating the husband's obligation to provide for his wife and the latter's legal duty to obey him.

The analysis in this chapter draws on data collected from interviews with 30 male and female plaintiffs (15 of each gender) in obedience cases, a focus group discussion with ten lawyers and observation of court proceedings in a Giza court.[6] In addition, statistical data on obedience cases were collected from five family courts in the governorates of Giza, Cairo and Sixth of October for the periods 2001 to 2009, and 30 court judgments were analysed. Finally, this chapter also draws on data collected from interviews with 100 Egyptian men and women (50 of each gender). These interviews focused on informants' marriage choices and marital roles, as well as their knowledge of recent reforms in family laws. Interviewees of different marital statuses were selected.[7]

1. *Qiwāma* in Islamic jurisprudence and Egyptian family laws

Islamic *fiqh* constructs marital roles in terms of a husband's *qiwāma* (i.e. authority and protection) over his wife and the latter's obedience (*ṭāʿa*) to him.[8] This construction is based on early jurists' interpretation of the following Qur'anic verse:

> Men are the protectors (*qawwāmūn*) and maintainers of women because God has given the one more strength (*faḍḍala*) than the other and because they support them from their means. Therefore the righteous (*qānitāt*) women are devoutly

> obedient and guard in the husband's absence what God would have them guard. As to those women on whose part ye fear disloyalty and ill-conduct, admonish them first. Next, refuse to share their beds. And last beat them lightly; but if they return to obedience, seek not against them means of annoyance (4:34, Yusuf Ali's translation).[9]

Therefore, a husband has a duty to provide for his wife, and in return the wife makes herself available to him, and puts herself under his authority and protection. The husband's exclusive right to his wife's sexual and reproductive labour is acquired through and conditioned upon his economic role. This model of marriage does not recognise shared matrimonial resources. Whatever possessions and assets the wife brings to the marriage remain hers. Likewise, apart from maintenance for herself and her children, the wife cannot make claims to resources acquired by the husband during marriage. In addition, the husband has unilateral right to repudiation and polygamy.

Marriage in modern Egyptian family laws reflects some of the main features of *fiqh*-based marriage. Article 1 in Egypt's Personal Status Law No. 25 of 1920 (amended by PSL No. 25 of 1929 and PSL No. 100 of 1985) stipulates that 'maintenance shall be the wife's right and due on her husband from the authentic date of the contract if she shall have given herself to him in marriage even if virtually and despite her being wealthy or different from him in religion'. Thus, marital roles are also defined as the husband being a provider for his wife, while the role of the latter is to be sexually available to the husband. To fulfil this role, the wife is expected to be 'obedient' to her husband. The code defines wifely obedience indirectly by defining its opposite, namely disobedience or *nushūz*. Article 11 in the code stipulates that 'if the wife refrains from obeying the husband unjustifiably and without any right, the wife's alimony shall be discontinued from the date of disobedience'. The article adds that 'a wife shall be considered refraining from obedience to her husband if she does not return to the matrimonial house after her husband calls her to return by serving on her person or on her proxy, a notice via a bailiff. He shall indicate the location of the matrimonial house in this notice.' Thus, the code defines wifely disobedience (*nushūz*) as a wife's illegitimate refusal to reside in the matrimonial house. Moreover, a wife who is found to be disobedient (*nāshiz*) by the court loses her right to spousal maintenance.

Among the legitimate grounds that permit a wife to leave the matrimonial home and thus entitle her to contest her husband's ordinance for her obedience are: (1) if the husband has not paid her the prompt dower (*mahr*), (2) if the matrimonial house is not safe or adequate, (3) if the husband does not protect her or her money (e.g. abuses her and/or unlawfully takes her money or possessions), or (4) if her leaving the matrimonial house is for reasons sanctioned by the social norms (*'urf*). However, the law does not spell out what these reasons are. But it is commonly understood that some of the acceptable reasons would include leaving the matrimonial house to visit extended family or to seek education or health care. However, whether a wife's leaving the matrimonial house for work is considered a socially acceptable reason has been contested by litigants and judges. But the explanatory memorandum of PSL No. 100 of 1985 points out that in the case when a wife has written in her marriage contract that she holds a job, her husband cannot bring an obedience-ordinance case against her on the basis of her going out to work. It is noteworthy that up until 1967, a wife who was found to be disobedient by the court faced the threat of forcible return to the conjugal home by law enforcement officials should her husband so wish. Nowadays, while the forcible return of a disobedient wife to the matrimonial house has been abolished, her loss of spousal maintenance remains sanctioned by the law.

But how do these legal marital roles, which obligate a husband to be a provider for his wife in exchange for her obedience, actually work in court cases on the one hand, and in the real marriages of Egyptian couples on the other?

2. Courtroom practices and realities of marriage: obedience ordinances

To initiate an obedience-ordinance case, a husband needs to file for a claim with the court bailiff who then sends a notice to his wife. The notice should specify the matrimonial house where his wife is supposed to fulfil her role of residing and being physically available for her husband (*iḥtibās al-zawja*). The wife then has the legal right to contest the obedience ordinance within a period of 30 days from the time she has been served the notice. However, if the wife fails to contest the obedience ordinance within the defined period of time, the husband does not automatically win the obedience case. The next step for him is to file for a proof-of-*nushūz* case. And it is only after the husband wins this latter case that a wife loses her right to spousal maintenance. On the one hand, one could argue that this somewhat prolonged legal process seems to protect wives from an easy loss of their right to spousal maintenance. On the other, there are a number of ways in which husbands exploit the system to their advantage and to the detriment of the wife. For instance, it is not uncommon for husbands to have obedience ordinances sent to wrong addresses so that their wives do not receive them and thus fail to contest them within due time. In addition, in the new family court system, every family dispute case (including contesting an obedience ordinance) has to first go through mandatory pre-litigation mediation.[10] In theory, when a wife files for pre-litigation mediation, the filing should count as the beginning of her lawsuit to contest the obedience ordinance. But recent studies have reported that some judges do not consider the filing for mediation as constituting the plaintiff's fulfilment of the condition of contesting the obedience ordinance within the designated 30-day period.[11] Of course, the most obvious challenge that a wife faces in such a case is that she has to prove to the court the legitimacy of the grounds on which she is contesting the ordinance. But how do wives contest obedience ordinances? And is it difficult for them to establish legitimate grounds for their contestations? To answer this question, it is first necessary to shed light on the reasons why men file for obedience ordinances and why women contest them.

3. Reasons for filing for obedience cases and contesting them

The field data collected for this chapter show that husbands and wives use obedience cases for a variety of reasons that may or may not be directly related to the case itself. For instance, a husband may file for an obedience ordinance to offset a wife's efforts to seek judicial divorce; to negotiate for more advantageous financial settlement as the wife seeks judicial divorce; to respond to a maintenance claim, or as a pre-emptive legal tactic before the wife files for such a claim; or to affirm his position of power and authority before he negotiates (through legal and non-legal channels) for the return of his wife to the matrimonial home.

Most of the women who are served obedience ordinances from their husbands feel compelled to contest the ordinance. Their motivations, however, are diverse and go beyond protecting their right to maintenance. Some of these reasons include: facilitating their pursuit of divorce, claiming a matrimonial house that is separate from the dwelling of the in-laws and negotiating their right to work.

Some women leave the matrimonial house and are either considering or have started the process of seeking judicial divorce. These women (and their lawyers) believe that successfully contesting the obedience ordinance would strengthen their legal position in the divorce case. One of the main and common grounds on which a wife wins the contestation of an obedience ordinance is the husband's failure to protect her and/or her money. Proving the husband's failure to protect his wife means establishing that harm is inflicted on the wife, which improves the latter's chances of winning the divorce case. Interestingly, women who are seeking *khulʿ* are sometimes disputants in obedience-ordinance cases. This happens either because the husband files for obedience after the wife has filed for *khulʿ*, or because the wife files for *khulʿ* while in the process of the obedience lawsuit. What often happens in a number of these cases is that the wife first gets a *khulʿ* judgment, and, accordingly, wins the contestation of the obedience case on the grounds that a divorced wife does not owe 'obedience' to her husband. The following cases demonstrate how an obedience lawsuit evolves into divorce.

Case 1: Obedience and *khulʿ*

The plaintiff contested an obedience ordinance for which her husband filed on 14 October 2008. The plaintiff and her husband had been married for six years and have two young children together. The wife left the matrimonial house because the husband did not support her and the children, and he physically abused her. Two weeks after contesting the husband's obedience ordinance, the wife filed for *khulʿ*. Both lawsuits were combined and in September 2009, the wife received one court judgment both granting her *khulʿ* and approving her contestation of obedience on the grounds that a wife who has been divorced (irrevocably) through *khulʿ* owes her husband no 'obedience'.[12]

Case 2: Obedience and divorce on the grounds of harm

The plaintiff contested an obedience ordinance filed by the husband in 2005. The couple had been married for three years but had not consummated their marriage because the husband was still in the process of preparing the matrimonial house. In the obedience ordinance, the husband claimed that he had a matrimonial house ready and called his wife to 'obedience'. The wife contested on the grounds that the husband had seized the furniture which she had bought for the matrimonial house (the wife had a court judgment against the husband for the crime of seizing her furniture). The wife also provided police reports documenting her filing a complaint against her husband for assaulting her in the street. Three weeks into the contestation of the obedience case, the wife filed for prejudicial divorce. In 2007, the wife received one court judgment granting her prejudicial divorce and accepting her contestation of the obedience ordinance on the grounds that the husband had not 'protected her and her money' because 'he assaulted her and seized the furniture she bought for the matrimonial house'.[13]

Obedience ordinances are, of course, also closely tied to the issue of maintenance in multiple ways. For instance, in some of the cases where a wife has filed for spousal and child maintenance, the husband reacts by filing for an obedience ordinance and the wife accordingly contests the ordinance. In such court claims, the motivations and the goals of both partners are diverse and complex. Sometimes neither spouse wishes to end the marriage or to see the lawsuit through, but is instead using the court as a pathway for renegotiating their financial roles and responsibilities in the marriage. While some may succeed in obtaining their goal, others fail and find themselves on the way to divorce. The following case illustrates some of these issues.

Case 3: Obedience and renegotiating the husband's role as a provider

The couple had been married for five years and had two children. They had frequent arguments about the husband's financial responsibilities towards the wife. The husband did not want to pay for the fees of the hospital where his wife wished to give birth to their second child. This latest conflict escalated and the wife left the house a few days before giving birth to their second child. She stayed with her family who paid for her hospital fees, and refused to return until the husband agreed to giving her more adequate financial provision. A month later, the husband filed an obedience ordinance. The wife contested the ordinance. While the case was in progress, the couple reconciled on the condition that the husband would pay back to his in-laws half of the hospital fees.[14]

An interesting issue that I have found to be integral to obedience cases is the wife's financial contribution to the matrimonial house. The wife's financial role is often necessary for married couples, despite the ambivalence that both spouses feel about this role. Often women have to work before marriage to contribute to the financial costs of the wedding and the setting up of the matrimonial house.[15] After marriage, many husbands do not wish their wives to continue working, for a number of reasons, the most common of which are: (1) to have the wife devote her time to childcare and housework, and (2) to restrict the wife's mingling with other men. Women often feel ambivalent about maintaining their jobs because they lack work with good benefits and find the juggling of work and family too difficult, or do not feel their work strengthens or expands their marital rights (e.g. they cannot make legal claims on the grounds of their financial contribution).[16] But the harsh economic realities of many couples lead to situations where husbands (particularly those working in the informal labour market) are often unable to meet the needs of the family. Yet some of these husbands are reluctant for their wives to work for the reasons mentioned above. Some wives work despite their husbands' objections, and the conflict between the spouses escalates because of the husbands' sense of frustration at being unable to be an adequate provider. Also, both partners struggle for control of the wife's income. Other wives find themselves in a dilemma because they are unable to seek work due to their husbands' objections, and yet continue to have marital conflicts because of the husbands' failure to provide for the family. Women in both kinds of situations often end up leaving the matrimonial house. And, in response, the husband files an obedience ordinance. The following case demonstrates some of the above-mentioned challenges.

Case 4: Obedience and a wife's work

The woman plaintiff had been married for 15 years and has two children. She received no formal schooling. Before marriage she had a job in a factory, but stopped working afterwards because her husband did not want her to mingle with other men. The husband earned his living by installing tiles in houses. The couple had constant conflicts because of the husband's failure to provide adequately and his refusal to let the wife to go back to work. The husband worked intermittently, and also gave some of the income he earned to his extended family. Before the latest conflict, the husband had left the wife and children without support for several months, and moved back and forth between the matrimonial house and his parents' house. The wife and children left the matrimonial house and moved in with her family. The husband filed for obedience, and the wife contested it.

The wife was willing to resume marital relations if the husband agreed to her working and gave her and the children a monthly allowance. While the case was in progress, the wife started a small business buying and selling clothes to the women in the neighbourhood where her extended family lived.[17]

3. Obedience cases: procedures and outcomes for women

Once an obedience case reaches the court, the following procedures take place. The judge orders the court experts to:[18] (1) examine the matrimonial house to ascertain its adequacy and safety, and (2) meet with the disputants in order to gather more details about the marital conflict and to attempt a final reconciliation between the spouses. The court experts then submit written reports to the judge.

The arguments on which the legal representatives of wives commonly base their contestation of the husband's obedience ordinance faithfully follow the letter of the law. That is, the plaintiff's case is often based on the claims that: (1) the matrimonial house is not adequate, and/or (2) the husband has failed to protect the wife and/or her possessions.[19] In the reviewed court records, I found that the claim about the inadequacy of the matrimonial house was based on a number of reasons, the most common of which was that it was occupied by the husband's family. Another less common reason was that the husband was using the matrimonial house as his workplace. Yet another was that the matrimonial apartment was next to one that was occupied by Christian neighbours, and hence the wife claimed that she did not feel 'safe'.[20] The husband's failure to 'protect' his wife was based on the following grounds: his failure to support his wife and children, repeated physical and verbal abuse inflicted by him on his wife (substantiated by witness testimony and police reports) and/or his seizure of his wife's matrimonial furniture (also substantiated by a police report).

Contesting an obedience ordinance solely or mostly on the grounds of the 'inadequacy of the matrimonial house' was risky for a wife. Even in cases where the matrimonial house was occupied by family members, there were some factors that could persuade the court that the dwelling in question was still a legitimate matrimonial house. One factor was if the couple was still able to have privacy despite living with relatives, that is, if they had their own separate room, or their own door to their part of the dwelling. Other factors were whether the husband had the financial means to provide a separate dwelling for his wife, and if there were compelling reasons that led him to share residence with his extended family. Perhaps this explains why none of the 30 court records for obedience cases that I reviewed were solely based on the grounds of the inadequacy of the matrimonial house. Lawyers, however, gave a great deal of attention to building the case for the husband's failure to 'protect his spouse', with testimonies and police reports to prove the mentioned grounds.

4. Obedience cases: trends from statistical data

The statistical data on obedience cases in the five selected courts indicate,[21] first, that there are far more obedience-ordinance cases than proof-of-*nushūz* cases. Second, the obedience cases won by wives consistently outnumber those won by the husbands. Third, more men than women are winning *nushūz* cases, though the pattern is not consistent. And fourth, a fair number of obedience cases are dismissed. Also, some cases are resolved through reconciliation. I will elaborate on each of these findings and their implications in what follows.

If we look at the statistical data on Family Court A, covering the period from 2004 to 2009, we find far more obedience cases than *nushūz* cases. Moreover, obedience cases were more often won by women than by men. But slightly more men than women won *nushūz* cases, although this pattern was not consistent (see Tables 1 and 2).[22]

Table 1 Family Court A: Obedience Cases: 2004–9

Year	Total no. of cases	No. of cases won by women	No. of cases won by men	No. of dismissed cases	No. of reconciled cases
2004	112	18	7	15	9
2005	142	32	3	30	22
2006	119	36	7	22	17
2007	141	34	6	23	25
2008	131	42	11	25	34
2009	64	12	2	12	7

Table 2 Family Court A: *Nushūz* Cases: 2004–9

Year	Total no. of cases	No. of cases won by women	No. of cases won by men	No. of dismissed cases	No. of reconciled cases
2004	13	2	3	3	0
2005	20	2	3	5	1
2006	14	3	0	1	1
2007	20	1	5	2	1
2008	21	1	3	5	1
2009	16	2	3	3	2

While the numbers of the obedience and *nushūz* cases filed in Family Court B were much smaller than those in Family Court A, the same patterns were discernible. Consistently, more women than men won obedience cases. Accordingly, there were fewer *nushūz* cases. However, more men than women tended to win *nushūz* cases. In Family Court B, this latter finding seemed to be a consistent pattern, unlike the case in Family Court A (see Tables 3 and 4).[23]

Table 3 Family Court B: Obedience Cases: 2001–9

Year	Total no. of cases	No. of cases won by women	No. of cases won by men	No. of dismissed cases	No. of reconciled cases
2001	13	2	0	3	3
2002	11	2	0	5	1
2003	3	1	0	0	1
2004	4	2	0	0	1
2005	26	6	0	2	4
2006	69	5	1	6	10
2007	89	11	1	5	7
2008	88	7	1	8	9
2009	98	14	1	17	12

Table 4 Family Court B: *Nushūz* Cases: 2001–9

Year	Total no. of cases	No. of cases won by women	No. of cases won by men	No. of dismissed cases	No. of reconciled cases
2001	9	1	3	1	0
2002	7	0	3	1	0
2003	8	0	3	1	0
2004	11	1	4	1	2
2005	12	0	3	1	0
2006	16	0	3	0	0
2007	20	1	5	5	0
2008	14	0	5	2	0
2009	18	1	5	3	0

When we compare the data on obedience cases in Family Courts C, D and E, similar results are found (Table 5). For example, in 2008, of the 167 obedience cases that were reviewed by Family Court C, 31 were won by women and only five by men. In Family Court D, a total number of 56 cases were reviewed in 2008. Sixteen of these cases were won by women plaintiffs, while husbands won only three. Also, in Family Court D, 74 obedience cases were reviewed in 2009. Eleven of these cases were won by wives, while only two were won by husbands. Lastly, in 2009, 221 obedience cases were reviewed in Family Court E. Seven of these cases were won by wives, two by husbands, and over 150 cases were still pending.

Table 5 Obedience Cases in Family Courts C and D in 2008–9 and Family Court E in 2009

Court	Year	Total no. of cases	No. of cases won by women	No. of cases won by men	No. of dismissed cases	No. of reconciled cases
C	2008	167	31	5	53	20
D	2008	56	16	3	5	6
C	2009	177	pending	pending	41	—
D	2009	74	11	2	8	9
E	2009	221	7	2	54	5

Again, comparing data on *nushūz* cases in Family Courts C, D and E, the findings are relatively similar. In 2008, of the 60 *nushūz* cases that were reviewed in Family Court C, four cases were won by husbands, while five were won by wives. In Family Court D, 14 *nushūz* cases were reviewed in 2009.[24] Five of these cases were won by husbands, while one case was won by the wife. Lastly, in Family Court E, 16 *nushūz* cases were reviewed in 2009. Only one case was won by the husband, and none by the wife (see Table 6).

Table 6 *Nushūz* cases in Family Courts C and D in 2008–9 and Family Court E in 2009

Court	Year	Total no. of cases	No. of cases won by women	No. of cases won by men	No. of dismissed cases	No. of reconciled cases
C	2008	60	5	4	14	6
C	2009	56	pending	pending	9	15
D	2009	14	1	5	1	0
E	2009	16	0	1	4	—

A final point to note is that a considerable number of obedience cases were dismissed. Normally a case is dismissed if the plaintiff fails to proceed with the legal process, or there are technical grounds that do not permit the court to review the case in question (e.g., lack of jurisdiction). But, in interviews with lawyers and disputants, I found that it was common for disputants to reach an agreement outside the court, yet not notify the court or withdraw the case. Since the disputants stopped proceeding with the lawsuit, the case would then be dismissed by the court. Thus, one can assume that some of the obedience cases that were dismissed in the five selected courts were probably those that were also resolved through out-of-court settlement between the couple.

A number of cases (though fewer than those dismissed) were also resolved through court-recorded reconciliation in the five courts. This means that the disputants reconciled in front of the court while the case was in progress.

If we look at the data on dismissed and reconciled cases in Family Court A (Table 1), we see, first, that a fair number of cases were dismissed each year. Secondly, this number was relatively close to the number of cases won by the wife. Thirdly, the number of cases ending in reconciliation, though lower, was by no means negligible.

In the other four family courts, a somewhat similar pattern was found, but there were also some variations. For example, in Family Courts C and E, the number of dismissed cases was significant. In Family Court D, however, there were far fewer dismissed cases than in the other courts (Table 5). There were also variations in the number of cases resolved through court-recorded reconciliation in the four courts.

Lastly, a number of *nushūz* cases were also dismissed in the four courts. For example, in 2008 in Family Court C, 60 cases were reviewed. Fourteen of these were dismissed, while six ended in reconciliation (Table 6).

In short, the considerable number of dismissed obedience cases suggests that some of the disputants in these cases reconcile or reach a settlement on their own but do not record the reconciliation in the court. This probably does not mean that the marital conflict has been resolved, or that the disputants have closed the door on claiming their rights through litigation. It may mean that filing for an obedience ordinance, as well as contesting it, is often used by disputants as an initial legal tactic to send a particular message to the other party and start a process of pressure and negotiation. However, it is not uncommon for disputants to resort to the court room again if their out-of-court settlement fails. But what certainly needs to be researched is why some couples do not record their reconciliation in the court. Another issue that needs further research is the out-of-court settlement arrangements that are made by disputants, their sustainability, and their advantages and disadvantages for both wives and husbands.

4. Conclusion

The findings of this research corroborate the results of important studies on Muslim family laws and courtroom practices in Palestine, Iran and Morocco.[25] These studies report that similar reasons drive men to file for obedience ordinances and women to contest them, as well as some commonality in disputants' legal strategies. Another similar finding is that women often successfully contest obedience ordinances. But the key finding common to all the studies is the growing disconnect between the legal model of an Islamic marriage that is upheld in the family codes of these countries, on the one hand, and the actual practices of marriage, on the other. Contemporary family codes, drawing from classical *fiqh*, base marriage on the model of the husband/provider versus the financially dependent/obedient wife. But, in real life, husbands do not necessarily provide, and wives are increasingly playing an important role in the financial support of the conjugal home. This discrepancy between legal text and social practice, in addition to the unequal marital rights that husbands and wives are accorded by the codes (e.g. access to divorce), results in legal disputes, which husbands and wives strive to negotiate and resolve to their benefit.

To return to obedience disputes in Egypt, it seems that women, more often than not, *do* win contestation-of-obedience cases. They mostly win because their husbands fail to carry out the role of the 'protector', which the law assigns them in exchange for their right to wifely obedience. The role of the 'protector' is interpreted by the judges as one that entails providing for the wife, refraining from harming her (physically and verbally) and not seizing her possessions. But how should we read these findings? Do they mean that despite the hierarchical model of marital relations that is created through the concept of maintenance versus obedience, women are not disadvantaged by this legal construction of marital roles?

My answer is *no*. What is clear is that contestation of an obedience ordinance in many cases becomes part of a wife's pursuit of judicial divorce. For instance, more wives are winning obedience cases because they file for *khulʿ* and are able to obtain judicial divorce before the obedience case is concluded. It is noteworthy here that husbands file obedience ordinances against wives who are seeking *khulʿ*, although it is understood that the latter are forfeiting their financial rights by filing for this form of divorce. It is also interesting that the court allows both lawsuits to proceed. In such cases, the wife does not really gain anything from winning the contestation-of-obedience ordinance. And even if she were to lose it, it would not impact her lawsuit for *khulʿ*. Yet, these women do contest the obedience case and proceed with both lawsuits.

But what motivates women, who were in the first place only involved in a contestation-of-obedience case, to file for *khulʿ* during the course of the former lawsuit? Is it because their main goal is to obtain a divorce, and thus they decide during the progress of a contestation-of-obedience case to relinquish their financial rights and file for *khulʿ* because they can afford to? While many of these women are seeking divorce, they do not opt for *khulʿ* because they can afford to, but because they are forced to. *Khulʿ* is a quicker, cheaper and more guaranteed legal pathway. Moreover, *khulʿ* becomes a more sensible option for these women not only because they cannot afford the lengthy and more expensive process of prejudicial divorce, but also because they are very doubtful of the enforcement of court judgments for alimony, indemnity or deferred dower.[26] The women's lack of faith in being able to claim their financial rights through court judgments seems to be caused partly by the enforcement problems that family courts face in general, and partly by the inability of the husbands of these plaintiffs to undertake all the financial responsibilities of their legal role as the 'provider/guardian', on which their right to wifely obedience is based.

Contestation of obedience again becomes part of a woman's pathway to divorce on the grounds of harm. However, in this case, the question arises: does winning the contestation-of-obedience case actually help the wife with her divorce case? As mentioned previously, one of the main claims on which contestation-of-obedience ordinance is often based is a husband's failure to 'protect his wife and/or her money'. This suggests that winning a contestation-of-obedience case would help a woman with her suit for judicial divorce on the grounds of harm, since it would seem that, by proving her husband's failure to 'protect her', a wife will have substantiated a form of spousal harm that is being inflicted on her. Our data shows that, when a wife is concurrently involved in both a contestation of an obedience ordinance and a prejudicial divorce lawsuit, winning the contestation of obedience in itself does not automatically give the plaintiff the right to prejudicial divorce. Rather, the divorce suit also has to be reviewed and adjudicated. But what frequently happens is that both suits are combined (by the request of the plaintiff's legal representative), and, at the end of the legal process, the judge usually issues one court judgment that combines rulings on both cases. Three of the 15 women we interviewed for obedience cases filed for prejudicial divorce, but their cases were still pending. Six of the remaining interviewees filed for *khulʿ*, while the other six were only contesting the obedience ordinance. In the 30 court judgments on obedience ordinance that I analysed, there was one in which the plaintiff filed for both contestation of obedience and prejudicial divorce. She won both cases. The remaining court judgments concerned women who were either seeking *khulʿ* (25) or those who were only contesting the obedience ordinance (four). But it is evident that the relation between the contestation of an obedience ordinance and the process of seeking prejudicial divorce merits further research.

In other words, the connection between divorce (whether prejudicial or *khulʿ*) and obedience cases suggests that the hierarchical marital relation that is created by the concept of *qiwāma* is not confined to the idea of maintenance versus obedience but includes the right to divorce. Men have an unfettered right to it, whereas a woman's right is restricted because it is granted and managed through the court. And obedience ordinances are one of the mechanisms through which women's right to divorce is restricted. By filing for obedience, men force their wives to undertake the task of contesting the husband's right to obedience. This results in prolonging women's pathway to divorce. Moreover, by filing such a case, husbands impose on their wives a situation in which the latter may have to make difficult choices and concessions (e.g. opting for *khulʿ* rather than prejudicial divorce, thus forgoing their financial rights). Furthermore, because women's rights and choices within the law (pertaining to divorce) are limited, it becomes a necessary tactic for them to fit the legal script and strive to make the most of the role that the law constructs for them. That is, women strive to prove to the court that they have been 'obedient' wives, while their husbands have 'failed to protect them', even in cases when they know they will not be able to claim the financial rights that will be due to them if they win the contestation-of-obedience case.

Another point that is highlighted by the details of the marital conflicts between disputants in obedience cases is the issue of a wife's financial role in the family. While Egyptian family law does not explicitly forbid women from working, it does not give them any rights in return for supporting their husbands. A husband, however, can claim his wifely obedience on the grounds of his financial role within the matrimonial house. Yet many married couples of lower-middle class live with the daily realities of economic hardship. This results in the failure of the husband to fulfil the role of the provider, and the need for the wife to contribute to the provision of the family. Even in the process of getting married and setting up the matrimonial house, the financial roles that are undertaken by the groom and the bride also often depart from the *fiqh*-based or family law-based model. That is, husbands do not exclusively prepare the matrimonial house, pay the dower to their brides and maintain them, thus earning lawful right to their obedience. Rather, women work and save money in order to help their future husbands with the establishment of the matrimonial household. They contribute to the furnishing of the matrimonial house and the expenses of the wedding. Moreover, even when husbands pay dower, this money goes towards furnishing the house.

The disjuncture between the lived experiences of many married couples and the legal model of marital roles leads, in my opinion, to conflicts between the spouses. Some women want to work. Others need to work even though they make little income and lack the work benefits that would facilitate their juggling work, childcare, husband care and housework. These women feel ambivalent about work because they are caught in a situation in which their husbands fail to provide for them and their children adequately and thus relieve them (the wives) from being trapped in difficult and poorly paid work. Husbands are often reluctant for their wives to work, but feel frustrated that they cannot provide for them. Yet these men still want to claim the power and authority over their wives that they obtain from their roles as providers/guardian. And, in some cases, they even use this power arbitrarily and excessively, resulting in physical abuse. Consequently, wives leave the matrimonial house because they cannot sustain a situation in which they are not provided for, are subjected to abuse and are not allowed to earn their own income. Husbands respond by invoking the authority of their *qiwāma*, and filing an obedience ordinance against their wives.

In short, three issues underlie the injustice that Egyptian women suffer under the legal concept of *qiwāma*. One is the connection between a husband's maintenance and wifely obedience. Another is the imbalance between men's and women's right to divorce. And the third is the public discourse on *qiwāma*. Regarding the first, the solution needs to go beyond mere abolition of the concept of 'wifely obedience'. There is also the complex issue of redefining the roles of both spouses. Should equality in financial obligations of spouses be a goal? And what kind of equality should be sought? Should it be formal or substantive equality? And how do we take into account inhibiting factors, which limit or diminish the value of women's financial activities? Such factors include their restricted access to the private formal labour market; the precariousness of the work that many women do for a living in terms of its income, permanence and benefits; and discriminatory codes that discourage them from being economically active (e.g. laws governing the dispensing of the state's social welfare financial assistance). And there is also the issue of other marital roles, such as childcare and management of the matrimonial house. Should we revisit the legal gendering of such roles?

Secondly, having an equal right to a just and accessible divorce is necessary so that every spouse can exit a failing, abusive or unwanted marriage. But, more importantly, it is an essential basis for a healthy marriage based on *mawadda* and *raḥma* (love and mercy). It is hardly possible for this kind of marriage, which Allah decreed in the Qur'an (30:21), to exist when husbands – because of their religious and legal claim to *qiwāma* – not only have a unilateral right to repudiation, but can restrict and make women's limited judicial pathways to divorce more difficult. This, unfortunately, is partly made possible through the current Egyptian family laws on wifely obedience.

Lastly, a main challenge to changing the hierarchical and unhealthy marital roles that are created by present-day family laws is the dominant view of *qiwāma* in the public discourse.[27] This view contends that men have authority over their wives, have the right to unfettered divorce and may beat their wives for the purpose of disciplining them, and that the latter are obligated to obey their husbands. And, sadly, this ideological construction of marital relations is justified on the grounds that it is Allah's law.

Notes

1 There are eight other personal status laws for non-Muslim Egyptians, who mostly belong to different Christian churches (the largest being the Coptic Orthodox). Only the Muslim personal status law was promulgated by the Egyptian legislator, while personal status laws for non-Muslims were drafted and approved by Christian religious authorities. But state laws dictate that, in the case of family disputes between spouses belonging to different religious communities, Muslim personal status laws apply. In the past decade this has increasingly caused conflict between the Egyptian Coptic Church and state courts that granted divorce to Christian men or women who belonged or had converted to a different church than their spouse. To address this problem, there is an ongoing effort undertaken by different churches, some Christian public thinkers, activists, and some of the women's rights organisations to draft and advocate the promulgation of a unified religious-based family code for all Christian Egyptians.

2 See Sonbol, Amira, 'Women in *Shari'a* courts: a historical and methodological discussion', *Kelam Araştirmalari* 2/2 (2004), pp. 25–56; Hallaq, Wael, *Sharī'a: Theory, Practice, Transformations* (Cambridge: Cambridge University Press, 2009); Tucker, Judith, *Women, Family, and Gender in Islamic Law* (Cambridge: Cambridge University Press, 2008).

3 Egyptian personal status laws are divided into two types: 1) substantive laws, which define and regulate the rights of spouses and children, such as Law No. 25 of 1920 and its amendments, Law No. 25 of 1929 and Law No. 100 of 1985, and 2) procedural laws, which regulate the legal processes and courtroom proceedings, such as Law No. 1 of 2000 and Law No. 10 of 2004, which regulate the work of the new family courts.

4 This research is part of a larger study that the author undertook from 2007 to 2010, which sought to investigate if and how reforms that were introduced in Egyptian family law since 2000 empowered ordinary Egyptian women and activists. The study researched these reforms from two angles: 1) the process of law-making and feminist legal activism, and 2) the implementation of the new laws in courtrooms through litigants' strategies and court personnel's interpretations of the new codes and gender rights. This study was part of a larger research project entitled 'Pathways of Women's Empowerment', undertaken by the Social Research Center at the American University in Cairo, through its membership in a research consortium consisting of a number of research centres and universities in Egypt, Palestine, Bangladesh, Ghana, Brazil and the UK.

5 Since 2000, a number of reforms have been enacted, the most notable of which are the new family courts and the *khul'* law. Currently, there are efforts (on the part of the government and women's rights activists) to introduce a new substantive family code.

6 This part of the research (i.e. focus group discussion with lawyers, interviews with disputants in obedience cases and observation of court proceedings) was carried out in the period from October to December 2009. Courtroom observation and analysis of court records were carried out by the author of this chapter. Interviews and focus group discussions were conducted by a team consisting of the author and two research assistants.

7 These interviews were conducted in the period from April 2009 to October 2009.

8 Mir-Hosseini, Ziba, 'The construction of gender in Islamic legal thought and strategies for reform', *Hawwa* 1/1 (2003), pp. 1–25; Abu Odeh, Lama, 'Modernizing Muslim family law: the case of Egypt', *Vand. Journal of Transnational Law* 37 (2004), pp. 1043–7, *Oxford University Comparative Law Forum* 3 (2004); Tucker: *Women, Family, and Gender.*

9 For a linguistic and hermeneutic analysis of this verse and, in particular, of the terms *qawwāmūn*, *faḍḍala* and *qānitāt*, see Barlas, Asma, *'Believing Women'*

in Islam: Unreading Patriarchal Interpretations of the Qur'an (Austin, Texas: University of Texas Press, 2002), pp. 182–9; Wadud, Amina, *Qur'an and Women: Rereading the Sacred Text from a Woman's Perspective (Oxford: Oxford University Press, 1999)*, pp. 64–78.

10 For detailed analysis of the new family courts, see Al-Sharmani, Mulki, 'Egyptian family courts: a pathway of women's empowerment?', *Hawwa* 7/2 (2009), pp. 89–119.

11 See *A Report on Women's Problems in Family Courts* (Cairo: National Council for Women, Ombudsman's Office, 2007, in Arabic).

12 Data about the case collected from court records and lawyer's notes.

13 Data collected from court records and lawyer's notes.

14 Data collected from court records and lawyer's notes.

15 See Amin, Sajeda and Nagah Al-Bassusi, *Wage Work and Marriage: Perspectives of Egyptian Working Women*, Population Council Working Papers 171 (New York: Population Council, 2003); Singerman, Diane, *The Economic Imperatives of Marriage: Emerging Practices and Identities among Youth in the Middle East*, Middle East Youth Initiative Working Paper 6 (Washington, DC and Dubai: Wolfensohn Center for Development and Dubai School of Government, September 2007).

16 These statements are based on the findings of interviews with 100 men and women (50 of each gender), who were of different marital statuses. The interviews were about their marriage practices and knowledge of family laws.

17 Personal interview with the wife, December 2009.

18 In the new family court, a panel of three judges presides on each case. The senior judge is the one who runs the court proceedings. The two junior judges assist with questioning witnesses and deliberations before issuing final court judgments. Each family court has two court experts, one of whom is trained in social work and the other in psychology. The court experts attend all court sessions, meet with the disputants in some cases and submit reports to the judge. In addition, according to PSL No. 10 of 2004 (which introduced the new family court system), one of the court experts has to be a woman.

19 Article 11, PSL No. 100 of 1985, does not spell out what constitutes a 'legitimate' (*shar'ī*) matrimonial house, or what defines the husband's failure to 'protect her or her money'. However, the Court of Cassation judgments (which set precedents) have considered a separate dwelling for the couple that is used for their residence as a 'legitimate matrimonial house' (even if it is a room with its own door in a dwelling inhabited by husband's family). In addition, according to rulings of the court, a husband's failure to protect his wife would mean any of the following: failure to provide for her; physically and verbally abusing her; seizure of her money or possessions; making false accusations against her and/or committing immoral acts in the matrimonial house such as drinking and fornication.

20 Residence next to a Christian neighbour seems to have implicitly been considered by the Court of Cassation as a factor that would make the matrimonial house illegitimate. I came across a case reviewed by the court in which the wife appealed an obedience ordinance on such a ground. The court ruled that the contestation of the obedience ordinance was rejected because the wife failed to prove that her neighbour was Christian. See Court of Cassation, Appeal Case No. 8 for Judicial Year 54, Court Session 21/1/1985, cited in Al Tabakh, Sherif, *Personal Status Laws: Between Jurisprudence and Law* (Cairo: Dar al-Fikr al-Jamiʿ, 2006, in Arabic), pp. 303–4.

21 These five courts were selected on the basis of ease of access to court records and personnel. For anonymity, the names of the courts are not identified. For Family Court B, the data collected covers the period from 2001 to 2009; for Family Court A it covers the period from 2004 to 2009; for Family Courts C and D the period covered is from 2008 to 2009, and, lastly, for Family Court E the data collected covers the period from January 2009 to 17 December 2009. Thus, I do not claim that the findings I draw from the analysis of this data are representative. However, triangulation of the findings gathered from the different methods of data collection indicates that my conclusions suggest a general trend.

22 In the tables, the total number of cases includes pending cases which had not been concluded by the court at the end of the judicial year. Hence, the cases listed in the other columns do not add up to the total number.

23 Note 22 also applies to Tables 3 and 4.

24 Statistical data on *nushūz* cases in Family Court D in 2008 is not available.

25 See Mir-Hosseini, Ziba, *Marriage on Trial: A Study of Islamic Law* (London and New York: I.B.Tauris, 2002); Shehada, Nahda, 'House of obedience: social norms, individual agency, and historical contingency', *Journal of Middle East Women's Studies* 5/1 (2009), pp. 24–49; Welchman, Lynn, *Beyond the Code: Muslim Family Law and the Sharʿi Judiciary in the Palestinian West Bank* (The Hague: Kluwer Law International, 2000).

26 This opinion was expressed by the majority of female interviewees in the obedience cases as well as the 50 women interviewees who were interviewed about their marriage practices and knowledge of family laws.

27 For example, none of the interviewees or the lawyers questioned this view of *qiwāma*, which they justified on the grounds of religious doctrine. What some of them questioned was only a husband's abuse of this right.

3

EGYPTIAN WOMEN'S RIGHTS NGOS

Personal Status Law Reform between Islamic and International Human Rights Law[1]

Marwa Sharafeldin

This chapter is based on a field study of how a group of Egyptian women's rights NGOs are adapting a new discourse to the Egyptian context in order to reform the personal status law (PSL), using both religious and human rights frames of reference. The PSL is the law governing family relations in Egypt, including marriage, divorce and custody. Because it is based on what the law-makers conceive to be Islamic law, it is very difficult to critique it for reform, as this becomes synonymous with critiquing Islam itself. It is, however, one of the main sites where Islamic concepts like *wilāya* and *qiwāma* take legal shape and force,[2] in the form of rights and obligations such as the wife's obligation to obedience, the husband's obligation to maintenance, and his right of unilateral divorce. These legal stipulations have become problematic in Egyptian society today from the point of view of the NGOs studied. Here I investigate the complex process through which women's rights NGOs selectively borrow, mix and develop elements of both Islamic law and international human rights laws to advocate a reformed PSL with a new conception of what *wilāya* and *qiwāma* could be today.[3]

This chapter first discusses the main 'references' or sources of law on which NGOs base their suggested reforms of the PSL. It then focuses on their legal method, namely, how they appropriate the religious and human rights references to support their PSL reform proposal. It gives concrete examples of this work in relation to the discussion of particular rights and obligations. It ends with a brief analysis of the potential and challenges of making a new discourse.

The methodology of this research was multi-pronged. Fieldwork included participant observation of activities and meetings of a network of 11 NGOs, which, since 2007, has defined its mandate as working for PSL reform.[4] Interviews were also conducted with the NGO members in this network who specialise in law, as well as other NGOs and activists outside the network working on the same topic. A total of 15 NGOs were studied for this research. Additionally, I closely followed and analysed the development of the network's law reform proposal document and the different stages of its development.

It is important to note that divergences of opinion did exist between the different NGOs. It was rare to find a consensus on any one topic of reform in the PSL. However, there were general tendencies and majority opinions on certain issues.

1. The personal status law

This law deals with all family issues in Egypt including marriage, divorce, maintenance, custody, paternity and guardianship. The term PSL is misleading, because it is used to describe not one but several laws that govern personal status, such as Decree Law 25/1920, Decree Law 25/1929 and Law 100/1985, to mention a few. Since the 1920s, the 'law' has only undergone a series of gradual amendments, thus indicating the historical difficulty, due to societal resistance, of changing it comprehensively.[5] The sanctity with which the law is imbued, by its relationship with religion, is one reason for society's resistance. Personal status laws have always been based on what is perceived to be Islamic law,[6] and the primacy of men over women in marital affairs.[7]

The underlying philosophy of all these laws is that men, having the *qiwāma* and *wilāya*, provide financially for their wives and therefore command their obedience and have authority over them. Consequently, the relationship between the spouses is legislated as one of complementarity, not equality.[8]

This particular conception of male authority over women in the PSL can be seen to be legally reflected in the ease of divorce for men and its difficulty for women; the possibility of polygamy for men; the husband's obligation to maintain the family; the wife's obligation of obedience to her husband and the father's right of guardianship over the children.

NGOs find these conceptions problematic, in that they are no longer suited to the current Egyptian context. They are now proving to cause difficulties in practice, as the roles and responsibilities in the Egyptian family are radically changing.[9] Furthermore, they clash with contemporary sensibilities and understandings of equality and justice. They are also inconsistent with Egypt's international legal obligations as a signatory to CEDAW.

2. The frames of reference

In their effort to reform these laws, NGOs find that it is important to identify their *marji'iyāt*, that is, the sources and frames of reference for their legal reform. Identifying 'references' constrains the demands that NGOs can make. This is especially pertinent when attempting to reform a law that most people today believe to be divinely ordained. For example, a human rights reference will not enable NGOs to demand that women have the equal prerogative to physically discipline their husbands, but will enable them to demand equality between men and women in their right to bodily protection. A 'traditional' Islamic reference would not give space for NGOs to demand the abolition of the wife's duty of obedience to her husband, but what the NGOs call an 'enlightened' Islamic reference would. Therefore, NGOs' choice of references is fundamental, because it will set the parameters of the demands they can make, and determine how convincingly these can be supported.[10]

The interviewed NGOs mostly identified three references that guided their work on the reform proposal:

(1) The lived realities of Egyptian women who suffer under this law.

(2) An enlightened Islamic legal discourse.

(3) International human rights law treaties and conventions.

Regarding the first reference, which NGOs termed the 'lived reality reference', it appeared, from their day-to-day work providing legal and other services to their constituencies, that there were serious problems faced by women because of the law. These include: limited grounds on which women can ask for divorce as opposed to men; court cases taking too much time when women file for a divorce (up to seven years); the procedural difficulty of their proving harm to get a divorce; the fact that the law only allows a woman to ask for maintenance arrears for up to a year prior to the date of filing the lawsuit, and not from the date the husband stopped paying; the lack of enforcement of maintenance verdicts in favour of women; the abuse of the obedience clause in the law by husbands to spite wives' seeking separation; and the economic hardship faced by women who no longer have access to the custodial home or custodial fee after the child's custody is completed, and end up in the streets with no shelter.

In fact, the problems faced by women due to the law are the reason NGOs began taking action in the first instance. The suffering caused by the law was a loud and clear message that there was a need for change. NGOs therefore commissioned several studies to gather statistics and data that would reflect women's suffering and the cost to society, to bolster their argument and gain legitimacy for their work.[11] This reality reference was a strong uniting force for NGOs, but when it came to the remaining two references, religion and human rights, the discussion on adopting them was not so consensual. The NGOs studied recognise that, legally and socially, family and marriage relations are fundamentally ruled by religion, as is stipulated in the law (Article 3 Law 1/2000).[12] Hence, any current attempt at reform will inevitably have to address religion, notwithstanding the sensitivity of this subject.[13] Moreover, some of those interviewed regard themselves as observant Muslims who respect the principles of Islam, and see no contradiction with human rights conventions and no problem in having family relations governed by religious principle.

In early 2007, at the outset of the network's work on PSL reform, member NGOs decided to discuss what the main reference for their joint work should be. Was it only to be international human rights conventions – as it had been in the early phase of the network's formation (since 2005) – or was it also to include religion? Some NGOs only wanted to have a human rights reference. Others thought this would be detrimental to their work, due to the Western/colonialist stigma that human rights carried in Egyptian society. It would also be unrealistic, since the law itself was based on religious principles. One of the NGOs holding the latter view threatened to withdraw from the network if the religious reference was not included. They felt the network would be throwing itself into the fire, exposing itself to great risk from state and society. At the same time, another opposing NGO warned the rest that 'it is not useful to create the monster and scare ourselves with it' (i.e., it was not useful to avoid referring to human rights because of the assumption that such rights would not be accepted at large).[14] After much discussion and mediation, the compromise was finally reached that the references would be both human rights and 'enlightened' interpretations of religion.

However, no discussion took place on defining what the word 'enlightened' might mean. When asked during interviews, most NGO representatives took it as meaning gender-sensitive Islamic interpretations, but no details were agreed upon collectively. It seemed that all assumed at the time that there was agreement on what 'enlightened' was, but later on, in the course of my fieldwork and the drafting of the NGOs' law proposal, it became apparent that there was a divergence over what 'enlightened' religion's stance was on thorny issues like financial guardianship of mothers over children, obedience, inheritance and outright prohibition of polygamy. One of the reasons for this vagueness could have been what both Dupret and Singerman describe as a tendency of Islamic law to lend itself to changing and re-imagined meanings across time, space and persons.[15] 'Enlightened' may mean different things to different people, each of whom will be able to support their understanding just as validly from the multitude of different Qur'anic verses, their interpretation and the rich jurisprudence around these verses.

As a result, it was not clear which frame of reference would take precedence in the NGOs' joint work in case of a contradiction. What if human rights conventions gave women certain rights that religion, even if enlightened, took away, and vice versa? A case in point is lesbian women's rights, which most of those interviewed opposed, principally on religious and cultural grounds. Inheritance was another contentious issue, which most NGOs did not seek to change. It seems that there was an underlying assumption that 'enlightened' religion would naturally be in accordance with human rights conventions, and that the possibility of contradiction between the two was minimal.

Another important and related point that became evident was that not all NGOs were for total gender equality, as stipulated in human rights documents. As with 'enlightened', the definition of 'equality' proved elusive and differed from one person to another. The equality sought in human rights conventions sometimes seemed to clash with conceptions of equality that different NGO activists held in light of what they perceived as religion. Some even found that the kind of equality promoted in the human rights discourse included elements potentially harmful to women in Egypt. For example, the silence of NGOs on certain issues discussed below, such as the husband's obligation of maintenance, illustrates the clash of these two conceptions of equality within NGOs. As the work of the NGOs shows, judgment on religion or human rights cannot be reduced only to how each addresses equality. Each discourse has its importance and value in this particular context, and each was subject to a multitude of factors that affected its appropriation by NGOs. It became evident during my fieldwork that the meanings of 'enlightened' and 'equality' were determined by a constant process of negotiation between NGOs, as will be shown below.

To conclude, this discussion of references amongst network members showed that NGOs were well aware that the choice of references would dictate what demands they could make for the reform of the PSL; the issues on which they must be silent; the justification behind these demands; the public image of NGOs in the eyes of state and society and the general societal acceptance of their demands.

This discussion was also important because it highlighted how NGO activists seem to regard human rights and religion as frames of reference for their demands. First, they seem to think that religion gives more credibility to their demands. A human rights framework does not appear to share the credibility of a religious framework in the eyes of Egyptian society or even some NGO activists. However, a traditional religious framework, as opposed to an 'enlightened' one, is less accommodating to the kind of equality for which NGOs plead. Second, most NGOs find that more effort needs to be spent on reinterpreting Islamic sources in a different way from traditional classical jurisprudence. Nevertheless, most NGOs agreed that addressing religion was indispensable to their PSL reform work.

3. The religious discourse: Islamic feminism

When asked to describe the role of the religious discourse in their PSL reform work, all interviewees appeared to be talking about 'Islamic feminism'. I define 'Islamic feminism' here in its widest possible sense, recognising that it holds different meanings for different actors and locations. Agreeing with Ziba Mir-Hosseini,[16] I define it as an awareness of the injustice inflicted upon women because they are women, and the will to do something about it, whether in the form of new knowledge production, or advocacy and activism, or all of these. I use the word 'Islamic' here to mean that this effort finds inspiration and justification from Islam and its sources, guided by the principles of justice, equality and the preservation of human dignity found in the Qur'an and the practices of the Prophet.[17] This was what most of the interviewed NGOs were attempting to do, to varying degrees, but without labelling their efforts 'Islamic feminism'. Abou-Bakr's general description of Muslim feminist scholars and activists,[18] 'who are not just "critiquing [i.e. attacking or deconstructing] Islamic history and hermeneutics", but are also providing alternatives and seeking solutions inspired by Islamic values', applies to the activists studied here.

Most of them began taking action to reform the law because of the problems they found in reality from their work on the ground.[19] They went on to find considerable support for their demands in the human rights and reality references, and some support in religion.

Many of the interviewed NGO activists see themselves as believers of the Islamic faith. Most of them personally find that Shariʿa's basic principles are anti-patriarchal and, hence, are in congruence with human rights principles. For these activists, it is the *fiqh* (jurisprudence) produced by scholars in the classical era that contains patriarchal elements, echoing the social context of its production. That is why, throughout the course of their work, some of them try to clarify the distinction between Shariʿa, the work of God, the eternal divine message contained in the Qur'an, which does not change with time and space; and *fiqh*, the work of man, which encompasses the changeable human attempts at understanding this message. This group finds the distinction useful because it allows them to advance a new *fiqh*, which reinterprets the main sources of Shariʿa. However, during the interviews, I sometimes noticed a difference between activists' definitions of both Shariʿa and *fiqh*. Some of those interviewed felt that what are perceived to be clearly written verses in the Qur'an can constitute unchangeable Shariʿa and hence are not subject to human interpretation (such as those on polygamy and inheritance, as explained in the 'Examples' section below).[20] Others disagreed, arguing that interpretation of these so-called definitive verses should be permissible and uninhibited.

These latter cite several incidents where the rulings of clear-cut verses were suspended by ʿUmar ibn al-Khattab, the second caliph, because in his context they no longer served their purpose (*maqṣad*). They agree that some Qur'anic verses clearly treat women and men unequally, but find that this does not stop them from referring to Shariʿa in their work. Most seem to have faith in the justice and eternity of the general Qur'anic message, and argue that such verses need to be understood historically and contextually, because they refer to social relations prevalent at the time of the Prophet Muhammad, and are not general principles. They state that it is up to Muslims to create a new understanding of these verses, based on the overriding general Qur'anic principles of equality and justice, which they consider two of the main purposes (*maqāṣid*) of Shari'a.[21] In their view, classical jurists who undertook that work in the centuries after the death of the Prophet, should not, and indeed never meant to, have a monopoly over the interpretation of the Qur'an and Sunna. All Muslims have the right to debate what these sources mean, to question jurists' interpretations and to create new understandings that are more suitable to the exigencies of modern times. They refer back to Islam's elevation of the use of one's mind to work out things for oneself. One of them exclaimed: 'There is no *kahanūt* (priesthood) in Islam!'[22]

NGOs report that talking the language of the people, through the use of religious discourse, does facilitate their work. However, it also poses challenges. They realise that both they and their opponents use the same religious reference, and that neither of the two camps can make monopolistic claims to authenticity. Many of them are aware of being open to attack because they are not religious experts and do not have the perceived right to call for a different religious discourse than the prevalent one. They sometimes fear that by using such a discourse, enlightened or not, they are augmenting the rising power of religion in Egyptian society. By doing so they would be indirectly supporting their opponents, whose discourse justifying the unequal treatment of women appears just as authentic as that of the NGOs in its references to scripture and use of Islamic jurisprudential methodology.

Another challenge is that, as mentioned above, NGO activists are not religious experts, so it is not in their best interest to be dragged onto this playing field.[23] They are experts in the human rights discourse, and try to frame the discussion accordingly. But they are often asked by their audiences to justify their demands vis-à-vis religion, so they find that they have to be well-prepared for an 'enlightened' religious discourse too.

Such preparation can be said to be an individual effort on the part of those interviewed. Many of them started reading about Islam and women on their own initiative and coming up with their own conclusions. This process has been informed by the individual lives and upbringing of most of the women interviewed. One of them says that she became a feminist due to her Islamic upbringing, which had focused on the principles of equality and justice. On two occasions, interviewees referred to their fathers' actual practice of these principles with their wives and with their daughters while they were growing up. The Islam that they believe in and are familiar with is not one that is unjust or detrimental to the dignity of women.

It is, therefore, important to shift the discussion temporarily from abstract references and discourses, to the agents who are themselves appropriating such discourses. Understanding the agents, in this case the NGO activists involved in the PSL reform, and their relationship to these discourses, will shed more light on the complexities and intricacies of the process at hand. For it is the lived realities they experience that eventually shape the discourse they create in their work. It is especially important when we find that their reform demands are, in reality, significantly affected by their personal faith and spirituality.

4. Types of NGOs by their use of religious discourse

This brings us to an important distinction between activists working in Egypt on women's rights. Karam usefully divides the women's organisations in Egypt today into three types.[24] The first is the Islamist women's group, which works towards more Islamisation of the state. The oppression of women here is seen as part of a larger societal problem that has resulted from straying away from Islam, and, in particular, from women seeking to be equal to men. They see compatibility and complementarity between the sexes, not absolute equality, as the right path.[25]

The second type is Muslim feminist organisations. These women refer to the Qur'an and Sunna in their work to show that the concept of equality is, in fact, supported by Islam. They try to build a bridge between Islamist discourse and the human rights one. They call for a reinterpretation of Islamic texts and sources, and subject these to a contextual analysis that questions the validity of medieval interpretations in today's world. They are, therefore, regarded as serious threats to the power base of establishment Islam, which assigns itself a monopoly on religious interpretation.[26]

The final type of women's organisations is those who profess strong secular ideals. They believe in the human rights discourse and shun the religious one, whether Muslim or Christian. They do not engage in any bridging exercises between religion and human rights, which they regard as a waste of time. They are targets of dangerous and harmful accusations, such as being agents of the West and non-believers.[27]

The NGOs interviewed here could be put under either one of the last two types. None of them want an Islamic state, nor do they use Shari'a as the main frame of reference informing the rest of their non-PSL work. Instead, they all refer, either mainly or solely, to international conventions of human rights in their brochures and publications. When asked, all the interviewed NGOs, except one, found that an enlightened, feminist interpretation of Islam is in accordance with human rights, even if a lot of work needs to be done to demonstrate this.

While Karam's categorisation is useful for understanding the general picture, it does not account for the highly complex reality of both these 'Muslim' and 'secularist' activists' work as it has developed since her observations. For example, some secularists were willing to work with a religious discourse despite their secularism.[28]

Also, some Muslim feminists were not always constrained by the literal religious text and included 'secular' human rights references in their interpretations of it, as will be shown in the next section.

5. The human rights discourse

Most of the interviewed NGOs would agree with An-Naʿim that international standards of human rights are founded on fundamental values, which are shared by all cultures and religions.[29] One of the interviewees felt that it would be too arrogant of the West, and ignorant of the East, to assume that human rights are a particular, exclusive product of the West's own culture; another, who was veiled, viewed human rights as the crystallisation of the principles common to all religions. Therefore, many felt that a reform of the PSL based on an enlightened interpretation of Islamic sources would naturally be in accord with human rights principles.

Despite these NGOs' claim that religious principles of equality, justice and the preservation of human dignity are similar to those of human rights, there remains a flaw in this argument. For some NGOs, 'religion' does limit their demands for equality, even if such demands are strongly supported by a human rights discourse. Examples discussed below include the total prohibition of polygamy, as well as equality in inheritance shares between women and men, which most NGOs were not willing to include in their reform proposal. This stance largely stems from the fact that these two issues were addressed in what appear to be definitive 'clear-cut' scriptural verses in the Quʿran (*qaṭʿiyyāt al-dalāla*).

Again, most NGOs would agree with Al-Naʿim when he asserts that, in a legal system such as the Muslim one, 'policy arguments are insufficient bases for challenging the rules and replacing them with an alternative set of rules unless one can also rely on *scriptural* authority'.[30] He warns that Islam can motivate women themselves to challenge these seemingly 'Western' notions of women's rights. But 'the best way to challenge this, it would seem, is to show that the rights of women are Islamic and not alien western notions'.[31]

These NGOs, as An-Naʿim and Deng describe, are actors from within a culture who are interpreting human rights in a culturally sensitive language.[32] According to Merry, it is the role of NGOs to 'negotiate the spaces between transnational ideas and local concerns'.[33] They are innovative in their local application of global concepts and practices through this process of translation.[34]

In this process of translation and negotiation, NGOs find that the human rights discourse stimulates a different understanding of religious law. Many report that it was the former that clearly informed them of the concept of equality between the sexes. A veiled interviewee said: 'Human rights helped me to become me.' Some felt human rights had helped them bring out the positive, gender-egalitarian elements of religion, which had been overshadowed in *fiqh* by the patriarchal influences of time and place. One activist went as far as suggesting that this work on the women's question might reform Islam and return it to its *maqṣad* or purpose. Another interviewee said human rights helped some activists to start questioning everything related to women, including concepts that were regarded as *thawābit* (unquestioned pillars), such as unequal inheritance or the need for a *walī* (guardian) to contract the marriage on behalf of the woman. One woman mentioned how human rights helped activists to break the male monopoly on religious interpretation. It enabled her to go back to the sources of Shariʿa and work things out for herself. Another stated that human rights had primarily aided her to look at herself and her different ideas as 'respectful', and that she expected to be respected by society too. Human rights helped her to reject the elements in *fiqh* that reinforced unequal and unfair treatment between women and men. She found that most of the *fiqh* looked at women 'always as part of a whole' – a family, a society – and not as an individual. Another interviewee gave a political example: how the discourse of an Islamist group, like the Muslim Brotherhood, pertaining to the work of women has changed since the 1980s. Today the Brotherhood cannot afford to be as vocal against women's employment outside of the home as they were previously, and have had to change their stance on the issue, in her opinion, due to the rising importance of human rights in the world today.

Most NGOs find that a human rights discourse is, more often than not, comfortably conducive to demands for the reform of the PSL. This is partly because, unlike religion, it is not subject to fundamentally different interpretations. Many of them also agree with Abou-Odeh that the prevalent traditional religious discourse will limit the rights women can enjoy,[35] because it mainly comprises an old *fiqh* that was created in a different context where equality between men and women was not a priority.[36] A radical re-understanding and recreation of a contemporary *fiqh* needs to happen for it to be as conducive to their work today as the human rights discourse.[37] If that change happens, most of them believe religion will not pose any limitation. However, it became apparent to me during my fieldwork that many of those I interviewed who consider themselves observant Muslims, would not have been spurred into action to reform the PSL by human rights alone. In their eyes, Islam came to advance equality, justice and dignity, and, hence, that was the green light for many of them to contest this law and attempt to reform it.

Besides NGOs' awareness that human rights can be popularly regarded as a Western import, and potentially a new form of colonialism, some interviewees found that the concept of equality, as outlined in international human rights conventions such as CEDAW, could also be problematic and disadvantageous to Muslim Egyptian women. They usually cite the Islamic legal obligation of the husband to pay a dower, as well as maintenance during marriage and after its dissolution, as Islamic advantages to women. Another privilege is that female kin, starting with the mother, take precedence in custody cases over male kin of the children of divorced spouses, regardless of the former's financial ability, since the father of the children is obliged to maintain them fully (and to pay the mother or female custodian a fee for caring for the children based on traditional Islamic interpretations). If NGOs followed the principle of equality in CEDAW consistently, they would be bound to ask for the rescinding of these rights that Islamic legal tradition gives to Muslim women. Most of those interviewed were very reluctant to deprive Muslim women of these privileges, bearing in mind the financially disadvantaged position of most women in today's Egypt. Therefore, their critical stance towards human rights is not just faith-based, but also stems from a grounded assessment of the socio-economic situation of the women they serve.

6. Applications of the new discourse to legal issues

Departing from the lived reality of women suffering under the PSL, and mixing and merging Islamic and human rights discourses, Egyptian NGOs are forming new conceptions of *wilāya* and *qiwāma* that they want the PSL to reflect. I will briefly illustrate this process using specific issues in the PSL, concentrating on *qiwāma* and maintenance, obedience, wife-disciplining, polygamy and inheritance. The arguments below are a conglomeration of what NGOs presented either in their law reform document, in their public meetings with their stakeholders or in interviews.

When asked about *qiwāma*, most interviewees refuted the prevalent understanding of it as unconditional male authority over women. Some of them argue from the text (4:34) that one of the conditions for *qiwāma* is to maintain the family financially; however, in many Egyptian families today, both women and men share financial responsibility because of poverty, and accordingly, *qiwāma* should also be shared. They also refer to some *fiqh* works, which condition *qiwāma* upon a person's knowledge, not only financial ability. Since women and men today have equal opportunities to pursue knowledge, with women sometimes excelling over men, it would be irrational, for example, for an illiterate man to have *qiwāma* over a female university professor. NGOs agree with scholars like Abdel Moaty Bayoumy in defining *qiwāma* more as a responsibility than a privilege or authority.[38] They go on to critique the link that classical *fiqh* made between the *qiwāma* of the husband, as the responsibility to financially maintain his wife, and the obedience of the wife in return.

Most NGOs reject the wife's duty of obedience to her husband as stipulated in the PSL and based on classical *fiqh* conceptions.[39] The argument that the husband maintains his wife in exchange for her obedience is, in their view, not only outdated and unacceptable, but close to *shirk*,[40] because obedience should be to no one but God. One interviewee recalled how, in a public event that she organised to discuss the PSL, she had to stand up and publicly debate a famous hadith that encouraged women to obey their husbands. The hadith exalts the example of a wife who failed to visit her father on his deathbed because she lacked her husband's permission to do so. The interviewee justified her stance by reminding the audience that this was a weak hadith, that the Qur'an clearly ordered people to treat their parents well (17:23), and that there was no correspondingly clear Qur'anic indication for the obligation of obedience to the husband. This, she said, was a strong argument because the Qur'anic reference, being the word of God, is generally accepted as stronger than the hadith, which are the transmitted words and practices of the Prophet.

NGOs with legal clinics also noted that most of the obedience court cases against their female clients were filed by husbands in a spirit of vengeance and spite, in order to purposefully prolong the wife's misery in the slow court system, or to get back at them for having dared to file a *khulʿ* case against the husband. Today, then, this legal provision is being used to inflict harm, which in their view would never have been the purpose (*maqṣad*) of Islam.

Most NGOs hold that obedience should have practically no place in the law governing Muslim families in today's changed Egyptian society.[41] However, some of those interviewed saw that, to be consistent, if they called for the rescindment of the obedience rules in the PSL, they also had to call for both spouses to share the obligation of maintenance, not just men. One of the interviewees stated that women in Egypt would not welcome such a change, because it would put an additional financial burden on their shoulders. She asserted that many Egyptian women did not really care for equality, and NGOs should not be rash in asking for things for which the society is not ready. Another, however, stated that women were, in fact, already substantial contributors to household expenses, and sometimes sole providers, and that society was 'already there'. Also, most NGOs held that the economic value of women's domestic work should be counted as their financial contribution to the household. The NGOs, however, have remained silent on the husband's legal obligation to maintenance in their legal proposal, which, by default, signifies their official agreement to this duty of the husband.

The physical disciplining of wives is not governed directly by the PSL, but rather by the penal code. It was included in the interviews because it takes place within the family sphere and is widely thought to be sanctioned by Islam because of the husband's *qiwāma* and *wilāya* over his wife. All NGOs are unanimous in rejecting the concept of bodily castigation despite its Qur'anic sanction (4:34). They appeal to a historical and linguistic analysis of the verse, indicating that the word *ḍaraba* has many meanings in the Arabic language, not just 'to strike', but also 'to leave' or 'to ignore'. They sometimes refer to *fiqh* conditions on how the disciplining should take place, to show that it is not an unconditional right of the husband. They also undertake a contextual analysis of the state of Qurayshi society, which justified the revealing of this verse at the time, to indicate that the context has changed radically. Above all, they highlight the Qur'an's protection of human dignity, and show how such disciplining contradicts this general and overarching principle of the Islamic message. They bolster their case with the practices of the Prophet himself, who never struck any of his wives.

Another issue, polygamy, was heavily criticised by most of those interviewed for its harmful effects on the family. Some highlighted the Qur'anic indication that polygamy would be permissible if men were able to treat their different wives justly and equally (4:3), but that they would not be able to do so (4:129). Hence, most NGO activists concluded, the practice should not be allowed. Some of them referred to the incident when ʿAli ibn Abi Talib, the Prophet's cousin and son-in-law, wanted to take another wife besides Fatima, the Prophet's daughter, and the Prophet forbade him to do so, indicating that anything that harmed Fatima would harm him personally. Some used the work of Shaykh Muhammad ʿAbduh (1849–1905), the late nineteenth-century Egyptian Muslim religious reformer and state mufti, which highlighted the ills of polygamy on society. They also cited facts from today's reality, indicating how harmful this practice is to women, children and men. NGOs, however, are aware of hostile societal attitudes on this matter, and, therefore, most of them will not call for the total abolition of polygamy in the PSL.[42] Rather, they will ask for restrictive conditions that will make it very difficult for the husband to take another wife.[43]

Inheritance was one of the trickiest concepts to handle for some of the interviewees. This is because the Qur'anic verses are perceived to be very clear as to how the estate should be divided between women and men. Also, they know that challenges to this concept will be received in a very antagonistic manner by society. Almost all of those interviewed indicated that inheritance should be the last issue to tackle, partly because of popular hostility and partly because women do not inherit anything at all in many areas in Egypt, so the priority should be to make sure they do, even if only half as much as their male kin. However, I realised that some of the interviewees hid behind these two points to mask their own indecision about what they, as practising Muslims, should do about inheritance. When I probed further, and asked whether they would call for equal inheritance if women did start inheriting their religious share of the estate, some said no, because that would be going against a clear Qur'anic verse, while others uncomfortably indicated that they hadn't yet decided. Yet there were others, some of them religiously observant, who clearly stated that women should have the same inheritance rights as men nowadays, due to the change in context, family structure and financial obligations on the spouses. This last group, a minority, still thought that it would do more harm than good to tackle this explosive issue now, and that there were other priority issues that they should address first.

7. Analysis and conclusions

Initially, NGO activists set out to tackle the problems they saw women facing under the PSL in a practical way, but without a clear and coherent intellectual framework. They originally built their work on references that turned out to have some problematic elements, as well as sometimes being inconsistent. But in the process of interaction between these references in the NGOs' work on PSL reform, a new discourse has developed, in which the concepts of *wilāya* and *qiwāma* are being reconstructed and given new meanings and implications.

The main tools used by NGOs for adapting this new discourse were:

- A historical, contextual and linguistic analysis of Qur'anic verses.
- Checking the verse or ruling against its purpose (*maqṣad*).
- A reinterpretation of Qur'anic verses based on general Qur'anic principles such as equality, justice and the preservation of human dignity.
- Making a distinction between Shari'a and *fiqh*.
- A study of hadith, sifting the strong hadiths from the weak.
- Presenting elements of the Prophet's life and practice that support their demands.
- Augmenting this religious discourse with facts and statistics from social reality.
- Finding inspiration and guidance in the international human rights discourse.

The approaches and tools that they use are very similar to those used by the Islamic feminist scholars cited above. However, it is necessary at the outset to make a distinction between 'Islamic feminism as a discursive movement, and the distinct local, national or transnational social and political movements that are all increasingly referring to this discourse'.[44] Egyptian NGOs did not create the Islamic feminist discourse from scratch; rather, they are reaching similar conclusions. They also added to it two other discourses, namely, those of reality and human rights. For them, all three discourses were interrelated and mutually affected each other. One discourse was the reason another discourse had to be sifted through, questioned and sometimes recreated. However, it became apparent through the course of their work that it is one thing to develop a new discourse with new concepts, and another to articulate these into appropriate demands in political lobbying. Articulating demands seems to be a distinct process, separate from creating the knowledge upon which these demands are based. Demands are shaped by the context they are made in, and by the actors who make them and their position in that context. That is why such demands might sometimes diverge, to a greater or lesser extent, from the theory underlying them, as will be discussed below.

NGO activists hold that, as Muslim believers, they have the right to engage in creating and choosing the interpretation that suits their contextual needs. The monopoly on Islamic authority held by traditional religious experts and leaders is thus being questioned. Interviewed NGO activists – most of them declared observant Muslims – are reclaiming their agency as Muslim believers to determine what they see as Islamic or not. This is not to say, however, that NGOs have successfully challenged traditional authorities and become recognised sources of religious knowledge production themselves.

What constitutes a credible and authoritative methodology of producing religious knowledge is also being tested. Methodologies such as critical, historical and literary analyses of the text and unearthing the purpose/*maqṣad* of Islam, seem to be rising in importance.[45] Also, previously, religious knowledge production was not under much scrutiny or pressure from an international community flying the flag of international human rights. Today, it is becoming increasingly difficult to produce religious verdicts that condone and encourage practices like slavery, wife-beating and child marriage. Human rights have become a new measure for evaluating religious knowledge production. This measure does not go uncontested by Muslims and others, nor should it, in light of its current manipulation by the powers that be. But it seems that, today, it is no longer a given that religious knowledge can depend solely on traditional *fiqh* understandings of the Qur'an and Sunna for its authority and acceptance by Muslims everywhere. It appears from the NGO work that, at least, it should not clash with general sensibilities of what constitutes human rights and dignity today. It most certainly should not be used as a pretext for harm as seen, for example, in obedience court cases, which the NGOs handle in Egypt. In all this, we might have the beginnings of what Messick calls a 'discursive rupture',[46] where the relations of knowledge and power involved in religious knowledge production are changing.[47] The new discourse critically addresses discrepancies between traditional jurisprudence on women's issues and the contemporary changing needs of women. Based on their grounded reality, NGOs analyse, question and deconstruct the traditional religious discourse to reconstruct a new one that is gender-sensitive and suited to the current context. Likewise, they take from human rights what they find suitable and leave the rest. This choosing, mixing and matching between the religious and human rights discourses, with references tailored to the needs, perceived by NGOs, of their Egyptian context, is creating new conceptions, opportunities and, indeed, a new logic and potential.

Some NGO demands represent breakthroughs in Egyptian debate. These include: placing conditions on polygamy; calling for the principle of shared responsibility between the spouses, even if it is just a theoretical demand that is not reflected in their specific demands regarding obedience; that custody of the children remain with the mother after her remarriage; that financial guardianship of the children be shared by both parents and not just the father; and, finally, the regulation of the accumulated shared wealth within a marriage.[48]

However, at the same time, this discourse can sometimes create what may be perceived as messy inconsistencies. For example, under a strict human rights umbrella, polygamy would be totally abolished from the PSL, not merely made subject to conditions, as the NGOs are demanding. Inheritance would be equally divided between women and men, which is not what the NGOs are currently working towards. Maintenance would be a shared obligation of the spouses, but NGOs have made no clear indication of that in their law proposal. According to their 'enlightened' religious discourse, they should be calling for the abolition of the wife's obligation to obedience, but they are not.

I would, however, in the end not use the word 'inconsistency'. For, as Cowan, Dembour and Wilson state, in the socio-legal study of human rights and local cultures:

> It is time that more attention is paid to empirical, contextual analyses of specific rights struggles. This intellectual strategy allows us to follow how individuals, groups, communities and states use a discourse of rights in the pursuit of particular ends, and how they become enmeshed in its logic. It reveals the moral ambiguities that are not always noticed in purely theoretical accounts, as well as the unavoidable messiness of social life, where competing claims and contestation over meaning are not a sign of cultural or community failure but, rather, part of the human condition.[49]

So what might be contradictory or inconsistent in the realm of abstract thought and theory is not necessarily so in the realm of practice. Practice should take precedence and inform theory, not vice versa. This is especially valid with regard to the view of 'standpoint feminists', who argue that the lived realities of women give rise to systems of knowledge that describe reality with as much authority as what were previously considered proper forms of 'scientific knowledge'.[50] Instead of attacking NGOs for their sometimes 'inconsistent' and messy demands, it is more useful to understand the possible reasons behind them. Taking a feminist standpoint view on this means examining the underlying complexities and power dynamics. Possible reasons for this 'unavoidable messiness' include:

- personal religious faith that prohibits some activists from making certain demands for equality they feel are in contradiction with that faith;
- the perceived socio-political willingness, or unwillingness, of society to accept certain demands for women;
- concerns that some demands, although calling for equality, could be potentially harmful to women and would deprive them of some current advantages;

- NGOs' structural weakness and lack of ability to mobilise supporters and leverage to effect significant changes in the situation of women; and
- the fact that the discourse is still gradually taking shape, therefore 'inconsistencies' are to be expected during the process of building and developing it through practice.

NGOs, having to grapple with these very real, convergent issues, eventually get caught between the concept and its execution. An apparent 'inconsistency' in their work could, in fact, be one of the very few possible responses to such conflicting factors and pressures.[51]

Cowan, Dembour and Wilson's words clearly describe the serious struggle of some activists to reconcile their religious faith and their demands for equality. Interviewees explained this struggle as mainly due to the perceived clarity of the text on issues like polygamy and inheritance. This shows the power a text like the Qur'an holds over its believers, the power of traditional interpretations to portray themselves as the only right ones, and the power of the belief that only religious scholars can interpret the Qur'an. All this explains the compromises, silences or 'inconsistencies' in the demands NGOs eventually made in practice. It also means, however, that this new discourse will need to clearly define its relationship with such a powerful text, and with those who speak in its name, if it is to effect any significant change in the future.

On a different but related note, most of those I interviewed do not use a religious discourse in an instrumentalist fashion. With a few exceptions, they are critically engaging with religion, clearly seeing its patriarchal elements, yet nevertheless trying to come up with a better and more suitable interpretation for the current context. Some of them use a religious discourse to better reach their audience with their new ideas, while others do it as a matter of respect for their own cultural identity and that of their audience. And finally, many of them consider themselves to be believers in the Islamic message, and find it a credible frame to regulate their own personal lives. Instrumentalists using religion as a pragmatic tool, without a personal commitment, would instead have made use of the prevalent piety in society by professing religion as the main reference of their work, without engaging with problematic elements in that religion.[52]

For the time being, however, the development and articulation of this new discourse seems to be an embryonic, individual and sporadic effort. Every NGO is working on its own in that respect, and there is no concerted effort to develop a joint approach or school of thought by NGOs in Egypt today. There are several possible reasons for this. First, these are civil society organisations, which primarily focus on civil, public, activist and advocacy activities, not think tanks nor universities with knowledge production as their primary vocation. Second, they are NGOs whose organisational and legal structures place serious limitations on what they can do.[53] Financial sustainability is almost always a struggle. They mostly work on a temporary project basis, and are caught between foreign donors – with the stigma that their foreignness poses for the NGOs' work – and a state that does its best to limit their freedom with restrictive laws. Third, even within the same NGO there is not yet a consensus on the boundaries of equality, which remain subject to considerable negotiation among NGO members. Fourth, cooperation on the fragmented women's rights NGO scene in Egypt seems to be short-term at best.[54] All this poses a serious challenge for NGOs, and it remains to be seen how successful their efforts will be. The discourse developed by the NGOs, however, is full of potential, as it combines references some would think incompatible: Islamic law and international human rights law. As summed up by one of my interviewees, it is a discourse that 'shows women and society at large that, in fact, being an observant Muslim woman does not necessitate accepting inequality and being treated as a second class citizen, and Islam does support us in that!'

Notes

1 This chapter is based on the author's ongoing thesis work: Sharafeldin, Marwa, *Personal status law reform in Egypt: women's rights NGOs navigating between Islamic law and international human rights law* (DPhil thesis, Law Faculty, Oxford University, forthcoming).

2 On these concepts, see the introductory chapter to this volume.

3 For the purposes of this chapter, when referring to international human rights law, I will particularly focus on the United Nation's Convention on the Elimination of All Forms of Discrimination against Women (CEDAW).

4 The network started work in 2005. Today it covers 19 of the 29 governorates in Egypt with its advocacy activities, which mainly target women, government officials, law-makers and the media. The network is funded by the German Technical Cooperation Office (GTZ) in Cairo, based on an agreement between the Egyptian and German governments.

5 Bernard-Maugiron, Nathalie, *Personal Status Laws in Egypt: FAQ* (Cairo: German Technical Cooperation Office [GTZ], 2010), p. 5.

6 Article 3 Law 1/2000; Fawzy, Essam, 'Muslim personal status law in Egypt: the current situation and possibilities of reform through internal initiative', in Lynn Welchman (ed.), *Women's Rights and Islamic Family Law: Perspectives on Reform* (London: Zed Books, 2004), pp. 32–3; Zahw, Ahmed, *Al-Zawāj fi al-Sharī'a al-Islāmiyya* [Marriage in Islamic Law] (Cairo: Law Faculty Cairo University, 1999), pp. 5–6; Ghazaly, Ahmed and Roushdy Shehata (eds), *Mushkilāt wa Qaḍāyā al-Ahwāl al-Shakhṣiyya li al-Muslimīn* [Problems and Issues of Personal Status for Muslims] (Cairo: Maktaba al-Nahda al-Misriyya, 2005), p. 7.

7 Fawzy, 'Muslim personal status law', pp. 38–9.

8 The International Islamic Committee for Women and Children, 'A critique of CEDAW' (in Arabic), n.d., available at http://www.iicwc.org/lagna/iicwc/iicwc.php?id=960 (accessed 27 March 2012).

9 For example, due to high poverty levels, most Egyptian households nowadays find it very difficult to get by without the income of both partners. Additionally, in 2000, 22% of households were solely dependent on the woman's income, as confirmed by government reports, cf. Fawzy: 'Muslim personal status law', p. 31.

10 For more on the references and discourses used to legitimate demands in the Egyptian context see Singerman, Diane, 'Re-writing divorce in Egypt: reclaiming Islam, legal activism, and coalition politics', in Robert Hefner (ed.), *Remaking Muslim Politics: Pluralism, Contestation, Democratization* (Princeton: Princeton University Press, 2005).

11 Examples of such studies are: El Hennawy, Hamdy and Salwa Abdel Baky, *Al-Takālīf al-Iqtiṣādiyya wa al-Nafsiyya li al-Ṭalāq fī Maṣr* [Economic and Psychological Costs of Divorce in Egypt] (Cairo: Centre for Egyptian Women Legal Assistance [CEWLA], 2009); Zakareya, Hoda, *Al-Taklufa al-Ijtimā'iyya li al-Ṭalāq* [The Social Cost of Divorce in Egypt] (Cairo: CEWLA, 2009); El Sayed, Hend Fouad, *Al-Usra al-Miṣriyya wa-Qaḍāyā al-Aḥwāl al-Shakhsiyya: Dirāsa Taḥlīliyya Iḥṣā'iyya* [Personal Status Law Issues and the Egyptian Family: An Analytical and Statistical Study] (Cairo: Egyptian Foundation for Family Development [EFFD], 2009); Abu Teeg, Mervat, *Naḥwa Qānūn Usra Jadīd* [Towards a New Family Law] (Alexandria: Women and Development NGO [WAD], 2009).

12 Some scholars, such as Sonbol, contest the current 'Shari'a' applied in contemporary Egypt in the family realm. She finds that the Shari'a applied today is significantly different from that applied in Egypt before the reform of laws that began in the 1880s. Sonbol, Amira El-Azhary, *Women, the Family, and Divorce Laws in Islamic History* (Syracuse, N.Y.: Syracuse University Press, 1996).

13 For more on the difficulty of changing the PSL due to the link being made between it and Islam as a sacred religion, see Singerman: 'Re-writing divorce'; Al-Ali, Nadje, *Secularism, Gender and the State in the Middle East: The Egyptian Women's Movement* (Cambridge: Cambridge University Press, 2000); Badran, Margot, *Feminists, Islam, and Nation: Gender and the Making of Modern Egypt* (Princeton: Princeton University Press, 1995).

14 This NGO emphasised that one needs to speak the right language for the right place. They would not go to a village in Upper Egypt and talk about CEDAW, as it would be seen as a foreign, inappropriate and suspicious reference. Rather, they would translate such concepts into local frames and images to get the point across. For more on the importance of translating international concepts into local ones, see Merry, Sally Engle, 'Legal pluralism and transnational culture: the

Ka Ho'okolokolonui Kanaka Maoli tribunal, Hawai'i, 1993', in Richard Wilson (ed.), *Human Rights, Culture and Context: Anthropological Perspectives* (London: Pluto Press, 1997), pp. 24–48; *idem*, 'Changing rights, changing culture', in Jane K. Cowan, Marie-Benedicte Dembour and Richard Wilson (eds), *Culture and Rights: Anthropological Perspectives* (Cambridge: Cambridge University Press, 2001), pp. 31–55; *idem*, *Human Rights and Gender Violence: Translating International Law Into Local Justice* (Chicago: University of Chicago Press, 2006); Shaheed, Farida, 'The cultural articulation of patriarchy: legal systems, Islam and women', in Haideh Moghissi (ed.), *Women and Islam: Critical Concepts in Sociology* (London: Routledge, 2005), pp. 38–44; An-Na'im, Abdullahi, 'The dichotomy between religious and secular discourse in Islamic societies', in Mahnaz Afkhami (ed.), *Faith and Freedom: Women's Human Rights in the Muslim World* (London and New York: I.B.Tauris, 1995), pp. 51–60; *idem*, 'The rights of women and international law in the Muslim context', *Whittier Law Review* 9 (1987–8), pp. 491–516; An-Na'im, Abdullahi and Francis Deng, 'Preface', in An-Na'im and Deng (eds), *Human Rights in Africa: Cross-Cultural Perspectives* (Washington, DC: The Brookings Institution, 1990).

15 Dupret, Baudouin, 'Sexual morality at the Egyptian bar: female circumcision, sex change operations, and motives for suing', *Islamic Law and Society* 9/1 (2002), pp. 42–69; Singerman: 'Re-writing divorce'.

16 Mir-Hosseini, Ziba, 'Islamic legal tradition and feminism: opening a new dialogue', paper presented at the IV International Congress on Islamic Feminism, Madrid, 21–4 October 2010.

17 For more on deconstructing the term see Mir-Hosseini, Ziba, 'Beyond "Islam" vs. "feminism"', *Institute of Development Studies Bulletin* 42/1 (2011), pp. 67–77 (first published in *Contestations: Dialogue on Women's Empowerment* 1 [2010], issue on 'Islam and Feminism', accessed 1 December 2011, now defunct; *Contestations* was the e-journal of the Pathways of Women's Empowerment Research and Communications Programme, http://www.pathways-of empowerment.org/ (accessed 26 September 2012).

The term, and the efforts it describes, have been widely contested and discussed over the years. See Badran, Margot, 'From Islamic feminism' to a Muslim holistic feminism', *IDS Bulletin* 42/1 (January 2011), pp. 78–87; *idem*, *Feminism beyond East and West: New Gender Talk and Practice in Global Islam* (New Delhi: Global Media Publications, 2007); *idem*, 'Islamic feminism revisited', *Al Ahram Weekly Online* 781 (9–15 February 2006), available at http://weekly.ahram.org.eg/2006/781/cu4.htm (accessed 19 September 2011) ; *idem*, 'Islamic feminism: what's in a name?', *Al Ahram Weekly Online* 569 (17–23 January 2002), available at http://weekly.ahram.org.eg/2002/569/cu1.htm (accessed 19 September 2011); Tohidi, N., 'Islamic feminism: perils and promises', *Middle East Women's Studies Review* 16/3–4 (Autumn 2001/Winter 2002), pp. 13–15, 27; Abou-Bakr,

Omaima, 'Islamic feminism: what's in a name?', *Middle East Women's Studies Review* 15–16 (Winter/Spring 2001) available at http://www.historians.ie/women/amews%20abou-bakr.htm (accessed 19 September 2011); Moghadam, Valentine, 'Islamic feminism and its discontents: toward a resolution of the debate', *Signs* 27/4 (Summer 2002), pp. 1135–71; Mir-Hosseini, Ziba, 'Muslim women's quest for equality: between Islamic law and feminism', *Critical Inquiry* 32/4 (Summer 2006); *idem*, 'The quest for gender justice: emerging feminist voices in Islam', *Islam 21* 36 (May 2004), available at http://web.fu-berlin.de/gpo/pdf/tagungen/Mir_Hosseini.pdf (accessed 19 September 2011); *idem*, 'The construction of gender in Islamic legal thought and strategies for reform', *Hawwa* 1/1 (2003), pp. 1–28.

18 Abou-Bakr: 'Islamic feminism'.

19 They were vaguely aware of the scholarly work, mostly written in English – which the majority of them do not speak – that attempts to create a symbiotic relation between Shari'a and human/women's rights. Only one of them – a university professor – had studied this work in depth.

20 On this, one of the interviewees exclaimed: 'we are not going to be asking for *ḥarām* (religiously prohibited) things just for [the sake of] equality between the sexes!', indicating that for her, going against a clear Qur'anic verse sanctioning unequal treatment of women would be considered *ḥarām*, even if it were for the sake of equality.

21 For more on the precedence of such overriding principles over the actual scriptural verses see Abu-Zayd, Nasr Hamid, *Dawā'ir al-Khawf: Qirā'a fī Khiṭāb al-Mar'a* [Circles of Fear: A Reading in Women's Discourse] (Beirut: Al-Markaz al-Thakafi al-'Arabi, 2004).

22 Indicating that the relation between a person and Allah is a direct one with no intermediaries, and in that sense everyone is empowered to communicate directly with God and understand Islam in their own way.

23 In the advocacy events and activities they organise, two of the interviewees said they prefer not to respond to religious questions posed to them for fear of losing credibility by giving incorrect information. Rather, they bring with them an 'enlightened' shaykh to attend the event and respond to the questions.

24 Karam, Azza, *Women, Islamisms and the State* (London: Macmillan, 1998).

25 Karam, *Women, Islamisms and the State*, pp. 9–11. For a more recent and problematised categorisation of Islamist groups' discourse on women, see Ababneh, Sara, 'Islamic Political Parties as a Means of Women's Empowerment: The Case of Hamas and the Islamic Action Front' (D.Phil. thesis, Department of Politics and International Relations, University of Oxford, 2009).

26 Karam, *Women, Islamisms and the State*, p. 13.

27 It is worth noting that secular women constituted the majority of women's rights activists in Egypt in the 1960s and 1970s. Al-Ali, Nadje, 'Gender and civil society

in the Middle East', in Jude Howell and Diane Mulligan (eds), *Gender and Civil Society: Transcending Boundaries* (Oxford: Routledge, 2005). However, fieldwork for this chapter shows that the women's movement today has changed somewhat to include more women who do not use an exclusively secular frame of reference, and who see no problem in drawing on a religious reference in their activism as well as in their personal lives.

28 This is because the law itself is based on religious jurisprudence, with the acceptance of the majority of the population for now. Also, many of the local women these secularists work with are themselves believers who do not want to 'anger God' by not following 'God's commands'. These secularists' solidarity and feminism leads them to engage with religious law critically, instead of avoiding it altogether like most other secular feminists in Egypt. There is yet another distinct group among the 'secular feminists' I interviewed and observed who are privately observant believers, but nevertheless believe in the separation of state laws and religion. They do not find any paradox in this, holding that religious belief is a private matter. I develop this in my thesis.

29 An-Na'im and Deng, 'Preface', *Human Rights*.

30 An-Na'im, 'Rights of women', p. 497, emphasis added.

31 *Ibid.*, p. 501.

32 An-Na'im and Deng, 'Preface', *Human Rights*, p. xiv.

33 Merry, 'Legal pluralism', p. 134.

34 To illustrate the difficulty of this role, Al-Ali quotes one of her women activist interviewees, saying, 'The position of mediator is never comfortable. You are always in the position of the potential betrayer, translator, double agent. It carries lots of responsibilities and it's full of tensions, but it's also very creative.' Al-Ali, *Secularism, Gender and the State*, p. 210.

35 Abu-Odeh, Lama, 'Egyptian feminism: trapped in the identity debate', in Yvonne Haddad and Barbara Stowassser (eds), *Islamic Law and the Challenge of Modernity* (Oxford: Altamira Press, 2004).

36 However, most of them disagree with her about the presence of an alliance between feminists and Islamic forces. They do not see it as an alliance, but rather as the use of a religious discourse that conveys the point to their audience more clearly.

37 It is important to note here the work of Peters and Cockayne, who criticise scholarship that incriminates 'Islam' by using a human rights yardstick, and argue that it is anachronistic and orientalist to judge the rules of classical Islamic jurisprudence by today's standards. Peters, Ruud, 'Islamic law and human rights: a contribution to an ongoing debate', *Islam and Christian-Muslim Relations* 10/1 (1999), pp. 5–14; Cockayne, James, 'Islam and international humanitarian law: from a clash to a conversation between civilizations', *International Review of the Red Cross* 84/847 (September 2002), pp. 597–626. What these NGOs seem to be

doing, rather, is to engage in an interactive dialogue between the two discourses to create a more relevant new one.

38 Bayoumy, Abdel Moaty, *Min qaḍāyā al-mar'a* [Women's Issues] (Cairo: CEWLA, 2009).

39 There were two interviewees who did not find obedience itself to be problematic; for them, obedience was the wife's 'right' rather than 'obligation' to stay in the marital home. In the event of spousal discord, it would be the husband who had to leave the marital home, not the wife. They were, however, a minority.

40 *Shirk* is understood as worshipping a partner to Allah, or polytheism, which is a grave sin. Nadwi, A. A., *Vocabulary of the Qur'an* (Chicago: IQRA' International Educational Foundation, 1983).

41 Nevertheless, in the end, NGOs in the network did not call for the abolition of obedience in their final legal manual. This seems to be the result of the negotiated interplay of power relations between the differing factions within the network on this issue.

42 In a round table organised by one of the NGOs to discuss PSL reforms with Egyptian judges, the organisers were surprised to find that the judges present unanimously agreed that polygamy is to be considered the rule, while monogamy the exception. The only participant who disagreed was a university professor in Islamic law (the round table was held in the Flamenco Hotel, Cairo, 17 March 2009).

43 A minority of NGO interviewees expressed sympathy for polygamy, but only in certain cases, such as if the wife is unable to bear children. They also found it difficult to ask for its total prohibition because it was mentioned in the Qur'an, and their faith in the Qur'an led them to think that it must have been put there by God for a good reason.

44 Schneider, Nadja-Christina, 'Islamic feminism and Muslim women's rights activism in India: from transnational discourse to local movement – or vice versa?', *Journal of International Women's Studies* 11/1 (November 2009), pp. 56–71 at p. 56.

45 Moll, Yasmin, '"People like us" in pursuit of God and rights: Islamic feminist discourse and Sisters in Islam in Malaysia', *Journal of International Women's Studies* 11/1 (November 2009), pp. 40–55 at p. 42.

46 Messick, Brinkley, *The Calligraphic State: Textual Domination and History in a Muslim Society* (Berkeley: University of California Press, 1993).

47 Moll, 'People like us', p. 44.

48 I consider these breakthroughs because some are relatively new public demands for Egyptian society (excluding polygamy); they are in contradiction with settled traditional Islamic jurisprudence on the matter; and they run against the general sensibilities of what women's and men's roles in Egyptian society today are perceived to be. For discussion, see, chapter 5, in my forthcoming dissertation, Sharafeldin, *Personal status law reform*, see note 1.

49 Cowan, Dembour and Wilson, *Culture and Rights*, p. 21.

50 For more on this see Harding, S. and M. B. Hintikaa, *Discovering Reality: Feminist Perspectives on Epistemology, Metaphysics, Methodology and Philosophy of Science* (Dordrecht: D. Reidel, 1983); Harding, S., 'Is there a feminist method?', in *idem* (ed.), *Feminism and Methodology: Social Science Issues* (Indianapolis: Indiana University Press, 1987), Ramazanoglu, C., 'Improving on sociology: the problems of taking a feminist standpoint', *Sociology* 23 (1989), pp. 427–592; Hartsock, N., 'The feminist standpoint: developing the ground for a specifically feminist historical materialism', in S. Kemp and J. Squires (eds), *Feminisms* (Oxford: Oxford University Press, 1997), pp. 152–60; McRobbie, A., 'The politics of feminist research: between talk, text and action', *Feminist Review* 12 (1982), pp. 46–57; Roberts, H., *Doing Feminist Research* (London: Routledge, 1981); Stanley, L. and S. Wise, *Breaking Out: Feminist Consciousness and Feminist Research* (London: Routledge, 1983).

51 This raises important questions, albeit outside the remit of this chapter, on the efficacy of this kind of work by NGOs.

52 For a critical discussion, see Sholkamy, Hania, 'Islam and feminism', *Contestations* 1, available by searching http://web.archive.org for http://www.contestations.net/issues/issue-1/religion-and-gender-justice/ (archived 24 May 2010, cf. also note 17).

53 For more on this see Jad, Islah, 'The NGOization of the Arab women's movement', paper presented at the international workshop 'Feminist Fables and Gender Myths: Repositioning Gender in Development Policy and Practice', Institute of Development Studies, Sussex, 2–4 July 2003.

54 Augustine, Ebba, 'Analysis on legal rights of women in Egypt', unpublished paper commissioned by the GTZ office in Cairo, Egypt, 2005; Abdel Rahman, Maha, *Civil Society Exposed: The Politics of NGOs in Egypt* (Cairo: The American University in Cairo Press, 2004).

4

THE RELIGIOUS ARGUMENTS IN THE DEBATE ON THE REFORM OF THE MOROCCAN FAMILY CODE*

Aïcha El Hajjami

1. Introduction

Upon independence, Morocco undertook the codification of its family law, which had been managed by judges (*qāḍīs*) and based on the scattered collections of the Maliki school, one of the four Sunni schools of law. The personal status code, known as the Mudawwana, was drawn up by a commission appointed by King Mohammed V and consisting of scholars (*'ulamā'*) including 'Allal al-Fasi (d. 1974), the champion of Moroccan reformist Salafism. In various writings, [1] he had already promoted bold legal reforms regarding women's rights, such as abolishing matrimonial guardianship, banning polygamy and instituting compensation for the repudiated wife regardless of the grounds for repudiation, based on an effort to interpret the religious texts (*ijtihād*) in connection with the demands of contemporary social reality. However, these innovative ideas were not accepted by the other members of the commission, which included learned *'ulamā'* such as Mohammed Belarbi Alaoui (d. 1964) and Mukhtar al-Soussi (d. 1963). The Mudawwana enacted in 1958 faithfully reproduced certain dogmatic legal rules, made by Maliki jurisconsults

* Translated from French by Christian Moe.

for a bygone era and context, which were no longer suited to the social reality of Morocco in the twentieth century.[2]

The Mudawwana thus confined the woman to the status of an eternal minor. In marrying, she was subject to matrimonial guardianship; once married, she owed obedience to the head of the family, her husband, in exchange for maintenance (*nafaqa*). The practice of polygamy was unrestricted; there was only a fair-treatment requirement of a purely moral nature with no judicial oversight. The husband had the discretionary power of unilateral divorce, whereas the wife only had the right to judicial divorce, if she could provide evidence; or to separation through compensation (*khulʿ*). The *khulʿ*, in practice, often enabled a recalcitrant husband to financially and emotionally blackmail his wife, forcing her to give up all her rights, including child custody. Upon divorce, the mother would be given custody (*ḥaḍāna*) of the children only if she did not remarry or take up residence far from the father's home.

The state of legal insecurity instituted by the Mudawwana led to grave family problems. That is why, ever since its promulgation, various voices have been criticising its institutionalised inequalities and calling for change. From the late 1970s onwards, these demands from women's movements intensified, despite a climate of suspicion. It should be kept in mind that the articulation of family law within the Islamic reference frame, in a society where religion is omnipresent but is also very much influenced by the fallout of modernity, makes the reform of women's legal status a complex and sensitive question, as religious, political and socio-cultural factors intertwine.

Still, after several abortive initiatives, a Mudawwana reform saw the light in 1993, drawn up by a royal commission of *ʿulamāʾ* and jurists. Deemed insufficient by the women's movements, the reform was, nevertheless, original in that it desacralised the Mudawwana, the provisions of which had been equated with the Shariʿa, and thus held by a large fringe of Moroccan society, including the *fuqahāʾ* (religious jurists),[3] to be untouchable as the faithful rendering of the word of God.

Later, Morocco's political opening, which allowed opposition parties into government, made the improvement of women's legal situation in the private sphere a central issue in the development and modernisation of society. In March 1999, the prime minister of the new government announced the draft National Action Plan for the Integration of Woman in Development, prepared by the Family, Child and Social Protection Department. The draft's legal section included proposals for banning polygamy, abolishing the *walī* institution (matrimonial guardian), raising the marriage age of girls from 15 to 18 years, instituting judicial divorce and dividing conjugal property acquired during the marriage in case of divorce.[4]

This action plan, which was part of the implementation of the recommendations arising from the 1995 Beijing Conference platform, caused a virulent reaction from the Islamic movement. The concern focused on both the legal part, its frame of reference and the drafting procedure, which had not included *ʿulamāʾ* or political factors from the Islamic movement.

The ensuing debate was dominated by the clash between two views of women's rights and roles in society,[5] inspired by two seemingly incompatible reference frames: that of Islam, and that of human rights as set out in international conventions.[6] Nonetheless, the salience of Islam on all levels of Moroccan political[7] and social reality[8] meant that both camps would largely have to resort to religious arguments, though the use of scripture and jurisprudence to support one position or the other was rather superficial, and more often led to a battle of texts than an in-depth scientific debate.

On the other hand, the involvement of jurists/theologians in the reform debate, before and after the code was adopted, allowed a better analysis of the religious arguments. While all the *ʿulamāʾ* adhere to the precepts of Islam and *ijtihād* as sources of inspiration for any family law reform, some of them, like Ahmed El Khamlichi,[9] Mohammed El Habti El Mawahibi[10] and Idris Hammadi[11] took notable stands in favour of women's demands. In their writings, pleading for the supporters of reform, they held that the proposed measures would not in any way conflict with the categorical foundations of Islam, as they fell under what *fiqh* terms *al-masāʾil al-khilāfiyya*, where there is no definitive consensus among the classical jurisconsults. They could, therefore, be subject to an up-to-date *ijtihād*, taking into account the development of society and women's aspirations to equality and equity.

Other *ʿulamāʾ* rose up against some claims they judged to be against Islam and its jurisprudence, in particular professors Ahmed Raysouni,[12] Mohammed El Habib Toujkani[13] and AbdelKabir Alaoui Mdaghri.[14]

This chapter draws largely on the arguments developed by each side to illustrate the positions on the new family code, which includes all the legal proposals from the action plan draft except the abolition of polygamy.

A consensus on adopting the code was reached after the then prime minister asked for royal arbitration. King Mohammed VI nominated a consultative commission to draft the code,[15] consisting of *ʿulamāʾ*, lawyers and other experts in the human sciences, including three women. It was also fairly representative of the two camps that had clashed over the reforms.[16] In his speech appointing the committee, the king stressed the limits of reform, as his father had done in 1992: 'We cannot forbid what God has permitted, or make licit what He has proscribed …'.

It should be noted that in his 10 October 2003 speech to parliament, presenting the draft family code, the king accompanied the announcement of each new provision with a religious argument from the Qur'an or hadith.[17]

The draft code was submitted to parliament according to normal legislative procedure and unanimously adopted by both chambers on 16 January 2003. It was gazetted on 4 February 2004 as *Mudawwanat al-usra*.

The new code represents an effort to reconcile three demands imposed by the socio-political context: the Islamic principles on the matter, the human rights values in international conventions signed and ratified by Morocco, and the contemporary realities and aspirations of Moroccan society.

This chapter seeks to bring out the religious arguments over the innovations in the new family code, especially those used in the ongoing Moroccan debates over the reform. Despite the consensus formed around the code, its provisions are still seen by some in Moroccan society as contrary to Islamic precepts, which makes for resistance to its proper implementation, whether among the citizens or within the judiciary.

2. The main innovations in the family code

The egalitarian philosophy behind the new family code may be seen in its various provisions. Thus, from the start, the code introduced the joint management of the family by both spouses; matrimonial guardianship was made optional for women who have reached legal majority; the legal marriage age was set at 18 for both sexes; both spouses were made equally responsible for the family; strict conditions were imposed on polygamy, to be assessed by the judge; divorce was made available to both spouses and placed under judicial control; and the wife could claim a share of the assets acquired during the marriage in case of divorce, in ways provided by law.

In what follows, we will, in particular, discuss those innovations that have been contested and debated.

a. The joint management of the family by both spouses

The old Mudawwana considered the husband to be the head of the family, to whom the wife owed obedience in return for maintenance. The new family code instead places the family under the joint responsibility of the spouses. Article 4 stipulates that 'marriage is an act based on mutual consent with a view to establishing a lawful and lasting union between a man and a woman. Its goal is life in reciprocal fidelity, purity and the founding of a stable family under the management of both spouses, in accordance with the provisions of the present code.'

In an egalitarian perspective one might imagine the code introducing the corollary of this joint responsibility and obliging the wife to contribute to the maintenance of the family as the husband does. And yet, the retention in the code of the wife's right to maintenance is rather in the spirit of Islamic jurisprudence, which considers it an inalienable right, and a valid ground, if unpaid, on which the wife can file for judicial divorce. The wife is, nevertheless, required to maintain her children, to the extent the father is unable to do so (Article 199).

Furthermore, the code institutes reciprocal and equal rights and duties for the spouses. They are identically mentioned in Article 51, which cites inter alia: 'the wife's assuming jointly with the husband the responsibility of managing household affairs and the protection of the children; consultation in decisions concerning the management of family affairs, children and family planning',[18] whereas in the old code, the duties of fidelity, obedience, running the household and treating one's parents-in-law well fell only on the wife.

By making the family the joint responsibility of both spouses, the new code questions the notion of *qiwāma* as understood and interpreted in the classical exegetical tradition.

At the time of the debate, the *qiwāma* concept was not tackled directly, all the more so since the joint management of the family did not figure explicitly among the demands. This measure was introduced by the consultative commission, and was greeted by the women's organisations. Nonetheless, the *qiwāma* was implicitly at issue in every proposal or demand for egalitarian reform. It must be admitted that all these demands questioned the idea of definitive male 'authority' and 'advantage' over women in all spheres of life, and hence of *qiwāma* as generally perceived by Islamic jurisprudence. This sense of *qiwāma* has served as the ground for legal norms on family and social life, and as justification for resistance to demands that were in no way opposed to the Islamic values of justice and equity.

b. The legal age of marriage

In the Maliki school there is no fixed minimum legal age for marriage. A distinction is drawn between the pubescent girl (*bāligh*, *rāshida*) and the prepubescent. Only the latter is subject to her legal guardian's right to marry her by force (*jabr*).

On 'Allal al-Fasi's proposal, the personal status code broke with this legal tradition. The right to marry a young girl by force was abolished and the marriage age was set to 15, below which a marriage could not be validly concluded.[19]

The committee members did not refer to any religious textual argument for this choice. It was motivated solely by consideration of the interest (*maṣlaḥa*) of the young girl, which required the law-makers to put an end to the harmful effects of premature marriages. Still, taking the *maṣlaḥa* into consideration is a religious requirement, as 'Allal al-Fasi explained.[20]

Despite these restrictions in the Mudawwana, marriage before the legal age of 15 continued to be practised in Morocco, for reasons related to the ways and customs that made such marriages attractive, the absence of schooling for young girls in some backward parts of the country, and the precarious economic conditions that pushed families into marrying off their minor daughter to the first suitor.

The proposed raising of the marriage age for girls to 18 figured among the demands of women's associations and the measures of the action plan; it was justified by the harmful impacts of early marriage on the health of mother and child, as well as on the required education of young girls and on the well-being of the family, and it was dictated by the need to adapt Moroccan legislation to the Convention on the Rights of the Child, which Morocco had ratified in June 1993 without reservation as to the definition of 'the child'.

Ultimately, the new code set the legal age of marriage at 18 for both girls and boys, leaving judges the option of granting dispensation in special cases. Unlike the former code, which had underlined the fact that marriage below the age of 15 was formally prohibited, however, the new code remained silent on this point, leaving the door wide open to early marriages of little girls:

> *Article 19:* Boys and girls of sound mind acquire the capacity to marry at 18 full Gregorian years of age.
>
> *Article 20:* The family judge in charge of marriage may authorise the marriage of a boy and girl below the legal age of marriage stipulated in Article 19 *supra*, through a reasoned decision stating the interest and motives justifying the marriage (...)

It must be noted that the decision of the judge in this matter is not open to appeal. This shows the importance of the discretion granted to the judiciary over this crucial question.

Since the code entered into force, fieldwork in Morocco as well as statistics published by the Ministry of Justice show that the marriage of minors continues to be practised, especially in rural areas, even for those below 15.[21] The dispensations from the marriage age granted by judges are based on subjective criteria, especially those related to the precarious socio-economic situations of families and the resistance of the traditional mindset.

Supporters of child marriages rely essentially on two arguments: the Qur'anic verse that states the waiting time for divorced women, mentioning the case of those who have not yet menstruated (65:4); and the example of 'A'isha, the wife of the Prophet, who was proposed to at the age of 6 or 7 and joined the marital home at the age of 9.

According to those opposed to raising the marriage age for girls, the marriage of minors has been authorised by the consensus (*ijmāʿ*) of Muslim jurisconsults.[22] The four Sunni schools, as well as the Zahiris and the various Shiʿi schools (Imamiyya, ʿIbadiyya and Zaydiyya) clearly approve of this kind of marriage.[23]

The opponents of child marriage base their arguments on the advice of certain classical jurisconsults who opposed the marriage of prepubescent girls, including Ibn Shubruma (d. 761), the illustrious Kufan judge.[24] He categorically forbade a father from giving a prepubescent daughter in marriage, as her authorisation was absolutely required, and this she could not give before puberty. He refutes the argument that the Prophet married 'A'isha at the age of 6 by explaining that this is one of the matters specific to the messenger of God that cannot be applied generally to all Muslims.

Another argument for banning child marriage rests on the analogy (*qiyās*) with the unanimously accepted principle in Islamic jurisprudence of the personal autonomy of both males and females in managing their personal and financial affairs. If the person in question is a minor or lacks the requisite competence to manage her affairs, she may delegate the task to a representative, but only in everyday and urgent matters. But marriage is not such an urgent need for a minor that she needs to appoint someone to contract it for her, as Khamlichi explains.[25] He does not see verse 65:4 as entailing any recommendation that Muslims authorise child marriage. Nothing in this verse indicates that those who have not yet menstruated (*allā'ī lam yaḥiḍna*) are necessarily girls before puberty. In his view, it probably refers to women with some physical impairment that prevents them from menstruating, and they could well be over 30 years old.

Moreover, even supposing that the verse does speak of prepubescent divorcées, which did exist in society at the time of revelation, the Qur'an's indication of their waiting period should be seen simply as stating a fact, and by no means as legalising the marriage of girls before puberty. In support of this thesis Khamlichi cites another verse that says 'Make trial of orphans until they reach the age of puberty (*nikāḥ*); if then ye find sound judgment in them, release their property to them …' (4:6). This verse orders the guardians of orphans to hold back their inheritance until they become fit to marry and thus capable of managing their property. It follows that fitness to marry corresponds to civil and legal capacity. This confirms the prohibition against marrying girls below puberty, who have not attained the age of discernment that would allow them to make the decision of entering married life.

*c. Matrimonial guardianship (*wilāya*)*

The *wilāya* or matrimonial guardianship is considered a condition for the conclusion of marriage in Muslim law. There are two forms of *wilāya*, one entailing a right of coercion (*wilāyat al-jabr*) and one entailing a right to give consent.

The right to force a marriage is recognised in *fiqh*. This right is for males only. It is held by the father or, in his absence, by the guardian if specified in the will. If the father's will did not designate a guardian, a judge may exercise the right to marry a girl by force if he fears bad conduct on her part.

The justification for forced marriage stems from a concern to protect the young girl, with regard to her inexperience. This did not prevent the classical doctrine from giving the girl recourse to ask the *qāḍī* to annul the marriage in case the right-holder abused the right of *jabr*.

For all that the 1957 personal status code abolished the right of coercion, it did not abolish matrimonial guardianship. In this it remained faithful to the Maliki school, which demands that the woman not conclude marriage herself, whether her own marriage or that of her ward if she is the testamentary guardian. This school holds that a woman must be represented by a matrimonial guardian who takes care of conveying her consent when the marriage is concluded.

This question was discussed in the drafting committee for the Mudawwana. ʿAllal al-Fasi sought to include in the final text the distinction between the question of consent, or the absence of coercion, and the question of the woman concluding her marriage directly with the man of her choice on the condition that his social standing matched hers.[26] When this failed, he joined the commission's majority opinion, justifying it on social rather than religious grounds in his report: 'The Moroccan family is not yet sufficiently evolved to admit the solutions of the Hanafi school in this matter. For a woman of age to personally contract marriage without a guardian or representative would be considered in the eyes of public opinion as a hard-to-justify transgression of Islamic morality.'[27]

The institution of the matrimonial guardian was thus maintained, as the presence of the *walī* was considered a condition for the validity of the marriage contract, but, as intended by the legislators, the role of guardian was to be limited to protecting the interests of the young girl or boy and to backing their choice of spouse.

Article 12 (4) stipulated, in effect, that the *walī* could not oblige a nubile girl to marry without her consent. He could not give her in marriage unless she had authorised it. However, the Mudawwana did not specify how the girl would authorise it, an ambiguity that gave room for abuse, as many guardians marry their wards by force but pretend to do so at their behest.

Moreover, the same paragraph added: 'unless depravity is feared on her part', leaving a judge to determine if there is risk of depravity and, if so, to impose a marriage on a girl, with due regard to social equivalence (*kufʾ*), in order to prevent moral decay (*ṣadd al-dharāʾiʿ*).

This exception apart, it was up to the woman to give her consent to a marriage proposal, but in the case of a girl who had reached the age of marriage but not yet reached the age of civil majority (21 years), the guardian had to supplement her consent with his own.

It must be noted that, despite the abolition of the right of *jabr* in the old code, forced marriage has continued to be practised in some circles in Morocco, giving rise to insurmountable problems and destabilising families.

Therefore, the action plan took up women's demands that the use of a representative be optional for girls of age, and that the latter be able to conclude their marriage contract without the intervention of a matrimonial guardian. The latter institution, say those who would abolish it, was tied to the sexual division of space in traditional societies. There is no longer any reason for it to be obligatory, considering the new role of women in society and the increasingly advanced marriage age.

Already, the partial Mudawwana reform in 1993 had relieved the fatherless, marriageable young girl of the obligation to have the matrimonial guardian present, while leaving her the option of appointing a person of her choice to conclude her marriage contract. This reform was criticised for its incomprehensible unequal treatment of girls with and without a living father.

The new 2004 family code remedied the situation by explicitly stating the optional nature of the *walī* for the woman of age, whether fatherless or not:

> *Article 24:* Matrimonial guardianship is a right that belongs to the woman. The woman who is of age exercises this right according to her choice and interests.
>
> *Article 25:* A woman of age may contract her own marriage or appoint her father or one of her relatives to do so.

This new measure breaks with the logic of treating Moroccan women as minors that prevailed in the old code, and has been subject to intense debate between the defenders of matrimonial guardianship and those who would abolish it. There is no categorical text either imposing or preventing matrimonial guardianship, as was noted by the Andalusian jurisconsult Ibn Rushd.[28] There is but a single verse of the Qur'an that, paradoxically, serves as an argument for both sides. It is all a question of interpretation. The verse is: 'When ye divorce women, and they fulfil the term of their *'idda*, do not prevent them (*lā taʿḍulūhunna*)[29] from marrying their (former) husbands, if they mutually agree on equitable terms …' (2:232).

The circumstances of its revelation boil down to Maʿqil ibn Yasar al-Muzani having forbidden his divorced sister to remarry her ex-husband after her waiting period was over. The verse addresses him, exhorting him not to hinder the reunion of his sister and her husband.

Already the classical jurisconsults were divided. For Malikis and Shafiʿis,[30] the message contains a legal command addressed to Maʿqil as the legal representative of his sister, entitled to oversee her marriage, and, more broadly, to all male guardians of their female relatives. In support of their view, they also cite the *qiwāma* verse 4:34; the hadith reported from 'A'isha by Al-Zuhri, 'any woman who marries without her guardian's consent, her marriage is void';[31] and that of Abu Hurayra that says 'a woman cannot marry off a woman, as she cannot marry off herself'.[32]

The Hanafi school, on the other hand, considers the *wilāya* a constituent part of marriage, but nevertheless does not condition its validity on the *walī*'s approval if the woman is of age and of sound mind; this is only a condition for *kamāl* (perfection). Such a woman may contract her marriage without the presence or permission of the *walī* as long as she chooses a spouse of equivalent social rank (*kuf'*), and the dower (*ṣadāq al-mithl*) is adequate.

The family code has adopted this solution, without the two conditions. Articles 24 and 25 allow a woman who has reached majority (*rāshida*) to free herself of the *walī*'s presence.

During the reform debate, the advocates of this option invoked the Hanafi school's view, without really supporting it with scholarly arguments. The stress was always on sociological arguments about the development and maturity of Moroccan women and the need to give them freedom of choice in this matter.[33]

As the record of the drafting commission – which may put the religious argument more precisely – has not been published, we find it useful to highlight these arguments, all the more so because some people, especially judges, remain reluctant about this new right given to women.[34]

One of the major arguments[35] of the Hanafis is based on the verse cited above, 'do not prevent them from marrying their (former) husbands …' In their view this verse represents a message of women's liberation from the male authority that enchains their will and exercises a right of supervision over them, and which lacks legitimate grounds. The Qur'anic message upholds women's legitimate right to manage their personal lives. The fact that the verse cited above is addressed to Maʿqil ibn Yasar does not make him the legal guardian of his sister. He is addressed as a person who has performed an act that the Qur'an condemns, although it was accepted in Arab society at the time. Hanafis find the Qur'an to be clear in its condemnation of this practice, whether by the brother or the spouse. It is equally explicit as to the validity of the marriage contract of a woman who chooses a social equal for her spouse.

Fakhr Al-Din al-Razi (d. 1209) holds that the verse does not only address the woman's brother, but that it concerns all the believers. It forbids all men, not simply women's legal representatives, from mistreating women and doing *ʿaḍl*. In the same vein, Ibn Rushd maintains that the verse does not specify who the *walī* should be or how he is related to the woman concerned.

This view is corroborated by other verses that give women the right to freely contract marriage without the presence of the *walī*, as long as her choice is made in accordance with conventions and propriety (*maʿrūf*), such as:

> Those of you who die and leave widows should bequeath for their widows a year's maintenance and residence; but if they leave (the residence), there is no blame on you for what they do with themselves, provided it is reasonable. And Allah is Exalted in Power, Wise. (2:240)
>
> So if a husband divorces his wife (irrevocably), he cannot, after that, re-marry her until after she has married another husband … (2:230)

The way these verses attribute the marriage act (*nikāḥ*) to the woman, and use the expression 'what they do with themselves', clearly shows the possibility of women directly contracting their own marriages.

As to the hadith denying women this right, it is contested: its chain of transmission is weak to the point that al-Zuhri, who reported it, himself later disowned it, saying he did not know it.

Moreover, the Hanafis, like Ibn Rushd, hold that the condition of the *walī* only applies to minors, as stipulated in a hadith reported by Ibn ʿAbbas: 'The woman who has already been married or who is no longer a virgin (*thayyib*) decides for herself, whereas the virgin (*bikr*) must be consulted, her silence serving as consent.'[36]

Another edifying example is the hadith reported by Ibn 'Abbas that shows the father cannot impose on his daughter a husband of his choice. The hadith reports that a young girl went to complain to the Prophet because her father had required her to marry his nephew; the Prophet gave her the choice of accepting or rejecting this forced marriage.

Furthermore, it is told that the Prophet voided the marriage of a woman (Khansa' bint Khudam) who had come to complain that her father had married her by force even though she was *thayyib*.

The Hanafis also cite the fact that 'A'isha, the wife of the Prophet, concluded the marriage of her niece, the daughter of her brother 'Abd al-Rahman, and even did so in the presence of Companions of the Prophet, who did not disapprove. 'Abd al-Rahman, who was absent at the time, approved the marriage on his return.

The Hanafi school, furthermore, draws an analogy between the marriage contract and other civil contracts, such as the contracts of sale or of lease, both of which involve a fee. And as Muslim personal law does not contest the right of a woman of age to directly conclude a business contract, or to manage her inheritance as she pleases, there is no reason to forbid her from concluding her own marriage, which first and foremost concerns herself.

3. Polygamy

Regarding polygamy, the 1957 Mudawwana faithfully followed classical Muslim law. It allowed polygamy, but added that it was forbidden if there was reason to fear an 'injustice' to the wife. In addition, it gave the woman the right to include in the marriage contract the condition that her husband not take another wife; if the husband broke this commitment, she had the right to demand the dissolution of the marriage (Article 31).

In practice, this monogamy clause has been very little used by Moroccan women, on account of the heavy weight of tradition and customs, and the lack of information on the issue.

The second paragraph of Article 35 of the old Mudawwana also stipulated that the polygamous husband must ensure equal treatment of his wives, and that he was not allowed to lodge his new wife in the same house as the first one without the latter's consent.

One may note that these different precautions taken by the law-maker to ensure fairness between wives only relate to the material aspect, whereas the harm to women engendered by polygamy is primarily of a moral and emotional kind. It is no accident that the co-wife is called *ḍarra*, 'harm', in Moroccan Arab dialect!

The perpetuation of polygamy as instituted in the Mudawwana has been the source of many family conflicts, threatening the stability and harmony of the marital home.

It is true that with the breakdown of the patriarchal family, the emergence of the nuclear family and the spread of women's education and employment outside the home, the practice of polygamy has declined. Nonetheless, the fact that this is still an option for men, subject to no conditions or judicial control, is a permanent threat to the married woman and her children.

For this reason, the abolition of polygamy has, since the early 1990s, been at the forefront of the various demands of women's organisations, with the support of human rights activists, researchers and jurists.[37] It was adopted by the 1999 action plan.

Under the pressure of public opinion, and faced with the virulent reaction of the *'ulamā'* and the Islamic movement,[38] the abolition demand gave way to the demand that polygamy be limited by strict conditions, based on arguments drawn from the Islamic frame of reference and the interpretations of Muslim reformers such as 'Allal al-Fasi and al-Tahir al-Haddad (d. 1936).

The 1993 reform had already made some formal adjustments to the regulation of polygamy, but the women's organisations deemed them insufficient. The 2004 code does not explicitly ban polygamy, except in cases where the wife has inserted the monogamy clause into the marriage contract or into any later agreement. However, Article 40 reasserts the spirit of the Qur'anic verse that makes polygamy conditional on fair treatment, 'if ye fear that ye shall not be able to deal justly (with them), then only one ...' (4:3), by banning polygamy 'when there is a risk of injustice toward the wives'.

Article 41 sets out the conditions that must be fulfilled by a husband who wants to take a second wife:

> The court shall not allow polygamy in the following cases:
>
> - When an objective justification of an exceptional character has not been proven;
> - When the claimant does not have sufficient means to support both families and equitably guarantee their maintenance, housing, and other needs of life.[39]

The legislator seeks to limit polygamy to exceptional situations, but the use of vague terms like 'risk of injustice', 'objective justification' and 'exceptional character', which are left for the judge to assess, leaves the door open to it.[40]

It is true that the rate of polygamous marriages registered in Moroccan courts is decreasing, and made up not much more than 0.27 per cent of the marriages in 2008, but, on the level of principle, the women's organisations find it clearly discriminatory against women and a threat to the stability of the family and the well-being of children, especially since sociological studies and reports by monitoring centres show that the practice of polygamy is often not justified on valid grounds.

The case for restricting polygamy was argued based on the text of the Qur'an and the tradition of the Prophet. First of all, it was recalled that the verses on polygamy do not in any way form a recommendation or injunction to practise it (4:3).[41] At most, they simply tolerate a practice deeply rooted in the patriarchal mindset of the era. In a slave-holding society, polygamous marriage was a mark of power and affluence. From there, Islam went progressively on, first, to limit the number of women to which a man could aspire, initially to four; then, in another verse, to exhort husbands to treat their wives justly and equitably while at the same time denying that this was possible; and, finally, to assert that they could never treat their wives equitably and exhort them to stay monogamous (4:129).

Moreover, this verse (4:3) first and foremost aimed to protect orphans from abuse by their guardians. Its limiting of the number of legal wives to four was a considerable advance in a society that knew no limit on the number of wives.

Islamic jurisprudence considers polygamy a permissible (*mubāḥ*) act, but not an obligatory one. Scholars of *uṣūl* accept that a *mubāḥ* may become forbidden (*ḥarām*) from the moment its practice causes social problems. In this case, the legislator may intervene to limit or suspend the practice in the public interest (*maṣlaḥa*),[42] which is one of the main objectives of Islam (*maqāṣid al-sharīʿa*).

The Prophetic tradition shows that polygamy may be banned,[43] as he did not allow even his cousin ʿAli to take a second wife. The Prophet is reported to have said: 'The Banu Hashim ibn al-Mughira have asked my permission to marry their daughter to ʿAli ibn Abi Talib; I do not allow it, I do not allow it; I do not allow it, except if ʿAli ibn Abi Talib wishes to repudiate my daughter and marry theirs.'[44]

ʿAllal al-Fasi, whose arguments have served to plead for women's demands, advocated a ban on polygamy. His arguments relied on the Qur'anic text, which makes polygamy conditional on strict fairness (*ʿadl*) between wives. He added that the mere fear of failing to be fair was a valid reason for giving up the practice. Al-Fasi compared the social context of the revelation of the verse that justified allowing polygamy, with the context of our current societies, rife with abuse and injustice to women, and concluded that the legislature could put an end to this by banning polygamy through the legitimate principle of *ṣadd al-dharāʾiʿ*. He wrote:

> Whatever one may say about the benefits of polygamy in some circumstances, public or private, as far as I'm concerned I find that the Islamic and social interest demands that it be banned at the present time; I do not claim that this ban is a supplement to Islamic legislation, since the latter is comprehensive on this subject as on others, for the Qur'an explicitly bans polygamy every time there is a risk of injustice. In our time, the harms suffered by the family and other institutions as a result of polygamy have become glaringly obvious, and no-one can deny them ... Polygamy must not be allowed in a society

that guarantees the prohibition of any injustice or abuse, to the contrary, in societies where private family interests or the public interest are infringed in the name of satisfying desires, it is imperative that the principle of *ṣadd al-dharāʾiʿ* be applied to ban the practice of polygamy in order to push back against these crimes.[45]

4. Dissolving the marriage tie

The 1957 Mudawwana kept unilateral repudiation by the husband, judicial divorce for harm, and divorce obtained by the wife for compensation (*khulʿ*) from the Maliki school. It sought to limit abusive divorce practices by imposing restrictions on so-called Sunni repudiation, banning 'any double or triple repudiation' and obliging the husband to register his repudiation with two notaries (*adouls*).

Still, gender inequality in divorce rights was perpetuated through the husband having the privilege of legally repudiating his wife without giving reasons, and the wife only two options for ending a marriage: either buying back her liberty by *khulʿ*, or referring the matter to a judge, invoking one of the grounds envisaged by the Mudawwana and bringing proof of her allegations, which was often impossible in practice. In practice, *khulʿ* often led to financial and emotional blackmail by a recalcitrant husband.

This explains why, despite the measures taken by the code, some husbands continued to practice repudiation arbitrarily, doing wrong both to the wife and the children, and threatening the stability and harmony of the family.

Based on this unhappy social reality, women's groups developed demands that repudiation be regulated and made subject to judicial control, in order to put an end to its arbitrary and capricious practice by husbands.[46]

The opponents of this proposal rose against the substitution of judicial divorce for the husband's repudiation.[47] They held that restricting the husband's free exercise of repudiation went against the religious texts and Islamic jurisprudence. They also argued that judicial intervention in family affairs would be an invasion of the intimacy of married life, exposing marriage problems before the courts for everyone to see, contrary to Muslim family ethics.

The new family code of 2004 offered judicial divorce as a way for both spouses to dissolve their marriage on an equal footing. It imposed judicial control over all forms of divorce, with new guarantees such as reinforcing the requirement for the parties to meet, attempting reconciliation and judicial authorisation. Divorce is thus no longer the husband's sole privilege, but henceforth the right of both spouses.

The different ways of dissolving the marriage retained in the code are: *ṭalāq*, unilateral repudiation at the husband's discretion, or the wife's in case of *tamlīk* (if this clause, delegated divorce, is part of the marriage contract) or *khulʿ* (against compensation); *ṭalāq* by mutual consent; *taṭlīq*, divorce granted to the wife on grounds of harm; and *shiqāq*, divorce on grounds of discord, granted to both spouses.

Furthermore, the code has expanded the grounds on which the wife may claim divorce (*taṭlīq*) beyond the husband's failure to pay maintenance, unacceptable defects (impotence or dangerous disease), absence, abstinence from marital relations, or physical abuse. It has added the grounds of his failure to meet the commitments he made at the time of marriage, and it has widened the notion of harm to include psychological harm.

Concerning *khulʿ*, Moroccan legislators, seeking to protect wives from any abuse by their husbands, have granted them the right to have their compensation payment returned to them if it is shown that their *khulʿ* divorce was the result of coercion, or that they suffered harm from their husbands. It is also emphasised that the compensation payment must not be abusive or excessive.

*a. Divorce on grounds of discord (*shiqāq*)*

This form of divorce is one of the major, emblematic innovations in the new code. It offers women important advantages: a wife who wishes to separate from her husband can have recourse to the *shiqāq* procedure, particularly in cases where she is not able to prove the harms she has suffered. She no longer depends on her husband's goodwill for dissolving her marriage.

Although this innovation was adopted in order to protect women and give them equal divorce rights with men, the legislators, following Qur'anic prescriptions, have made the procedure available to both spouses.

Article 94 stipulates that 'When one or both spouses asks the court to settle a dispute that divides them and threatens to lead to discord, it is incumbent on the court to make every attempt to reconcile them, in accordance with the provisions of Article 82 supra.'

In such a case, the court must seek to reconcile the parties in the presence of the two arbiters mentioned in Article 95. If reconciliation fails, and the discord continues, the court declares divorce and rules on the payments due, taking into account the responsibility of each party for the causes of divorce when evaluating damages to be paid to the injured party (Article 97).

The novelty of this procedure, compared to divorce on grounds of harm, is that the parties are not required to cite particular grievances. The mere assertion that continuing marital relations would be intolerable suffices in the eyes of the law to justify the divorce ruling.

b. The arguments over the new divorce provisions

The arguments in support of expanded access to divorce for women and leaving this up to the judge,[48] found their justification, first, in the Islamic principles of justice and fairness, and second, in the texts of the Qur'an and Sunna.

Recall that, even if in Islam divorce is considered 'the permitted act that God hates the most', it is nonetheless a remedy for an anomalous situation where it becomes unbearable for the couple to live together. 'But if they disagree (and must part), Allah will provide abundance for all from His all-reaching bounty: for Allah is He that careth for all and is Wise' (4:130).

It must be done with respect for the wishes and dignity of both spouses, which is why all the verses on divorce,[49] without exception, contain recommendations for the man – to whom they are expressly addressed, since at the time, he was the one who held the power of 'repudiation' – not to do harm to the woman: 'either take them back on equitable terms or set them free on equitable terms; but do not take them back to injure them, (or) to take undue advantage; if any one does that; He wrongs his own soul' (2:231).

The verse relevant to *shiqāq* is: 'If ye fear a breach (*shiqāq*) between them twain, appoint (two) arbiters, one from his family, and the other from hers; if they wish for peace, Allah will cause their reconciliation: For Allah hath full knowledge, and is acquainted with all things' (4:35).

The Maliki *fuqahā'*, unlike the other Sunni schools, allowed divorce on grounds of discord by taking into account this verse and the hadith that forbids doing harm to others in general (*lā ḍarara wa lā ḍirār*).[50]

The provisions on divorce through compensation (*khul'*) were included in the code based on the verse: 'If ye (judges) do indeed fear that they would be unable to keep the limits ordained by Allah, there is no blame on either of them if she give something for her freedom' (2:229).

The tradition of the Prophet also throws light on the possibility of a woman obtaining divorce, whether on the grounds of the harm she has suffered or simply because she can no longer stand living with her husband. The hadith reported by Ibn 'Abbas about the wife of Thabit ibn Qays is the first case of *khul'* in Muslim history.[51]

The jurisconsults justify this form of divorce by arguing that the wife who seeks to free herself from the marriage tie is causing harm to the husband, and must compensate him accordingly.[52]

The code's adoption of divorce on grounds of discord has undeniably brought relief to many women victims of domestic violence, who faced the obstacles tied to the other forms of divorce. *Shiqāq* is a solution in complete agreement with the values of fairness and justice advocated by Islam.

After the promulgation of the code, it was found that repudiation was being replaced by *shiqāq* divorce in almost all the courts of Morocco. It was also noted that men, too, largely use this procedure, despite having access to other means of divorce, in order to get out of paying their wives their dues, and to be indemnified if they succeed in proving that the separation is the fault of their wife. In order to limit this circumvention of the law and to protect the rights of women whose husbands claim divorce on grounds of discord, the Marrakech court, bucking the trend in other Moroccan courts, has innovatively required the husband to first deposit the amount due to the wife with the court.[53]

5. The division of property acquired during marriage

In Muslim law, marriage does not create common property. The married woman retains the right to freely manage and dispose of her property. The principle of separate property stems from the Qur'anic verse: 'That man can have nothing but what he strives for; that (the fruit of) his striving will soon come in sight' (53:39–40).

Accordingly, upon the dissolution of marriage, be it by divorce or by bereavement, the wife who had contributed to the growth of family property would have the right to a determined share of this property in exchange for her labour. Although the Maliki school prevents the wife from making a donation of more than a third of her holdings without her husband's permission, the 1957 personal status code did not retain this restriction (Article 5, para 5), giving her instead 'the full liberty to manage and dispose of her property without any control by the husband, as the latter has no power over the property of his wife'. Article 39 gave instructions on how to settle disputes over property ownership.

The new family code, while upholding the principle of separate property, adds a clause tending to protect the economic interests of the wife, by allowing her to claim a part of the family property acquired during marriage.

> *Article 49:* Both spouses have their own property. However, the spouses may agree on conditions for the investment and division of property they will acquire during their marriage.
>
> This agreement shall be set out in a document separate from the marriage contract.
>
> The *adouls* shall inform both parties of the above provisions at the time of marriage.
>
> In the absence of the aforementioned agreement, recourse is had to the general standards of evidence, taking into consideration the work of each spouse, the efforts invested and the responsibilities assumed in the development of the family assets.

This is a major innovation that consecrates the principle of justice and equality between the couple, referred to in Article 400 of the code. It is also in line with the jurisprudence practised in certain regions of Morocco, variously known as *al-kadd wa al-siʿāya*, *ḥaqq al-shqā* or *tamazālt*, that is, the right of effort.

And it is adapted to the current social reality of Morocco, where women are entering the economic field and making an active contribution to the maintenance of their families and to the family assets.

By adopting Article 49, Moroccan legislators met, to an extent, one of the major demands of the women's movement,[54] namely, putting an end to the financial loss suffered by the wife because her contribution to the family assets is not taken into consideration at the dissolution of marriage or at the death of the husband.

a. The arguments pro and contra

Those opposed to the division of assets between the spouses deem this demand to be unfounded and contrary to the principles of justice and fairness. The wife has no right to the husband's fortune, according to Islamic jurisprudence, as the husband is required to maintain his wife in exchange for her housework. Her direct or indirect participation in the development of these assets is in return for the duty of maintenance. On the other hand, custom (*ʿurf*) would have the wife offer her husband the fruits of her labour of her own free will. For the Qur'an says: 'And give the women (on marriage) their dower as a free gift; but if they, of their own good pleasure, remit any part of it to you, take it and enjoy it with right good cheer' (4:4).

Under these conditions, laying claim to a part of the husband's fortune would be seen as earning money for nothing, and would boil down to unjustly dispossessing another of what properly belongs to him,[55] which is illicit and forbidden in Islam, as indicated by the verses that warn believers not to 'eat up' their property among themselves (2:188, 4:29).

Those in favour of dividing the assets between the spouses at the moment of separation retort that these same verses rather support their argument. In our time, the women who work outside the home contribute to the growth of the family assets by their efforts: they take on providing for the family and contribute to the everyday expenditures of the household. To deprive them of part of these assets is a flagrant injustice, condemned by these very verses that forbid appropriating other people's property for no reason.

Moreover, they say that the husband's duty to provide for the wife was not instituted in exchange for household chores, as is claimed, for the wife is not under obligation to do any work at all, whether in the marital home or outside it.[56] They quote Ibn Hajar: 'To oblige the wife to work of any kind lacks a valid foundation. The consensus (*ijmāʿ*) holds that it falls to the husband to support the wife completely, and Tahawi reports the consensus that the husband has no right to dismiss his wife's housemaid, which proves that he is obliged to pay for the housemaid as needed.'[57]

It should be kept in mind that the division of assets acquired during marriage between the spouses at the time of divorce or death has been a customary practice in certain regions of Morocco, notably in the northern Rif region (Ghmara) and in the south (Souss). It was consecrated by jurisprudence in the celebrated fatwa of the Moroccan jurisconsult Ibn ʿArdun, and has been applied by the courts up to the present day.[58]

In these two regions of Morocco, *fiqh* accords a woman who participates in farm work with her husband up to half the assets acquired during marriage upon divorce or the husband's death.[59]

This right is justified through the *ijtihād* of ʿUmar ibn al-Khattab, who rendered justice to Habiba bint Zurayq by taking into consideration the fact that her manual labour had contributed to the assets of her deceased husband. He thus granted her half of what her husband had left behind as compensation for her work, in addition to her heritage, which was one fourth.[60]

This *ijtihād* was taken up by Imam Malik and his disciples, who held that the wife has the right to part of the assets acquired during marriage, independently of their nature, in proportion to her contribution to their growth.[61]

Thus, the principle of division of assets upon divorce adopted by the new family code draws its legitimacy from the Islamic frame of reference, via *ijtihād* and Maliki jurisprudence. It also takes into account the evolution of Moroccan society and the role played by women in public and private spheres.

Nevertheless, one is not convinced that this measure will be effective, insofar as Article 49 requires the general standards of evidence to be met, which is not always easy to do. Whereas in the past, the traditional judge applying the principle of *al-kadd wa al-siʿāya* had wide latitude to assess the wife's contribution based on the Islamic standards of evidence, such as witness testimony or declarations under oath, the power of the contemporary positivist judge is severely limited by Article 49's condition.[62]

6. Conclusion

The analysis of the religious arguments used during the debate on family law reform shows the sensitivity and complexity of this question in a traditional society that is largely dominated by the patriarchal mindset, but at the same time drawn to 'modernity' in all its dimensions. The question of women's rights is only the visible part of an iceberg that crystallises the ideological and conceptual debates over modernity and tradition, universality and particularity, and an Islamic frame of reference versus secularism (*laïcité*).

This ambivalence is reflected in the contents of the new code which, while continuing to give primacy to the Islamic frame of reference in an innovative reading (*ijtihād maqāṣidī*), has opened itself up to the human rights set out in international conventions. This approach has supposedly contributed to the emergence of a new culture and new behaviours within society, and yet, one finds that, even after the code entered into force in 2004, there are still several obstacles to its proper implementation.

These obstacles are as much to do with cultural resistance and the socio-economic environment as with the functioning of the judicial apparatus. Moreover, practice has shown that there are lacunas, inadequacies and contradictions in the legal text itself, which may limit the scope of certain measures,[63] including measures favouring the restriction of polygamy, the institution of a legal marriage age, and the division of marital assets between spouses upon the dissolution of the marriage.

Where polygamy is concerned,[64] when the judge does not allow a husband to take a second wife after having assessed whether his application is based on objective and exceptional grounds, the husband bypasses this refusal by having recourse to other articles of the code concerning recognition of marriage[65] or recognition of paternity.[66] In this case, the judge is faced with a *fait accompli* and has to grant an exception from the principle of monogamy.

As to the legal age of marriage, the judges are often forced against their wish to permit the marriage of a young girl, especially in rural areas, because of the precarious economic situation and the traditions that drive parents to marry off their daughters at an early age.

In addition, when it comes to safeguarding the financial interests of the wife upon the separation of spouses through the division of assets envisaged in Article 49, this intent of the lawgivers is thwarted by the standard of evidence required by the text, as well as by the text's silence on whether the wife's housework should be considered in the assessment of the family assets. It is also hobbled by the weight of tradition and social conventions opposed to this measure.

This shows that promoting the social change expected from the adoption of the new family code requires a global approach, addressing the various socio-cultural and economic barriers.

Notes

1 Notably in al-Fasi, 'Allal, *al-Naqd al-Dhātī* [Self-Criticism] (Beirut: Dar al-Kashaf, 1966).

2 'Allal al-Fasi had described the sources that should inform the Mudawwana as follows: 'If we wish to codify Muslim law in Morocco in order to facilitate its application by the Moroccan courts, we must refer as far as possible to the Maliki school, but at the same time take into consideration the general principles of Muslim law and public interest …'. See the text of his report in *Prologues* special issue 2, *La réforme du droit de la famille: Cinquante années de débat. Anthologie des textes* (Casablanca: Al-Najah al-Jadida, 2002), pp. 46–74.

3 See the statement by a group of '*ulamā*' addressed to the prime minister and to the president of the House of Representatives in response to the 8 March 1992 press release of the Union de l'Action Féministe (UAF), which had demanded gender equality in family law, including inheritance. The '*ulamā*' statement declared any reform of the personal status code a direct attack on the Shari'a. *Arrāya* 25 (6 July 1992), pp. 8–10; also published in El Habib El Toujkani, Mohammed, *Qaḍiyyāt*

Mudawwana al-Aḥwāl al-Shakhṣiyya bi al-Maghrib [The Question of the Personal Status Code in Morocco] (Casablanca: Al-Najah al-Jadida, 1994), pp. 81–97.

4 See the legal section of the action plan draft in *Prologues* special issue 2, pp. 219–27.

5 The demands of women prior to the 1993 reform were later taken up by other civil society bodies that defended the contents of the action plan, particularly the several women's and human rights groups in the 'Collectif du Printemps de l'Egalité'. Some other organisations formed a network named 'L'instance pour la défense de la famille marocaine', with the aim of fighting the adoption of the action plan and the gender approach, to which they opposed 'the family approach'. The positions and arguments of these actors are published in the special issue of *Prologues*. The polarisation of the conflict culminated on 12 March 2000 with two giant marches, one held in Rabat by the defenders of the action plan, the other in Casablanca by its opponents.

6 It should be stressed that the positioning of the actors with regard to the two frames of reference was not clear-cut. A detailed analysis of the debate shows convergences and cross-references between the two camps. See El Hajjami, Aïcha, ' La problématique de la réforme du statut juridique de la femme au Maroc: entre référentiel et procédure', *Revue de Droit et d'Economie* 19 (Fes, 2002), pp. 33–53.

7 According to the constitution Islam is the state religion and the king is *amīr al-mu'minīn* (Commander of the Faithful).

8 More than 99% of Moroccans are Muslims, and strongly attached to Islam. See the national values survey in *Le Maroc possible* (Editions Maghrébines, 2006), pp. 52ff.

9 Professor of law and theology, director of Dar al-Hadith al-Hasaniya, family law expert and member of the consultative commission tasked with drafting the family code reform.

10 Theology professor at Kénitra. See especially El Habti El Mawahibi, Mohammed, 'What possibilities does the Maliki school offer for a substantial reform of Moroccan family law?' (in Arabic), in *Prologues* special issue 4, *Les possibilités d'une herméneutique favorable à une réforme substantielle du droit de la famille. Actes de la rencontre organisée le 18 mai 2002* (Casablanca: Al-Najah al-Jadida, 2002), pp. 33–52.

11 Theology professor at Allal Ben Abdellah University in Fès. See Hammadi, Idris, *Al-Buʿd al-Maqāṣidī wa Iṣlāḥ Mudawwanat al-Usra* (Casablanca: Ifriqia al-Sharq, 2005).

12 The then president of the Islamic movement al-Tawhid wa al-Islah and theology professor in Rabat. See his views in Raysouni, Ahmed, *al-Fikr al-Maqāṣidī* (Rabat: Al-Zaman, 1999). See also the Islamic movement's *Mawqifunā* … [Our Position on the So-called National Action Plan for the Integration of Women in Development] (Rabat: Top Presse, 2000).

13 Professor at the University of Theology in Tetuan. See El Habib El Toujkani, *Qaḍiyyāt Mudawwana.*

14 Minister of Islamic Affairs and Waqf (*habous*) in the new opposition government; law and theology professor at Mohammed V University in Rabat. He broke with his government in rejecting its proposed action plan, giving his argument in Alaoui Mdaghri, AbdelKabir, *Al-Marʿa Bayna Ahkām al-fiqh wa al-Daʿwa ilā al-Taghyīr* [Woman between *Fiqh* Rules and the Appeal for Change] (Mohammadia: Fedala, 1999).

15 In 1992, King Hassan II had declared that the Mudawwana reform fell under the remit of the king in his capacity as Commander of the Faithful, according to Article 19 of the constitution, which mandated him to 'ensur[e] respect for Islam'. See the text of his speech in *Al-ʿAlam*, 30 September 1992.

16 It is regrettable that the drafting history of the consultative commission has not been published, which would have allowed a more faithful reflection of the viewpoints of the experts of the two camps as they were expressed within the commission.

17 See the speech in *Le Matin du Sahara*, 11 October 2003.

18 Translator's note: quotations from the Mudawwana are translated from the French. I have made use of the unofficial English translation published by Global Rights (http://www.globalrights.org/site/DocServer/Moudawana-English_Translation.pdf), but have followed the official French translation from the Moroccan Ministry of Justice where they diverge. The Arabic original has been consulted in a few cases of doubt.

19 The (old) Mudawwana, Article 2 (2).

20 He explains his disagreement with the Maliki school on this point, and the reasons why the law must institute a minimum marriage age for girls, in al-Fasi, *Al-Naqd al-Dhātī*, pp. 279–82.

21 See the courtroom fieldwork led by El Hajjami, Aïcha, *Le Code de la famille à l'épreuve de la pratique judiciaire* (Marrakech: El Wataniya, 2009), pp. 46–50. See also the study of judicial practices in *idem*, *Le code de la famille: Perceptions et pratique judiciaire* (Rabat: Publications Friedrich Ebert and ImprimElite, 2007).

22 The September 2008 fatwa of Dr Maghrawi, a Salafi shaykh and theology professor in Marrakech, which authorised the marriage of small girls 'from ten years and up', raised an outcry in Morocco, causing the High Council of *'ulamā'* to intervene with a press release condemning the advice and reminding the public that it had jurisdiction over fatwas. It also pointed out that the family code was the only frame of reference in this matter. See the fatwa on Maghrawi's website (http://maghrawi.net/?taraf=fatawi&file=displayfatawi&id=371).

23 See al-ʿAsqalani, Ibn Hajar, *Fatḥ al-Bārī* (Cairo: Al-Maktaba al-Salafiyya), Vol. 9, pp. 124 and 190.

24 See Professor Khamlichi's discussion of Maghrawi's fatwa (http://www.dafatir.com/vb/showthread.php?p=217388).

25 *Ibid.*

26 In his writings, 'Allal al-Fasi defends the woman's right to choose her spouse and contract marriage. In this he adopts the Hanafi position and refutes the Maliki thesis that it is the matrimonial guardian's right to force a marriage. Al-Fasi, *Al-Naqd al-Dhātī*, pp. 272–80.

27 See the text of the report in *Prologues*, p. 54.

28 Ibn Rushd, Abu al-Walid, *Bidāyat al-Mujtahid wa Nihāyat al-muqtaṣid* (Beirut: Al-Maktab al-'Asriyya, 2004), Vol. 1, pp. 11ff.

29 *Al-'aḍl*, according to Ibn Manzur, *Lisān al-'Arab* (online at http://www.baheth.info) means to unjustly prevent someone from doing what he or she wants, e.g. to unjustly prevent a woman from returning to her husband.

30 For more details on the arguments for *wilāya* as an obligation, see the book by Al-Fandlaoui, Yusef ibn Dunas, *Kitāb Tahdhīb al-Masālik fī Nusrāt Mahhab Mālik, Tahqīq Aḥmad al-Būshikhī* (Mohammadia: Fedala, 1998), Vol. 1, pp. 10ff.

31 Cited by Abu Dawud, Tirmidhi and Ibn Baja.

32 Cited by Ibn Maja, in the chapter *Al-Nikāḥ.*

33 See, in particular, El-Mawahibi, 'What possibilities', pp. 38–9. Idris Hammadi cites in support the position of Ibn al-Qasim, see *Al-Bu'd al-Maqāṣidī*, p. 128.

34 As we found in our study of court practice, see El Hajjami, *Le Code de la famille à l'épreuve*, pp. 42–3.

35 These arguments are given in Al-Juzayri, 'Abd al-Rahman, *Kitāb al-Fiqh 'alā al-Madhāhib al-Arba'a* (Cairo: Al-Maktaba al-Tawfiqiyya), Vol. 4, pp. 34–41 and 49–57. See also Al-Fandlaoui: *Kitāb Tahdhīb al-Masālik*, pp. 7–14.

36 Cited inter alia in Malik's *Muwaṭṭa'* and by Abu Dawud.

37 See the second communication of the UAF, and the responses it provoked in El Habib El Toujkani, *Qaḍiyyāt Mudawwana.*

38 El Habib El Toujkani, *Qaḍiyyāt Mudawwana.*

39 The expression 'both families' shows that the legislators intended to limit to two the number of wives a man can marry.

40 See El Hajjami, *Le Code de la famille à l'épreuve*, p. 51.

41 In this regard, see El Habti El Mawahibi, 'What possibilities', pp. 39–40; see also Hammadi, Idris, 'Maqāṣid al-sharī'a fī binā'i al-usra wa al-mujtama'' [Objectives of Sharia in the construction of the family and society].

42 El Habti El Mawahibi, 'What possibilities', pp. 39–40.

43 *Ibid.*, p. 40.

44 Cited by Bukhari.

45 Al-Fasi, *Al-Naqd al-dhātī*, pp. 291–3.

46 A symbolic trial on divorce was held in Rabat on 9 March 1996 on the initiative of the UAF, convicting the Moroccan legislation on this matter and appealing

for reform in accordance with human rights. Professor Khamlichi and other professors took part, along with some ten organisations. See the document in Mdaghri, *Al-Marʿa Bayna Aḥkām al-Fiqh*, pp. 102–14.

47 See the communication of the *ʿulamā'* (Toujkani, Raysouni and others) and those of the Islamic movements and the right-wing parties in El Habib El Toujkani, *Qaḍiyyāt Mudawwana* and in *Prologues* special issue 2.

48 Hammadi, *Al-Buʿd al-Maqāṣidī*, pp. 130–2.

49 The translation of *ṭalāq* by 'repudiation' seems incorrect, as it lends the word a connotation of expulsion and rejection that is humiliating to the woman. The etymological sense of *ṭalāq* is connected with *ṭalīq*, which means 'free'; the verb *ṭallaqa* means to liberate or set free. This is the sense it is given in the Qur'an when it recommends that husbands stop doing harm to their wives upon divorce: 'or set them free on equitable terms …' (2:231). Admittedly, in practice, the unilateral divorce exercised by men in Muslim societies takes the form of rejection and expulsion of the woman from the marital home.

50 See Al-Juzayri, *Kitāb al-Fiqh*, Vol. 4, pp. 378–9; El Habti El Mawahibi, 'What possibilities', p. 41.

51 The wife of Thabit came to the Prophet to say: 'I have nothing to reproach Thabit ibn Qays for, either where his piety or his good behaviour is concerned, but I fear committing a transgression against Islam (if I stay with him).' The Prophet asked her: 'Can you give him back his garden (which was his dower)?' She agreed, and the Prophet then ordered her husband to repudiate her. Cited by Bukhari and Ibn Maja.

52 See al-Zuhayli, Wahba, *Al-Fiqh al-Islāmī wa ʿAdillatuhu* (Damascus: Dar al-Fikr, 1996), Vol. 7, pp. 480–2.

53 On this, see El Hajjami, *Le Code de la famille à l'épreuve*, pp. 55, 142–5.

54 This demand came up towards the end of the 1990s in the draft action plan, was supported by the 'Spring of Equality' umbrella group of eight women's organisations, and was published on 29 October 2001. See the text of the communication in 'La réforme du droit de la famille', *Prologues* special issue 2, pp. 404–9.

55 See the communication from the Islamic movement Al-Tawhid wa al-Islah, published in *Al-Tajdīd* 50 (5 January 2000).

56 El Habti El Mawahibi, 'What possibilities', pp. 44–7; Hammadi, *Al-Buʿd al-Maqāṣidī*, pp. 132–3.

57 See *Nawāzil al-ʿAlamī*, Vol. 2, p. 102. Cited by El Habti El Mawahibi, 'What possibilities', p. 45 (see note 11).

58 In particular the rulings of the Supreme Court: decision no. 410 of 30 March 1985; decision no. 177 of 12 May 1980; decision no. 44 of 28 November 1978; as well as decisions by local courts across Morocco. In a recent ruling, the Supreme Court has held that 'the principle of *al-kadd wa al-siʿāya*, contrary to the ruling of the Safi Appeals Court (no. 244 of 4 April 2000), applies as much to rural women

as to urban women, in accordance with the objectives of the Islamic Shariʿa and jurisprudence, which apply only the criterion of the work and effort contributed by the wife to assess what is due to her'. Cited by Zhor El Horr in *Colloques et Rencontres* (Rabat: Ministry of Justice), Vol. 8, p. 386.

59 The fatwa books (*Nawāzil al-fiqhiyya*) testify to the abundant jurisprudence on the matter: *Nawāzil al-ʿAlamī*, 2/101–6; *Nawāzil al-Sarmūkī*, booklet no. 16 (Bibliothèque generale; 3566); *Al-Manhal al-ʿAḍb al-Salṣabīl*, pp. 257–66. See also El Habti El-Mawahibi, Mohamed, *Fatāwa Tatahaddā al-Ihmāl fī Shafshāwen wa mā Hawlahā mina al-Jibāl* (Rabat: Ministry of Islamic Affairs, 1998), pp. 161–2. For more detail, see Houssain, Milki, *Niẓām al-Kiddi wa al-Siʿāya*, 2 vols (Rabat: Dar al-Salam, 2001).

60 Cited by El Abbadi, Hassan, *'Amal al-mar'a fī Sūs* (Rabat: Top Press, 2004), p. 25.

61 See El Habti El Mawahibi, 'What possibilities', p. 47.

62 El Hajjami, *Le Code de la famille à l'épreuve*, p. 58.

63 For more detail on the application of the code in the courts, see El Hajjami, *Le Code de la famille à l'épreuve*; *idem*, *Le code de la famille: Perceptions*.

64 Less than 2% of marriages contracted each year are polygamous.

65 Article 16 deals with the recognition of non-formalised marriages for a limited five-year period, renewable for five more years. Such marriages are common in rural areas, and are formed simply by reading *Al-Fātiḥa*.

66 Article 156 allows the establishment of paternal filiation for children born from sexual relations in the engagement period.

5

FROM LOCAL TO GLOBAL

Sisters in Islam and the Making of Musawah: A Global Movement for Equality in the Muslim Family

Zainah Anwar

1. Herstory

It started with a question: if God is just, if Islam is just, then why do laws and policies made in the name of Islam cause injustice? This was the burning question that faced the founding members of Sisters in Islam (SIS) when we began our search for answers to discrimination against Muslim women made in the name of Islam.

There were eight of us, all active professional women in Kuala Lumpur, outraged at the persistent message of misogyny coming from preachers over the radio and television, and confronted with complaints from women, friends and strangers, about the misogyny they suffered at the hands of religious bureaucrats when seeking redress for their marital problems.[1]

It was in 1987 that we first met, looking at the problems surrounding the implementation of the Islamic Family Law and the difficulties women faced in accessing their rights under the law. But, as we went on, we realised that working with the law alone was not enough. In religious classes, talks over the radio and television, in interaction with those in the religious departments and Syariah Courts, women were often told that men are superior to women, men have authority over women, a woman must obey her husband, a man has the right to beat his wife, the evidence of two women equals that of one man, the husband has a God-given right to take a second wife and therefore it is a sin for a woman to deny him that right, that a wife has no right to say no to sex with her husband, that hell is full of women because they leave their heads uncovered and are disobedient to their husbands …

Where is the justice for women in all these pronouncements? This question, and, above all, the conviction that Allah could never be unjust, eventually led us back to the primary source of our religion, the Qur'an. We felt the urgent need to read the Qur'an for ourselves and to find out if the text actually supported the oppression and ill-treatment of women.

The process SIS went through was a most liberating and spiritually uplifting experience for all of us. We took the path of *iqrā* ('read', the first word revealed to the Prophet Muhammad, cf. Qur'an 96:1) and it opened a world of Islam that we could recognise, a world for women that was filled with love and mercy, with equality and justice.

For us, it was the beginning of a new journey of discovery. It was a revelation to us that the Qur'anic verse on polygamy (4:3) explicitly said '… if you fear you shall not be able to deal justly with women, then marry only one …' How is it that one half of the verse, which says a man can have up to four wives, becomes universally accepted as a right in Islam and is codified into law, but the other half, which promotes monogamy, is unheard of – until women begin to read the Qur'an for themselves. It dawned on us that when men read the verse, they only saw 'marry up to four wives'. In that phrase, they saw the word of God that validated their desire and their experience. When women read the verse, we clearly saw '… if you fear you cannot deal justly with women, then marry only one'. These were the words of Allah that spoke to our fears of injustice. We understood that the supposed right to polygamy was conditional, and that if a man could not fulfil those conditions of equal and just treatment, then Allah said 'marry only one'. In fact the verse goes on to say that '… this will be best for you to prevent you from doing injustice'. What further validation do we need to argue that polygamy is not an unconditional right in Islam, but is actually a responsibility allowed only in very exceptional circumstances?

It was empowering for us to read the Qur'an through a feminist lens and to discover that our yearning to be treated as human beings of equal worth and dignity were rooted in our tradition, in our faith. We felt validated in our struggle. We were more convinced than ever that it is not Islam that oppresses women, but interpretations of the Qur'an influenced by cultural practices and values of a patriarchal society, which regard women as inferior and subordinate to men. For much of Islamic history, it is men who have interpreted the Qur'an and the traditions for us. The woman's voice, the woman's experience, the woman's realities have been largely silent and silenced in the reading and interpretation of the text. This human silence was mistaken as the silence of the text, that is, as if God did not speak to women's suffering and questioning.

During this initial process of studying and rediscovering our religious texts, we were lucky to have with us a theologian who had completed her Ph.D. thesis on the Qur'an and women.[2] Dr Amina Wadud, an African-American *mufassira* who was then teaching the Qur'an in the Department of Revealed Knowledge and Comparative Religion at the International Islamic University in Kuala Lumpur, guided us in our reading and understanding of the Qur'an and its message. We engaged in Qur'anic hermeneutics, a model which looks at the socio-historical context of revelation as a whole and of relevant Qur'anic verses, and we looked at syntactical structures and grammatical compositions within the text (how it says what it says), and at the whole text to understand its worldview. From this hermeneutical approach, we derived the values and principles that underlie the Qur'anic message. It is these values and principles that are universal and eternal and that serve as our guide, rather than the cultural and historical specificities of the seventh-century Arabian context. This experience also gave Dr Wadud an opportunity to develop an interface between her theology and methodology and our experience of the socio-legal context and realities of lived Islam: the problems faced, the contradictions, the challenges of being Muslim women in a modernising society where Islam is increasingly shaping and defining our lives.

This was really the beginning of our struggle to stand up for women's rights within the Islamic framework. Through our readings, through consultations and studies with Islamic scholars, theologians and jurists, inside and outside the country, we developed a framework and a methodology through which we could stand up and argue for justice and equality for Muslim women in contentious areas such as polygamy, equal rights, dress and modesty, obediehce, domestic violence, *ḥudūd* laws, freedom of expression, freedom of religion and other fundamental liberties.

The work in the Malaysian context was all the more urgent in the late 1980s because women's groups in the country had formed a coalition to campaign for a domestic violence law, to make domestic violence a crime. The Joint Action Group against Violence against Women (JAG), which was formed in 1985, had come up against opposition from representatives of the federal government's Islamic Affairs Department, who asserted that such a law could not apply to Muslims because a Muslim man, it was claimed, had a divine right to beat his wife. Therefore, no man-made law could take that right away by making domestic violence a crime.

The verse cited to justify wife-beating was the Qur'anic verse on *nushūz* (4:34), commonly interpreted as disobedience, which reads: '… As for those from whom you fear *nushūz*, admonish them, then banish them to beds apart and 'strike' them [*aḍribuhunna*, from the verb *ḍaraba*] …' As Muslims brought up to believe in a just God and a just Islam, it was hard for us to believe that God could sanction any injustice, any oppression, any violence against women. Turning back to the original text of the religion and arguing for a nuanced and contextual understanding of the verse became an imperative. When we did our research, it was heart-warming to find that the dominant interpretation of 4:34 that justified domestic violence was inconsistent with the overall Qur'anic ethos of justice and equality, compassion and mercy; that there were other, equally valid, interpretations of 4:34 that were not premised on allowing domestic violence; that the word *ḍaraba* was open to many different meanings; and that there was no hadith that reported any act of violence by the Prophet Muhammad against his wives.

2. Knowledge becomes action

Empowered and elated by the liberating message of the Qur'an, we felt compelled to share our findings with the larger public, in order to break the dominant belief that Islam discriminated against women. We felt it was important that the Malaysian public, and Muslims in particular, become aware of the diversity of interpretations and juristic opinions that exist within the Islamic heritage. And we felt that if we, as Muslims, wanted Islam to be a source of law and public policy, there must be a public debate and discussion on these issues. But how best to do this when there were just eight of us, with no traditional authority and no access to the traditional platforms for religious teaching? The opportunity presented itself in 1990, when the Selangor Syariah Appeal Court in the case of *Aishah Abdul Rauf* v *Wan Mohd Yusof Wan Othman* decided that the husband did not have the right to take a second wife as he had not fulfilled all the four conditions under the Islamic Family Law to ensure that justice would be done.[3]

SIS decided to use this judgment to write to all the newspapers as a strategy to get our alternative voice heard in the public space. The judgment had led to much debate on whether the state had the right to impose man-made restrictions on what was supposedly a God-given right for men to practise polygamy. Many men were critical of the court judgment, but we wanted to welcome this judgment publicly and to explain our position on polygamy.

We felt the best way for us to create a public voice was through the daily newspapers, which reached a wide audience. We also made a calculated decision not to issue a press statement, but to use the 'letters to the editor' page, which provided space for longer statements. It was thus in August 1990 that the group officially and publicly became Sisters in Islam, when the eight of us decided to write a letter to the editor welcoming the Syariah Appeal Court judgment and providing an alternative understanding that polygamy is not a man's right in Islam, but a responsibility.

It was a measure of the news-worthiness of the SIS voice that the letter was published in all four Malaysian mainstream daily newspapers in both English and Bahasa Malaysia.[4] It generated a buzz: people were asking each other if they had read it and we proudly admitted to its authorship. The letter, of course, also generated its share of criticism from those who felt that questioning the practice of polygamy was going against God's teachings.

3. No turning back

But there was no turning back for Sisters in Islam. We continued with our intensive weekly readings and research on the Qur'anic text, *tafsīr* literature, Islamic law, Islam and women's rights. We took classes with other scholars, including another visiting professor at the International Islamic University, the late Dr Fathi Osman,[5] the Egyptian legal and Qur'anic scholar, who was based in Los Angeles.

The focus of the research was to address two issues of urgent concern: equality between men and women and domestic violence. Convinced of the message of equality and justice in Islam, we decided to share our findings in two short question-and-answer booklets: *Are Women and Men Equal before Allah?* and *Are Muslim Men Allowed to Beat their Wives?* Given the complexities of understanding a religious text, and our mission to promote an understanding of Islam that recognises the principles of justice and equality, we felt it was important that we communicate with the general public in language that was easy to understand. The first booklet was intended to be a basic understanding of the message of equality in the Qur'an and how human effort at understanding God's intent in a patriarchal world has led to inequality. The second booklet was part of the SIS effort to build a Muslim public constituency to support the national campaign by the women's movement to make domestic violence a crime.

By 1991, these two seminal question-and-answer booklets on women's rights in Islam were ready to be launched publicly. There was some trepidation about revealing our identities to the public, as we were already being criticised in Islamist publications, especially after our second letter to the editor in 1991 on 'Islam and women's rights', which criticised the misogynistic views of Haji Nik Aziz Nik Mat, the spiritual leader of the Islamist party PAS, who asserted that Islam granted men greater ability to lead than women, and that women were best suited to stay at home to look after their husbands and children.[6]

We knew by then that a struggle for equality and justice for Muslim women, which involved challenging religious orthodoxy and its message of misogyny, was going to be an uphill battle. We were ready to accept the natural consequence of this struggle – that we would be attacked and condemned as going against Islam, God's teachings and Islamic law. But it was our knowledge and our conviction in a just God and a just Islam, and our outrage that our religion was being misused and abused to maintain patriarchy, that gave us the confidence to come out publicly and be identified individually.

We were lucky to have the support of the then minister in charge of women's affairs, Datuk Napsiah Omar, who agreed to launch the booklets. The response was tremendous. Over 200 women and men from civil society, academia, government and business attended the launch and the one-day public forum on the rights of women in Islam. Many women told us how heartened they were to hear publicly, for the first time, of an Islam that spoke to their own sense of fairness and justice. The launch received wide media coverage and SIS work took off as the demands for our input on many emerging contentious issues intensified.

This was the 1990s, when the radicalisation of the Islamist movement in Malaysia, and the Islamist party, PAS, in particular, was at its height. In the 1980s, the party's leadership had been taken over by radicals who demanded that Malaysia be turned into an Islamic state, with the Qur'an and the traditions of the Prophet Muhammad as the Constitution of the country. The success of the Iranian Revolution had provided an impetus to Islamist movements all over the world. By the mid-1980s, PAS was expounding the concept of an Islamic state led by the *'ulamā'*; it declared the Malaysian Constitution an infidel document and the ruling party an infidel party for being in alliance with non-Muslims. The National Front Malaysian government responded by adopting its own Islamisation policy, using Islam as a source of legitimacy to face the challenge of an Islamist party that was undermining its rule by declaring it a secular government that acted against Islam.

Thus, the 1990s saw an escalating holier-than-thou battle between the ruling party and the Islamist party to disprove each other's religious credentials. As could be expected, the status, role and rights of women became the casualty in this battle for Islamic legitimacy. A slew of laws or amendments to existing laws were introduced that discriminated against women or chiselled away at the rights Muslim women enjoyed in Malaysia. Several amendments were made to the Islamic Family Law that made it easier for men to divorce their wives and to commit polygamy,[7] and the Syariah Criminal Offences Act was also amended, turning more sins into crimes against the state and making it an offence to disobey or dispute a fatwa once it was gazetted as law.[8]

SIS concern with this punitive and misogynistic Islamisation process and the challenge it poses to change and modernity within a democratic system led it to organise, in 1992, its first national conference on 'Islam and the Modern Nation State'. This conference, which brought together international scholars of Islam and Malaysians of all faiths, further enhanced SIS reputation as a women's group that combined activism with scholarship and that was inclusive in its approach, looking at the Islamisation process and the rise of political Islam as a national issue of critical importance to nation-building and democratisation.[9]

Thus, from its first phase of knowledge-building work, SIS expanded into advocacy to influence public policy, as more laws or amendments to existing laws, which discriminated against Muslim women, were being introduced. SIS submitted its first memorandum, in 1993, to the then prime minister, Datuk Seri Dr Mahathir Mohamed, on the Kelantan Syariah Criminal Code (the so-called *Ḥudūd* law), arguing from religious, legal, human rights and socio-historical perspectives against such draconian punishments and discrimination against women, and also providing empirical evidence of injustice and gender discrimination in Muslim countries where the *Ḥudūd* law was in place.[10] In 1994, SIS submitted its second memorandum to the government on the Domestic Violence Act, arguing on religious and legal grounds that Muslims should be included within the jurisdiction of the proposed law.[11]

By the end of the 1990s, SIS activism had expanded into the larger issue of upholding democratic principles and fundamental liberties as guaranteed by the Federal Constitution, human rights principles, and international treaties and conventions signed by the Malaysian government. It was thus that SIS began to take public positions on freedom of religion and freedom of expression in the face of efforts to criminalise Muslims who attempt to leave Islam, and to silence differences of opinion regarding Islam.[12]

Underlying this was the firm belief that an activist group such as SIS could not isolate itself from the larger human rights and democracy movement in the country. A movement for gender justice must necessarily be a part of the larger human rights movement and vice versa. Thus, protecting and expanding the democratic space that enables civil society to thrive, and protecting the values of fundamental liberties upheld in the Constitution are important, as they provide the overarching framework that enables a group like SIS to exist.

For the first 11 years of its existence, the SIS members worked on all its projects without pay, without an office and without support staff. It was love, passion, and emotional and financial support from family and friends that sustained the eight SIS members, their activities and their publications. As political Islam continued to impact the lives of Muslims and people of other faiths throughout the world, the demand for SIS work and its strategy of working within an Islamic framework grew at the national and international level. In 1998, SIS finally set up an office with paid staff.

From a focus on research and advocacy, SIS began to expand its work into the area of public education. In 2000, it began work on a training module on women's rights in Islam and it revived its study sessions. The impetus came from the expansion of SIS membership to include younger women, many of whom were fresh graduates who had just started a career. At the same time, more and more people, Muslims and those of other faiths, men and women, had become interested in the SIS voice for change. Many were concerned at the impact of political Islam on women's lives, the rights of non-Muslims and the democratisation process in Malaysia. SIS then set up a two-day training programme on women's rights in Islam, to reach a wider audience and build a public constituency that would support the Islam of justice and equality for which SIS stands. The revived SIS study sessions, open only to Muslim women in the first year, soon after opened its doors to everyone, Muslim men and women and people of other faiths.

Another expansion took place in 2003 when SIS established a service arm with the launch of its legal clinic, which offers legal counselling via email, fax, letters, telephone calls and face-to-face meetings. The clinic has since served over 6,000 clients.

From its letters to the editor on gender justice in Islam in 1990 to issues of freedom of religion and freedom of expression, from its first memorandum to the government in 1993 on the injustice of the *Ḥudūd* law to its call for the repeal of the Syariah Criminal Offences Act,[13] from its first national conference in 1992 on 'Islam and the Modern Nation State' to its international round table on 'Trends in Islamic Family Law Reform in the Muslim World' in 2006, SIS had gained recognition, by the mid-2000s, as a Muslim feminist group at the forefront of a growing international movement that seeks to develop an understanding of Islam that stands for justice and equality in this modern world. As women have been the group first and most affected by the rise of political Islam in our own communities, it is no surprise that in many Muslim countries it is women's groups that are at the forefront in challenging Islamists and the misogynist and punitive Islam they propagate, because it is our lives and our well-being that are most at stake. Women's groups, working with progressive Islamic scholars, are organising and networking at the national and international levels to build support and to share knowledge and strategies to develop a more egalitarian and just vision of Islam.

4. From local to global

But this was not how it was some 20 years ago, when Sisters in Islam first began to attend meetings of women's groups from South Asia and the Arab world. When I spoke publicly on finding equality and justice in Islam in the 1990s, a common response was 'why bother?' Many Muslim feminists said it was a waste of time because religion is inherently patriarchal: for every alternative interpretation SIS could offer to justify equality, the *'ulamā'* could counter with a hundred others. And to work with religion where patriarchal interpretations prevailed and *ijtihād* was forbidden was a waste of time. It was a losing battle. Moreover, the secular feminists felt it was dangerous to engage in matters of religion, as it would give legitimacy to the position of religion in the public arena. A feminist working within the religious framework, they argued, would never be recognised as having any authority to speak on Islam. For many Muslim feminists, then, justice and equality could only be fought for through a human rights framework.

But this decision of so many feminists and human rights activists to ignore religion has had detrimental consequences. It has left the field wide open for the most conservative and intolerant forces within Islam to define, dominate and set the parameters of what Islam is and what it is not. They decide what a good Muslim is, they dictate how to be a good Muslim woman, wife and daughter, and then prescribe laws and policies that keep women shackled as second-class Muslims, indeed, second-class citizens. When we protest, they silence us by saying we have no authority to speak about Islam.

But 20 years later, modernisation and development in Muslim countries have not led to less religion in the public sphere, but more. The rise of political Islam in all Muslim countries, and even in minority Muslim communities in the West, eventually led many Muslim feminists to review their approach to religion. Religion has not gone away. In fact, it is increasingly reshaping and redefining the lives of Muslims in the modern world, both in Muslim majority countries and among Muslim minorities living in the West. Many activists have come to realise there is a need to understand Islam better, and to better equip themselves to engage in the public discourse in order to reshape the meaning and place of religion within their societies. To remain silent is to cede the discourse on Islam to those who believe that men and women are not equal in Islam, that Muslims must live in an Islamic state and be governed by Islamic law, that there can only be one truth and one interpretation of Islam, which must be codified into law, and that any digression from it must be punished.

This ideological strategy of the Islamists has impacted politics, governance, law-making, women's rights and human rights in a powerful and adverse manner. In most Muslim societies and communities, gripped by Islamic revivalism and political Islam, women – their rights, status, role in private and public life, dress and behaviour – have become the first battleground of the return to Islam. In many Muslim countries, laws and policies are being introduced or amended in the name of Islam, which, more often than not, discriminate against women and infringe fundamental liberties and human rights principles. In some countries, where a culture of public debate on Islam does not exist, those who speak out against Muslim extremists and who demand the reform of discriminatory and unjust laws, face threats to their lives and even death.

By the 2000s, more and more Muslim feminists and human rights activists began to realise the need to understand Islam better. There was a growing interest in the SIS work and much demand for SIS members to give talks at international meetings. A stream of scholars, researchers and journalists visited the SIS office to try and understand our work better and share it with the world. In 2003, SIS organised its first international meeting, to document and analyse the impact of Islamic extremism on women's rights. The meeting, in Bellagio, Italy, brought together activists from Southeast Asia, the Middle East, Iran and Turkey to discuss the legal and social impact of political Islam and the strategies adopted by women's groups to deal with this challenge against women's right to equality and justice.[14] It was shocking for SIS to discover that in some Muslim countries women's groups had not organised a single meeting to discuss the impact of political Islam on women's rights, because of a determination to ignore the place of religion in public life.

The meeting in Bellagio provided an open and safe platform for women's rights activists from across the Muslim world to frankly discuss and acknowledge how the legal and social rights, status and roles of Muslim women have been impacted adversely by the rise of political Islam. We explored the idea of creating an international platform for Muslim women to assert an empowered cultural identity and demand equality and justice. We felt it important to bring everyone together and create a visible international presence, and we also recognised the need to equip more women activists with the emerging progressive scholarship, which recognises equality and justice in Islam. The participants felt that a deeper rights-based understanding of Islam, in the areas of Qur'anic interpretation, jurisprudence and hadith, would enable them to challenge more effectively the Islamist strategy of using Islam to justify discrimination against women and delegitimise women's demands for change.

5. Musawah takes shape

Three years later, in 2006, the idea of Musawah, a global movement for equality and justice in the Muslim family, began to take shape. In March that year, SIS organised an international consultation in Kuala Lumpur on 'Trends in Family Law Reform in Muslim Countries'. It was here that the SIS idea for a global initiative was first proposed, and was endorsed by activists and scholars from different countries and contexts.

The meeting brought together Muslim activists and scholars from Turkey and Morocco (two Muslim-majority countries with recent successful family law reform campaigns), Iran, Pakistan, the United Kingdom, the United States and Southeast Asia, to share knowledge and strategies on family law reform. We felt the time had come for us to build an international network of women's groups in the Muslim world that have, for decades, been working on family law, in order to share scholarship, challenges, strategies and best practices.

We felt it was important for us to bring to international attention the fact that there was already a 'paradigm shift' in Muslim theological and jurisprudential scholarship, that there was a possibility of reconciling the teachings of Islam with human rights, with women's rights. This sharing, we hoped, would help build an international discourse and public voice asserting that equality is possible within Islam, build the momentum to propel forward our efforts to protect existing rights in Muslim family laws and practices, and promote our demands for the reform of discriminatory provisions at national, regional and international levels.

The trigger was the success of the Moroccan women's movement in 2004 in pushing for a new Muslim family law that regarded marriage as a partnership of equals. If they could do it, why couldn't we? we asked ourselves. The *Guide to Equality in the Family*,[15] produced by the Collectif 95 Maghrebi network of women's groups in Morocco, Tunisia and Algeria, also provided a model of a holistic four-pronged approach to family law reform: how to justify equality and non-discrimination grounded in Islamic, constitutional and human rights principles, and the lived realities of women and men today.

In August 2006, SIS organised its first two-week short course in 'Understanding Islam from a Rights Perspective'. Some 14 Muslim women leaders, from 11 countries, participated. The course, which was designed for activists who were already grounded in gender and human rights principles, but wanted to understand the possibility of working for justice and equality within the Islamic framework, was a huge success, and a life-changing experience for many of the participants.[16] Once again, SIS presented the idea of a global meeting that would bring women's groups in Muslim countries together to push for family law reform. Everyone felt the time had come for such collective action.

SIS initially felt that this initiative should be organised by an international network for it to be a successful global meeting. But this did not work out, so SIS decided to take responsibility for initiating the movement. As there was universal support for such an initiative from everyone SIS consulted, the SIS team set things in motion.

Because SIS is not an international organisation, we felt it was important to form an international planning committee that would be representative of the diverse stakeholders for such an initiative. Given SIS international networking and reputation, we were able to invite some leading scholars and activists with whom SIS had worked over many years, from diverse regions of the Muslim world and minority contexts. From the start, we felt it important for the success of the movement that we follow the SIS tradition of combining scholarship and activism, and that the planning committee be as inclusive as possible. Some jumped at the opportunity to be a part of what they saw as an exciting, groundbreaking initiative; others demurred, not so sure, not so comfortable about working and engaging with religion in this very public way.

We were pleased to be able to bring together a credible planning committee comprising members from Egypt, the Gambia, Indonesia, Iran, Malaysia, Morocco, Nigeria, Pakistan, Qatar, Turkey and the United Kingdom. We had our first meeting in Istanbul, Turkey, in March 2007. The initial idea was to organise an international conference on Muslim family law reform with about 100 participants. But, by the second day of the meeting, the members realised that what we were actually talking about was movement-building for equality and justice for Muslim women, not a one-off international conference.

We looked at the Violence against Women movement as a model: how, some 25 years after it began, more than 60 countries in the world have laws that make domestic violence a crime. How, as an international movement, it developed an analysis of all forms of violence – physical and emotional – against women, and gave support to national groups to provide shelter services and share strategies in law reform and awareness-raising.

Similarly, the planning committee wanted Musawah to be able to provide theoretical concepts, resources, tools and an action plan to those advocating women's rights in the Muslim family. The approach needed to be a nuanced one, tenable for women living in both Muslim-majority and Muslim-minority countries, women pushing for family law reform, and women resisting the backlash against the advances they have already made. We also wanted the movement to be an inclusive one, where both women who worked with religion and women who worked exclusively within the human rights framework would be able to come together to work towards a common cause.

We were clear from the start that we would not prescribe a model Muslim family law. That would be left to the groups at the national level to decide, given their particular contexts. There would be those who were ready to push for a comprehensive law based on marriage as a partnership of equals, others who could only work at piecemeal law reform, dealing with the most discriminatory aspects of their family law, and yet others who were only beginning to campaign for a codified family law. What we wanted to provide were concepts, tools and arguments that would make equality and justice possible within the Muslim family.

The committee members spent almost two years building a foundation for the initiative. We wanted the process to be as inclusive as possible, and we wanted our scholarship and theoretical framework to be watertight. The planning committee envisioned a movement that would build knowledge and offer a holistic approach to law reform, with arguments grounded in Islamic teachings, human rights principles, constitutional guarantees of equality and non-discrimination, and the lived realities of women and men today. Those who had past experience in working on family laws and practices could share their successes, failures and strategies, and anyone with a common mission to uphold justice and equality for Muslim women could adopt and adapt this knowledge to support their work on the ground at the local and national levels.

As a movement, the committee felt it was important to have a framework for action to guide its work, and that this should be drafted in consultation with a wider group of stakeholders. Towards this end, we held a meeting of Qur'anic and *fiqh* scholars and activists in December 2007 in Cairo, Egypt, to develop the theoretical concepts, principles and justifications concerning why equality in the family is necessary and why it is possible. The scholars presented commissioned papers on why equality is possible through a rereading of the Qur'an and rethinking of *fiqh* principles to deal with contemporary challenges, and, together with the activists, developed the principles and ideas for the *Musawah Framework for Action*.[17]

Throughout the following year, 2008, this document was shared with national and international women's organisations, scholars and activists, generating feedback and intensive discussion by email, in order to ensure the accuracy and relevance of our vision, and our conceptual tools and arguments for change.

6. Challenges and tensions

There were challenges throughout, of course, as Musawah wanted to include both feminists who work with Islam and those who work only with international principles of human rights. Some secular feminists were initially apprehensive about the idea of supporting a global movement that engaged with religion. They feared their members and networkers would think they were straying from their secular principles and human rights framework.

The planning committee was very sensitive to the many leading feminists and women's organisations in Muslim countries that do not see religion and human rights as compatible. We wanted a framework and a movement that would be inclusive and be able to bridge the divide between religion and feminism, between Islam and human rights. We did not want Musawah to be seen as supplanting other women's groups, but to build on what already exists. What Musawah hopes to bring to the larger women's and human rights movement is this:

- An assertion that Islam can be a source of empowerment, not a source of oppression and discrimination.
- An effort to open new horizons for rethinking the relationship between human rights, equality and justice, and Islam.
- An offer to open a new constructive dialogue where religion is no longer an obstacle to equality for women, but a source for liberation.
- A collective strength of conviction and courage to stop governments, patriarchal authorities and ideological non-state actors from the convenience of using religion and the word of God to silence women's demands for equality.
- A space where activists, scholars and decision-makers, working within the human rights or the Islamic framework, or both, can interact and mutually strengthen our common pursuit of equality and justice for Muslim women.

There were moments of tension even within the Musawah planning committee, as it included both members who worked with religion and those who exclusively worked within the human rights framework. In the end, our belief in our ability to reconcile the teachings of Islam with human rights within the holistic approach of the

Musawah framework, and the realisation that we were offering new and compelling ideas to advance the rights and status of Muslim women within the larger global women's movement, kept us together.

Musawah was launched at the Global Meeting in Kuala Lumpur, Malaysia, in February 2009. About 250 activists and scholars from all over the Muslim world and from minority contexts participated in this groundbreaking event. We launched three key Musawah publications: the *Framework for Action*, which was translated into five languages; a book called *Wanted: Equality and Justice in the Muslim Family*, which includes writings by scholars and activists on the possibility and necessity of equality and justice in the Muslim family;[18] and *Home Truths: A Global Report on Equality in the Muslim Family*, which contains summaries of reports from 30 countries on the status of their family laws and practices, the challenges faced and the possibilities for reform.[19] The five-day Global Meeting provided an exciting and stimulating intellectual journey of possibilities for equality and justice, with intense discussion and debate on a wide range of issues, from the Qur'an and *fiqh* to gender and human rights, from text to context, from theory and concepts to practice and strategies.

One year after its launch, the Musawah planning committee was transformed into an International Advisory Group. Three key areas of work were defined: knowledge-building, movement-building and international advocacy. *Musawah Vision*, a quarterly newsletter devoted to issues surrounding family law reform and developments in the Muslim world, is distributed to Musawah Advocates and allies.[20] Musawah Affinity Groups have been established in at least twelve countries.[21] Inquiries are coming in from other countries expressing interest in formal links with Musawah. Thematic Affinity Groups for Minorities North and the Young Women's Caucus have also been formed. The Musawah website continues to attract visitors with its wealth of information and scholarship on the necessity and possibility of reform to ensure equality and justice in the Muslim family (http://www.musawah.org).

What Musawah brings to international attention is a rich and diverse Muslim heritage of interpretations, juristic opinions, concepts and principles that make it possible to read equality and justice in Islam, and ground these arguments for reform in human rights principles, constitutional guarantees of equality and fundamental liberties, and the lived realities of women and men today. It brings to international attention the fact that there is already a deep shift in perspective in Muslim theological and jurisprudential scholarship, and that reform is not alien to the Muslim tradition. It is producing new feminist knowledge to overcome the tension between Islam and human rights and the disconnect between law and reality. The Musawah scholarship and activism represent a vital contribution to the women's and larger human rights movement at a time when democracy, human rights and women's rights constitute the modern ethical paradigm of today's world.

At the time of writing, it has been over two years since the launch of Musawah as a global movement in 2009, and over four years since we began preparations for it. What has been most heartening is the response it is getting at the national and international levels. Many Muslim women, caught in a world where human rights and Islam are seen in opposite polarity, have found in the holistic Musawah Framework for Action an approach that enables them to comfortably make the public claim to be Muslim and feminist at the same time. For others, the holistic framework represents a major step forward, as it enables activists and policy-makers to justify the possibility and necessity for law reform towards justice and equality in language and arguments that can generate broader appeal in countries, and in Muslim minority contexts, where Islam is a source of law and public policy governing the Muslim population.

The joint Musawah and SIS training on 'Understanding Islam from a Rights Perspective', led by progressive Islamic scholars of the Qur'an, *fiqh* and hadith, is much in demand. Participants found the training transformative, as they are exposed to concepts and tools that open the possibilities for reform in their understanding of Islam. It gives participants the knowledge and courage to speak publicly on Islam and women's rights. Since the 2009 Global Meeting, the two-week course has been held for Musawah Advocates, and a shorter version was organised in Cairo for activists from a network working on family law reform. Plans are now under way for regional training for those in the Horn of Africa and South Asia.

In international advocacy, Musawah made inroads in Geneva in 2010, when senior officials of the Office of the High Commissioner for Human Rights, and members of the CEDAW Committee, welcomed its offer of scholarship and seminars on women's rights in Islam. The Musawah report on *CEDAW and Muslim Family Laws: In Search of Common Ground*, which critically examines state parties' use of Islam and Shariʿa to justify reservations and resist demands for law reform, and offers the Musawah framework as a possible way of moving forward, is used as a resource by CEDAW Committee members, and in training on CEDAW shadow reporting by regional and international groups.[22] The report is also used by activists in the area of reproductive health and rights, and children's rights.

In its key knowledge-building area of work, Musawah is engaged in a major research project to produce new understandings concerning the twin concepts of *qiwāma* and *wilāya* (commonly understood as men's authority over women and children), which underpin much of the discrimination against women in the legal framework that has governed Muslim family laws to the present day. The team has commissioned research papers on Muslim legal traditions, and will be conducting participatory research on life stories, in order to document how *qiwāma* and *wilāya* impact the lived realities of women and men. A main output will be a Musawah viewpoint document on *qiwāma* and *wilāya*, which will synthesise the results of the research and forge a new contextual understanding of these concepts relevant to women's realities, and demands for equality and justice in the twenty-first century.

In its outreach work, Musawah seeks to build a critical mass of supporters that work with and advocate for the Musawah framework. The Secretariat reaches out to build the movement in countries where Advocates have expressed a critical need for the Musawah Framework to aid their advocacy for family law reform and women's rights in Islam. A Musawah toolkit has been developed to enable Advocates to critically engage with the key ideas in the Musawah framework and promote the Musawah key messages. Advocates keep the Secretariat informed of developments at the national level, and the Secretariat responds to requests for progressive scholarship in family law, and links Advocates doing similar work with each other.

Musawah, as a movement, is growing steadily, with its holistic framework offering hope especially to those involved in family law reform, who feel the necessity of reconciling the teachings of Islam with human rights and women's rights in order to advance their advocacy and build public support for their campaign. What makes Musawah empowering for many Muslim women is its bold endeavour to reclaim the spirit of equality and justice within Islam, which it sees as compatible with international human rights standards. In highlighting women's realities, amplifying women's voices (both historical and contemporary), and striving to legitimise these perspectives, Musawah is filling a void that exists in the discourses on human rights and on Islam in much of the Muslim world and in intergovernmental international organisations, such as the UN system. Instead of just condemning the injustices arising from patriarchal customs and laws that take their legitimacy from particular readings of Islam's sacred texts, Musawah offers a constructive way forward through a holistic framework based on new understandings of Muslim jurisprudence, laws and practices in ways that are responsive to women's needs and in concord with Islamic teachings and human rights principles.

Notes

1 These were mostly front desk officers and counsellors women dealt with in the Syariah Courts and Religious Affairs Department.

2 Since published as Wadud, Amina, *Qur'an and Women: Rereading the Sacred Text from a Woman's Perspective* (Oxford: Oxford University Press, 1999).

3 These four conditions are: that the proposed marriage is 'just and necessary'; ability to financially support all wives and dependents; ability to treat all wives equally; and that the proposed marriage will not cause harm to the existing wife or wives.

4 'Islam and polygamy', SIS letter to the editor, *The Star*, 18 August 1990, available at http://www.sistersinislam.org.my/comment.php?comment.news.816 (accessed 26 September 2012).

5 Sisters in Islam took private weekly classes on the Qur'an and *fiqh* with Dr Fathi Osman in the summers of 1993 and 1994. Dr Fathi passionately believed that the Qur'an, in taking humankind beyond the age of ignorance, oriented human thinking towards change. He was concerned that in a world of dramatic change, Muslim thinking had stagnated. He feared that if the text did not engage with reality, it would become a dead text. *Ijtihād* then becomes nothing more than an exercise in 'linguistics gymnastics' by an exclusive group of people who very often not only isolate the text out of the socio-historical context in which it was revealed, but isolate the text from the context of the contemporary society we live in today.

6 'Islam and women's rights', SIS letter to the editor, *New Straits Times*, 12 January 1991, available at http://www.sistersinislam.org.my/comment.php?comment.news.287 (accessed 26 September 2012).

7 Islamic Family Law (Federal Territories) Act 1984 [Act 303], amended in 1994 by the Islamic Family Law (Federal Territories) (Amendment) Act 1994 [Act A902] and in 2006 by the Islamic Family Law (Federal Territories) (Amendment) Act 2006 [Act A1261], which was enacted by parliament in December 2005, with royal assent granted by the Yang di-Pertuan Agong (king) in January 2006.

8 Syariah Criminal Offences (Federal Territories) Act 1997 [Act 559].

9 See the collection of conference papers in Othman, Norani (ed.), *Shariʿa Law and the Modern Nation State* (Kuala Lumpur: Sisters in Islam, 1994).

10 See Ismail, Rose (ed.), *Hudud in Malaysia: The Issues at Stake* (Kuala Lumpur: Sisters in Islam, 1995).

11 See 'Domestic violence is a crime', SIS letter to the editor, *New Straits Times*, 16 March 1996, available at http://www.sistersinislam.org.my/comment.php?comment.news.313 (accessed 26 September 2012).

12 See 'Islam, apostasy and PAS', SIS letter to editor, *New Straits Times*, 24 July 1999, available at http://www.sistersinislam.org.my/comment.php?comment.news.302 (accessed 26 September 2012).

13 Syariah Criminal Offences (Federal Territories) Act 1997 [Act 559].

14 See the collection of conference papers in Othman, Norani (ed.), *Muslim Women and the Challenge of Islamic Extremism* (Kuala Lumpur: Sisters in Islam, 2005).

15 English translation: Collectif 95 Maghreb-Egalité, *Guide to Equality in the Family in the Maghreb*, trans. Chari Voss, WLP Translation Series (Washington, DC: Womens Learning Partnership, 2005), available at http://learningpartnership.org/guide-to-equality (accessed 13 September 2012).

16 The short course was held in Bellagio, Italy. It consisted of critical coursework on the Qur'an, hadith and *fiqh*, with a focus on the possibilities for change and for justice and equality. The resource persons were Muhammad Khalid Masud, Ziba Mir-Hosseini, Amina Wadud and Abdullah Saeed. Participants came from

Egypt, Yemen, Palestine, Sudan, Nigeria, the Gambia, Tanzania, Afghanistan, Bangladesh, the Philippines and Thailand, with facilitators from SIS.

17 The Framework is available at http://www.musawah.org/framework_action.asp (accessed 26 September 2012).

18 Anwar, Zainah (ed.), *Wanted: Equality and Justice in the Muslim Family* (Petaling Jaya: Sisters in Islam, 2009), available online at http://www.musawah.org/background_papers.asp.

19 Rumminger, Jana, Rozana Isa and Hadil El-Khouly (eds), *Home Truths: A Global Report on Equality in the Muslim Family* (Petaling Jaya: Sisters in Islam, 2009), available at http://www.musawah.org/home-truths-global-report-equality-muslim-family (accessed 26 September 2012).

20 'Advocates' share Musawah's goal of equality in the family, and have a stake in and commitment to the growth of the movement. All Advocates agree with the Musawah Framework, use the Framework in their activities, and contribute to the achievement of Musawah's strategic goals and objectives. 'Allies' are individuals and organisations who broadly support Musawah's work, vision and principles, though they are not working specifically on issues related to Muslim family laws and practices.

21 'Affinity Groups' are self-formed groups of individual Advocates or organisations who share a national, regional, thematic or contextual focus.

22 Available at http://musawah.org/sites/default/files/CEDAW%20%26%20Muslim%20Family%20Laws_0.pdf (accessed 28 September 2012).

Part II
Approaches to Reform

6

GENDER EQUALITY AND THE DOCTRINE OF *WILĀYA*

Muhammad Khalid Masud

1. Introduction

Muslim scholarship has been divided over the status and rights of women in Islam, with issues ranging from polygamy and the right of divorce to gender equality. Even though the majority of religious leaders (*'ulamā'*) have taken a conservative position, a growing number of scholars and jurists regard gender equality as the basic Islamic principle,[1] and reject discrimination on the basis of gender. Unfortunately, this large diversity of Muslim voices is usually ignored, and writers on Islam generally describe the religion as incompatible with modernity and human rights, especially with regard to the principle of gender equality. Essentialising a legal tradition in this manner overlooks the social evolution of that tradition and its doctrines. This chapter studies the diversity of views among Muslim jurists about the doctrine of *wilāya*.[2] This diversity also reflects the changing social perception of gender over time. From case laws of the early colonial period in India, when British judges were mostly prejudiced against gender equality and regarded the rights given to women by Muslim family law as immoral,[3] to family law reforms that began in Muslim societies after independence, the perception of gender equality has changed considerably. The reformist governments in Muslim countries adopted the methodology of Islamic modernism that stood for compatibility between Islam and modernity while the conservatives continue to oppose these reforms. The change in gender perception under the rising influence of Islamism in the late twentieth century has once again impacted the principle of gender equality. In Pakistan, legislation during the Islamisation of laws (1980–90) and a significant judgment (1997) on the requirement of a marriage guardian exemplify this influence.

Ignoring the inner dynamics of Muslim discourses, one tends to simplify the social and intellectual diversity in Muslim societies. The interest and focus on gender equality in current debates on Islamic law in fact points to the disturbing phenomena of forced marriages, honour killings and domestic violence that go unchallenged under traditional laws. To reduce this focus on reforms in Muslim societies to a Western impact, and to interpret Islamic modernist and 'progressive' Muslim discourses for gender equality as apologetic and Westernised, is to overlook this inner dynamism. Debates on gender equality, especially about *wilāya* (marriage guardianship) in the wake of the 1997 judgment in Pakistan, which I discuss below in this chapter, also reveal the ongoing tension about gender equality between reformists and the conservatives, who have renewed their emphasis on Islam's incompatibility with modernity. They describe gender equality as a Western agenda that disrupts Muslim family structure, and defend *wilāya* as a divine law. In this chapter I argue that Muslim jurists have been interpreting gender equality over time in ways informed by their respective social contexts, and that the doctrine of *wilāya* is a social construction. The chapter is divided into three sections. The first offers a brief summary of the classical doctrine of marriage guardianship. The second analyses this doctrine, showing that social contexts informed the doctrine. The third looks at the issue of gender equality in some recent reconstructions of the concept of marriage guardianship.

2. The classical doctrine of *wilāyat al-ijbār*

The classical doctrine of marriage guardianship (*wilāyat al-ijbār*) is highly complex, as the jurists are divided over the meaning and interpretation of the terms *wilāya* (guardianship) and *ijbār* (coercion), as well as over the nature and authority of the marriage guardian. The following is a very brief summary of the doctrine.

a. Wilāya

Guardianship (*wilāya/walāya*) means the legal authority to manage the affairs of another person who lacks the required capacity. The presence of a marriage guardian (*walī al-nikāḥ*) is a formal requirement for the valid contract of a marriage.

Mustafa Ahmad al-Zarqa' distinguishes 'guardianship' (*wilāya*) from 'legal representation' (*niyāba*), despite the fact that, in principle, a 'guardian' is like a 'legal representative' who is acting on behalf of someone else. However, agency (*wakāla*) is created by individuals and is voluntary (*ikhtiyārī*). Guardianship, on the other hand, is a legal requirement.[4] Subhi Mahmasani explains that guardianship is legally required in cases where the ward lacks legal capacity. The law authorises a near relative to act as a guardian in the minor's interest and on his/her behalf. In ancient legal systems like Roman law and customary practices like in pre-Islamic Arabia, guardianship was also extended to such legal matters as marriage and divorce, since, in those systems, women lacked legal capacity and guardianship was required to fill that gap.[5]

b. Marriage guardian

Muslim schools of jurisprudence differ as to whether the authority of a marriage guardian is final and absolute, which means that a marriage contract concluded by the guardian cannot be annulled, or that no marriage contract is valid without his consent. On account of this authority, the marriage guardian is also called *al-walī al-mujbir* (guardian with coercive power). The doctrine of *wilāyat al-ijbār* (compulsory guardianship) has been in the process of continuous construction in the history of Islamic jurisprudence. Consequently, coercion (*ijbār*) as a technical legal term is used in three meanings: (1) that guardianship is an absolute right that cannot be waived; (2) that the guardian has absolute power to compel his ward against his/her will into marriage; and (3) that this authority makes the contract complete and final even though one of the parties lacks legal capacity. Adults of sound mind are generally considered as having the legal capacity to contract marriage, but the jurists are divided even on these criteria in the case of the marriage contract. Of course, gender is also contested as a criterion.

Wilāyat al-ijbār or *al-wilāya al-ijbāriyya* is defined as 'enforcing one's will on another person whether he or she agrees or disagrees'.[6] In contrast to *wilāya ikhtiyāriyya*, in which the ward has the option to challenge the contract concluded by the guardian on his/her behalf, the contract under *wilāyat al-ijbār* is final. The authority of *ijbār* in marriage contract means that a guardian is not legally required to seek the consent of the ward for a marriage to be final and valid. It also includes the power to withhold his consent (*'aḍl*). It is difficult to translate the term *ijbār* into European languages. The French scholars usually translate the term as *contrainte matrimoniale*,[7] and the English translation is often 'compulsion' or 'force'.[8]

The power of a pre-Islamic father and head of the family who could pawn his children, and had the right, though rarely exercised, to kill them, illustrates the extent of the meaning of *ijbār*. Therefore, the right to contract marriage also belonged to the father or to the head of the family. The purpose of this right was to protect the honour of the family or of the tribe, and not of the individual spouse. The marriage was considered a tribal obligation rather than an agreement between two individuals.[9] The marriage guardian (*al-walī al-mujbir*), then, has the right of both *ijbār* and *'aḍl*. *Ijbār* means the right to marry the ward to someone without his or her consent, and *'aḍl* means to intervene in the marriage or refuse permission to a marriage concluded by the ward on his/her own. The father is unanimously regarded as the guardian possessing this power. The Hanbali school does not extend this power to anyone else. The Shafiʿi school extends it only to the grandfather in the absence of the father. The Maliki school considers the executor of the father's will also entitled to represent the father in this capacity. In his absence the power of *ijbār* belongs to the ruler (or to the court). The Hanafi school allows *ijbār* only in case of minor and insane wards, and the right of *ʿaḍl* in cases of incompatible marriage.

As mentioned already, the jurists are divided on whether insanity, minority, gender and religion are the only valid legal grounds for the incapacity of the ward, justifying the guardian's power of coercion. Insanity is unanimously considered incapacity and hence a ground for *ijbār*. According to Hanafi and Hanbali jurists, minority is the main ground for coercion. For Shafiʿis the ground is virginity (being unmarried), hence a marriage guardian has coercive authority even in the case of an adult unmarried female. Malikis regard both 'minority' and 'virginity' as grounds for coercion. They explain that maturity (*rushd*), which is their criterion for legal capacity, is not achieved by adulthood or marriage. According to them, a married woman remains under the authority of her father until she is both married *and* has stayed with her husband. They rule that the father can declare his daughter legally capable and terminate the *ijbār* when, after due deliberation, he finds her mature enough to take care of her own interests. Hanafis and Hanbalis consider *ijbār* terminated when the ward is adult. In their diverse opinions, the jurists' basic concern seems to be to protect the vulnerable ward in the marriage contracts.

According to the Maliki school, a guardian has the power to compel the following wards into marriage: a virgin girl (minor or adult), a minor divorcée or widow, and a girl of unsound mind. The Hanafi and Hanbali schools allow a guardian this right in the case of minor wards, both male and female. The Hanafi school also extends it to mentally incapacitated wards. Furthermore, they allow other agnate relatives to be guardians, in the same order of priority as regulated by the order of succession. Forced marriage is, however, revocable by a minor ward on attaining adulthood, according to the Hanafis (*khiyār al-bulūgh*, 'option of puberty'). As I will discuss later, a Pakistani court has challenged this view. The Shafiʿi school allows this power only in case of virgins, regardless of whether they are minor or adult. The Maliki and Shafiʿi schools do not allow a guardian to compel a male ward to marry, because an adult male cannot be married without his consent and a minor male is not in immediate need of marriage. According to the Maliki, Shafiʿi and Hanbali schools, guardians other than *al-walī al-mujbir* cannot marry off a minor orphan girl; they must wait until she is of marriageable age.

A guardian loses his authority to compel his wards to marry when he loses his sanity, is absent or disappears for a long time, exercises his power without legal justification or withdraws his authority. A guardian also loses this power in the absence of grounds of *ijbār*. In cases where the marriage contracted by the guardian is disadvantageous to the ward, or the intended spouse is not of equal status or the dower is not proper, the ward or one of the relatives could apply to a court of law for intervention. Also, if the guardian is abusing his powers or is unnecessarily and unlawfully withholding his consent, the ward can approach the court for investigation. If the guardian cannot satisfy the court, his guardianship can be terminated. The court can appoint another guardian or can proceed on the ward's behalf.

3. Analysis of the legal reasoning

Legal reasoning in Islamic law has been largely analogical, employing the method of *qiyās* based on the theory of the four sources for Islamic law: the Qur'an, Sunna, *ijmā*ʿ and *qiyās*. The first three are considered material sources, while the fourth, *qiyās*, is a formal method of justifying a conclusion on the basis of a precedent in the Text (the Qur'an and Sunna) and the Islamic history of jurisprudence (the consensus of jurists or their doctrines). Legal reasoning, be it a doctrine, an expert opinion (fatwa) or a judgment (*ḥukm*), is a process of continuing legal reconstruction. As I understand it, 'reconstruction' is part of a three-phase juristic reasoning: interpretation, construction and reconstruction.

Interpretation is a language activity that focuses on a text in order to determine its meaning. Theories of meaning that informed classical methods of interpretation concentrated on word–meaning relations.[10] Recent theories of language have advanced our understanding of meaning. These theories suggest that there are at least three approaches to the quest for meaning. One, which I will call the 'objectivist' approach, stresses an essential semantic relationship between words and their meaning. It focuses entirely on the text and its semantic contents because it believes that meaning is transmitted in the text. This quest for meaning is essentially linguistic. The second approach may be called 'subjectivist', as it stresses that the readers create the meaning. In other words, it is the readers who assign meaning by selecting and prioritising the various semantic contents. This happens quite often in jurisprudence when developing legal concepts and definitions. This apparently subjectivist interpretation is transformed into objectivist meaning within a school or group of jurists by convention and practice. The third approach may be called 'teleological' because it explores the reason behind the usage of the word. It is in some sense related to the subjectivist approach because it prioritises some of the semantic contents over others, but it is not completely subjectivist, because it provides criteria for this priority. In jurisprudence, the teleological approach explores the meaning by asking why the particular law or rule was enacted.

The phase following interpretation, which may be called 'construction', explores the rule in the text on the basis of this interpretation. Construction moves on from the semantic content to the legal content. In other words, it is concerned with applicative meaning in a certain legal framework; it refers to the legal implications that a text has for a particular case.

'Reconstruction' is a phase in which the earlier interpretation and construction are both revisited under changed circumstances. Interpretation now re-explores the semantic content of the legal text and construction selects, and specifies the range of these meanings within a given legal framework. Reconstruction, then, is a phase of legal reasoning in which a jurist revisits the construction, reviewing its framework and redefining it from the perspective of the intent of the Lawgiver or the purpose of law. The latter is known as the *maqāṣid al-sharīʿa* (objectives of law) approach, which will be discussed below. As the perception of the intent of the lawgiver may differ from one jurist to the other, their opinions may also differ. This diversity, known as *ikhtilāf al-fuqahā'*, illustrates the divergence in the process of reconstruction. As a jurist's individual perception of the purpose of law is informed, among other things, by the social construction of law in his society, reconstruction may also vary with social changes. Therefore, the development of *fiqh* is a continuous reconstruction. The *maqāṣid* approach argues on the basis of the objectives of the law as a whole, rather than referring to a specific text. This approach regards the Shariʿa as being for the benefit of human beings. I will now analyse the doctrine of *wilāya* in this framework of legal reasoning, namely interpretation, construction and reconstruction.

a. Interpretation

The term *wilāya* shares a semantic field with *walī* and *walā'*. Let me, therefore, first present an overview of its various meanings.

The Qur'an uses the word *walī*, often as an attribute of God, paired with synonymous terms like *naṣīr* (helper, for instance, 4:45, 4:89, 4:123, 9:116, 29:22, 33:17, 42:31), *shafīʿ* (one who intercedes, for instance, 32:4), *wāq* (shield, for instance, 13:37) and *murshid* (guide, for instance, 18:17). It has also been used with reference to human beings in the following meanings: defender of rights (17:33), a watcher over someone's interests (2:282), ally (5:51, 5:81, 4:144), closely related (9:71) and master (in a negative sense with reference to Satan, 7:30).

The semantic field of the term *wilāya* thus includes the following meanings: control and authority, help, relation, succession and alliance. In the Arabic language, the term *walī* is used with reference to an orphan (*walī al-yatīm*) and a woman (*walī al-mar'a)*; in the former case it means managing the ward's affairs, and in the latter it means 'authority to conclude her marriage and to not allow her to proceed to the marriage contract independently without him'.[11] *Mawlā*, a derivative from the same root, is used as a synonym for *walī*, and also in the meaning of successor, as well as ally and protector. Ibn Manzur (d. 1312), author of the dictionary *Lisān al-ʿArab*, finds six different meanings in the usage: agnate relative, helper, caretaker, client, patron (of a freed slave) and freed slave. A freed slave is like a cousin whose protection is obligatory and whose property is inheritable.[12]

We find further vital evidence about the institution of *walā'* in the hadith literature. The literature reveals that *walā'* was also closely associated with the practice of slavery. *Walā'* and *wilāya* were legal rights belonging to the slave owner. A freed slave was called *mawlā* and remained under the guardianship of the owner. Imam 'Ali's statement that '*walā'* is a form of slavery' affirms this observation.[13] Several stories narrated by 'A'isha also suggest that a slave, even after manumission (freedom), owed his/her *walā'* to the chief of the tribe. At succession, the right of *walā'* was inherited along with property.[14] If a freed slave died and had no one to succeed him, his previous owner inherited all his property if they followed the same faith.

When discussing the marriage guardian, the jurists refer to different verses from the Qur'an (2:221, 2:232, 2:234, 2:237, 4:2–3, 4:6, 4:25, 24:32, 60:10, 65:4); none of these uses the term *walī* or *wilāya*. They cite the following verse most frequently: 'And when you have divorced women and they reach their term, *do not prevent them from marrying their husbands*, if it is agreed between them in kindness' (2:232). Apparently, this verse forbids guardians from preventing their wards marrying the person of their choice, even their previous husbands. The jurists who consider marriage guardianship a requirement also cite the same verse. The latter argue that the prohibition in the verse implies that the guardians do have this right, or they would not be forbidden from exercising it. Another point of difference is the use of masculine and feminine forms in the above verses. The Hanafis cite 2:232, 2:234 and 65:4, which use the feminine form, to rule that women have the right to conclude their own marriage and do not need a marriage guardian.[15] Others use 2:221, 2:232, 2:237, 4:2–3, 4:25, 24:32 and 60:10, which use the masculine form, to deduce the right of male guardians. I need not analyse the jurists' discourse on these verses.

In order to establish the validity of the marriage of a minor and the need for a marriage guardian, the jurists refer to 4:2–3 and 65:4, which require guardians for orphan and minor girls respectively. Once the requirement is established, the jurists proceed to prove *ijbār*, as follows: since a minor has no capacity to contract a marriage, his or her consent is immaterial. As the minor's lack of capacity may give unlimited power to the guardian, the jurists feel the need to propose various restrictions on this power. Firstly, Abu Hanifa allows the option of puberty to a minor girl if a guardian other than her father compelled her into marriage.[16] Secondly, most of the jurists allow *ijbār* of a minor only in extreme cases, arguing that a minor is not in immediate need of marriage and hence can wait until marriageable age.[17] The Hanafis argue that the guardian has a heavy responsibility to find a suitable mate for his ward. He may find a suitable one when his ward is still a minor, he may lose him if he waits or he may fear his own death. In such cases, early marriage is in the interest of the minor.[18] Early marriage does not, however, mean consummation of the marriage. Al-Nawawi (d. 1278) calls such marriage 'perpetual captivity' as the ward does not have the legal capacity to consent to this contract.[19] Two judges in the eighth century, Ibn Shubruma (d. 761)[20] and Abu Bakr al-Asamm (d. 816/17), are reported to have disallowed such marriages. Among other arguments, these judges cited 4:6 to argue that the verse implies a certain marriageable age.[21]

The verse 2:237 mentions the term 'marriage tie', meaning the power to contract a marriage:

> And if you divorce them before having touched them, but after having settled a dower upon them, then half of what you have settled – unless it be that they forgo their claim or he in whose hand is the marriage tie forgoes his claim. And to forgo what is due to you is more in accord with God-consciousness.

The verse does not specify whether the person with the 'marriage tie' is the husband or the guardian. This has been another point of differing interpretations among the jurists. In reference to this verse, Ibn al-ʿArabi (d. 1347), a Maliki jurist, notes that the scholars are divided on its meaning. Some say that the verse refers to the husband; others claim that it alludes to the guardian. Ibn al-ʿArabi argues that after divorce the husband does not hold the right to affect the marriage contract, and hence the verse cannot be addressed to him.[22] Also, as the verse refers to the remission of dower, it cannot refer to the husband, because it is he who owes this to the wife. He cannot remit what is obligatory for him. The Hanafis, who hold that the marriage tie refers to the husband, explain that remission of dower means that the husband can pay more than is due. The remission may also mean that if the dower has already been paid in full, and the wife has to return it, the husband is willing to forego his claim to half of it.[23] In fact the term 'marriage tie' implies both the power to contract marriage and the power to dissolve the contract and deal with its consequent effects, including the authority to remit the dower. Such power belongs to spouses and not to the guardian.

This range of opinion among the jurists shows how legal interpretation may limit or extend the semantic field of a word. These diverse interpretations also suggest that this method of argument by syntax is not conclusive. Jurists can select verses suitable to their arguments. This also suggests that the verses are selected and interpreted in view of the doctrine of the school. This is construction rather than interpretation, as I mentioned above. It is quite significant to note that none of these verses mention the term 'marriage guardian' (*walī*). The term is, however, expressly mentioned in the hadith literature. I now turn to exploring jurists' interpretations of the following six hadiths, sayings of the Prophet Muhammad, which they commonly cite on the subject.

1. Any woman who is married (or marries herself) without the permission of her guardian, her marriage is void, void, void. If the marriage is consummated, the

woman is entitled to dower because the man took her as his lawful wife. If they are in dispute, the ruler is guardian for those who have no guardian. (Reported by 'A'isha.)[24]

2. No marriage (is valid) without a guardian. (Reported by Ibn 'Abbas.)[25]
3. A single woman (*ayyim*) who has been previously married is entitled regarding herself more than her guardian [that is, she is more entitled to look after her affairs than her guardian is, meaning that she no longer requires the guardian's protection]. The virgin's consent regarding herself must be sought, her silence is her consent. (Reported by Ibn 'Abbas.)[26]
4. The virgin's permission regarding herself must be sought, her silence is her permission.[27]
5. The orphan must be consulted regarding herself. If she is silent it is her permission. If she refuses no one is entitled to compel her.[28]
6. A widow or divorcée (*thayyib*) is entitled to her rights more than her guardian.[29]

The first two hadiths are cited more frequently with reference to the requirement of guardianship. The other jurists who do not subscribe to this doctrine find them weak on technical grounds, however. One of the transmitters of the first hadith, Ibn Shihab al-Zuhri (d. 741), denied reporting this hadith to Ibn Jurayj (d. 767), the next transmitter. Ibn Hazm (d. 1064) dismisses this criticism by saying that Zuhri might have forgotten he did so. However, this suggestion renders Zuhri's authority as a transmitter and collector of hadith doubtful. The hadith has been further contested because Prophet Muhammad's wife 'A'isha (d. 678), the narrator of this hadith, is herself known to have contracted the marriage of her niece Hafsa without the permission of her brother, who was Hafsa's father and guardian.[30]

The chain of transmission in the second hadith is not complete; the critics maintain that it is, at best, a saying of one of the Companions of the Prophet.[31] This hadith is not reported in the most authentic collections. Zayla'i (d. 762) refers to Ibn al-Jawzi, the well-known critic of hadith, who observes that, although these words have been reported by other transmitters, all the reports are technically defective.[32] *Al-Muwaṭṭa'* reports a similar statement but attributes it to Caliph 'Umar, not to the Prophet.[33] In addition to the technical objections, the Hanafis regard it as contradictory to the Prophet's own practice.[34] Ibn Hazm observes that the hadith has been reported with varying words by other transmitters, and claims that it is authentic enough to repeal any other contradicting hadith.[35]

As to the third hadith, Ibn Humam (d. 1457)[36] and Zurqani (d. 1687),[37] belonging respectively to the Hanafi and Maliki schools, explain that the term *ayyim* in this hadith means all unmarried women including virgins, divorcées and widows. Shafi'is read the third and sixth hadiths together and argue that the phrase that a divorcée or widow has more rights than her guardian simply means that the guardian should consult them. In other words, seeking their permission is only commendable, not mandatory. Shafiʿi and Maliki jurists hold that the hadith only distinguishes between virgins and those previously married to stress two different modes of their consent; it does not exempt the divorcée and widow from the requirement of a guardian.[38] Al-Nawawi (d. 1278) further explains the phrase 'she has more right than the guardian' in the above-mentioned hadiths (3 and 6) by saying that it, in fact, prescribes that both share this right, but the woman's share is larger, and hence she cannot be forced into marriage.[39] The Maliki jurist ʿIyad (d. 1144) comments that the phrase 'having more right' means that while the guardian has the right to contract marriage, the woman has more rights in other matters.[40]

One notices, however, that, similar to the cited Qur'anic verses, none of the hadiths provides a clear Text for or against the requirement of a marriage guardian. Ibn Rushd (d. 1198) also concludes that the doctrine of guardianship is not derived from the Qur'an and Sunna. He implies that it has its origins in social practice.

> Jurists differ because there is no verse of the Qur'an or the Sunna of the Prophet that clearly stipulates guardianship as a condition for the marriage contract, let alone any explicit text on the point. Rather, the verses and the Sunna cited by the proponents of guardianship and their opponents are equally ambiguous and probable. The authenticity of the cited hadiths is also debatable.[41]

Ibn Rushd, even though a Maliki jurist, is not satisfied with the rational justifications given by both sides. He observes that the frequency of cases referred to the Prophet in this respect would have required the Prophet to spell out explicitly and in detail the qualifications and categories of the guardians, if he considered it such an essential condition that their absence could invalidate a marriage.[42] He therefore concludes that guardianship means general supervision; it is not an essential requirement for a marriage contract.[43]

The above analysis, though brief, reveals that references to the Text and its legal interpretation are, in fact, informed by social considerations of the period in which the jurists lived. The interpretations constructed the legal norms of marriage guardianship with the prevailing social policies of the time in mind. This process of legal reasoning may be considered to be social construction of the doctrine. In the following section I shall refer to some prominent jurists to show how they explain the social need for the institution of the marriage guardian.

b. Construction

The above analysis notes that none of the verses and hadiths cited by the jurists is explicit about the coercive authority of the guardian; the Qur'anic verses do not even mention the term *walī*. Jurists have, nevertheless, developed diverse and complex sets of views on marriage guardianship. The question is: how did the jurists construct this doctrine? A cursory summary shows wide differences on the issues of the nature and need for a marriage guardian.[44] Looking at the gender distinction and their different criteria for the ward's incapacity on the basis of minority and virginity, one does not need to go far to find that the doctrine was developed within the framework of local social practices and tribal social structure. In this section, I refer to Imam Malik, Imam al-Shafiʿi, al-Sarakhsi, al-Ghazali and a recent Pakistani court judgment to illustrate the social construction of *wilāya*.

Imam Malik (d. 795), the founder of the Maliki school, justifies the doctrine as a social practice in Medina and points to the incapacity of females as a ground for the guardian's authority.

> It was the practice in Medina that virgins were not consulted about their marriage. If a father marries his virgin daughter to someone, the contract becomes binding on her. A virgin had no right in her property until she had her own home and her financial experience (*ḥāl*) became known.[45]

Imam al-Shafiʿi refers to *walā'* justifying the authority of guardianship.

> There is evidence in the Sunna of the Prophet that the guardian has common interest (*sharika*) in her vulva (*buḍʿ*). The marriage cannot be complete without him as long as he withholds his permission. Partnership in her vulva does not mean ownership. It only means additional care to guard the situation lest the woman contacts a person who is not equal to her. That is the meaning relied upon by those who hold equals (*akfā'*) necessary [for the marriage contract].[46]

He elaborates further that 'since the guardian has a joint interest in the commodity about which the woman is concluding the contract she cannot conclude marriage without the consent of the guardian'.[47] Refuting the argument that the Qur'an forbids guardians preventing their female wards from marrying the person of their choice (2:232), Imam al-Shafiʿi again argues as follows:

> The verse *falā taʿḍulūhunna an yankiḥna azwājahunna* (Do not prevent them from marrying their husbands) is the best evidence in the Qur'an indicating the fact that the guardian has a common right with the woman in her self and that it is the guardian's duty not to refuse permission when she agrees to marry according to the known practice (*maʿrūf*). The verse refers to the guardian because only the guardian has the right to refuse. The husband does not have that right after he has divorced her and she has completed the waiting period.[48]

The foregoing brief analysis suggests that the classical jurists, in general, were constructing guardianship in the tribal structural framework. It explains why Maliki and Shafiʿi jurists interpreted marriage guardianship in terms of absolute authority. The Hanafi construction differed because it was based on *kafā'a* (equality of status) rather than *walā'*, a tribal framework. Nevertheless, Al-Sarakhsi (d. 1106) explains the concept of a marriage guardian as follows.

> That is because marriage is a contract for the whole life and is founded on aims and objectives like companionship, familiarity, living together, and building relationships. That can be accomplished only between equals (*akfā'*). The principle of ownership of a woman is a kind of slavery (*riqq*). Marriage is slavery. One must, therefore, be careful where one places one's noble ward because humiliating oneself is forbidden. No believer is allowed to humiliate oneself.[49]
>
> (…) The guardians have the right to challenge [the contract of marriage concluded without their permission] to prevent dishonour (*'ār*) to them so that such persons as are not equal to them may not become relatives through marriage.[50]

Al-Sarakhsi mentions five criteria for judging equality (*kafā'a*): lineage (*nasab*), freedom, wealth, vocation and noble birth (*ḥasab*).[51] These are all social considerations.

In later periods, when the social structures in some areas of the Muslim world had changed, we find new reconstructions, which move away from tribal social concepts. I will illustrate this with some examples from the fourteenth century in the next section. It is, however, pertinent to stress that even in modern settings, the social structure may return to authoritative and patriarchal constructions to protect the institution of the family. Let me illustrate this point with reference to the recent case of *Abdul Waheed* v *Asma Jehangir* in Pakistan,[52] which shows the tension between legal and social norms.

In Pakistan, classical Hanafi *fiqh* governs marriage guardian laws. An adult Hanafi Muslim woman can contract her own marriage without the *walī*'s consent. The essential requirement for the validity of the contract is the woman's consent and not the *walī*'s. However, the influence of custom has been very strong.

Saima Waheed, a fourth-year student in the Government Lahore College for Women, contracted marriage with M. Arshad in 1996 without the knowledge of her father, Hafiz Abdul Waheed. A month after the alleged marriage, she left the family home and went to live in 'Dastak' (a women's refuge), managed by the first respondent, Asma Jehangir. The petitioner, Saima's father, commenced proceedings in the High Court, claiming that, in accordance with the Holy Qur'an and hadith, the marriage (*nikāḥ*) was not valid because he had not given his consent as her guardian (*walī*). The petitioner submitted that a previous Federal Shariat Court ruling – that adult Muslim women be allowed to marry without the consent of their *walī* – was not binding, as it had been delivered in the exercise of the court's appellate jurisdiction. He also contended that children are under an obligation to obey their parents and that marriage in Islam is not a civil contract. The respondents argued that marriage between men and women can be performed validly without the intervention of a *walī* and that restraints on the movements of women against their will violated their fundamental rights under the Constitution. The petition was considered by the High Court with reference to the following three questions: (1) The parent's right to obedience by the children. (2) The nature of the marriage contract: civil or sacred. (3) The guardian's permission as a necessary requirement for the validity of the marriage contract.

The advocates for the petitioner argued on the grounds of morality ('The runaway marriages offend all norms of a Muslim society')[53] and parental rights to obedience ('virgin girls stepping out of parent's house without their consent').[54] Advocates for the respondent argued on the basis of Hanafi law, according to which 'an adult girl is at liberty to marry'.[55]

The judgment constructed the dispute as a family issue, as can be seen in the following extracts:

> The family is the basic sphere of human activity. The child normally is said to learn good manners, discipline and follow religion which he finds his parents and other members of the family practicing. Therefore, all religions have laid special emphasis on the preservation, strengthening and protection of family.[56] (...)
>
> The Nikah is uniting/linking not only two individuals but also two families. The rights and obligations in Islam are not according to the sex but according to its contribution to the family.[57] (...)
>
> The parents are responsible for marriage of the children generally and girls particularly.[58] (...)
>
> The view that marriage was simply a contract of sale purchase was rejected without keeping in mind that the womenfolk have been driven to the status of slaves by this theory of sale purchase. This was not only inhuman but most disgraceful and was completely in derogation to teachings of Islam.[59]

The judgment explains that the consent of the *walī* is one of the conditions of a valid *nikāḥ* according to the Qur'an (2:221–2, 24:32), hadith (Bukhari, Abu Da'ud, Tirmidhi and Ibn Majja) and *tafsīr* (Ibn Kathir, Qurtubi).

> It is a matter of common knowledge that this mode [requiring the *walī*'s consent] is in vogue in the Muslim Society including this Sub-Continent till today. What more clear, strong and direct evidence is required to uphold the rule that *la nikāḥa illa bi-walī*. This is the only mode of marriage prevalent in our society and to disturb this arrangement would if not wreck then completely shake the structure of the society rather than strengthening it.[60]

In Pakistan, even in cases where a women is not legally required to have a marriage guardian, since she cannot appear in public during the marriage ceremony she requires a male relative, representing her, to convey her consent to the registrar of marriage. The need for a *wakīl* (representative) in the marriage ceremony is explained as follows:

> The purpose seems to be that as the female is not to appear in the assembly herself, therefore, a male must represent her.[61]

The judgment elaborates the parents' right of obedience on the basis of the Qur'an (4:1, 6:151, 17:23–4, 31:14–15) and hadiths, concluding that 'children are bound to obey their parents'.[62] The judgment holds that 'the obedience [to] the parents could be enforced by the Courts'.[63] The court ruled that 'It is, therefore, held that Mst. Saima Waheed and Arshad were not validly married.'[64] The other judge in this case also endorsed this line of argument, although he allowed the marriage.

> The parents sacrificed their rights and pleasures so that their children flourished. Should the children then insist on exercising their rights and pursuing their pleasure in a manner, which sinks the parents in shame, is a question not difficult to answer.[65]

On appeal, the Supreme Court ruled that adult Muslim girls were free to marry of their own free will, adding that they did not need to seek the consent of their *walī* (guardian) or other relatives. The apex court declared the marriage of Arshad Ahmad and Saima Waheed valid. The question put before the court was whether or not an adult Hanafi Muslim woman may contract her own marriage without the consent of her *walī*. In this particular case, the woman was an adult Hanafi Muslim of 22 years of age, who contracted a marriage with a college lecturer.

Modernity has influenced the institution of the Muslim family in diverse ways. Trends towards the independence of young people and gender equality have introduced a tension, which is often termed a clash between Western and Islamic values. The conservatives feel threatened by these developments, which they see as leading to promiscuity and immorality. The revival of a strong sense of family values has reintroduced the institution of the marriage guardian, even in a society like Pakistan that had followed the Hanafi school, according to which a guardian could not compel an adult girl into marriage. This renewed emphasis on the authority of parents as guardians is responsible for an increasing number of forced and unhappy marriages. The Saima Waheed case, in which judges of the High Court reintroduced the doctrine of *wilāyat al-ijbār* in a Hanafi society, is a good example of 'the regard for changing social norms', although their decision was ultimately reversed by the Supreme Court. It is significant that, unlike classical jurists, who interpreted and reinterpreted the injunctions of the Qur'an and hadith relating to the *walī*, these judges focused on the injunctions about parents and obedience towards them.

Analysing the above constructions, one finds two sets of reasoning. One set, namely *walā'*, in al-Shafi'i's construction mentioned above, relates to the concept of ownership based on biological relationship, especially between parents and children. From this perspective, the ward has no rights and the guardian has absolute authority. The other set of reasons relates to the concept of the protection of the weak. Minors and females do not have the capacity to contract a marriage, and therefore need the protection of a guardian. Both sets of reasons respond to the issue of inequality, and guardianship provides protection to ensure their wards have equality in their dealing with others. Patriarchy employed all these justifications, but in the process focused excessively on the weakness and inequality of the female. The jurists viewed these social conditions as natural norms that do not change. In the Pakistani case, it is the family that is under threat and needs protection. The court used the doctrine of guardianship to enhance the parental control of youth.

c. Reconstruction

The above summary also points to another, very important, continuing phenomenon in the development of Islamic jurisprudence: the diversity of opinions in the classical doctrine (*ikhtilāf al-fuqahā'*). It is the most cherished principle of Islamic jurisprudence, as every traditional text abides by it, faithfully reporting different views about each legal doctrine. The principle of diversity facilitated the accommodation of local social norms in Islamic laws in different Muslim societies. It also allowed later jurists to revisit and reconstruct the classical doctrine of *wilāya*. As I am not able here to go into this in depth, I will mention only two jurists in the fourteenth century, who illustrate the shifting framework of reasoning.

Ibn Qayyim (d. 1350), a Hanbali jurist, views the absolute authority of a guardian as akin to slavery and rejects it as a requirement for adults. He finds it contrary to the objectives of law and the interests of the community.

> An adult virgin cannot be married by force. She can be wedded only with her consent. This is the view of the majority of the ancient scholars followed by Abu Da'ud and Ahmad ibn Hanbal. This is what Allah has willed to be the law. We do not accept anything else ... It is in consonance with the judgment of the Messenger of God, with his injunctions and prohibitions, with the fundamentals of his laws and the interests of the community. Her father cannot dispose of a virgin girl, who is adult, sane and mature, in the least part of her property except by her consent. She cannot be forced to alienate a right without her permission. How can it be lawful that her father can enslave her or alienate herself from her without her consent to anyone he wishes. She may be the worst compelled person and he may be the most

> abhorred thing in the world to her. Regardless, her father marries her with him, forcing her without seeking her permission and reducing her to his captive.[66]

Another important jurist of the fourteenth century, Abu Ishaq al-Shatibi (d. 1388), developed the doctrine of *maqāṣid al-sharīʿa*, and shifted the framework of legal reasoning from deductive to inductive and from *qiyās* to *maqāṣid.* He identified *maṣlaḥa* as the main objective of Shariʿa. Let me briefly introduce this doctrine.

Abu Hamid al-Ghazali (d. 1111) was probably the first to analyse the contents and levels of *maṣlaḥa* in his work *al-Mustaṣfā.*[67] He defined the following five as areas of public interest that Shariʿa aims to protect: faith (*dīn*), life (*nafs*), intellect (*ʿaql*), family and children (*nasl*) and property (*māl*). He also suggested three mutually reinforcing levels of protection of the above-mentioned five contents. The first level identifies these five as core basic needs (*ḍarūrāt*) that Shariʿa aims to protect by prescribing laws and by fixing punishments for those who violate these laws. The second level builds a system of (legal) requirements (*ḥājiyyāt*), for example, the marriage contract, to institutionalise this protection. The third level incorporates (social) preferences (*taḥsīniyyāt*) to make the laws of protection acceptable in society. It was within this framework that al-Ghazali placed marriage guardianship among the *ḥājiyyāt* – the second level – not among *ḍarūrāt.*[68] It is significant to note that al-Ghazali regarded *maṣlaḥa* as an 'imagined' principle, not properly rooted in the revealed texts. He called *maṣlaḥa mursala* a public interest that was not explicitly prescribed in the scriptures; it is valid only if it is regulated by the texts of the Qurʿan and Sunna. Following Imam al-Shafiʿi (d. 820), who rejected the Hanafi principle of *istiḥsān*, al-Ghazali disallowed the Maliki principle of *istiṣlāḥ.* According to Imam al-Shafiʿi, *istiḥsān*, reasoning on the basis of the common good, was arbitrary and hedonistic. To al-Ghazali, *istiṣlāḥ* was similar to *istiḥsān*; both were imagined principles (*uṣūl mawhūma*).

Al-Shatibi refined al-Ghazali's views and systematised their structure in his work, *al-Muwāfaqāt.*[69] Contrary to al-Ghazali, who considered it an 'imagined' principle, al-Shatibi identified *maṣlaḥa* as the main objective of law and intent of the Lawgiver. Textual approaches use the deductive method of *qiyās* to determine the cause or the grounds for legal reasoning, which they restrict to the specific texts of the Qur'an and hadith. Al-Shatibi, on the other hand, defined the *maqāṣid* approach as more definitive because it employs the inductive method. Using this method, he came to conclude that *maṣlaḥa* was the overall objective of Shariʿa. He developed *maqāṣid al-sharīʿa* as a systematic theory of five aspects of the intent of the Lawgiver and three levels of the objectives of law. He defined the protection of faith, life, intellect, family and property as five basic needs, which are universally recognised natural necessities. The law protects them both prescriptively, by prescribing rules, and proscriptively, by forbidding their violation.

Al-Shatibi also explained the three levels as protective zones.

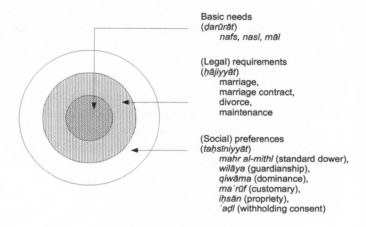

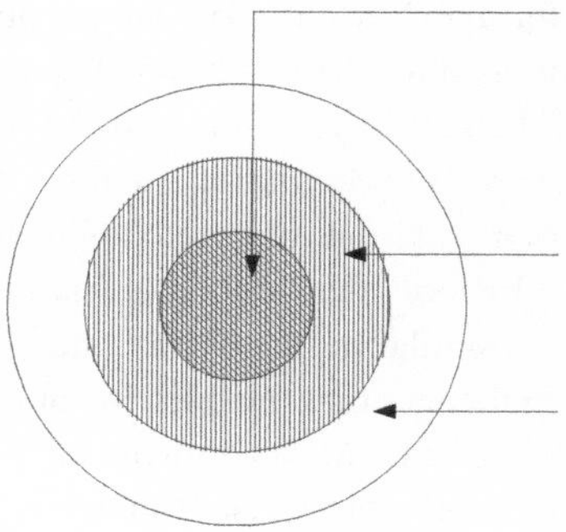

The three protect each other. The innermost circle, *ḍarūriyyāt*, consists of the five basic needs of a human society. The next, middle, circle, *ḥājiyyāt*, consists of values which are requirements of the innermost circle. The outermost circle, *taḥsīniyyāt*, which protects the other two, consists of values that refine the needs at the first and second level. In each circle values are defined further as requisite, substantive, subsidiary and complementary.

Al-Shatibi places family, as a basic need, in the innermost circle. The second circle protects this institution by constructing laws, for example, about marriage, divorce and inheritance. It also protects the family by developing further laws to punish the violation of these laws. Al-Shatibi thus places the laws of marriage in the second circle at the level of 'requirements', as a legal institution to protect the fundamental, natural institution of the family. Child marriage is, therefore, placed in the third level, because it is considered a social practice, neither a basic need nor a legal requirement. Child marriage is usually justified on the basis of considerations such as social compatibility (*kuf'/kafā'a*), as it is argued that a child, especially a girl, should be married as soon as a compatible mate is available. S/he may not get a suitable mate if the parents miss that opportunity. Similarly, the practice of standard dower (*mahr al-mithl*) is a social consideration. Legally, it is only complementary, and not an essential legal requirement for the marriage of a minor girl. Al-Shatibi places all these social norms in the third circle, protecting the second circle that contains legal norms.[70]

4. Gender equality

The above-mentioned concepts of *walā'*, in the case of al-Shafi'i, and *kafā'a*, in the case of al-Sarakhsi, as the legal grounds for marriage guardianship are not applicable to the social systems of today. *Walā'* applied to tribal patriarchal systems that are not the basis of the modern concept of the family. *Kafā'a* is also fast losing its rationale. The concept of equality before the law is undermining the idea of status-based rights. For instance, several court cases in Pakistan interpreted *khul'* in terms of gender equality, referring to verse 2:228.[71] In 2008, the Council of Islamic Ideology recommended a right of divorce for wives similar to that of husbands.[72] Recent reforms in Muslim countries illustrate the challenges that the doctrine of marriage guardianship faces in the modern legal environment.[73] Most countries have banned child marriages. Some countries have restricted the marriage of minors by fixing the minimum marriageable age. It ranges from 17 to 20 years for males and from 12 to 18 for females. In exceptional cases it can be relaxed, however, and in many countries the violation of this rule does not invalidate a marriage. The role of the marriage guardian has been restricted generally to one of protecting the interest of the ward. The consent of the guardian is essential only in cases where the parties have restricted capacity. The practice has, however, varied from time to time and country to country.

Recent studies of the doctrine vigorously challenge its deep roots in social norms, especially in patriarchy and the resulting concept of limited capacity of women.[74] Hammudah 'Abd al-'Ati explains the absolute authority of a marriage guardian from the perspective of women's incapacity and vulnerability in a male-dominated society.[75]

> Simply stated, marriage guardianship is the legal authority invested in a person who is fully qualified and competent to safeguard the interests and rights of another who is incapable of doing so independently. It is the authority of a father or nearest male relative over minors[, the] insane, or inexperienced persons who need protection and guardianship.[76]

A recent study argues that *fiqh* consists of individual exercises of *ijtihād* that fill the gaps in state laws, but also offers itself as an alternative law. *Fiqh* earned supremacy through the doctrines of *taqlīd* and *madhāhib* (following the teachings of established schools), but its application remained limited to certain areas of law.[77] These diverse approaches point towards an inner dynamism in Muslim thinking that provides new possibilities for revisiting traditional frameworks of gender roles.

During the debates generated by the social and legal changes, some new approaches to Islamic legal interpretation, especially with reference to gender equality, have also emerged. For illustration, I will mention a few of these, which offer an alternative to the traditional approach. Muslim jurists focus on the Text and its divine nature. They hold the Text to be revealed, and therefore eternal and immutable. Consequently, no *ijtihād* is allowed in the presence of a clear Text (*naṣṣ*).[78] The new approaches, on the other hand, maintain that *fiqh* texts are the individual opinions of the Muslim jurists; they cannot be regarded as revealed texts, and therefore immutable. Similarly, the majority of Muslim jurists regard the hadith (sayings of the Prophet Muhammad) as Text in addition to the Qur'an. Most new approaches regard only the Qur'an as the revealed Text; they consider hadith texts controversial. The traditional approach tends to view *fiqh* texts as definitive, and closed to further interpretation. In contrast, the new approaches have developed several hermeneutical approaches to emphasise the dynamism of the Qur'an as a Text. Nasr Hamid Abu-Zayd (d. 2010) defined the Qur'an as a discourse (*khiṭāb*), rather than a Text. He explained that the Qur'anic discourse was made in a patriarchal framework because the society was patriarchal; patriarchy, according to Abu-Zayd, is not the essence of that discourse.[79] Another Egyptian scholar, Hasan Hanafi (1935–), takes a phenomenological approach and distinguishes the Text (*naṣṣ*) as ideal from the realities (*wāqiʿ*) as context. A literalist approach idealises the Text and ignores the realities.[80] A Syrian scholar, Muhammad Shahrur (1938–), suggests a structural semantic approach to the meaning and interpretation of the Qur'an. He reads the Qur'anic verses as sets and subsets. For instance, the Qur'an consists of two sets: *al-Qur'ān* and *al-Kitāb* (the Book), and its injunctions fall into two subsets: (1) *ḥudūd* are definitive rules that define the upper and lower limits and (2) *taʿlīmāt* are ethical instructions that are open. All the Qur'anic verses are divided into a system of similar sets and subsets. This semantic structural approach enables Shahrur to present an ungendered interpretation of guardianship. He argues that guardianship is a universal rule, not specific to Islam. He elaborates that the Qur'an gives two conditions for *qiwāma*, namely physical and financial strength. The traditional jurists have presented these conditions as justifications for patriarchal domination, but to Shahrur these reasons are not gender specific; they apply to both men and women. Arguing that *qawāmiyya* is gender neutral, he concludes that if the husband is not in good health or the wife is financially stronger she qualifies for *qiwāma*. Whoever is stronger of the two on these two grounds is responsible for guardianship.[81]

A Tunisian scholar, Mohamed Talbi (1921–) suggests a mathematical concept (*sahm muwajjah*, the 'ray method') to extend Qur'anic reforms to contemporary issues.[82] In mathematics a 'ray' is a straight line that has a starting point but no end point. He gives examples of slavery and inheritance; the Qur'anic reforms, according to the ray method, should lead to equality. An Iranian scholar, Abdolkarim Soroush

(1945–), speaks about the epistemological crisis in Muslim thought and offers a new paradigm in epistemology to reinterpret the meaning of the revealed Text.[83]

Let me also mention here the historical approach to the study of the revealed Text. Those who adopt this approach insist on historicising the Qur'an and its rulings; the historical context of a verse clarifies its fuller meaning. The Pakistani Islamic scholar Fazlur Rahman (d. 1988) exemplifies this approach, as he explained that Islamic legal reasoning moves back and forth between past and present to develop analogies. Other historical approaches also look into the development of Islamic law and distinguish between Shari'a (the revealed law in the Qur'an and its explanations in the Sunna) and *fiqh* (the schools of law) and the *qānūn* (state legislation and administrative laws). Joseph Schacht points to a gap between theory and practice in Islamic law.[84] He regards Shari'a and *fiqh* as theory, and state legislation, such as commercial law and administrative law, as practice.

During this period, al-Shatibi's doctrine of *maqāṣid* has also become increasingly popular. Approaches based on this doctrine stress the spirit or the philosophy of the revealed law, rather than the words in the Text. They have reintroduced the jurisprudential principles of *istiqrā'* (inductive search for meaning), *sukūt* (silence) or *ibāḥa* (assumption of permissibility) where there is no clear word to explain the text.

Al-Shatibi's description of three zones of *maṣlaḥa* has become more relevant than ever before in the modern context because it is possible to understand the zones as three concentric circles, which refer to three levels of normativity: natural law, legal norms and social norms. His systematic treatment is extremely relevant to the question of normativity. That is why the *maqāṣid* approach has become more popular in recent years: it is not only more open than the textual approach, but, more significantly, it distinguishes different levels of norms, especially legal and social norms.

5. Conclusion

In recent years, social changes in Muslim societies have called for a new approach to the doctrine of guardianship, especially with reference to gender equality. *Maqāṣid al-sharī'a* is one such possible approach. Contrary to the analogical deductive method of legal reasoning (*qiyās*), it employs an inductive method of interpretation. Rather than arguing from one Qur'anic verse or a single hadith, it looks at the intent of the lawgiver in the whole legal system. It studies history and social norms, and develops a systematic understanding of legal concepts and doctrine.

Abu Ishaq al-Shatibi's discussion of *maqāṣid* and *maṣlaḥa* as the common good provides valuable insight into Islamic reasoning. His systematisation of the three levels of *maṣlaḥa* as a method of legal reasoning is also helpful in applying the *maqāṣid* approach to the modern context. The three levels, or concentric circles, indicate not only the grades of importance of the norms they contain, but the different fields to which those norms belong. The innermost circle comprises norms that are basic and natural. The second circle denotes legal norms, and customs treated as laws. The third refers to social and cultural norms. The second and third type of norms may differ from one society to another and from one time to another. The third circle, in particular, is quite specific to a given society.

Seen in al-Shatibi's system of concentric circles, the doctrine of marriage guardianship defines its role and position in accordance with the social values of the time. Guardianship is not an essential requirement, as its absence does not damage the essential objectives of the law, but it imbues those laws with a cultural and aesthetic value. Thus, it facilitates the grounding of laws in society's values and cultural tradition. This position simultaneously explains that social and cultural change in a society may influence social values such as guardianship, which may require reconstruction of these values in order to better serve the purpose of the law. As we have seen above, the guardian was required to protect the interest of the ward. In other words, guardianship was a measure adopted to provide gender equality, in the sense that the guardian created a balance to protect the vulnerable gender. This concept of justice, as keeping order and balance in society, created a hierarchy. That was in accordance with the pre-modern notion of justice, which aimed at a social balance created by social hierarchy. Modern concepts of equality before the law, and justice based on individual rights, rather than on hierarchy, require a redefinition of the role of parents, who would not need the authority of *wilāyat al-ijbār* to keep that social balance today.

Al-Shatibi places the traditional norm of marriage guardianship, as well as the issue of denying leadership positions to women (in al-Shatibi's words, 'not allowing a woman to take the position of leadership and to conclude her marriage'), in the third circle of *taḥsīniyyāt*. 'On the whole', according to him, 'these values (*taḥsīniyyāt*) pertain to the noblest values in addition to *ḍarūriyyāt* and *ḥājiyyāt*.'[85] In other words, social norms and practices represent the additional cultural values that are required to protect the essential objectives of a society. They are additional because their absence does not violate the legal norms, but they are cultural requirements. That also means that these values may change with time, and the new cultural values may replace the old ones as *taḥsīniyyāt*.[86]

Notes

1 See, for instance, al-Hibri, Azizah, 'A study of Islamic herstory: or how did we ever get into this mess?', *Women's Studies International Forum* 5/2 (1982), pp. 207–19; Rahman, F., 'Status of women in the Qur'an', in G. Nashat (ed.), *Women and Revolution in Iran* (Boulder, CO: Westview Press, 1983); Hussain, F. (ed.),

Muslim Women (New York: St Martin's Press, 1984); Mernissi, F., *Beyond the Veil* (Bloomington, IN: Indiana University Press, 1987); Ahmed, L., *Women and Gender in Islam: Historical Roots of a Modern Debate (New Haven: Yale University Press, 1992)*; Hassan, R., 'An Islamic perspective', in J. Belcher (ed.), *Women, Religion and Sexuality* (Geneva: WCC Publications, 1990); Ali, S. S., *Gender and Human Rights in Islam and International Law: Equal Before Allah, Unequal Before Man?* (The Hague: Kluwer Law International, 2000); and the studies mentioned below.

2 Lane mentions that *wilãya* and *walãya* are both verbal nouns for *walī*, that inter alia means guardian of a woman. He further clarifies that *wilãya* signifies office and authority. Lane, Edward William, *An Arabic English Lexicon* (Beirut: Librarie du Liban, 1968), Supplement, p. 3060.

3 Flavia Agnes has shown how male economic privilege and Christian religious concepts informed the evolution of Anglo-Muhammadan law in India through the British notion of public policy. Some British judges were shocked at Islamic laws that gave women access to inheritance, to delegated or negotiated divorce (*tafwīḍ, khul'*), and to some property upon divorce (*mut'a*). In their view, these laws encouraged divorce and allowed property rights to women, contrary to universally accepted norms of the time. Agnes, Flavia, 'Economic rights of women under Muslim personal law in India', *Economic and Political Weekly* 31/41–2 (12–19 October, 1996), p. 2832.

4 Zarqa', Mustafa Ahmad, *Al-Madkhal al-Fiqhī al-'Āmm: Al-Fiqh al-Islāmī fī Thawbihi al-Jadīd* (Damascus: Matba'a Jaṃi'a Dimashq, 1963), Vol. 2, p. 818.

5 Mahmasani, Subhi, *Al-Awḍā' al-Tashrī'iyya fī Duwal al-'Arabiyya* (Beirut: Dar al-'Ilm li al-Mala'in, 1962), p. 52.

6 The Hanafi jurist Al-Haskafi's (*Al-Durr al-Mukhtār*) traditional definition of the term, cited in Zarqa': *Al-Madkhal*, p. 818.

7 See Bousquet, G.-H., *Abrégé de la loi musulmane selon la rite l'imâm Mâlek* (Paris and Algiers: Édition algérienne Nahda, 1958), p. 17.

8 See Ruxton, F. H., *Maliki Law, Being a Summary from the French Translation of the Mukhtasar of Sidi Khalil* (London: Luzac and Company, 1916); Anderson, N. D., *Family Law in Asia and Africa* (London: George Allen & Unwin, 1967).

9 Subhi Mahmasani finds the concept of this authority in pre-Islamic Arabia quite similar to that of Roman law before the Republic period. The Arab head of family had the same powers as that of the Roman *pater familias*. Mahmasani, *Al-Awḍā' al-Tashrī'iyya*, pp. 51–2.

10 Masud, Muhammad Khalid, 'Shāṭibī's theory of meaning', *Islamic Studies* 32 (1993), pp. 5–16.

11 Ibn Manzur, *Lisān al-'Arab* (Beirut: Dar Sadir, 1882), Vol. 15, p. 407.

12 Ibn Manzur, *Lisān al-'Arab*, p. 408.

13 *Al-walā' shu'ba min riqq* ('*Walā'* is a branch of slavery'). Ibn Qudama, *Al-Mughnī* (Cairo: Hajr, 1992), Vol. 9, p. 217.
14 Malik, *Al-Muwaṭṭa'* (Cairo: 'Isa al-Babi, 1951), Vol. 2, p. 781.
15 Al-Sarakhsi, Abu Bakr, *Al-Mabsūṭ* (Beirut: Dar al-Kutub al-'Ilmiyya, 2001), Vol. 5, p. 12; al-Nawawi, Abu Yahya Sharaf, *Al-Minhāj bi Sharḥ Ṣaḥīḥ Muslim*, on the margin of al-Qastallani, Irshad al-Sari, *Sharḥ Ṣaḥīḥ Bukhārī* (Cairo: Bulaq, 1886).
16 Al-Sarakhsi, *Al-Mabsūṭ*, Vol. 4, p. 236.
17 Al-Nawawi, *Al-Minhāj*, p. 149. Ibn Shubruma's view (*lā yajuzu inkāḥ al-abi ibnatahū al-saghīra illā ḥatta tablugh wa ta'dhanu*), cited in Ibn Hazm, *Al-Muḥallā* (Beirut: Dar Ihya al-Turath al-'Arabi, 1997), Vol. 11, p. 20.
18 Al-Sarakhsi, *Al-Mabsūṭ*, Vol. 4, p. 236.
19 Al-Nawawi, *Al-Minhāj*, p. 149.
20 Cited by Al-Sarakhsi, *Al-Mabsūṭ*, Vol. 4, p. 236.
21 Al-Sarakhsi, *Al-Mabsūṭ*, Vol. 4, p. 236.
22 Ibn al-'Arabi, *Aḥkām al-Qur'ān* (Beirut: Dar al-Kitab al-'Arabi, 2000), Vol. 1, pp. 267–8.
23 Al-Sarakhsi, *Al-Mabsūṭ*, Vol. 6, p. 73.
24 Abu Da'ud, *Sunan Abi Dā'ūd* (Riyaḍ: Dar al-Salam, 2000), Ḥadīth 'Ā'isha no. 2083, p. 1376; Tirmidhi, Abu 'Isa, *Jāmi' al-Tirmidhī* (Riyad: Dar al-Salam, 2000), Ḥadīth 'Ā'isha no. 1102, p. 1757.
25 Ibn Majah, Abu 'Abdullah, *Sunan ibn Mājah* (Riyad: Dar al-Salam, 2000), Ḥadīth ibn 'Abbās no. 1880, p. 2589; Tirmidhi: *Jāmi' al-Tirmidhī*, Ḥadith ibn 'Abbās no. 1108, p. 1759, Ḥadīth Abū Mūsā no. 1011, p. 1757.
26 Muslim b. Ḥajjaj, *Ṣaḥīḥ Muslim* (Riyad: Dar al-Salam, 2000), Ḥadīth ibn 'Abbās no. 3476, p. 914; Abu Da'ud, *Sunan Abi Dā'ūd*, Ḥadīth ibn 'Abbās 2098, p. 1377; Tirmidhī, *Jāmi' al-Tirmidhī*, Ḥadīth ibn 'Abbās 1108, p. 1759.
27 Muslim b. Hajjaj: *Ṣaḥīḥ Muslim*, Ḥadīth Abū Hurayra no. 3473, p. 914.
28 Abu Da'ud, *Sunan Abi Dā'ūd*, Ḥadīth Abū Hurayra no. 2093, p. 1377; Tirmidhi, *Jāmi' al-Tirmidhī*, Ḥadith Abū Hurayra no. 1109, p. 1759.
29 Muslim b. Hajjaj: *Ṣaḥīḥ Muslim*, Ḥadīth ibn 'Abbās no. 3478, p. 914; Tirmidhi, *Jāmi' al-Tirmidhī*, Ḥadīth no. 1107, p. 1758; Ibn Qasim, 'Abd al-Rahman, *Al-Mudawwana al-Kubrā* (Beirut: Dar al-Kutub al-'Ilmiyya, 1994), Vol. 2, p. 103.
30 Zayla'i, *Naṣb al-Ra'ya fī Takhrīj Aḥādīth al-Hidāya* (Cairo: Al-Majlis al-'Ilmi, 1938), Vol. 3, pp. 185–6.
31 *Ibid.*, pp. 182–3.
32 *Ibid.*, p. 182.
33 Malik, *Al-Muwaṭṭa'*, Vol. 2, p. 525.
34 Al-Sarakhsi, *Al-Mabsūṭ*, Vol. 5, p. 12.
35 Ibn Hazm, *Al-Muḥallā*, Vol. 11, p. 19.
36 Ibn Humam, *Sharḥ Fatḥ al-Qadīr* (Quetta: Maktaba Rashidiyya, n.d.), Vol. 3, p. 159.

37 Al-Zurqani, *Sharḥ Muwaṭṭa' Imām Mālik* (Cairo: Matba'a al-Istiqama, 1954), Vol. 3, p. 126.
38 Al-Shafi'i, *Al-Umm* (Beirut: Dar al-Kutub al-'Ilmiyya, 1993), Vol. 5, p. 22.
39 Al-Nawawi, *Al-Minhāj*, p. 147.
40 Zurqani, *Sharḥ*, Vol. 3, p. 126.
41 Ibn Rushd, *Bidāyat al-Mujtahid*, trans. M. K. Masud (Cairo: Maktaba al-Kulliyyat al-Azhariyya, 1969), Vol. 2, pp. 10, 28ff.
42 *Ibid.*, p. 11.
43 *Ibid.*, p. 13.
44 The source for this summary is al-Zuhayli, Wahba, *Al-Fiqh al-Islāmī wa Adillatuhu (Damascus: Dar al-Fikr, 1996)*, Vol. 7, pp. 186–228.
45 Malik, *Al-Muwaṭṭa'*, Vol. 2, p. 525. The Malikis subject an unmarried women's legal capacity to *rushd*, 'maturity'. Ibn Qudama, *Al-Mughnī*.
46 Al-Shafi'i, *Al-Umm*, Vol. 5, p. 179.
47 *Ibid.*, p. 11.
48 *Ibid.*, p. 179.
49 Al-Sarakhsi, *Al-Mabsūṭ*, Vol. 5, p. 23.
50 *Ibid.*, p. 25.
51 *Ibid.*, pp. 23–4.
52 *Abdul Waheed* v *Asma Jehangir*, PLD 1997, Lahore 301; *Hafiz Abdul Waheed* v *Mrs. Asma Jehangir*, PLD 2004, Supreme Court 219.
53 *Abdul Waheed* v *Asma Jehangir*, PLD 1997, Lahore 317.
54 *Ibid.*, 313.
55 *Ibid.*, 322.
56 *Ibid.*, 323.
57 *Ibid.*, 326.
58 *Ibid.*, 326.
59 *Ibid.*, 333.
60 *Ibid.*, 340.
61 *Ibid.*, 343.
62 *Ibid.*, 351. Hadiths were cited from *Ṣaḥīḥ Bukharī.*
63 *Ibid.*, 351.
64 *Ibid.*
65 *Ibid.*, 375.
66 Ibn Qayyim, *Zād al-Ma'ād fī Hadī Khayr al-'Ibād* (Beirut: Mu'assat al-risāla, n.d.), Vol. 5, pp. 96–7.
67 Al-Ghazali, Abu Hamid, *Al-Mustaṣfā min 'Ilm al-Uṣūl* (Baghdad: Maktaba al-Muthannā, 1970), Vol. 1, pp. 284–315.
68 Al-Ghazali, *Al-Mustaṣfā*, Vol. 1, p. 289.
69 For a detailed discussion see Masud, Muhammad Khalid, *Shatibi's Philosophy of Islamic Law* (Islamabad: Islamic Research Institute, 1995).

70 Al-Shatibi, *Al-Muwāfaqāt* (Cairo: Maktaba Tijariya, 1975), Vol. 2, p. 13.

71 For instance, see *Mst. Khurshid Bibi* v *Baboo Muhammad Amin*, PLD 1967, Supreme Court 97.

72 See the report, Council of Islamic Ideology, *Muslim 'Ā'ili Qawānīn Ordinance 1961, Naẓr Thānī awr Sifārishāt* (Islamabad: Council of Islamic Ideology, Government of Pakistan, 2009), especially pp. 3–9.

73 See for details, Mahmood, *Family Law Reform in the Muslim World* (Bombay: N.M. Tripathi, 1972).

74 See 'Abd al-'Ati, Hammudah, *Family Structure in Islam* (Lagos: Islamic Publications Bureau, 1982), p. 96.

75 'Abd al-'Ati, *Family Structure*, pp. 70–2.

76 'Abd al-'Ati, *Family Structure*, p. 70, referring to modern authors like Farrukh,'Umar, *Al-Usra fī al-Shar' al-Islāmī* (Cairo: Matba'a al-Maktaba al-'Ilmiyya, 1951), and Mughniya, Muhammad Jawad, *Al-Zawāj wa al-Ṭalāq 'alā al-Madhāhib al-Khamsa* (Beirut: Dar al-'Ilm li al-Mala'in, 1960).

77 Masud, Muhammad Khalid, '*Ikhtilaf al-fuqaha*: diversity in *fiqh* as a social construction', in Z. Anwar, *Wanted: Equality and Justice in the Muslim Family* (Selangore: Musawah, 2009), pp. 65–91.

78 The word is capitalised to distinguish it from 'text' in the ordinary meaning.

79 See Abu-Zayd, Nasr Hamid, *Mafhūm al-Naṣṣ: Dirāsa fī 'Ulūm al-Qur'ān* (4th edn, Beirut: Al-Markaz al-Thaqafi al-'Arabi, 1998); and *Naqd al-Khiṭāb al-Dīnī* (Cairo: Maktaba al-Madbuli, 1995).

80 See Hanafi, Hasan, *Min al-Naṣṣ ilā al-Wāqi'*, Vol. 1: *Takwīn al-Naṣṣ* (Cairo: Markaz al-Kitab li al-Nashr, 2004), Vol. 2: *Bunyat al-Naṣṣ* (Cairo: Markaz al-Kitab li al-Nashr, 2005).

81 Shahrur, Muhammad, *Al-Kitāb wa al-Qur'ān: Qirā'a Mu'aṣira* (Beirut: Sharikat al-Matbu'a li al-Tawzī' wa al-Nashr, 1992), p. 620. See also Christmann, Andreas, *The Qur'ān, Morality and Critical Reason: The Essential Muḥammad Shaḥrūr* (Leiden: Brill, 2009), pp. 279–92.

82 See Talibi, Muhammad (Mohamed Talbi), *'Iyāl Allāh, Afkār Jadīda fī 'Alāqat al-Muslim bi Nafsihī wa bi al-Ākharīn* (Tunis: Dar Sirar al-Nashr, 1992), pp. 143–4. Janjar translates it as 'vecteur orienté', oriented vector; Janjar, Muhammad al-Saghir, 'Lāhūt, ba'ḍ jawānib al-tajdīd fī al-fikr al-dīnī 'inda Muḥammad al-Ṭālibī', *Muqaddimāt* 10 (1997), pp. 5–12. I prefer to translate it as 'ray' because a ray, according to its mathematical definition, has a direction but no end point. A 'vector', on the other hand, also has an end point. The point of emphasis in Talbi's argument is on a line showing direction in the past to an indefinite future.

83 See Soroush, Abdolkarim, *Qabḍ-u-Basṭ-e ti'urik-e Shari'at* (Tehran: Mu'assasa Farhanagi Sirat, 1990); Cooper, John, 'The limits of the sacred: the epistemology of 'Abd al-Karim Soroush', in John Cooper, Ronald Nettler and Mohamed Mahmood (eds), *Islam and Modernity: Muslim Intellectuals Respond* (London:

I.B.Tauris, 1998), pp. 38–56; and Dahlén, Ashk, *Deciphering the Meaning of Revealed Law* (Uppsala: Uppsala University, 2002).

84 Schacht, Joseph, *An Introduction to Islamic Law* (Oxford: Clarendon, 1965).

85 Al-Shatibi, *Al-Muwāfaqāt*, Vol. 2, p. 11.

86 *Ibid.*, p. 12.

7

THE STATUS OF WOMEN BETWEEN THE QUR'AN AND *FIQH*

Nasr Abu-Zayd

Editors' note: Nasr Abu-Zayd passed away half a year after opening our January 2010 workshop in Cairo with the thoughts that follow. We are honoured to be able to include in this book one of the last contributions of his distinguished career. This chapter is based on the draft he presented, as well as on his substantial contributions to the workshop discussions, a few short extracts of which are given at the end. The reader will appreciate that this is not the polished scholarly argument that Dr Abu-Zayd would have made had he been granted the time to revise it as planned, nor does it not cover the full set of issues he intended to address. It sets out in some detail how the Qur'an should be read with attention to its different discourses and domains of meaning, and how its linguistic form opens a space for divergent opinions, rather than certainties. It goes on to sketch how a new, contextual ijtihād *could be applied to gender issues in law such as inheritance and male guardianship.*

1. Introduction

In a brilliant remark, the Egyptian reformist Muhammad 'Abduh (1845–1905) compares the jurists' definition of marriage with the Qur'an's view of the marriage relationship. Marriage, according to *fiqh*, is a contract that renders the female vagina the property of a male. The Qur'an's view, however, is that marriage is one of the divine signs (*āyāt*): 'Among His Signs is this, that He created for you mates from among yourselves, that you may dwell in tranquility with them, and He has put love and mercy between you; verily in that are Signs for those who reflect' (30:21).[1] ʿAbduh emphasises the responsibility of *fiqh* for downgrading women's status from the high level it has in the Qur'an.

ʿAbduh's choice of this specific verse of the Qur'an to make his point is indicative of the objectives of the reformist project in the nineteenth and the twentieth century. It was to open the meaning of the Qur'an, and, consequently, the meaning of Islam, to accommodate the positive values of modernity, rationalism, freedom and equality. In this attempt, the reformist thinkers had to emphasise the historical gap between the modern world and the traditional world of classical Islam. *Fiqh*, in their view, belongs to the traditional worldview that is in need of rethinking. *Fiqh* is no more than the earlier Muslim generations' attempt to unfold the meaning of the divine source in order to sustain and accommodate their worldview. In our modern context, the reformists preached, we have not only the right but the obligation to do the same – that is, to unfold the meaning of the Qur'an to accommodate the values of our modern time.

The verse quoted by ʿAbduh to emphasise the high status of women in the Qur'an belongs to the high ethical and spiritual domain of meaning. This differs from the legalistic domain of meaning, to which belong the passages that the *fuqahāʾ* highlighted. In the following, I will first present the Qur'an's different domains of meaning. Then, I will elaborate on the reformists' attempt to historicise *fiqh* by extending it to *uṣūl al-fiqh*, the legal theory that was constructed to systemise *fiqh*. The final section will be devoted to issues of gender equality.[2]

2. The worlds of the Qur'an: domains of meaning

To return to ʿAbduh's attempt to draw a distinction between the Qur'an and *fiqh*, it should be pointed out that the worlds of the Qur'an, or its multi-dimensional worldview, were separated, in fact fragmented, in the classical disciplines. Theology took over the world of Godhead; philosophy took over the world of metaphysics, that is, the cosmos, the grades of existence, nature and so on; Sufism took over the ethical–spiritual world; and legal theory took over the legislative world. Thus fragmented, the Qur'an's worldview is in need of defragmentation. To reconnect the worlds of the Qur'an, we need to approach the Qur'an differently. The Qur'an was communicated as series of oral discourses during the last 20 years of the Prophet's life (612–632);[3] each discourse has its occasion, audience, structure, type, mode and message. These discourses were later collected, arranged and written down in the *muṣḥaf*. The difference between the *muṣḥaf* arrangement and the chronological order of these discourses is a well-known fact. The *muṣḥaf* gave the Qur'an the form of a book, which in its turn redefined the Qur'an as a Text.

As a revealed divine Text, the Qur'an maintains that it has no contradictions (4:82). Yet the phenomenon of contradiction does exist. The theologians realised this, and took pains to solve it with the duality of clarity/ambiguity. So did the jurists, who tried to solve it by the doctrine of abrogation. In modern Qur'anic studies in the Muslim world, the solution proposed is to distinguish between two dimensions in the Qur'anic worldview: the 'universal' and the 'historical'. In all these efforts, the phenomenon is realised, acknowledged, but not fully solved.[4]

My assessment is that the concept of 'text', with its underlying assumption of authorship, is the cause of this paradoxical entrapment between historicity and divinity, or between the chronological order and the *muṣḥaf* order. Realising the fact that the Qur'an was originally a series of discourses, each of which has a certain historical context and a certain degree of independence, I have suggested a redefinition of the Qur'an as discourse(s). These discourses reflect polyphony rather than monophony, and reflect not only different situations, but different addressees. A humanistic hermeneutics, I suggest, is to consider in every discourse unit: (1) who the speaker is and who the addressees are; (2) the mode of discourse under investigation, whether argumentative, persuasive, polemical, proscriptive, prescriptive, descriptive, inclusive or exclusive and so on. Thus I do not deal with the *sūra* or with the *āya* as independent units; the unit is the discourse identified by these suggested criteria.

From such a perspective, the achieved chronological arrangement of the Qur'anic chapters presents only an introductory step towards a chronological arrangement of discourses, a project that needs to be accomplished in the future. This approach, however, does not entirely depend on the chronological order, nor does it disregard the *muṣḥaf* order. Both the synchronic and the diachronic dimensions are taken into consideration, as the different domains of meaning exist everywhere in the Qur'an. For now, I propose dividing the worlds of the Qur'an – its multi-dimensional worldview – into five interdependent domains, each of which reflects one level that has been taken away and disconnected from the other levels in one of the Islamic disciplines, namely *fiqh*, theology, philosophy and mysticism.

1. *Cosmology*. Here the Qur'anic worldview of the cosmos, the universe, nature, creation and recreation, the creator, death and resurrection are presented.

2. *The divine–human relationship*. Here closeness and distinction are both emphasised. Despite this emphasised closeness, mediation between the divine and the human is presented in poetic language, describing the angels filling the space between heaven and earth bringing down God's *amr* or command. The fact that God always sends guidance to humans via the mediation of angels is a token of His care for them. Humans in return are expected to be grateful. The Qur'anic narratives, *qaṣaṣ*, which are scattered throughout almost every chapter, represent the textual space for this manifestation. In the covenant narrative, all human beings

acknowledge their obligation to obey God: 'When your lord took from the children of Adam, from their loins (*ẓuhūrihim*) their seed and called them to testify of themselves: "Am I not your lord?" They said, "Indeed yes! We testify"; lest you should say on the day of resurrection, "we were unaware of this!"' (7:172).[5] Due to this primordial commitment to obedience, humans are morally responsible from birth.

3. *The ethical and moral dimension*. Here the Qur'an maintains a certain tension between the possibility of human perfection and the reality of human moral deficiency. The complex image of God as merciful and mighty could be understood as a parallel or reflection of human nature, but it could also be said that the Qur'an mentions God's mercy to remind humans of the possibility of repenting of evil. Thus, human nature and divine nature are not in tension; rather, they are interwoven.

4. *The societal level*. Here the Qur'an deals with specific practical issues such as marriage, divorce and inheritance and so on. This is the domain of meaning contained in the Qur'anic passages with legal rulings. This domain is the domain of *ijtihād*, independent rational reflection, which should not be limited to the classical concept of *qiyās*, analogy. We know that these legal stipulations originally addressed the seventh-century milieu and the nascent Muslim community, which needed certain regulations after moving from Mecca where Muslims were a minority group. We should always have this context in its totality in mind. Such contextualisation is far beyond the classical legal theory, which built a hierarchical structure of the legal sources, *uṣūl al-fiqh*, with very limited space for *ijtihād*. Even the theory of objectives (*maqāṣid*) of the law discussed below is a theory of preservation or protection (*ḥifẓ*), not a theory of development.

On this level we find legal rulings interwoven with ethics, as with divorce: 'Divorce twice, then take back with *ma'rūf* or release with *iḥsān*' (2:229). Divorce as a dramatic event of separation between husband and wife should be conducted with ethical common sense (*ma'rūf*, an important ingredient in Qur'anic ethics), and with benevolence (*iḥsān*). The ethical aspect is also connected to worship (*'ibādāt*). Prayers are intended to prevent the believer from committing indecent or reprehensible acts (*fāḥisha/munkar*; 29:45). The blood and flesh of the animal sacrificed on hajj (i.e. the ritual in itself) is not as important as its inner intended significance, *taqwā* (22:37).

5. *Punishment* (ḥudūd). This level exists in the Qur'an, but it does not belong to the worldview of the Qur'an. It does not even belong to the category of 'legal rules'. Cutting off the hands of the thief, or flogging the adulterer and those who falsely accuse others of adultery (*qadhf*), are not genuine Qur'anic rulings, let alone stoning (*rajm*), which is not a rule in the *muṣḥaf* but is claimed to have been abrogated in its textual form only (*nusikha lafẓan la ḥukman*). These forms of punishment existed before the Qur'an, and the Qur'an borrowed them in order to protect society against crimes.

These levels – and there may be more – are all intrinsically interwoven in the Qur'an, and the Qur'anic worldview could not be reconstructed without them.

3. The legal theory and the *maqāṣid*

a. The legal theory: uṣūl al-fiqh

Fiqh literally and originally denotes 'knowledge' and 'understanding'. It later became a term that only applied to knowledge of law. The early Muslim jurists, or *fuqahā'*, by applying the method of deduction, were able to build a legal system, Shari'a, out of the limited legal issues addressed in the Qur'an. While the extent of the legal matter in the Qur'an is debated, the fact remains that it is limited.[6] The *fuqahā'* tried their best to deduce the implicit out of the explicit in the Qur'an by developing certain concepts, such as *maṣlaḥa* (pl. *maṣāliḥ*),[7] the community public interest, and *istiḥsān* and *istiṣlāḥ*, preference.[8] They gradually built what is known as the legal theory of Islam, *uṣūl al-fiqh*, in which they supplemented the Qur'an with other legal sources, that is, the Prophetic tradition (Sunna); the consensus (*ijmā'*) of the first Muslim generation (the *ṣaḥāba*) and the scholars of the following generations; as well as *ijtihād*, independent rational effort to deal with legal issues not dealt with in the above three sources. The first construction of the Islamic legal theory, *uṣūl al-fiqh*, was accomplished by Muhammad b. Idris al-Shafi'i (767–820). He is believed to be the first jurist who systematically established analogy (*qiyās*) as the only methodological means by which *ijtihād* is to be performed. Thus, he limited the scope of *ijtihād* by excluding *istiḥsān*, *istiṣlāḥ* and *ra'y* (opinion).[9]

So, the sources of the legal theory are of two types; the Qur'an and the Sunna are the main textual sources, while *ijmā'* and *ijtihād* are auxiliary explanatory sources. Being the main textual sources, the Qur'an and the Sunna are not immediately comprehended; linguistically, they are in need of explanation, elucidation and interpretation, which can lead to diverse conclusions (*ikhtilāf*). Ibn Rushd (d. 1198) summarises the structure of Shari'a before indicating the cause of the legal diversity in the introduction to his *Bidāyat*.[10] His summary, freely quoted and restructured, runs as follows. First, Ibn Rushd identifies the five rules (*aḥkām*) of Shari'a in relation to the human subject (*al-mukallaf*).[11] The second issue is to identify the sources through which these rules are expressed. Ibn Rushd differentiates between textual and non-textual sources. The textual sources are the Qur'an and the verbal Sunna, that is, the sayings of the Prophet, hadiths. Non-textual sources are the non-verbal practical Sunna, consensus, and *ijtihād* by analogy.

1. The textual sources are not as clear and obvious as expected; they contain different linguistic forms (*ṣiyāghat al-alfāz*) such as command (*amr*) and prohibition (*nahy*);[12] different types of wording, or rather styles (*aṣnāf al-alfāẓ*), such as general (*'āmm*) and particular (*khāṣṣ*);[13] as well as different semantic domains.[14] For

each of these, the *fuqahā'* have differed over the implications, such as whether the *amr* denotes obligation or recommendation.

2. As for the second, non-verbal channel, the Prophet's actions (*afʿāl*), approvals and disapprovals (*iqrārāt*), some jurists maintain that the reports of the Prophet's actions do not indicate rulings, as they do not have linguistic forms. Those who maintain that rulings can be received through *afʿāl* differ over the kind of ruling indicated by them. Some say that they indicate obligation, while others say that they indicate recommendation (*mandūb*).[15]

3. As for the third source of Shariʿa established in the legal theory, *ijmāʿ*, it has no independent authority; its proof (*ḥujja*) is derived from one or more of the textual sources. Its role is, therefore, limited to strengthening an unclear or non-decisive (*ẓannī*) ruling into one that is definitive and decisive (*qaṭʿī*).

4. Lastly, recourse may be had to *ijtihād* by applying analogy (*qiyās*). Legitimate *qiyās* is assigning an existing ruling to a legal issue about which the sources are silent. This is the only legal method to connect the limited rules provided by the two basic sources with the unlimited demand of life. *Qiyās*, therefore, has to be based either on a resemblance between the issue waiting for a *ḥukm* and one on which the law has already provided the *ḥukm*, that is, *qiyās shabah*, or on the existence of an explicit or implicit ground (*ʿilla*) for both the Shariʿa ruling and the issue under consideration, that is, *qiyās ʿilla*.

The Zahiri school maintains that analogy in law (*sharʿ*) is illegal; they argue that when the Shariʿa is silent, there is no *ḥukm*. Ibn Rushd eloquently explains the difference between legal *qiyās* based on analogy, refuted by the Zahirites, and the linguistic process of deducing the general intended meaning from the type of particular statement (*khāṣṣ*) that is intended as a general one (*ʿāmm*). The latter is a linguistic procedure of explicating the intended or the implied (*mafhūm*), out of the expressed (*manṭūq*); the expansion of the *ḥukm* according to this linguistic methodology is not *qiyās*, as it is based on the implicit meaning in the expression (*dalālat al-lafẓ*). *Qiyās*, on the other hand, expands the *ḥukm* of an explicit Shariʿa rule to a new case by analogy, not by linguistic explication. Because analogy can depend on a ruling derived from a particular statement with particular intent, these two kinds of expansion of the *ḥukm*, by *qiyās* or by explication of the *manṭūq*, are very close and often cause confusion. Ibn Rushd concludes that it is possible for the Zahiris to dispute the first type, that is, *qiyās*; they are not entitled to dispute the second, explicating the general meaning intended in the specific statement, for it belongs to *samʿ*,[16] and he who rejects this, rejects an Arabic style of communication (*khiṭāb*).

After providing this concise summary of the structure of Shariʿa, Ibn Rushd briefly, but adequately enough, explains that the reason for divergence of opinion (*ikhtilāf*) is the linguistic structure of the textual sources, namely the Qur'an and the verbal Sunna. *Ikhtilāf* is even greater in the verbal Sunna, on the one hand because of the way it is transmitted, and on the other because of the possibility of conflict (*taʿāruḍ*) in the reported texts from which the law derives the rulings. Moreover, the conflict may exist between reported acts (*afʿāl*) or approvals (*iqrārāt*). As for analogy, *ihktilāf* rather than agreement is the norm; it depends on the jurist's personal capacity to discover the similarities or to deduce the *ʿilla*. Lastly, a conflict may occur between one of these four channels and another channel: that is, a conflict between a text and a reported act, or a conflict between *iqrār* and *qiyās*.

b. Maqāṣid al-sharīʿa

Quite possibly, it was in order to bypass the *ikhtilāf*, or at least to minimise its negative consequences, that a great attempt was made to rationalise the legal theory by finding the comprehensive underlying objectives of Shariʿa (*al-maqāṣid al-kulliyya li al-sharīʿa*). This notion was proposed by the Shafiʿi al-Ghazali in the eleventh century, and was later developed and sophisticated by al-Shatibi (d. 1388). It is rightly stated that

> the doctrine of *maqāṣid al-sharīʿa* has its roots in early Muslim attempts to rationalise both theology and law. In terms of theology, the ideas of the Muʿtazila undoubtedly influenced the emergence of the *maqāṣid* doctrine. The Muʿtazili doctrine that God's decrees are subject to, rather than the origin of, the ideas of good and evil (...) ultimately resulted in an assertion that God is compelled to act in the interests (perhaps the best interests) of humankind. His law must be of benefit to his creation, for if it was not, his qualities of justice and goodness would be compromised.[17]

Al-Shatibi takes the analysis of 'benefits' accruing from the institution of the Shariʿa – used by previous jurists in relation to *qiyās*, *istiḥsān* and *istiṣlāḥ* – and declares, uncompromisingly, that the whole Shariʿa is to promote the welfare of the believers. The benefits that are promoted and preserved when the Shariʿa is instituted are of three basic types: those that are 'necessary' (*ḍarūriyyāt*); those that are 'needed' (*ḥājiyyāt*) to make the obedience to Shariʿa less demanding; and the 'improvements' (*taḥsīniyyāt*) on the benefits already enjoyed by the believers.

Firstly, the five necessary objectives (*ḍarūriyyāt*) are the preservation (*ḥifẓ*) of life (*nafs*), property (*māl*), progeny (*nasl*), sanity (*ʿaql*) and religion (*dīn*). These five objectives are centred on the concept of preservation, *ḥifẓ*, and are based on the divine intention of realising the interest (*maṣlaḥa*) of humans in general and of the believers in particular. The second type of objectives (*ḥājiyyāt*) includes, for example, relieving the sick person from the obligatory fasting against the compensation of providing a pauper with a daily meal during Ramadan (2:184). The third type (*taḥsīniyyāt*) includes, for example, freeing a slave as compensation for many sins (4:92, 5:89, 58:3).

Whereas rulings (*aḥkām*) are produced by deduction, the theory of *maqāṣid* attempts to introduce a method of induction, through which the deduced rulings can be positively judged when they sustain one or more of the *maqāṣid*; deduced rulings that contradict one or more of the *maqāṣid* could be abandoned. The concept of the human underlying this legal worldview is the concept of the *mukallaf*, the duty-bound being, whose destination is determined in accordance with his actions; if he is obedient, he will attain happiness in the afterlife, while misery and punishment await him in case of disobedience.

This view of Shariʿa has been celebrated by modern Muslim reformers all over the Muslim world, because, being based on *maṣlaḥa* and preservation, it provides them with the traditional impetus to reform classical Shariʿa rules, especially in the domain of personal and family code, to make them less discriminatory and closer to the modern legal norms.

But a deeper insight would reveal that these five objectives are deduced from the penal code of Shariʿa (*ḥudūd*), without taking into consideration the moral, ethical and spiritual components of the Qur'an's worldview. The first objective, preservation of life, is deduced from the penalty for illegal killing; retaliation (*qiṣāṣ*), according to the Qur'an, is in fact to maintain 'life' itself (2:178–9.) The second objective, preservation of progeny, is based on the penalty for committing adultery, whether the 100 lashes mentioned in the Qur'an (24:2) but later explained to apply only to the unmarried, or the stoning penalty for the married, which has no Qur'anic ground, but is based on the practical Sunna or on a supposedly abrogated verse.[18] As for the third objective, preservation of property, it is obviously deduced from the penalty for theft, cutting off the hands of the thief (5:38). The fourth objective, preservation of sanity, is deduced from the prohibition against consuming alcohol products, for which there is no penalty in the Qur'an; the penalty of 80 lashes was introduced by the Companions, copying the penalty for false accusation of fornication, *qadhf* (24:4). Preservation of religion, the fifth objective, is based on the death penalty for committing apostasy, *ridda*, which was developed later by the jurists, based on reports with but a single narrator (*ḥadīth āḥād*); no worldly punishment is mentioned in the Qur'an for those who turn their back on Islam after accepting it. What is mentioned is a punishment in the afterlife (3:90, 4:137).

A contextual historical reading, however, reveals that all the penalties mentioned in the Qur'an are borrowed from the pre-Qur'anic Arab tradition. They were borrowed as means, not as ends, and are subject to change in accordance with the changing historical, socio-political and cultural conditions, as long as the ends are secured and sustained.

In the modern Muslim world, where theology, philosophy and mysticism have been marginalised for centuries, the Shariʿa paradigm, whether the legal theory or the substantive law (*furūʿ*), became the only representative of Islam. The two vocabularies, Shariʿa and Islam, became synonymous. However, the legal worldview

– as well as the theological worldview – has concentrated on a very limited portion of the Qur'an.

4. The Qur'an

The world of the Qur'an, on the cosmological level as well as on the ethical–spiritual level,[19] sustains absolute human equality. On the cosmological level, it is stated in the opening verse of the chapter 'Women' (*Al-Nisā'*, 4:1), which addresses humans: 'O mankind! Reverence your Lord Who created you from a single soul from which He created its mate and from them He emanated countless men and women; reverence Allah through Whom you demand your mutual (rights) and (reverence) the wombs (that bore you): for Allah ever watches over you.' It is quite significant that the term 'soul', *nafs*, is a feminine word, and that the mate created from it is named *zawjahā*, which is a masculine word that could be translated as 'twin' or 'husband'. The second meaning is highlighted in 7:189: 'It is He who created you from a single soul and made out of it its mate that he might dwell with her (in love).' As the chapter about women opens with absolute cosmological equality, the entire chapter, which contains most of the legal regulations concerning marriage, should always be connected to the principle of equality. Another point to support this proposition is the frequent reference to justice, *'adl*.

On the ethical–spiritual level, equality is also sustained; both men and women receive the same reward for their righteous actions. In a cluster of verses presenting a discourse of admonition, divine justice is put forward as the governing principle: 'Allah commands justice, the doing of good, and liberality to kith and kin, and He forbids all shameful deeds, and injustice and rebellion: He instructs you, that ye may receive admonition' (16:90). The admonition concludes: 'Whoever works righteousness, man or woman, and has Faith, verily, to him will We give a new Life, a life that is good and pure and We will bestow on such their reward according to the best of their actions' (16:97). See also 4:124, 40:40, 3:195 and 9:71–2, where the believers are presented as one unified community of males and females in mutual intimate guardianship:

> The Believers, men and women, are protectors one of another: they enjoin what is just, and forbid what is evil: they observe regular prayers, practise regular charity, and obey Allah and His Messenger. On them will Allah pour His mercy: for Allah is Exalted in power, Wise.
>
> Allah hath promised to Believers, men and women, gardens under which rivers flow, to dwell therein, and beautiful mansions in gardens of everlasting bliss. But the greatest bliss is the good pleasure of Allah: that is the supreme felicity. (9:71–2)

On the societal level, however, differentiation is acknowledged. In the case of religious difference, there exists a discourse of discrimination. Gender differentiation, however, is free from any discrimination. Qur'anic gender differentiation developed into discrimination in the *fiqh* literature due to a certain cultural and sociohistorical context.

5. Case study: inheritance[20]

An illustrative case is women's inheritance share in the Qur'an. One of the objectives of Islam, deduced from the contextual reading, is 'equality'. If certain Qur'anic stipulations take into account the immediate context of revelation, which was not ready for the full-fledged implementation of equality, they nevertheless allude to a certain future direction to be attained. To start with, one has to understand why, in the middle of the detailed exposition of shares of heirs, the Qur'an states 'your parents and your children; you are not aware who is closer to your benefit' (*ābā'ukum wa abnā'ukum lā tadrūn ayyuhum aqrabu lakum naf'an*, 4:11). Before trying to answer this question, several points should be made.

First, the inheritance system of the Qur'an is obviously based on blood kinship in the male line (*'aṣabiyya*). However, the direction alluded to by the Qur'anic statement above seems to contradict this established system. Looking at this from a wider perspective, one may emphasise that Islam, in fact, has created a higher kinship within the community of believers, the bond of 'faith' as a spiritual–ethical bond. Second, prescribing a half share for the female was a great forward step in a context when inheritance was for males who were able to fight; male children and females were excluded. Third, the early community did not really appreciate including children and females when sharing the wealth of the deceased.[21]

To conclude, it seems to me that the statement alludes to the direction of disregarding the inheritance system based on blood kinship in the male line, and encourages developing an equality-based system in the future, sustained by the objective of equality in the Islamic worldview.

The above analysis presents only one example of the proposed *ijtihād* method, which starts by contextualising the passage not only in the micro-context of *'ulūm al-Qur'ān*, but also in the macro-context of Arabia in the seventh-century milieu. This step will allow unearthing the original historical meaning, that is, the meaning addressing the early community. I have to clarify that this uncovered historical meaning is not final; it is based on *ijtihād* and is open to further *ijtihād* with the discovery of new historical material. The second step is to discern the significance of the uncovered meaning in the context of our modern milieu, taking into account the different socio-political and cultural context of every society.

6. Guardianship *(qiwāma)*

Another case in point is the *fiqh* articulation of the issue of *qiwāma* (guardianship, oversight)[22] as expressed in a key verse:

> Men are the protectors and maintainers of women, because Allah has preferred the one over the other, and because they support them from their means. Therefore the righteous women are devoutly obedient, and guard in (the husband's) absence what Allah would have them guard. As to those women on whose part ye fear disloyalty and ill-conduct (*nushūz*), admonish them, refuse to share their beds and beat them; but if they return to obedience seek not against them means (of annoyance): for Allah is Most High, Great (above you all). (4:34)

In his comprehensive study, Mahmoud rightly pointed out that the traditional exegesis has no problem with the patriarchal nature of the Qur'anic discourse in general, or of this verse in particular.[23] Patriarchy is taken for granted in the classical milieu; a change to this has had to wait until the paradigm change in our modern era of gender equality and feminism. The issue that bothered Islamic legal and exegetical tradition was that of 'beating' as the last solution for bringing a rebellious wife back to obedience if the other two solutions, that is, admonition and deserting the wife's bed – should fail.

The classical discussion starts by trying to contextualise the meaning of the verse by reference to the 'occasion of its revelation' (*sabab al-nuzūl*). According to this occasion, the verse presents an attempt to ease the consequences of the Prophet's immediate response to a woman who came to him complaining of being slapped in the face by her husband, namely, that 'she must retaliate by slapping the husband back',[24] which might have caused powerful protest from the male community. Knowing the occasion of revelation does not mean limiting the legal power of the stipulation in the verse to its historical occasion. According to the exegetical rules, what counts is the general significance of the wording (*'umūm al-lafẓ*), rather than the specific occasion (*khuṣūṣ al-sabab*). Still, beating one's wife to discipline her was not easy to accept within the moral norms of the Qur'an and the practice of the Prophet, who never raised his voice, not to mention his hand, to any of his wives.

In the end, the 'beating' stipulation was limited by the advice to be 'light', not harsh. This is very obvious in Yusuf 'Ali's translation, which adds '(lightly)'. Such attempts by classical as well as modernist interpretation concluded with a virtual abrogation of the 'beating'.

As for the *qiwāma*, which is the foundation of the right to discipline by 'beating', there are two justifications provided by the verse: God's preference for males over females (*bi mā faḍḍala Allāh ba'ḍahum 'alā ba'ḍ*), and the males' responsibility for financially supporting females. There is no problem within the second justification;

for the preference justification, however, the question is: does the verse stipulate a divine, unconditional preference for males over females? Traditional exegesis would sustain the positive answer; modern exegesis would try either to condition or to contextualise it. Again, Yusuf 'Ali's translation does not translate *faḍḍala* as 'preferred'; the translation is 'Allah has given the one more (strength) than the other'. So, according to this interpretation it is male physical power versus female tenderness that justifies the male responsibility.

The question is, why should we demand of the Qur'an that it violate the established rules in the societal domain of meaning? It should be recognised that when the Qur'an sustains absolute equality in both the cosmological and the ethical-spiritual domain, this is the direction in which the Qur'an would like Muslims to upgrade the societal domain of inequality. Traditional law-makers failed to do so because there was no socio-cultural development in this direction. They were able to move in this direction in the domain of physical punishments (*ḥudūd*), because the primitive nascent Muslim community, which the Qur'an initially addressed, was developed into a cosmopolitan civilised empire. By explaining the near-impossible conditions placed on the punishments, they upgraded the penal code, and achieved the same end as in the case of 'beating' wives, that is, virtual abrogation.

The demand for gender equality is a product of our modern era of human rights. The challenging question is: are Muslims able to exert the same courage to upgrade the societal domain of meaning to the high level of the cosmological and the ethico-spiritual domains?

7. From the discussion

How can freedom, equality and justice be established as objectives (maqāṣid) *of Shari'a?*

Abu-Zayd: I have written on the possibility of reaching new *maqāṣid*, by rereading the Qur'an. I established the concept of *freedom* by looking into the wider context of the emergence of Islam in the seventh century. Islam put itself at odds with the *jāhiliyya*. This is sometimes wrongly translated as ignorance. But *jāhiliyya* refers to blind following, adherence to the tribal code … The tribal code is about following in the ways of the fathers – the Qur'an is *against* that (2:170, 5:104). This I think is very important. Freedom is *reasonable* conduct, as opposed to the tribal code.

Another thing about freedom is the fact that every Prophet *invites* other people, whether they belong to a religion, or they are *mushrik*, to convert. So there is this assumption that people are free to change their religion … Freedom is something essential, as one of the *maqāṣid*, like equality and justice. We need to look to freedom not in the context of the classical concept of freedom, but the modern concept of freedom. The modern concept of freedom entails not only freedom from need, but freedom of decision …

The entire universe is constructed on the basis of *justice*. I recommend you read *Sūrat al-Raḥmān*. Justice is a scale, *mizān*, and this image of the scale (55:7–8) is very important in all I have presented here. A scale is very practical to have in the marketplace, but also a very cosmological image.

Equality, as I explained, is maintained in the Qur'an on three levels: the cosmological, the spiritual and the ethical. It is only negotiated – but not disregarded – on the societal level.

*How can we use the approach to different levels of meaning in the Qur'an to deal with the problem of unequal marital roles and rights? How does it help us to go into technicalities about whether something is 'unclear' (*mutashābih*) or 'apparent' (*ẓāhir*) and so on?*

Abu-Zayd: Of course, I cannot encourage you to take up what I'm trying to do ... As I mentioned, the Qur'anic meaning has been fragmented in the history of Islamic law, and we need some sort of 'defragmentation'. But it's very hard work and I don't encourage you to do it – and *never* to mention my name. (*Laughter.*) We're dealing with reality, and I have already been declared an apostate for lesser things. I've become more careful. I'm very proud of being able to do this in the service of Islam.

What I'm trying to do is to provide something useful in any discussion concerning women and women's rights; to tell you that when you hear the phrase *qaṭʿī al-dalāla* ('definitive meaning'), don't be frightened. When someone says, *lā ijtihād fī-mā fīhi al-naṣṣ* ('no independent judgment where there's a clear text'), don't be intimidated.

It is true that the *fuqahā'* have said this, but they said it in the context that the *naṣṣ* is one among at least five semantic categories ranging from absolute ambiguity to absolute clarity. When the classical *fuqahā'* say 'this is *naṣṣ*', it means that it is a very clear statement in the Qur'an that doesn't need any interpretation. But they also say that clear texts are rare. Clear texts are very, very rare in the Qur'an; they are not the entire Qur'an.

The entire Qur'an as a *naṣṣ* is a modern concept, not a classical concept. *Al-naṣṣ al-qur'ānī* is a modern concept that belongs to the twentieth century, to the development of linguistic study, literary criticism. The *fuqahā'* were not aware of it. It is very important how the word is used in a specific domain of meaning that belongs to a specific discipline.

So don't be intimidated when someone quotes a Qur'anic verse and says 'this is definitive in meaning' or 'no *ijtihād* where there's a clear text'. Because all these texts, all these phrases need interpretation. I quote here the great Iranian scholar Mohammed Mojtahedi Shabestari: There is not one single word in the Qur'an that is clear by itself. You need to go to the context, to the phrase, to the syntax, and to move from the syntax to the style, from the style to the mode of narrative. Here you have hermeneutics, rather than *tafsīr*. If you deepen your knowledge about this, you will not be frightened by all this yelling.

Notes

1 The author used various Qur'an translations, including (as here) Yusuf 'Ali's, with modifications – Eds.

2 Abu-Zayd had intended to revise his chapter to analyse marriage, divorce and guardianship (*wilāya*) in addition to the subjects covered here – Eds.

3 Counting from the beginning of Muhammad's public preaching of the Qur'an. – Eds.

4 Fazlur Rahman's double movement is a representative example of this effort. First, the Qur'an is recognised as 'the divine response through the Prophet's mind to the moral–social situation of the Prophet's Arabia, particularly to the problems of the commercial Meccan society'. In order to bring its meaning to our modern situation, the process of the 'double movement' is suggested, first to move 'from the present situation to Qur'anic times, then back to the present. (…) The first step of the first movement, then, consists of understanding the meaning of the Qur'an as a whole as well as in terms of the specific tenets that constitute responses to specific answers. The second step is to generalise those specific answers and enunciate them as statements of general moral-social objectives that can be "distilled" from specific texts (…) The second movement is to be from the general view to the specific view that is to be formulated and realised now.' Rahman, Fazlur, *Islam and Modernity: Transformation of an Intellectual Tradition* (Chicago: University of Chicago Press, 1982), pp. 5–7.

5 Reinhart, A. Kevin, 'Ethics and the Qur'an', in Jane Dammen McAuliffe (ed.), *Encyclopaedia of the Qur'ān* (hereafter *EQ*), Vol. 2, p. 57, from which is also taken the translation of 7:172 and that of 2:229 below.

6 According to Abu Hamid al-Ghazali, there are 500 verses of legal import, while others count only 150. Al-Suyuti explains, 'if they mean the explicit rules, the Qur'anic verses are limited in number; however, so many rules are deduced from the Qur'anic narratives and parables'. Suyuti, *Itqān fī 'ulūm al-Qur'ān*, chapter 65. Wael Hallaq has argued from the length of the legal verses and from the repetition in the non-legal matter that the Qur'an contains no less legal material than the Torah. Hallaq, Wael, 'Law and the Qur'an', in *EQ*, Vol. 3, p. 150.

7 For the earlier application of the concept without employing the word, see Khadduri, M., 'Maṣlaḥa', in *Encyclopaedia of Islam, Second Edition* (hereafter *EI2*), Vol. 6, p. 738.

8 For the development of this concept, see Paret, R., 'Istiḥsān and Istiṣlāḥ', in *EI2*, Vol. 4, pp. 255–95.

9 Cf. my *Al-Imām al-Shāfi'ī wa al-Ta'sīs al-Īdyulujyā al-Waṣaṭiyya* [Imam al-Shāfi`ī and the Establishment of the Middle Position Ideology] (2nd edn, Cairo: Maktabat Madbuli, 1996), pp. 129–46.

10 Ibn Rushd, *Bidāyat al-Mujtahid wa Nihāyat al-Muqtaṣid*. English translation: Ibn Rushd, *The Distinguished Jurist's Primer*, trans. Imran Ahsan Khan Nyazee, 2 vols (Garnet, 2000), pp. xliii–xlix.

11 The obligatory (*wājib*), recommended (*mandūb*), permitted (*mubāḥ* or *muhkayyar*), disapproved (*makrūh*), and prohibited (*ḥarām*).

12 Jurists differ over whether the form of *amr*, demanding commission of an act, indicates an obligation (*wājib*) or a recommendation (*mandūb*). Similarly, they differ over whether the form of a *nahy* indicates that an act is disapproved (*makrūh*), unlawful (*ḥarām*) or neither.

13 Following Ibn Rushd, these two types of wording create four levels of meanings: (1) the general term (*lafẓ ʿāmm*) applied to all its categories (*yuhmalu ʿalā ʿumūmihi*); (2) the specific term (*lafẓ khāṣṣ*) applied to a single case (*ʿalā al-khuṣūṣ*); (3) the general term intended to be specific in its application (*yurādu bihī al-khuṣūṣ*); and (4) the specific term intended to be general in its application (*bihī al-ʿāmm*). In Ibn Rushd's examples, the general term 'swine' (*khinzīr*) is applied generally to prohibit all kinds of swine in 5:3, whereas in 9:103, *zakāt* is not made obligatory on all kinds of 'wealth', but on *māl* in particular. The fourth category, the specific term to be applied generally, includes (a) the use of the higher meaning to indicate the lower meaning, (b) use of the lower meaning to indicate the higher, and (c) the indication of equivalent meanings. For instance, the prohibition of verbal insult to parents in 17:23 is a case of using the lower meaning to indicate the higher, as it includes the prohibition of beating and abuse.

14 Four semantic domains arranged according to the level of ambiguity and/or clarity of a word or a phrase: (1) *naṣṣ*, which has a single clear definite explicit meaning; (2) *mujmal*, which has two possible meanings, the immediate and the non-immediate, with no indication how it should be interpreted; (3) *muḥtamal*, wherein the non-immediate meaning is the most probable; and (4) *ẓāhir*, wherein the immediate meaning is the most probable. There is no dispute that the *naṣṣ* indicates a ruling, whereas the *mujmal* does not imply any ruling (*ḥukm*) because of its ambiguity.

15 Ibn Rushd is of the opinion that if the actions occur as an explication of an obligatory *mujmal* Qur'anic enjoinment, they indicate an obligation, and if they occur as an explication of a recommended *mujmal* Qur'anic enjoinment, they indicate a recommendation. If they do not occur as an explanation for a *mujmal*, but belong to a recommended category, they indicate recommendation. If they belong to the classification of *mubāḥ* – permissible acts – they indicate permissibility. As for the *iqrārāt*, they only indicate permissibility.

16 *Samʿ*: 'hearing'; what has been orally transmitted; authoritative transmissions, often the Qur'an and hadith – Eds.

17 Gleave, R. M., 'Maḳāṣid al-sharīʿa', in *EI2*, Vol. 12, p. 569 (spelling adapted).

18 This is one example, perhaps the only one, of abrogating the text but keeping its rule in force. The supposedly abrogated verse is '*wa al-shaykhu wa al-shaykhatu idhā zanaya fa irjumūhumā al-battata nikālan mina Allāh*'. For me, it is not sound Qur'anic style at all.

19 A domain of meaning which should *not* be considered as expressing the Qur'an's view on the position of males and females is the polemic discourse that ridicules the veneration of female deities (53:19–28, 37:149–160, cf. 3:117) by Arab pagans who assigned daughters to God, while they preferred males for themselves (43:16, 16:57–59).

20 Abu-Zayd's draft discussed *qiwāma* before inheritance. The present structure, with a brief example of an approach to inheritance leading up to the longer discussion of *qiwāma*, better reflects the focus of his talk – Eds.

21 For these two points, see al-Tabari's *Jami' al-Bayān 'an Ta'wīl āy al-Qur'ān*, 8:30–31.

22 Abu-Zayd had intended to continue with a discussion of *wilāya* in the marriage contract, based on Ibn Rushd, *Bidāyat* – Eds.

23 Mahmoud, Mohamed, 'To beat or not to beat: On the exegetical dilemmas over Qur'ān, 4:34', *Journal of the American Oriental Society* 126/4 (2006), pp. 537–50.

24 *Ibid.*, p. 539.

8

GENDER EQUALITY AND THE HADITH OF THE PROPHET MUHAMMAD

Reinterpreting the Concepts of *Maḥram* and *Qiwāma*[1]

Faqihuddin Abdul Kodir

> We do not say, and any reasonable person cannot say, that women are above men or lower than men by a degree or more. But we have seen people who revile [women] the worst of revilements and disdain them and deny them most of their rights. – Al-Jahiz (d. 869)[2]

1. Introduction

As I was trained in an Islamic boarding school by the religious scholar Husein Muhammad, who has later become known as an emerging Indonesian Muslim feminist,[3] I have for quite some time been disturbed by the ambiguity of Islamic jurisprudence (*fiqh*) in dealing with issues related to women. For example, on the one hand, Islamic jurisprudence, referring to the Qur'an (2:282), considers two female witnesses equal to one male witness in terms of testifying for financial contracts. On the other hand, the sciences of the Hadith (*'ulūm al-ḥadīth*) prescribe that one woman is equal to one man in terms of the reception and delivery of *ḥadīth* (pl. *aḥādīth*, hereafter simply 'hadith'),[4] the second source of Islamic teachings. Since testifying about financial contracts is not nearly as important as testifying regarding traditions that have been passed down to generations of Muslims, the opinion disqualifying a lone woman from giving evidence in the case of financial contracts is questionable. However, this inconsistency within Islamic jurisprudence in dealing with women's issues opens up possibilities of rereading the texts of the Hadith in order to argue for justice for women.

The images of women in Islamic jurisprudence (*fiqh*) are established by Muslim theologians far more often using the Hadith than the Qur'an, which deals mostly with principles of Islamic teachings.[5] Nevertheless, reinterpretations of Islamic texts, establishing what Amina Wadud calls a 'tawhidic paradigm'[6] underpinning gender equality in Islam, have proliferated with regard to the Qur'an, but have largely passed over the Hadith, even though the Hadith has played a very important role in prescribing Islamic teachings throughout Muslim history.

Some scholars, like Asma Barlas, dismiss the Hadith as a possible source for a paradigm of gender equality in Islam as it has been corrupted by political interests, and it has texts that contradict each other and are influenced by Mediterranean cultures as well as by Judaism and Christianity.[7] Others dismiss the the Hadith as being of minor importance compared to the Qur'an. Wadud, for instance, concentrates her 'gender jihad' exclusively on the Qur'an, which is, she argues, 'congruent with the orthodox understanding of the inerrancy of Qur'anic preservation versus historical contradiction within the Hadith literature'.[8]

To the contrary, as I will be arguing in this chapter, the Hadith is very important to advocacy for gender equality in Islam, for the classical sciences of the Hadith (*'ulūm al-ḥadīth*) and the principles of Islamic jurisprudence (*uṣūl al-fiqh*) offer a hermeneutical basis for a contextual reading. As the Hadith has played a very important role in prescribing Islamic teachings throughout Muslim history,[9] its reinterpretation for the purpose of arguing for gender justice should be a central concern in the face of contemporary changed conditions of Muslims' lives. While many progressive Muslims have established a hermeneutical basis for reading the Qur'an for gender justice, this chapter supports those who call for a rereading of the Hadith to encourage equal relationships between women and men.[10]

For the purpose of rereading, this chapter takes the Hadith to be a scholarly effort (*ijtihād*) by classical *'ulamā'* to shape and interpret the concept of following (*ittibā'*) the Prophet. The *ijtihād* here is not only about the interpretation of the Hadith and the implementation of its meaning, but also its transmission from one generation to another and its collection in the period of codification of early Islamic knowledge. The transmission, as well as the collection of hadiths, should, accordingly, be perceived as the *ijtihād* of the collectors within the historicity of their context-based understanding. Moreover, works of interpretation of hadiths are obviously perceived as human scholarly efforts by the majority of scholars and jurists.

Within the complex grey areas of *ijtihād*, a contextual reading of the Hadith as a hermeneutical process should be applied to develop the ethical guidelines of

Islamic family law known as the 'objectives of Islamic law' (*maqāṣid al-sharīʿa*) and the 'logic of the rulings' (*ʿillat al-aḥkām*). As regards this reading, many progressive Muslims have noted that the Qur'an emphasises the universality of the principle of justice. As it relates to the relations between women and men, this principle is seen in at least three aspects. First, women and men are created from the same entity (4:1), and for that reason they are of equal standing. Second, both women and men have the obligation to live good lives and to do good works (16:97). Third, women and men have the same right to be rewarded for their works (33:35).

The suggestion of rereading the Hadith in this chapter will be based on the universality of this principle of justice as the ethical purpose of Islamic teachings. Accordingly, this chapter calls for a reinterpretation of the Hadith that should be made in line with those aspects established by the Qur'an to ensure the principle of gender justice. Arguably, as mentioned by Ibn Qayyim al-Jawziyya (d. 1350), the ideals of justice and the welfare of the community are the foundational principles of Islam.[11] Thus, interpretations that are contrary to the principles of justice must be challenged and rectified. In this work, reinterpretation also highlights the inevitable historicity of the Hadith, that is, the essential, intrinsic, socio-historical embeddedness of much of the content.

2. What is the Hadith?

The term 'Hadith' is usually defined as an action, in the form of words, deeds or manifestations of approval, that can be traced to the Prophet Muhammad. Other terms used to refer to Hadith include *sunna*, *khabar* and *athar*. The term *sunna* is most common, which is why Hadith is sometimes also known as the Sunna of the Prophet. The literal meaning of *sunna* is 'way' or 'road', and it is therefore often translated as 'tradition' in the sense of a course of action commonly followed by the Prophet. *Khabar* literally means 'news', and *athar* means 'heritage'. The term *ḥadīth* itself means 'something that is new' or 'something that is reported', but it has come to refer to something reported from or about the Prophet.

Later scholars of Hadith, particularly after al-Shafiʿi (d. 819), arrived at a consensus that the Sunna is identical with the corpus of hadiths, and refers only to the Prophet, whereas in early Islam the Sunna had been more broadly defined as the ways of the Prophet, the Companions and the community ('the people of Medina'). Scholars of Hadith, pioneered by al-Shafiʿi, then proposed an interplay between the Qur'an and the Sunna in shaping Islamic teachings, and argued that the former should be explained and interpreted by the latter. Because of this development, the majority of Muslim scholars were convinced that the Hadith, as synonymous with the Sunna, was one of the authentic sources of Islamic rulings and teachings.[12]

However, in the hierarchy of sources the Hadith ranks second after the Qur'an. The Hadith serves as a clarification of the revelations contained in the Qur'an.

Insofar as the Hadith is also regarded as revelation according to some scholars – though it is problematic to have revelation other than the Qur'an – it is perceived by the majority as an indirect and secondary source, the accuracy of which is not necessarily guaranteed. The accuracy of the Qur'an as the very word of God as revealed to Muhammad, by contrast, is unquestionable, because the chain of transmission of the Qur'an from the time of its revelation to Muhammad, to its being written down in definitive form, included a large number of transmitters of the same text in each generation.

There is less certainty that the Hadith contains accurate reports of the Prophet's actual words and actions, simply because the number of individuals in each generation who orally relayed those reports from one person to the next is smaller. In most cases, there were only one or two transmitters in each generation. The fewer the links between the Prophet's words and the permanent written record, the greater the possibility of a mistake, an omission or an outright untruth.

In his analysis of the sources of Islamic law, for instance, al-Shafi'i categorised the Hadith as 'individual reports' (*akhbār khāṣṣa*), in the sense that they were heard and reported by a limited number of individuals, sometimes only one. This differs from the Qur'an, which al-Shafi'i termed a 'general' or 'public' report (*khabar 'āmm*) because it was heard, witnessed and transmitted publicly, and therefore accepted by and acceptable to all Muslims. The fact that knowledge of the Prophet's actions was much more limited than knowledge of the contents of the Qur'an makes it more difficult to justify applying the terms of the Hadith to all Muslims. Thus, the authenticity of the Hadith is 'strongly presumed' rather than axiomatic. It is for that reason that al-Shafi'i said, 'We are not justified in demanding repentance of one who is doubtful as to the truth of a hadith.'[13]

The Hadith carries less legal authority than the Qur'an but more than either the consensus of Muslim scholars (*ijmā'*) or the process of analogy (*qiyās*), which form the other sources of Islamic law. For that reason, scholars of Islamic jurisprudence (*fiqh* and *uṣūl al-fiqh*) have held that the authority of the Hadith only extends to matters of religious practice and not to matters of faith and creed.[14] The authority of the Hadith as evidence of God's will derives from the fact that the Prophet Muhammad possessed a special understanding regarding the meaning of the Qur'an, and thus these texts have primary significance as explanations and elaborations of the meaning of God's revelation. The Hadith serves a number of different functions in relation to the Qur'an. Sometimes it confirms the revelations given in the Qur'an, sometimes it supplies an interpretation of the Qur'an, and at other times it refers to new legal matters, which are not mentioned in the divine revelation but which have to be judged in accordance with its basic spirit.

Only a few hadiths were transmitted through multiple narrators (*tawātur*) like the Qur'an. The larger part of the Hadith – if not the whole – is only transmitted through a solitary link (*āḥād*). However, the solitary character of the transmission of a hadith is, according to the scholars, not an obstacle to its authority as a source of Islamic law. According to al-Shafiʿi, even though a hadith is the report of a single individual, it can still be accepted and put into practice, just as the testimony of a single witness is sufficient in a court of law, or as we rely on information from a single individual in daily life. However, he also wrote that

> If anyone can say that there is a consensus (*ijmāʿ*) by the religious scholars (*ʿulamāʾ*) confirming the authority of the solitary report (*al-khabar al-wāḥid*), it should be me. But that is not the case, I only say that as far as I know the legal experts do not disagree (i.e., there is no *ijmāʿ*) that the solitary report is a source for Islamic law (...)[15]

The quotation above implies that the authority of the Hadith is accepted by most but not all Muslim scholars (*ʿulamāʾ*), while the Qur'an, on the other hand, is accepted by all. The Hadith is far from gaining recognition as a revelation besides the Qur'an by a consensus of scholars and jurists. At best, the Hadith is considered as a vital source for exegesis of the revelation – the Qur'an – and as a crucial criterion for flourishing Islamic jurisprudence.

In sum, the discussion above at least shows the scholarly assumption that the establishment of the Hadith, especially a particular hadith, as a source of Islamic teachings is a matter of *ijtihād*. Many of the scholars and the jurists even consider the Hadith as 'largely transmitted in the words of the narrators themselves'.[16] These features will be more noticeable in the following section, which discusses efforts made by scholars of Hadith in selecting, compiling, accepting, rejecting and critiquing texts according to their chain (*sanad*) and content (*matn*).

3. Studying the *sanad* and *matn* of the Hadith

At the time of the Prophet, the Hadith consisted solely of its content: the text (*matn*) or the message embodied in the Prophet's words or actions. After his death, the Hadith typically came to comprise two parts: the content and the chain of narrators, the *sanad*. With the passage of time, the evaluation of the authenticity of a hadith has become more and more difficult. The categorisation of a particular text as valid (*ṣaḥīḥ*), sound (*ḥasan*) or weak (*ḍaʿīf*) is based on the reliability of the content (*matn*) and on the narrative chain (*sanad*). In short, a text is not considered to be valid, nor can it be implemented as the basis for a legal ruling, until both its *sanad* and *matn* have been subjected to critical evaluation.

The critique of the *sanad* and *matn* should be inseparable in the narration and implementation of a hadith. While this critical methodology has been employed by Hadith scholars from the early period of Islam, they typically concentrate on the transmitters of the hadith, while the Islamic legal experts (*fuqahā'*) focus on the content. Critiquing the *sanad* involves investigating the integrity of the individuals named in the chain of transmission, from the last person in the chain who recorded the text, to the first person who had direct contact with the Prophet. In the evaluation of a *sanad*, the links in the chain of transmission must all be directly connected to the previous narrator, and each one must also meet a standard of integrity measured by his reliability (*thiqa*), honesty (*'adāla*) and good memory (*ḍābiṭ*).[17] Al-Shafi'i added the requirement that the transmitters of a hadith must comprehend its meaning.[18] If this is not the case, the hadith is considered weak (*ḍa'īf*), even if the deficiency relates to only one of the criteria in one generation of transmitters. In other words, if one or more of the following deficiencies are found in a transmitter, a text would be described as 'weak': the transmitter is unknown by Hadith scholars; disapproved of by the scholars; considered corrupt or of limited integrity; known to have produced invalid hadiths; or known to have lacked sufficient knowledge of the particular text. A weak hadith does not constitute a legal proof (*ḥujja*).[19] Generally speaking, Hadith scholars agree that the validity of a *sanad* does not inevitably indicate that the *matn* is valid, and vice versa. As stated by the Hanbali scholar Ibn Qayyim al-Jawziyya (d. 1350): 'It is understood that the validity of a *sanad* is one condition for the validity of a hadith, but it does not automatically guarantee that the hadith is valid.'[20]

For instance, internal inconsistency and confusion of the *matn* can add to the acknowledged weakness of a hadith. Accordingly, from the beginning, Hadith scholars have conscientiously evaluated the *matn* of each text for possible inconsistencies and confusion, known as defects of the Hadith (*'ilal al-ḥadīth*). In his work *al-Mawḍū'āt al-Kubrā*, Ibn al-Jawzi (d. 1201) mentions forms of defect that occur in *matn*. These include inconsistencies with a verse of the Qur'an, a more valid text of the Hadith or a contrary historical fact; inconsistencies in logic; and inappropriate linguistic formulation.[21]

These evaluations were subsequently further developed by Islamic legal scholars and theologians, who often had a greater interest in the correct implementation of a hadith, particularly when it affected the other foundations of law, such as the Qur'an, the consensus of Muslim scholars (*ijmā'*) and analogical reasoning (*qiyās*).[22] A text is considered inconsistent when it differs from a text related by another narrator with greater integrity, or from another hadith that is related by a larger number of narrators with the same level of integrity. There are several types of inconsistencies in *matn*: they can take the form of additions to the text, an inversion, a manifest discrepancy, a writing error or the inclusion of a narrator's interpretation within the hadith itself.

Thus, the critique of the *sanad* and the *matn* of reports related to the Hadith has been recognised and practised since the time of the Companions of the Prophet.

Indeed, the Companions debated whether the validity and truth of accounts communicated among them required confirmation. Some Companions readily accepted accounts coming from other Companions, while others demanded verification in the form of the testimony of another person or an oath in support of the transmission. Some Companions rejected hadiths narrated by their fellow Companions because they were deemed not credible, were considered to violate the demands of the Qur'an, or were inconsistent with reason or historical fact.

In his book *al-Ijāba*, al-Zarkashi (d. 1392) has recorded that 'A'isha, the wife of the Prophet, objected to certain hadiths from the Prophet narrated by 24 Companions, including hadiths that are available in *Ṣaḥīḥ al-Bukhārī*.[23] Among these is a hadith that states 'the sources of misfortune are three: horses, women, and houses'.[24] The text is rejected by 'A'isha based on the following verse from the Qur'an:

> No misfortune can happen on earth or in your souls but is recorded in a decree before We bring it into existence: that is truly easy for Allah (57:22).[25]

The method of comparing Hadith reports with verses from the Qur'an was developed most extensively by scholars from the Hanafi school. For them, Qur'anic texts that have a broad meaning (*'āmm*) could not have their meaning narrowed down by a hadith.[26] For example, the statement in the Qur'an that any Qur'anic verse may be recited in prayer (73:20) must be understood to have a broad purpose fulfilled by the recitation of any verse or chapter during prayer. The hadith stating that the recitation during prayer has to include the opening chapter (*Sūrat al-Fātiḥa*) cannot thus restrict the meaning of the Qur'ànic verse, which has always been broad. Accordingly, unlike the Maliki, Shafi'i and Hanbali schools, recitation of the *Fātiḥa* in ritual prayer is not considered obligatory by the Hanafi school.[27]

Scholars often compare a *matn* or a text with historical fact and with other texts in order to critically evaluate the text. Muhammad al-Ghazali (1917–1996), a contemporary Muslim scholar, used this technique to critically assess a valid hadith, which suggests that it is preferable for women to perform their prayers in a secluded place.[28] In critiquing this hadith, al-Ghazali argued that the *matn* does not accord with historical fact as shown by other, more valid hadiths, which demonstrate that throughout the Prophet's lifetime, his wives and his female Companions regularly joined in congregational prayers without ever being excluded or reprimanded. Indeed, a special entrance had been constructed for women to enter the Prophet's mosque. On one occasion the Prophet heard a baby crying while he was leading the prayer. He quickly completed the prayers out of concern for the baby and its mother. An even more pointed indication of the inauthenticity of the hadith above is the fact that the Prophet issued a directive that women could not be prevented from entering the mosque.[29]

To sum up this section, the discussion of *sanad* and *matn* in the sciences of the Hadith opens up possibilities to reevaluate prevalent texts that disregard women and to centre Islamic thought, accordingly, on those that promote equality and kindness to women. In other words, a reformulation of the compilation of hadiths regarding gender issues, in accordance with an ethic of justice, is not only possible but is grounded in the classical intellectual tradition of hadith criticism in both the sciences of the Hadith and the theories of jurisprudence. In turn, the work of ʿAbd al-Halim Abu Shuqqa (1924–1995), *Taḥrīr al-Mar'a fī ʿAṣr al-Risāla*,[30] should be acknowledged as a novel compilation of authentic hadiths on liberating women in the period of revelation. How Islamic theoretical jurisprudence (*uṣūl al-fiqh*) provides a contextual reading of the Hadith will be discussed in the next section.

4. Contextual reading of the Hadith

Through a critical reading of the *matn*, the scholars of Hadith and the jurists have also made attempts (*ijtihād*) to arrive at a more precise appreciation of the meaning contained in the hadiths, which can help to clarify the correlation between particular hadiths and other sources. A hadith's text, scholars of Islamic jurisprudence argue, is also a linguistic text, and its meaning is thus related to the structure, character and vocabulary of the language in which it is expressed. Every language is a product of the culture to which it belongs, and functions within a cultural environment. In addition, the communication of ideas by means of linguistic symbols, and the interpretation of those symbols by readers, entails the inevitable risk of diverse, incompatible, and even reductionist and distorted understandings. As a result, diversity of interpretation is inescapable.

This diversity in interpretation is something that the Prophet himself observed and acknowledged. That point is illustrated by an incident commonly cited by scholars of Islamic legal theory (*uṣūl al-fiqh*). As the Companions were departing to return home after the Battle of Ahzab, the Prophet told them that no person was allowed to perform the first evening prayers (*ʿaṣr*) unless they had reached the village of Banu Qurayza.[31] Later, when the time for completion of the *ʿaṣr* prayer was nearly past and the group of Companions had not yet reached Banu Qurayza, they fell into disagreement. Some insisted that they were not to perform the *ʿaṣr* prayer along the way, and that the prayer must be performed in Banu Qurayza as commanded by the Prophet, even if that meant praying after the proper time had passed. Others in the group were of the opinion that the Prophet had instructed them to pray in Banu Qurayza in order to encourage them to travel swiftly, and that the *ʿaṣr* prayer should be performed at the proper time even if they had not yet reached the village.[32]

These two different approaches towards the interpretation of the hadith – one literal and the other contextual – are also evident among the scholars of the generation after the Prophet and the Companions within the disciplines of law (*fiqh*), exegesis (*tafsīr*) and religious doctrine (*ʿaqīda*). Within Islamic jurisprudence, for example, a hadith regarding the almsgiving at the end of the fasting month (*zakāt al-fiṭr*) was interpreted in different ways by different scholars. While some Shafiʿi scholars interpreted a hadith regarding the obligation to provide wheat and dates at the end of the fasting month as a fixed and unvarying requirement, others adopted a slightly broader interpretation of the hadith, allowing payment with other staple foods besides those mentioned in the text.

The Hanafi school, however, interpreted the hadith as imposing a more general obligation to fulfil the needs of the poor at the close of the fasting month. According to this interpretation, the form of the *zakāt* is unimportant. It can be paid in wheat, dates or other staples having equal value, provided that the needs of the poor are satisfied. Indeed, the *zakāt al-fiṭr* can even take the form of cash equal to the value of wheat or dates, since the poor know best what their needs are, and cash can be used to supply those needs.

Similar differences regarding interpretive approaches have been adopted with respect to the hadith stipulating the payment of *zakāt al-fiṭr* in the early morning, that is, the payment that should be made after sunrise but before the communal prayer of the first day after the end of the fasting month. Some scholars regard this as a hard and fast rule. Others interpret the text within the social context in which it was first articulated – that is, in which people lived simply, in small, close-knit communities, and had limited access to food. They suggest that charity can be distributed earlier too, including at the beginning of Ramadan. The only stipulation is that it be paid or delivered within the time frame specified by the Prophet, which made it possible to collect and distribute the *zakāt al-fiṭr*.

The discussion above illustrates that a particular hadith can be given a literal, textual meaning or can be interpreted substantively, according to its broader purpose. The use of a textual approach will generally have the effect of narrowing the scope of its application. The use of such approaches undermines the notion that Islamic law can be received and implemented at all times and in all places. Indeed, calls to avoid such literal and simplistic interpretations of hadith are heard with increasing frequency in the Muslim world.

It is in this context that Muhammad al-Ghazali has sharply criticised the growing tendency to use an overly literal approach to the interpretation of the Hadith. In order to provide some guidelines for using interpretative as opposed to literal approaches, his student, Yusuf al-Qaradawi, a prominent contemporary Muslim scholar, proposed eight basic guidelines for arriving at a proper understanding of hadiths: comparing the text with verses from the Qur'an; comparing the text with other texts that have similar themes; classifying texts that are contradictory in meaning; investigating the causes, circumstances and purposes of a particular hadith; distinguishing texts that concern particular as opposed to general matters; distinguishing texts that are literal and metaphorical; distinguishing texts that concern the supernatural from those that concern the natural world; and finally, and most essentially, ascertaining the meaning of a hadith with a dictionary of Arabic.[33]

These guidelines are a blueprint for a contextualised interpretation of the literal terms of the Hadith. The words of hadiths do not change. What changes are the conditions of social life within which the hadiths are implemented. That is the reason why the inquiry into the circumstances that prompted the emergence of the hadiths, known as *ʿilm asbāb al-wurūd*, has become such a critical area of investigation in Hadith studies.

The texts are historical records. As such, they are intimately connected to the social dynamics of Arab society at the time of the Prophet. Consequently, in light of the fundamentally contextual character of the Hadith, a number of scholars have adopted an understanding informed by the essential purpose of the text and the root problem that it addresses. The meaning inscribed in the literal language of the text is not regarded as definitive and need not be applied in an unconditional manner. In essence, then, as social contexts change, the essential purpose of the Hadith, rather than its literal meaning, should be emphasised.

Ibn Khaldun (d. 1406) illustrated this point using the hadith that states, 'Leadership is in the hands of the Quraysh.' While some read the text literally and considered one who does not accept the political leadership of the Quraysh as an apostate,[34] Ibn Khaldun understood it within the context of the time, when the Quraysh dominated the political sphere. The hadith, according to him, should be taken to refer to leadership qualities and not to eternal tribal hereditary rights to political office. Accordingly, later, as political power became more dispersed, even though the language of the hadith remained the same, the texts did not provide a mandate for Qurayshi hegemony but a comment on the leadership qualities required for Muslim rule.[35]

Muhammad al-Ghazali made the same point in connection with the hadith that states, 'A people that turns over leadership to a woman will never be happy.' He argued that this hadith must be understood in context; otherwise, it does not accord with the reality that women have often achieved positions of leadership in the world. The hadith addresses a situation in which a Persian queen was in line to succeed to the throne. At the time, the social and political circumstances in Persia were chaotic. The country had been defeated by the Romans and there was a general state of unrest. The times demanded a leader who was strong, disciplined and had a deep understanding of the political problems at hand. The throne, however, was given over to a young woman, who was inexperienced and had little understanding of the problems of the realm. In the hadith, the Prophet was addressing these realities, and not delivering a legal ruling prohibiting women in general from holding positions of political leadership.[36]

According to the Tunisian scholar Muhammad ibn ʿAshur (1879–1973), other hadiths concerning prohibitions, particularly those referring to body ornamentation, should also be understood within the context of Arab society at the time. He argues that these hadiths were revealed at a time when certain fashions such as particular hairstyles, shaved eyebrows and the use of hair extensions marked women as commercial sex workers, but that such practices cannot be considered eternally forbidden. In other words, the prohibitions were not directed at specific markers of identity but rather at the associated amoral behaviour. After all, cutting one's hair or lengthening it are simply ways to make one attractive. Thus, if it is grooming that is to be prohibited, then all forms of grooming must be forbidden for everyone. But Islam allows us, including women, to make ourselves more attractive, provided it is not for the purpose of engaging in behaviour that lowers our self-respect or inhibits justice.[37]

Using this contextual reading method, we may go further to reinterpret all texts of the Hadith commonly understood as sources of discrimination against women in Islam. This method deliberately adopts the ethical principles of Islam as the light by which to understand the messages of its revelation, which were presented, interpreted and applied within the realities of political, social, historical, cultural and economic contexts. In the next two sections, I will reread the text that forbids women from travelling unless accompanied by their relative (*maḥram*) and the text that outlines the concept of household leadership (*qiwāma*) in the light of the principle of justice within the changed realities of our contemporary social context.

5. The ethic of the concept of *maḥram* on women's journeys

Contemporary interpretations of many hadiths continue to engender inequality and unfairness in the relationship between men and women. This inequality violates the most fundamental principles of the Qur'an and Hadith. For that reason, a reinterpretation of hadiths that address the relations between women and men is imperative in order to turn the ideal of social justice embodied in Islam into a practical reality. The hermeneutical ground for the project of reinterpretation is, in the word of Sa'diyya Shaikh, to 'unearth [the] construction of a religious anthropology in which humanity, male and female, is presented in ways that are holistic, non-hierarchical, egalitarian and, I dare to say, Islamic!'[38]

Take, for example, the hadith of Abdullah bin 'Umar, which prohibits women from going out by themselves:

> It is impermissible for a woman who believes in Allah and the Day of Judgment to travel the distance that can be covered in a journey of one day and one night without being accompanied by a close relative whom she may not marry (*maḥram*).[39]

In a feminist perspective, it would seem clear that a patriarchal way of thought lies behind this text and its interpretation among scholars and jurists. In the patriarchal view, the woman's body is problematic and not only should be covered to limit the perilous temptation (*fitna*) it represents, but should be prohibited from public space, and, moreover, from a long-distance journey on her own. A quick reading of the book of *Subul al-Salām* (Paths to Peace), a commentary on hadiths of legal import (*aḥādīth aḥkām*) by al-San'ani (d. 1768), confirms this assumption. This book links the above hadith with the nature of bodily temptation of women. The book also mentions the opinion of al-Nawawi, who views the matter as a general restriction without any consideration of the duration mentioned in the text. The opinion that prohibits only young, not older, women, mentioned in the *Subul*, also justifies, obviously, the feminist assumption that the text was produced and interpreted on patriarchal grounds.[40]

However, as I discuss in the following, the issue was disputed among Hadith scholars and jurists, and this dispute uncovers the possibility of a less gender-biased interpretation. In the account of Ibn Hazm (d. 1064) in his magnum opus *Al-Muḥallā bi al-Āthār*, versions of the above hadith as well as opinions of jurists on the matter differ. One version states that the Prophet prohibits a woman from journeying unaccompanied by a *maḥram* for more than three days and three nights; another mentions a journey of three days; yet another, two days; one states the prohibition even for a journey of only one day; and there is also a version that unconditionally forbids an unaccompanied woman from making any journey.[41]

In the report of al-Zuhri (d. 742), however, 'A'isha, the beloved wife of the Prophet, disavows the text by saying: 'Not every woman has a *maḥram*.'[42] This saying of 'A'isha is considered by al-Zarkashi (d. 1392) as her criticism against her fellow Companions who narrate the above hadith from the Prophet. Moreover, some reports state that 'A'isha made a journey and was not accompanied by her *maḥram*.[43]

Though the majority of jurists have adopted a literal understanding of the prohibition rather than seeking the reason (*'illa*) behind the text, legal opinions vary on 'the issue of an unaccompanied woman', particularly with regard to the matter of hajj. We may reveal an ethical purpose of the ruling from the features of this dispute. Interestingly, literalists such as Ibn Hazm avow the possibility of a woman travelling alone on hajj. He opens the discussion by saying:

> A woman who has no husband nor close relative performing hajj with her may travel without any requirement (to find a *maḥram*); if she has a husband obliged to do hajj, he should travel to accompany her; if he does not do so, he becomes disobedient towards God the Almighty. Therefore, she may travel alone without him for the hajj and he has no right to forbid her.[44]

In arguing his opinion, Ibn Hazm interprets the hadith concerning the prohibition with reference to the Qur'an (3:97), which describes hajj as a religious duty for men and women (*al-nās*); to hadiths about women being permitted to go to mosques; and to the hadith that commands a man to accompany his wife, rather than forbidding her from the journey of hajj.[45]

However, in the absence of an ethical perspective on the issue, and as part of the patriarchal context of his society, Ibn Hazm takes a stance only on the direct literal logic of the rulings. Accordingly, he limits the permission only to performing the hajj, and even then only the obligatory one. He still encourages women to stay at home and asks them to obey their husband. In the case of non-obligatory hajj, for instance, he argues that women are not allowed to leave their home without their husband. Indeed, according to Ibn Hazm, to obey the husband is the highest religious duty for the wife, and it ranks above performing the non-obligatory hajj.

A contextual reading entitles one to link the hadith on the *maḥram* to the ethical principle that vulnerable people should be protected from the possibility of violence, particularly in the chaotic social context of wars. This principle is not only advocated by many verses of the Qur'an, but found amid the diversity and complexity of the classical scholarly debate on the issue. For example, protection is linked to the issue of accompanying women on their journeys in the Shafiʿi school of law, under the rubric 'safety of ways' (*amn al-ṭuruq*).

In the commentary on the hadith that 'A woman should not travel', Ibn Hajar al-ʿAsqalani (d. 1448) quotes in his *Fatḥ al-Bārī* the opinion of al-Karabisi (d. 859), the student of al-Shafiʿi, who sees no problems with a woman travelling alone on her hajj or *ʿumra*, as long as her safety is guaranteed during her journey; al-Qaffal (d. 1026) and Abu al-Mahasin al-Ruyani (d. 1107) extend the argument to travel for any purpose.[46] Thus, the security of a woman's journey should be posited as the objective of the hadith, not the literal prohibition of the journey itself. It stands to reason, accordingly, that all components of society would be under a common obligation to ensure the protection and security of the entire populace.

In addition, the literal reading of the hadith that prohibits women from travelling should be critiqued with reference to other texts of the Hadith. The two following hadiths provide further evidence that women have the right to travel without any religious restriction because the *maḥram* rulings are only a matter of suggestion in the context of tribal society. First, in the hadith of Abu Saʿid al-Khudri, the sentence 'A woman should not travel without being accompanied by her close relative', is followed by 'Journeys should not be conducted unless to three mosques; the mosque al-Haram, the mosque of al-Aqsa, and my mosque.'[47] Both sentences are mentioned in one hadith reported by al-Bukhari. Although both use the same negation, *lā*, many jurists interpret the former sentence as prohibition, but the latter only as a suggestion. The latter sentence, according to the jurists, only suggests the best places in religious terms for Muslims to travel. Accordingly, no Muslim is prohibited from travelling to other than the three mosques, or even to other places than mosques. If the second sentence should be taken as a suggestion, I submit the same should apply to the first sentence. Thus, the first sentence also merely suggests a woman not travel without her close relative. A woman, therefore, is not prohibited from travelling alone, particularly if the journey is safe and good for her.

Moreover, it is reported by 'Adi ibn Hatim in the reliable collection of al-Bukhari that

> Once a man came to the Prophet, peace be upon him, complaining of the condition of poverty, while another came with the case of brigandage. Then the Prophet asked his companion 'Adi bin Hatim: 'Have you seen the city of al-Hira?' 'No,' he replied, 'I have just been told about it.' The Prophet then replied: 'If you have a long life, you will see a woman who makes a journey from al-Hira and circumambulates the Ka'ba; for she does not fear anyone except God.'[48]

The quotation above discloses the context of why women, and even men, should be accompanied when they make a journey, namely the risk of highway robbery. When the way becomes safe, people, including women, will travel comfortably from one place to another. It is a clear statement, I think, that shows the literal understanding of the hadith to be a mistaken *ijtihād*, because it not only misses the context of the text but negates the ethical principle advocated by Islam. Moreover, the subject should be discussed in light of the rights of women to work and to learn, which are principles of Islam advocated not only by the verses of the Qur'an but also, as mentioned in the work of Abu Shuqqa, by the Hadith.

Unlike the conservatives, who refer to the text above for the notion of women's domestication, the contextual reading argues for the protection and security of all people. At the time the hadith was narrated, the category of those in need of protection included women. In the tribal social system at the time, accompanying women was the only possible and reasonable way to keep them safe on long-distance journeys.

Unlike tribal society, the social order of our society no longer depends upon self-help and communal solidarity, but on the existence of rational institutions and systems, which include law enforcement and equal rights for all. Today, the state is expected to provide safety and protection for all of its citizens. Accordingly, the hadith needs to be understood as having emerged from a tribal context in which the family, the clan and the tribe protected their own. Now that society has significantly changed, the challenge today is how to interpret and integrate these older directives and sanctions within emerging civil societies. In essence, the time-honoured tradition of patriarchal authority is being significantly challenged by notions of gender equality and rule of law, and the interpretation and application of the Hadith has thus become a topic of considerable contention.

6. Reinterpretation of the concept of *qiwāma* in the household

In the main schools of Islamic jurisprudence, the marital relationship tends to be a hierarchical one in which the husband becomes the head of the household, while the wife is subordinate to him. The jurists have formulated, accordingly, a set of obligations of the wife towards the husband, as distinct from those of the husband towards the wife. The main duty of the husband, to provide maintenance (*nafaqa*) – shelter, food and clothing – is juxtaposed with the wife's main duty of submission (*ṭāʿa*), that is, obedience to please the husband at least in terms of his sexual needs.

This unequal model of the relationship leaves the wife vulnerable to violence, as the husband has power to chastise, even to beat, the wife, while she has no power to chastise the husband. In the account of al-Nawawi of Banten (d. 1897), for instance, the husband has the right to beat his wife for trivial reasons such as the wife's refusal to dress when the husband asks her to do so; her refusal to immediately engage with her husband in sexual intercourse; going out without her husband's permission; tearing her husband's garment; touching her husband's beard; saying the word 'donkey' or 'stupid' to her husband even when he has just shouted at her; showing her face to others; talking to a non-*maḥram* (a person other than a close relative whom she may not marry); talking to her husband loudly so that others can hear; or giving away something to others from the house of her husband which she should have taken care of or kept.[49]

The obedience of the powerless wife and the possibility of violence by the powerful husband are derived from the literal concept of *qiwāma*, namely, the leadership of men in the household, which is contrary to the principle of justice and equality of Islam. The concept of *qiwāma* should, accordingly, be revised to implement the principle of justice. As it relates to marriage, for example, the implementation of the principle of justice includes, among other things, the consent of both parties to the marriage contract (2:232–3); the assumption of responsibility (4:58); a shared commitment to create a peaceful family life that is full of love (30:21); an obligation to treat each other with kindness (4:19); consulting each other in order to resolve problems (2:233, 3:159, 42:38); and, lastly, sharing the tasks of daily life in order to avoid saddling one party with an unfair burden.

In the Indonesian context, besides verse 4:34 of the Qur'an, many religious preachers maintain the subordination of women in the domestic realm with reference to the hadith of ʿAbdullah ibn ʿUmar:

> I heard Allah's Apostle saying, 'All of you are guardians and responsible for your wards and the things under your care. The Imam (i.e. the ruler) is the guardian of his subjects and is responsible for them and a man is the guardian of his family and is responsible for them. A woman is the guardian of her husband's house and is responsible for it. A servant is the guardian of his master's belongings and is re-

> sponsible for them.' I thought that he also said, 'A man is the guardian of his father's property and is responsible for it. All of you are guardians and responsible for your wards and the things under your care.'[50]

Consistent with the commitment to the principle of justice, this hadith should be interpreted to develop the ethics of rulings rather than used for its literal meaning. Unlike the conservative reading, the contextual reading of the above hadith is centred on the ethic of responsibility rather than on the ruling of guardianship. The text, as clearly mentioned in the first and the last sentences, highlights the moral responsibility of everyone as a guardian. The scopes of guardianship mentioned in the text – the caliph over his people, the husband over his family, the wife over her household, the servant over his master's wealth and the man over his father's wealth – are only examples of where people should apply their responsibility. The ethic of moral responsibility is fixed regardless of persons, place and time, while the scope of guardianship, on the other hand, is changeable due to the conditions in the context.

Literally, the text highlights that the wife can be the guardian of the household of her husband (*rāʿiya fī-bayt zawjihā*) while the husband is the guardian of the whole family (*rāʿin fī-ahlihi*). In another narrative, reported by al-Bukhari, the wife is also the guardian of the family of her husband (*rāʿiya ʿalā ahli bayt zawjihā*).[51] Again, the scopes are not the crux of the message of the hadith; for the wife also can be the guardian either of the household or the family, though both are within the scope of the house of her husband. In the absence of the husband, for instance, the wife, practically, becomes the guardian of the whole family. She is not the guardian of only the internal household, but is also responsible for working outside it to provide everything needed by the members of the family. Of course, in our time there are many families with both husbands and wives working outside the home. Therefore, the scopes of guardianship of each member of the family should be changed in accordance with their capability, while the ethic – that everyone should be responsible for his or her guardianship – remains as the main purpose of the rulings of Islam.

The conservative concept of *qiwāma* in the Islamic jurisprudence was obviously established on the basis of the fundaments of philosophical, metaphysical, social and legal assumptions and theories developed in the social context of patriarchal systems. Therefore, the nascent reinterpretation of the hadith of Abdullah ibn ʿUmar, above, will be insufficient to purge the concept of *qiwāma* of its patriarchal elements. However, discussion of the ethical meaning of the hadith discloses the possibility of changing the concept of *qiwāma* to be more suited to the principles of marital relationship advocated by the Qur'an: equality, justice, peace and shared responsibility for one another. The concept of *qiwāma*, accordingly, should be interpreted as a responsibility of those who are physically and mentally better qualified to protect and guide those members of a family who are less qualified, regardless of gender and age. This is beside the principles that members of the household are obliged to treat each other with kindness, respect, love and mercy.

7. Conclusion

The discussion above argues for the reinterpretation of texts of the Hadith in terms of gender equality, as the possibility of gender-equal interpretation is opened up within the diversity of classical Islamic scholarship. Indeed, in my opinion, this reinterpretation contributes more to the agenda of gender equality among Muslims than does challenging Muslims about the issues of the authority and validity of the Hadith. The authority and the authenticity of the Hadith – the assurance that the Hadith convey an accurate account of actual words and deeds of the Prophet – have, in fact, been discussed broadly by Muslim scholars since the early centuries of Islam. To reiterate, according to the sciences of the Hadith, for example, the sayings and deeds of the Prophet cannot be considered to be reliable as a second source of Islamic law unless they pass two main categories of assessment; namely, those relating to the chain of transmission (*sanad*) and those relating to the text (*matn*). Scholars of Islamic jurisprudence (*fiqh*), in this respect, have also extended the eligibility criteria of the Hadith to insist that it not be contrary to the Qur'an or the dictates of reason and natural law, which excludes some accepted texts of the Hadith of al-Bukhari.[52] While the grounding of the evaluation of even the authentic hadiths in the Qur'an is quite obvious in the works of al-Ghazali and al-Qaradawi, the use of reason in such an evaluation may, to some extent, be found in the work of Rashid Rida (d. 1935).[53] However, as Daniel Brown argues, what they do is not outside of classical criticism of the Hadith, but is rather 'explicitly grounded in the Islamic intellectual tradition itself'.[54]

In sum, any work of reformation of Islamic understanding simply cannot disregard the significant role of the Hadith as a source of Islamic teachings. This is to say that reinterpreting the Hadith, especially those texts which address the relations between men and women, is necessary work in order to achieve gender equality in Islam. It is also likely to be fruitful work, as the number of positive texts on women's issues is far greater than the number of negative ones, most of which are, in any case, weak. I am suggesting that we work for interpretation as the Hadith, according to Siddiqi, 'still [wield] a great influence on the minds of the Muslims, and is bound to influence them in the future also'.[55] In this respect, Khaled Abou El Fadl notes that '[it] is fair to say that considering the wealth of historical and legal sources that are yet to be studied, edited, or published, our understanding of gender dynamics and the way that these dynamics influenced the development of Islamic jurisprudence is still in its nascent stages'.[56] I hope that there will be many more attempts among Muslim feminists to address the lack of scholarship with regard to reinterpreting the Hadith to advocate gender equality within Islam.

Notes

1 I would like to express my thanks to Amber Engelson and to the editors for their comments and suggestions how to make this article more readable.

2 I got this quotation from *Rasāʾil al-Jāḥiẓ* (3/312) from my close teacher K. H. Husein Muhammad, the prominent Muslim scholar feminist in Indonesia. English translation from Abou El Fadl, Khaled, *The Search for Beauty in Islam: A Conference of the Books* (Lanham: Rowman & Littlefield, 2006), p. 10.

3 On those who struggle for Muslim feminism in Indonesia, see: Feillard, Andree, 'Indonesia's emerging Muslim feminism: women leaders on inheritance and other gender issues', *Studia Islamika* 4/1 (1997), pp. 83–111; Robinson, Kathrin, 'Islamic influences on Indonesian feminism', *Social Analysis* 50/1 (Spring 2006), pp. 171–7; and Nurmila, Nina, 'The influence of global Muslim feminism on Indonesian Muslim feminist discourse', *Al-Jāmiʿah* 49/1 (2011/1432), pp. 33–64.

4 In this chapter I capitalise the term 'Hadith' to denote the concept of an authoritative source of knowledge in Islam traced back to the Prophet Muhammad, while the lower-case term 'hadith' represents a particular text of the Hadith. I often substitute the term 'text' for 'hadith'.

5 Stowasser, Barbara Freyer, 'The status of women in early Islam', in Freda Hussain (ed.), *Muslim Women* (London and Sydney: Croom Helm, 1984), pp. 1–43.

6 Amina Wadud uses the term 'tawhidic paradigm' to describe claims for the equality of human beings in Islam without distinctions of race, class and gender. The term *tawḥīd* denotes the unity of God, the essential doctrine of Islam. In the concept of *tawḥīd*, God is one and He is the Creator, while all human beings are His creation and thus equal before Him. The concept overarches both the horizontal and the vertical relationships of human beings. On a vertical axis, *tawḥīd* relates to the transcendent reality, the unity of Allah. On a horizontal axis, as an ethical term, *tawḥīd* relates to relationships and developments within the social and political realm, emphasising the unity of all human creatures beneath one Creator. See: Wadud, Amina, *Inside the Gender Jihad: Women's Reform in Islam* (Oxford: Oneworld, 2006), pp. 14–32.

7 Barlas, Asma, *'Believing Women' in Islam: Unreading Patriarchal Interpretation of the Qur'an* (Austin: University of Texas Press, 2002), pp. 44–5.

8 Wadud, Amina, *Qur'an and Women* (Oxford: Oxford University Press, 1999), p. xvii. (Originally published in 1992 by Penerbit Fajar Bakti Sdn. Bhd., Kuala Lumpur, Malaysia.)

9 Siddiqi, Muhammad Zubayr, *Ḥadīth Literature: Its Origin, Development, Special Features and Criticism* (Calcutta: University of Calcutta, 1961), p. xviii; Graham, William, A., *Divine Word and Prophetic Word in Early Islam: A Reconsideration of the Sources, with Special Reference to the Divine Saying or Ḥadīth Qudsī*, Religion and Society 7 (The Hague and Paris: Mouton, 1977).

10 See Clark, L., 'Hijab according to the ḥadīth: text and interpretation', in Sajida Sultana Alvi, Homa Hoodfar and Sheila McDonough (eds), *The Muslim Veil in North America: Issues and Debates* (Toronto: Women's Press, 2003), pp. 214–86.

11 Ibn Qayyim al-Jawziyya, Muhammad ibn Abi Bakr, *I'lām al-Muwaqqi'īn 'an Rabb al-'Ālamīn*, ed. Muhy al-Din 'Abd al-Hamid (Beirut: Dar al-Fikr, n.d.), Vol. 3, p. 14.

12 Kamali, Mohammad Hashim, *Principles of Islamic Jurisprudence* (Kuala Lumpur: Ilmiah, 1998), pp. 47–8.

13 Al-Shafi'i, Muhammad bin Idris, *Al-Risāla*, ed. Abd al-Fattah bin Zafir Kabbarah (Beirut: Dar al-Nafâ'is, 1999), p. 235, text no. 1261.

14 Al-Suyuti, Jalal al-Din 'Abd al-Rahman, *Tadrīb al-Rāwī fī Sharḥ Taqrīb al-Nawawī*, ed. Ahmad Umar Hisham (Beirut: Dar al-Kitab al-'Arabi, 1989), Vol. 1, p. 54.

15 Al-Shafi'i, *Risāla*, text no. 1249–50.

16 Kamali, *Principles*, p. 59.

17 Al-Suyuti, *Tadrīb al-Rāwī*, Vol. 1, pp. 43–4.

18 Al-Shafi'i, *Risāla*, p. 201 no. 1040.

19 Kamali, *Principles*, p. 82.

20 Quoted from al-Khayr Abadi, Muhammad Abu al-Layth, 'Al-manhaj al-'ilmī 'ind al-muḥaddithīn fī al-ta'āmul ma'a mutūn al-Sunna', *Islamiyyat al-Ma'rifah* 4/13 (1998), pp. 14–18 (Kuala Lumpur: IIIT).

21 *Ibid.*, pp. 22–6.

22 See Kamali, *Principles*, pp. 58–65 and 75–6.

23 Al-Zarkashi, Badr al-Din, *Al-Ijāba li Īrād mā Istadrakathu 'Ā'isha 'alā al-Ṣaḥāba*, ed. Sa'id al-Afghani (Beirut: al-Maktab al-Islami, 2000).

24 The hadith was narrated by Abdullah ibn 'Umar in Al-Bukhari, Muhammad ibn Isma'il, *Ṣaḥīḥ al-Bukhārī*, numbered by Muhammad Fu'ad 'Abd al-Baqi (Cairo: Dar ibn al-Haytham, 2004), book 56, ch. 47, text no. 2858.

25 The hadith of 'A'isha on the matter is available in al-Bayhaqi, Ahmad ibn al-Husayn, *Al-Sunan al-Kubrā*, ed. Muhammad 'Abd al-Qadir 'Ata (Beirut: Dar al-Kutub al-'Ilmiyyah, 2003), Vol. 8, p. 241, book of *al-Qasāma*, ch. 20, hadith no. 16525. See also al-Zarkashi, *Al-Ijāba*, pp. 124–7.

26 The position of the Hanafi school is that the broad meaning cannot be narrowed by a solitary hadith (*āmm al-Qur'ān lā yukhaṣṣaṣ bi al-khabar al-wāḥid*). See al-Khin, Mustafa Sa'id, *Athar al-Ikhtilāf fī al-Qawā'id al-Uṣūliyya fī Ikhtilāf al-Fuqahā'* (Beirut: Mu'assasat al-Risala, 1998), pp. 204–14.

27 In the Hanafi school, the obligatory (*farḍ*) recitation in prayer, based on 73:20, is any verse of the Qur'an. The recitation of the *Fātiḥa* in particular, which is considered obligatory in other schools based on a hadith, is only a duty (*wājib*) in two units (*rak'a*) of prayer, while in the remaining units it is neither obligatory nor a duty, according to the Hanafi school. The term 'duty' here is similar to the term 'strongly recommended' or *sunna mu'akkada* in other schools, as prayer without

the *Fātiḥa* is still valid in the Hanafi school. See Al-Jaziri, ʿAbd al-Rahman, *Al-Fiqh ʿalā Madhāhib al-Arbaʿa* (Egypt: Dar al-Hadith, 2004), Vol. 1, pp. 181–3.

28 Al-Haythami, Nur al-Din bin ʿAli bin Abi Bakr bin Sulayman, *Majmaʿ al-Zawāʾid wa Manbaʿ al-Fawāʾid*, ed. Muhammad ʿAbd al-Qadir Ahmad ʿAtha (Beirut: Dar al-Kutub al-ʿIlmiyyah, 2001), Vol. 2, p. 118. A footnote in that work notes that the hadith is also reported by Ahmad ibn Hanbal in his *Musnad* (6/371), by al-Mundhiri in his *al-Targhīb* (1/225) and by Ibn Khuzayma (no. 1689).

29 Al-Ghazali, Shaykh Muhammad, *Al-Sunna al-Nabawiyya bayna Ahl al-Fiqh wa Ahl al-Ḥadīth* (Beirut: Dar al-Shuruq, 1992), pp. 62–4. The text of the hadith affirming that women may enter the mosque can be found in Ibn al-Athir, Abu al-Saʿadat Mubarak ibn Muhammad, *Jāmiʿ al-Uṣūl min Aḥādith al-Rasūl* (Beirut: Dar Ihya al-Turath, 1984), Vol. 6, p. 155, no. 3283, and Vol. 11, p. 467, no. 8698.

30 Abu Shuqqa, ʿAbd al-Halim Muhammad, *Taḥrīr al-Marʾa fī ʿAṣr al-Risāla*, 6 vols (Kuwait: Dar al-Qalam, 2002).

31 Al-Bukhari, *Ṣaḥīḥ al-Bukhārī*, book 12, ch. 5, no. 946.

32 Al-ʿAsqalani, Ahmad ibn ʿAli ibn Hajar, *Fatḥ al-Bārī Sharḥ Saḥīḥ al-Bukhārī* (Beirut: Dar al-Fikr, 1993), Vol. 3, pp. 109–10.

33 Al-Qaradawi, Yusuf, *Kayfa Nataʿāmal maʿa al-Sunna al-Nabawiyya: al-Maʿālim wa al-Ḍawābiṭ* (Egypt: IIIT, 1999), pp. 93–183.

34 Al-Shahrastani, Abu al-Fath Mohammed bin ʿAbd al-Karim, *al-Milal wa al-Niḥal*, ed. Ahmad Fahmi Huwaidi (Beirut: Dar al-Kutub al-ʿIlmiyyah, 1992), Vol. 1, p. 108.

35 Al-Qaradawi, *Kayfa Nataʿāmal*, p. 130.

36 Al-Ghazali, *Al-Sunna al-Nabawiyya*, pp. 55–8.

37 Al-Khayr Abadi, ʿAl-manhaj al-ʿilmīʾ, p. 44.

38 Shaikh, Saʿdiyya, ʿKnowledge, women, and gender in the ḥadīth: a feminist perspectiveʾ, *Islam and Christian-Muslim Relations* 15/1 (January 2004), pp. 99–108 at p. 107.

39 Al-Bukhari, *Ṣaḥīḥ al-Bukhārī*, book 18, ch. 4, no. 1088.

40 Al-Sanʿani, Muhammad ibn Ismaʾil, *Subul al-Salām Sharḥ Bulūgh al-Marām*, ed. Muhammad ʿAbd al-Qadir ʿAta (Beirut: Dar al-Kutub al-ʿIlmiyyah, 2002), Vol. 2, pp. 371–3.

41 Ibn Hazm, Abu Muhammad ʿAli bin Ahmad, *Al-Muḥallā bi al-Āthār*, ed. ʿAbd al-Ghaffar Sulayman al-Bandari (Beirut: Dar al-Kutub al-ʿIlmiyyah, n.d.), Vol. 5, pp. 19–27.

42 *Ibid.*, p. 19.

43 Al-Zarkashi, *Al-Ijāba*, pp. 143–4.

44 Ibn Hazm, *Al-Muḥallā bi al-Āthār*, Vol. 5, p. 19.

45 Al-Naysaburi, Muslim ibn al-Hajjaj, *Ṣaḥīḥ Muslim*, in Yahya ibn Sharaf al-Nawawi (ed.), *Sharḥ Ṣaḥīḥ Muslim*, numbered by Muhammad Fuʾad ʿAbd al-Baqi (Beirut: Dar al-Kutub al-ʿIlmiyyah, 2003), book 15, ch. 74, no. 424/1341. See also Al-Bukhari, *Ṣaḥīḥ al-Bukhārī*, book 28, ch. 26, no. 1862.

46 Al-ʿAsqallani, *Fatḥ al-Bārī*, Vol. 6, p. 88.
47 Al-Bukhari, *Ṣaḥīḥ al-Bukhārī*, book 28, ch. 26, no. 1864.
48 Al-Bukhari, *Ṣaḥīḥ al-Bukhārī*, book 61, ch. 25, no. 3595.
49 Nawawi, Muhammad Umar, *Syarḥ ʿUqūd al-Lujjain fī Bayān Huqūq az-Zawjayn* (Indonesia: Syirkat Nur Asia, n.d.), p. 5.
50 Al-Bukhari, *Ṣaḥīḥ al-Bukhārī*, book 11, ch. 11, no. 893.
51 The last narrative is available in al-Bukhari, *Ṣaḥīḥ al-Bukhārī*, book 93, ch. 1, no. 7138.
52 Siddiqi, *Ḥadīth Literature*, pp. 93, 194–204 and 201–3, cited in Kamali, Mohammad Hashim, *Hadith Methodology: Authenticity, Compilation, Classification and Criticism of Hadith* (Kuala Lumpur: Ilmiah Publishers, 2002), pp. 290–1. In his account, due to lack of *matn* criticism in the sciences of the Hadith, there are still found weak or forged hadiths even in the standard collections, such as that of al-Bukhari. He gives the example of three hadiths in al-Bukhari's collection that are questioned by scholars of the Hadith and jurisprudence. (1) The hadith that the Qur'anic verse (49:9) refers to ʿAbd Allah b. Ubayy. This is criticised because ʿAbd Allah b. Ubayy had not accepted Islam even outwardly at the time when the verse was revealed. (2) The hadith that if Ibrahim, the son of the Prophet Muhammad, had lived, he would have been a prophet. The hadith was considered a forgery by al-Shawkani, among others. (3) The hadith that Adam's height was 60 yards, as it conflicts with the fact that the measures of the homes and dwellings of some of the ancient nations do not show that their inhabitants were enormously tall.
53 Brown, Daniel, *Rethinking Tradition in Modern Islamic Thought* (Cambridge, New York and Melbourne: Cambridge University Press, 1996), pp. 116–32.
54 *Ibid.*, p. 132.
55 Siddiqi, *Ḥadīth Literature*, p. xviii.
56 Abou El Fadl, Khaled, 'Legal and jurisprudential literature: 9th to 15th century', in Suad Joseph (ed.), *Encyclopedia of Women in Islamic Cultures* (Leiden and Boston: Brill, 2007), p. 41.

9

RETHINKING MEN'S AUTHORITY OVER WOMEN*

Qiwāma, *Wilāya* and their Underlying Assumptions

Hassan Yousefi Eshkevari

In Islamic culture and legal tradition, the men in the family (father, husband and, in some instances, brother or even grandfather) have a kind of authority or guardianship right over women. This view is supported by some Qur'anic verses and sayings of the Prophet and other religious authorities, which will be referred to later. Such a notion has prevailed, in different manifestations, throughout history, in all religions and in all societies, and it still exists, even in more progressive and developed countries; therefore, it is necessary to explore its sociological, historical and epistemological origins in religion and in other areas. Given the interconnection between systems of thought, beliefs, rituals and cultures, an investigation of their origins and analysis of the reasons for their existence will help us to understand this patriarchal view, and the legal tradition that grants men authority over women.

* Translated from Persian by Ziba Mir-Hosseini.

1. The epistemological assumptions of male authority

The assumptions underlying the idea that men have authority and guardianship over women are numerous and varied; here I will only list, in the briefest possible way, the three salient ones.

1. *Men are created superior to women and women are evil, possess an evil essence, or can create evil, and must therefore be controlled.* Such a belief is reflected in the literature and proverbs of varied peoples and nations. It is both supported by, and the product of, certain assumptions, notably with regard to women's weakness in reason, the strength of their emotions, their sexuality and its power to corrupt men, and some features of their sexual physiology, such as menses and childbirth, which involve blood and are considered to be polluting.[1]

2. *The patriarchal family is the basic unit of society, and must be protected for its survival.* The family, which at first was natural and inevitable and was formed due to necessity, has, in the course of history, gone through many transformations, with the changing conditions of human social life and interaction with many direct and indirect factors. In these changes, assumptions like those discussed here played a role in defining the purpose and philosophy of the family, in developing an intricate set of rules and laws to regulate relations within it, and eventually in giving the institution and its continuation an aura of sanctity. These fundamental beliefs and teachings naturally and openly led to the emergence of a family with a hierarchical structure, with the man in charge, as provider and protector. In Islamic legal tradition this becomes the man's right of guardianship (*wilāya*) over the family. The principle is that the family is the basic unity of society and must be protected: how this principle is interpreted can have an important role in defining the position of women and their rights in relation to men (father, husband, brother).

3. *Aristotelian justice.* Although the Aristotelian notion of proportional justice is no longer as significant as it was with respect to women's rights and status in the family, its influence on philosophers and religious and social thinkers in the last two millennia has been immense. Aristotle's ideas and teachings have had an impact on many philosophical, political, social and religious branches of knowledge, including those developed by Muslims. We know that Aristotle believed in the doctrine of essentialism, according to which things and beings have essences that are unchangeable. This doctrine influenced Greek, Christian and Islamic philosophies throughout the Middle Ages. Humans, Aristotle considered, have an unchangeable essence, but are created in different racial and social groups for the fulfilment of certain duties in human society. He believed in a hierarchal, caste-like social order in which slavery was a natural part; humans are born to be masters or slaves. In this framework, justice, which for Aristotle was of great importance, was also interpreted in an essentialist way. That is to say, 'justice is to maintain everything in its proper place', and since

the place of everything and everybody was fixed and essential, justice meant keeping that place, and treating people accordingly. Injustice meant going against the essence and not granting individuals the rights they were due. According to such notions of humanity and justice, a slave rebelling against a master or a woman rejecting a man's authority (be it her father's, husband's or even her brother's) threatens the social order and family organisation, and is thus behaving unjustly and is subject to punishment.

These epistemological assumptions, shaped and consolidated over several millennia, became the basis of an authoritarian ethical and legal system that is premised on the notion that, if women fail to obey men in the family and society, justice will be compromised, as both family organisation and social order will disintegrate. It was in such a context that the notions of *wilāya* and *qiwāma* found their proper meaning in Islamic language and legal thought, and became the backdrop to a set of rulings that required women to submit to their husbands and to ask their permission for many things, including leaving the house. Numerous restrictive legal rulings in *fiqh* and religious-based ethics, such as the requirement for women to cover their entire body and not to display their beauties (*tabarrūj*),[2] are premised on such epistemological notions. Other rulings allow polygamy for men; grant the guardianship of minor children to the father, or even the grandfather; prevent women from being judges or political leaders; and ordain different inheritance shares for males and females.

These assumptions, thanks to constant reiteration, now appear to be common sense. But if, for whatever reason, we question them or interpret them differently, it is evident that we must completely transform the laws derived from them.

2. Alternative assumptions

If we admit that (a) the above assumptions play a significant role in determining relations between men and women, (b) they are, in turn, the product of historical and legal legacies, and (c) we must transform the situation in the interest of women and the health of society, then we must modify the assumptions, or at least interpret them in a more humane and beneficial way. In my opinion these assumptions are flawed. In what follows I shall refute them and introduce other principles (in particular from within Islamic legal thought) to create a way of rethinking the issue of women's rights in Islamic legal tradition.

1. *Men and women are created essentially equal.* Fortunately there is little need to provide justification for this assertion, as there is no sound argument or textual proof for the absence of essential equality between men and women. On the contrary, in particular in Islam, there is ample textual and rational evidence to support the idea that the two human sexes are essentially equal. This is so self-evident that the burden of proof is on those who deny it. A number of Qur'anic verses clearly say 'we have created you from the same *nafs* (soul)' (4:1, 6:98, 7:189,

31:28, 39:6). It is noteworthy that there is an entire chapter with the title 'Women' (*Al-Nisā'*), which starts with this sentence, and there are a number of hadith to support this. In Qur'anic ontology, no human is distinct from other humans; neither race, nor colour, nor status brings distinction, as clearly stated in a famous verse (49:13). Salvation, as the ultimate objective of religion, depends only on righteousness (*taqwā*) and righteous action (*'amal ṣāliḥ*); men and women have the same potential and qualifications for salvation (4:124), and are addressed as male (*mū'minūn*) and female (*mū'mināt*) (e.g. 9:71–2). This assertion is endorsed by what humans have gained through knowledge and experience; among these important gains are Articles 1 and 2 of the Universal Declaration of Human Rights (adopted by the UN in 1948) that fortunately have been ratified by almost all peoples and nations, making this a universal consensus.

2. *Women are not inherently weak in reason or ruled by their emotions.* If we pay attention to the arguments of those who are against women participating in political and social matters, serving as judges, or even having the right to the custody of their own children, we see that they are generally based on the proposition that women are weak in reason and are controlled by emotions; thus they do not have the required capacity for such tasks, which can only be performed by men, who are rational and not emotional.

The fact is, such a belief is a historical construct, the product of the age of men's domination and the fading of women's role in society. Such a historical mindset also influenced the religious sources and traditions after the Prophet's time. Many traditions were fabricated and then attributed to the Prophet or other religious personalities,[3] as is attested by rigorous research on the history and genealogy of such traditions. In recent years, with the expansion of Western natural sciences in Muslim countries, some base their views about women's inferior rationality on arguments drawn from science; for instance, they say that women are inferior to men because their brains weigh less than men's, or because they are physically weaker than men. However, there is no rational or scientific basis for assuming women to be mentally inferior; rather, in the course of history, women generally had fewer opportunities than men for intellectual and rational growth. This, in turn, was the product of men's historical domination, which, in practice, gave fewer opportunities to women, who were secluded and marginalised in social and political life. It has nothing to do with men's or women's natural abilities. From 'what is', an ideological and eternal 'ought' cannot be derived. Experience (also in our time) shows that once women have enough room to grow, to become aware, to acquire the knowledge and skill to assume responsibility, they have proven their capacity to do so.

This does not mean that men and women are identical in creation and have exactly the same attributes. Certainly their bodies, as sexual and physical structures, are different, and these differences inevitability lead to certain differences in individual, collective or sexual behaviour. But the point is that men and women are created as 'humans' and are equal in humanity (i.e. none is more human than the other); more importantly, natural and genetic differences (even if it were true that men and women differ in their capacity for reason or emotion) are not the basis of the rights of men and women or the family organisation.

3. *The family is a joint enterprise.* The question of the 'family' is a sensitive and important one. There is no doubt that it emerged as an institution and went through various forms and fundamental changes over time. The concept of the family as we know it, and laws governing relations among its members, have been through many changes and, as already stated, are the product of socio-historical processes. But they are premised on certain assumptions that are no longer valid. Therefore, we now need to rethink these assumptions, to correct the theoretical and practical errors in them, and to come up with a new definition and a new set of rulings.

If we take into account the primary principles of Islam (the universal and general principles taken from the Qur'an and valid Sunna), there is no doubt that this religion has stressed the importance of the family and its integrity. Islam brought important transformations to family organisation and customs among the Arabs in the Hijaz. On the one hand, it reformed and restricted some areas of laxity and promiscuity in relations between men and women; on the other, it removed some restrictions. On the whole, it enhanced women's position in the family and society, and gave them more rights.

We are now at a very different historical juncture, but, arguably, there is still a need to preserve the family as the basic unit of society and the prime locus of socialisation and education. We can even claim that the 'Islamic family' can provide a good model; but what we cannot provide is a reasonable Islamic defence for those archaic traditions and rulings whose time is past. This is the case because these rulings – whether they are Shariʿa-based (*aḥkām sharʿī*) or attributed to the Shariʿa – are compatible with neither our theological and epistemological assumptions nor contemporary notions of justice. Justice, which is one of the fundamental principles of Islam, cannot have a fixed and unchanging meaning and expression. In seventh-century Arabia, family organisation had a pyramid-like structure, with the man as the head; he had authority over women and children. Family members were naturally assigned rights in accordance with the patriarchal ethos on which the social order was based. This was the case in most societies then, and continued to be so more or less everywhere.

Since we need laws regulating the family and relations among its members, I suggest the following. That is, we admit, as a general presumption and a religious principle, that the realm of the family is a joint enterprise (*mulk mushāʿ*) in which no one – husband, wife, children or others – is distinct from the others in essence or natural rights. In effect, the rights of each member should be decided according to what is accepted as good practice in our time and cumulative human reasoning (which includes the joint interests of husband and wife as the two main elements of the family). These rights should also be consistent with a definition of justice that is both local and contemporary. In the Qur'an, many social and family matters are referred to *ma'rūf*, which in Qur'anic language denotes the best accepted practices of the time (*'urf al-zamān*); these are not necessarily covered by religious law.

The intention is not to elevate the best practice of the time, but to suggest that laws and social systems in different human societies carry weight because they represent the sum of collective knowledge and accumulated experience of successive generations. For this reason, they are not only less prone to error than the impulsive ideas of an individual, but provide a better basis for continuity, reform and gradual change in society. There is no other way to bring about change of any kind or extent than to build on the customs and practices of the time. This is what all the prophets did. This kind of appeal to tradition or *'urf* does not, of course, mean the blind following of, or submission to, ancestral traditions; the Qur'an has given numerous interdictions of ignorant imitation of past traditions. However, reflecting on the causes of the revelation of these verses indicates that the Qur'anic interdictions largely related to the realm of dogma, *tawḥīd* (the unity of God) and polytheism. A large majority of religious laws are in fact *imḍā'ī* (endorsed) – those that endorse already existing practices. In short, what we have in mind by appealing to *'urf* is based on four elements: (1) awareness of *'urf* (etymologically *'urf* means 'the known'); (2) critique of *'urf*; (3) a rational approach to *'urf*; and (4) a search for better alternatives. But we should not forget that this is an ongoing and fluid process; therefore, in the course of time *ma'rūf* practices are transformed, and what was commended and optional (*mamdūḥ wa mukhtār*) can become the opposite: abhorred and proscribed (*madhmūm wa munkar*).

In a religious society, laws and practices that can be defended in the name of religion can also be part of socially accepted customs. In practice, of course, a division of labour and responsibilities in the family is unavoidable, but what is important is that, in the theory of the family as a joint enterprise, it is the collective logic and custom of the time that determines rights within the family, not a set of fixed and immutable laws.

4. *No one should dominate another.* If we go back in history, we clearly see that the phenomenon of patriarchy (like other types of supremacy) and the notion of men's authority over women stem from a crucial belief that we now call the 'right of dominion' (*haqq-e solteh*). The belief that certain persons, groups, races or families are inherently superior to others, was part of common sense in the past; thus men's 'right of dominion' and authority over women was presumed to be natural and common sense. But if we reject this presumption as unnatural, and start from the notion that no individual or group should dominate another, then we prevent the emergence of any social or family organisation based on the notion of the intrinsic

superiority of one person over the other. In fact, such a notion was clearly stated and stressed in the Abrahamic and monotheist religions. In Islamic thought any submission apart from submission to God is a heresy. If we take into consideration numerous Qur'anic verses and hadith, and the whole logic of the principle of *tawḥīd* (unicity, monotheism), negation of any type of domination becomes an undeniable religious tenet. The same sources also indicate that the meaning of submission to God is not merely an abstract theological notion, but is manifested in concrete, social affairs.

How are we to understand notions such as *wilāya* and *qiwāma* in a way that is compatible with the principle of *tawḥīd*? If we look at the kinds of family structure and relations between men and women in Muslim cultures and societies, we see that at least some of the laws that are attributed to God and the practice of the Prophet, in effect require the submission of one human being to another; they require a woman to submit to her husband's desires. In Islamic legal discourse a woman is considered as property that can be possessed and occupied; terms such as *tamlīk* (possession) and *tamattuʿ* (enjoyment) in the marriage formula (*ʿaqd*), and *taṣarruf* (conquest) in referring to consummation, speak of an androcentric mindset in which a woman is the object of male pleasure.

5. *Women enjoy economic autonomy.* One of the important issues is that of women's economic independence, the absence of which in the course of history has created many problems for women, children, and even men. Although in religious legal discourse women have always had the right to economic autonomy, in practice it was denied to a large majority of women. Women in the past were not considered part of the labour force, as they were not allowed to take part in wars and their maintenance was the duty of men. Men's access to wealth and economic success was one of the main reasons that enabled them to have several wives. This state of affairs found its way into the *fiqh* rulings. When Islam gave women rights to inherit, traditional-minded Muslim men objected and saw it as unjust; their argument was that, because women did not participate in wars and jihad, they were not entitled to inherit from the wealth produced by men.

It is evident that such a state of affairs has disintegrated with women's access to education and entry into the labour market. This is, of course, in the interests of women, and ultimately of men and society. Now we Muslims admit that women have the right to acquire education and skills, and to enter the labour market as men do, which means that we have accepted and acknowledged the social and economic imperatives of our time. Hence, we can no longer defend many of the legal rulings that are attributed to the Shariʿa and are part of traditional *fiqh*. For instance, how can we explain and justify legal rulings such as women's lesser share in inheritance, men's right to polygamy, *mahr*, men's obligation to provide maintenance for their wives, women's obligation to obey their husbands, men's right to prevent their wives from leaving the house without permission? What is the meaning of *qiwāma* and *wilāya* when men and women as equal human beings unite for the best interests of their family?

6. Fiqh should not be maximalist. One of the basic quandaries that we face is the a priori belief that Islam is all-inclusive. After the Prophet's death, Muslims gradually came to think of Islam as a comprehensive religion with a programme and a legal ruling (*ḥukm*) for every aspect of human life; therefore, believers must live their lives in accordance with these rulings. This idea was based on Islam's universal appeal, as the most complete religion (5:3) and 'the seal' of all religions (33:40), and on an expansive and novel interpretation of the Prophet's conduct. It was thus claimed that the religion of Islam has perfected and completed the other, earlier monotheist religions and abrogated their laws, and that the path to salvation is in absolute obedience to the Prophet of Islam and the laws that he brought. From the outset, on the basis of 'You People', a general address that appears many times in the Qur'an, it was claimed that Islam is a universal religion and is for the salvation of all human beings, hence its laws and commands are perfect, for all people and for all times. It was in order to conform to these theological claims that the Prophet's conduct, Sunna, acquired a universalist meaning.

These claims, which are based on interpretations of certain Qur'anic verses, on the principle of Muhammad as the last Prophet, and on the necessity to follow his example, gradually became part of Muslim dogma and belief. But they all are open to disputation and can be refuted through textual and rational arguments.[4] Between the second and fourth centuries after Hijra, the science of Islamic jurisprudence or *fiqh* was shaped and the specialist class of *fuqahā'* emerged, claiming to be the only ones with religious knowledge and the right to determine the duties of believers in the context of the five rulings (*wājib*, *ḥarām*, *mustaḥabb*, *mubāḥ* and *makrūh*). Thus Islam became conceptualised as a complete and all-inclusive religion that has an exact ruling for every aspect of life from birth to death. Denial of such claims was regarded as heresy, although they were all based on certain readings and understandings of Islam's textual sources that were shaped in interaction with the needs and conditions of the time, not least the expansion of the Arabo-Islamic empire. In this process, *fiqh* became the totality of Islam, and the *fuqahā'*, as experts in Islam, became the exclusive point of reference for resolving all religious, legal and social problems.

Now the time has come to ponder and rethink this historical legacy so that we can cut the Gordian knot in *fiqh*, *ijtihād* and Qur'anic interpretation. We need to question such perfectionism and the totalising aspects of *fiqh*, as well as the need for 'religious authority', at least in the way it exists and functions now. Once we realise that we do not have to refer to religious authorities and their fatwas for decisions on every issue, the domain of *fiqh*, and by extension the role of the *fuqahā'*, will be curtailed. Did people refer to *fuqahā'* or interpreters of the Qur'an in the first century of Islam in order to make decisions?

Such an attitude can resolve many problems with legal rulings relating to women's rights and the rights of spouses in marriage, most of which were certainly devised after the second century. If we accept the premise that all human beings – including believers – are endowed with free will and can decide for themselves, and that they – not the men of religion – are accountable for their choices and deeds, then, to use a *fiqh* idiom, the realm of *mubāḥāt* (religiously neutral or permissible acts) will be expanded and many restrictive laws will become redundant.

7. Mutability of social rulings in the Shariʿa. One important question in *fiqh* and in Islam is the mutability or immutability of religious-based laws (*aḥkām sharʿī*); any answer to this question has social and political implications, including in the realm of women's rights. In the face of developments mentioned in the previous section, the idea that all laws that are derived from the Qur'an and Sunna are eternal and unchangeable has remained more or less intact.

However, from the very outset, Muslims in everyday experience came to the realisation that many of the laws stated in the Qur'an and the hadith cannot be applied in all places and at all times. For this reason, they found ways to make them relevant and applicable to circumstances different from the time of revelation. When ʿUmar, the second caliph, declared 'what was licit to you at the time of the Prophet is now illicit', it originated from a concrete and tangible social need. The notion of *ijtihād* was one device that, for the first few centuries, was able to resolve the problem. Other ways to accommodate change were also devised; in my research I have come across the following solutions that the Shiʿa jurists, both past and present, came up with to resolve the incongruity between rulings and changing contexts.

- Divisions of rulings into changeable and unchangeable, as advocated by prominent scholars such Mohammad Hossein Naʿini (d. 1860), ʿAllameh Hossein Tabataba'i (d. 1981) and Morteza Motahhari (d. 1979). This is a solution that is recent to Shiʿa *fiqh*; there are no clear criteria for determining what is changeable and unchangeable, and perspectives differ. Yet such a division makes religious law more fluid and flexible.

- Dynamic jurisprudence (*fiqh-e puya*) as opposed to traditional jurisprudence (*fiqh-e sonnati*). This was promoted by a number of young scholars in Qom seminaries before the 1979 Revolution and had a great deal of appeal, but in practice its advocates have not yet come up with a clear and workable formulation.

- Absolute rule of the jurist (*velayat-e motlaqeh-ye faqih*), which was introduced by Ayatollah Khomeini after the establishment of the Islamic Republic, to resolve the problem of the non-applicability of some *fiqh* rulings in Iran. In effect, according to this theory, whenever the ruling jurist (*vali-e faqih*) discerns that the application of primary and secondary rulings is not possible and endangers the political system, then he can intervene and suspend those rulings temporarily. The only criterion is that of the 'interest of the state', and the right to discern this rests with the ruling jurist.

- The state ruling (*hokm-e hokumati*). Although such a theory existed in *fiqh*, it was only after the Iranian Revolution that it became more pronounced, as an extension of the political system based on the absolute rule of the jurist; it is now frequently employed. In effect it removed the deadlock and contradictions between religious rulings and the necessities of the time.
- The absence of the infallible Imam. In this situation, it is argued, some rulings, especially penal ones, are not to be implemented, as Muslims do not yet live in a just society; thus they are suspended (perhaps for ever).[5]
- Conditional suspension. While believing in the eternal validity of religious laws (*aḥkām sharʿī*), some Muslim intellectuals contend that their implementation is contextual, contingent on the existence of certain conditions. Therefore, while the right context is not provided and all necessary conditions are not fulfilled, these rulings must not be implemented.
- The view that certain rulings are not for implementation. In the context of traditional *fiqh*, some jurists hold that harsh rulings (including punishments for sex outside marriage and theft) are designed as deterrents, to scare those tempted to do wrong.
- The distinction between religion (*dīn*) and Shariʿa, as raised by some of the Muslim intellectuals. In this view, religion is general, beyond time and place, thus eternal, but Shariʿa is time- and space-bound, thus evolving and subject to *ijtihād*.
- Separating essentials from accidentals. Different variations on this notion have been introduced by religious intellectuals – for instance, the distinctions between religion and Shariʿa, or fundamentals (*uṣūl*) and auxiliaries (*furūʿ*) in *fiqh*. Religious intellectuals have employed this, using different sets of criteria, in order to find a solution to align the understanding of Islam with the needs of our time.
- Maximalist and minimalist interpretations of religion.[6]
- The changeability of social Shariʿa rulings. Although this theory contains elements of the previous ones, it holds that no rulings related to social life (that is to say, laws legislated and implemented in the realm of politics, society and family) are eternal; rather, they all have the capacity to evolve and be

transformed. In effect, the fundamental premise of this theory is that, from the outset, these rulings were not meant to be forever; and after the death of the Prophet, for certain reasons Muslims have misinterpreted them.

The only viable solution, in my view, is the last one: to put aside the illusion that all social rulings of the Shari'a are eternal.[7] Through scientific and rational inquiry, we need to rethink some of the epistemological assumptions and theories that inform our understanding of religion and *fiqh* so that we can resolve past and present contradictions and put an end to the inconsistencies between Islamic law and the demands of time and place. This is in the interest of religion, believers and the societies of faith. There is no *bid'a* – deviation from religion – in this proposal. On the contrary, it is a rejection of all deviations that came about after the Prophet, which are in contradiction with the spirit and philosophy of religion, and in opposition to the initial invitation to Islam. Let us return to the eternal principles and dogmas of religion, and, as in the time of the Prophet, accept the premise that people are free and recognise the right of the believers to regulate the manner of their daily lives. In the language of the Qur'an, let us leave 'people's affairs' to them, so that they make their own decisions and live in a world guided by high religious and ethical principles and the notions of justice and rationality that reflect the best practice (*ma'rūf*) of the time.

It is within this framework, of course, that legal rulings relating to the family and women's rights will find their rational and proper solutions.

3. The meaning of men's authority over women *(wilāya* and *qiwāma)*

Having laid the groundwork, we can now turn to the notions of *wilāya* and *qiwāma* in Islamic legal culture. If the reader agrees with my critique of conventional assumptions and my proposal for new approaches to understanding Islamic textual sources (the Qur'an, the Prophet's Sunna and hadith), then we have already taken a giant step along the difficult road of evaluating religious traditions and legacies, including religious-based laws relating to women.

What inferences are to be drawn from the principles and presumptions delineated in the preceding section? If we admit the following three points, then logic mandates that no law that claims to be part of the religion of Islam can go against these undisputed principles.

(1) In Islamic thought, men and woman are created as humans from the same essence, and numerous Qur'anic verses affirm the equal humanity of men and women.

(2) Freedom, the right to choice in all personal and collective matters and the responsibility that comes with it, and the possibility of salvation, are

inherent to humans, and numerous Qur'anic verses recognise these basic principles and dogmas of the religion of Islam equally for men and women without discrimination.

(3) One of the main objectives of prophethood – and one of the fundamental dogmas of Islam in particular – is to bring justice, and therefore every religious-based law, in effect, is an interpretation of what justice entails.

In other words, in Islam laws regulating personal and societal matters are to enable human beings to achieve freedom and the right to choice and responsibility, which will ultimately lead to the realisation of justice in the social and political realms.

The family is one of the most important social and civic institutions, and the laws governing it cannot be divorced from the general laws governing the social order. The demands of justice entail equality between man and woman as the two pillars of the family, and their equal access to all human resources and rights. The understanding of justice is, of course, temporal and, to some extent, local; in particular the convention (*'urf*) of the time determines its instances or its manifestations. But the criteria for any understanding of justice are equal rights to freedom and the right to choice and responsibility. As we have seen, the Qur'an also recognises *'urf* as a primary criterion, and refers many affairs to regulation by *'urf*, which in Qur'anic idiom is *ma'rūf* (good practice). In fact, the term *ma'rūf* in the Qur'an is most often used in relation to the family and relations among its members, including regulations regarding divorce, inheritance, and the suckling and care of children (such as 2:229, 240, 180; 4:6–8). In the Qur'an it is said that *'āshirūhunna bi al-ma'rūf* (4:19), that is, consort with them (your wives) according what is accepted as good practice.[8]

This means that the *'urf* of the time was the context for the revelation, and that the Prophet worked to shape social order and laws, introducing reforms and the value system of Islam and *tawḥīd*. Hence, logically we must admit that the basis and background for legislation in the social and political realm is not religion but tradition and customary practices. God's commands and the religious law do not encompass all human affairs. Why? Because it would be neither possible nor beneficial; the civil laws in the Qur'an, or those that were implemented at the time of the Prophet, in *fiqh* idiom, were nothing more than 'guidance according to reason', and guidance on the basis of the traditions of the Hijaz Arabs. The historical record tells us that during the Prophet's time, people, whether Muslim or non-Muslim, followed existing customs and laws in their daily lives; when there was a need, the Prophet intervened and changed the conventions through revelation or his own judgement. In other words, existing laws in the Hijaz were the basis and the content of legislation, and what Islam did was to add and make some amendments (of course, important ones). In this way, the Prophet's practice (*sunnat al-nabawī*) is the continuation – in a more elevated, just and humane form – of the traditions of seventh-century Hijaz, which, over time, became the source of some important reforms. The conclusion that we can derive from this analysis is that Islam's social and legal rulings at the time of the Prophet (part of the *aḥkām sharʿī*) were all local and temporal, and cannot be regarded as eternal and beyond time and place. In other words, laws were legislated, amended or endorsed on the basis of the needs and 'realities' of the time, not on the basis of Islam's eternal egalitarian 'truth'. Muslims and believers in revelation and prophethood – on the basis of reason and logic, and even on the basis of the Prophet's practice – must always give due weight to the tradition and conventions of the time. In the light of the essentials of religion as well as extra-religious principles such as nature (*fiṭra*), reason (*ʿaql*), ethics (*akhlāq*) and justice (*ʿadāla*), they must examine and rely on human experience, and learn from the good conventions and laws of other nations and people. Whatever convention or law is most just and reasonable, is inevitably more Islamic. This is the Prophet's practice, contrary to what some Muslims insistently but wrongly perceive and believe. It is not the Prophet's practice to remain frozen in history as a prisoner of the customs and conventions of the Arabia of fourteen centuries ago.

This principle extends to the family and the laws regulating the rights and obligations of spouses, expressed in the Qur'an as following the custom and best practice of the time (*ʿurf wa maʿrūf*); it is evident that custom and best practice, by definition, cannot be fixed and constant. What remain constant are the essential rights and equality of all human beings, men and women, as well as the pursuit of justice, which in current world conditions entails the realisation of equal rights and non-discrimination. It is noteworthy that in some Qur'anic verses there are explicit indications of equal and mutual rights between men and women, including 2:228: 'Women shall have rights similar to rights against them according to what is *maʿrūf*.'[9]

In the Qur'an, the concept of *wilāya* is not used in the sense of male superiority or a man's unilateral and authoritarian guardianship rights over his wife and daughters. What we find in the sacred text is an equal and bilateral notion: 'the believers, men and women, are protectors of one another' (9:71). In the common language, tradition and mindset of Muslims, however, this relationship of mutual protection is understood as men's authority over women. But this has no firm place in Islam, *fiqh* and its principles, particularly if we take the conventional legal meaning of *wilāya* in *fiqh* – that is, the unilateral, and unequal, supervision and care of a major over a minor, of a sane over an insane person, or of master over slave.

To justify men's control over women the jurists use the first part of verse 4:34: 'Men are *qawwāmūn* of women because God has favoured the one more than the other, and because they support them.' *Qawwām*, generally used for someone who stands and serves, is variously translated as maintainer, provider, manager, guardian, protector. The theme of the verse is that men are to protect, manage and guard their wives. Two reasons for this duty are mentioned; one is that God has granted more favours to some than to others, and the other is that men spend their wealth on women. The second part of the verse, apparently building on the first, specifies the duty of a righteous woman to her husband when he is absent: to remain chaste and faithful. It is for this reason that the issue of *nushūz* (disobedience) is raised: how a man should deal with a wife who is neither righteous nor faithful. Assuming what is said in the first part of the verse to be a fixed state of affairs, it is concluded that men have a kind of authority over women.[10]

Let us pause and reflect on the two reasons given for men's authority over women. The verse states that 'God has favoured some more than others.' The best evidence suggests that what is meant is men's superiority over women, but what is meant by superiority? It seems that there can be no other reason than that offered by most interpreters, namely, men's greater physical strength. I do not know whether men's physical superiority over woman is constant, essential and eternal, but if, for the sake of argument, we suppose that it is, then we need to take into account two things. The first is that, in the past, physical strength had a unique and privileged role in the performance of vigorous tasks such as hunting and warfare. More recently, however, this faculty has undergone intense transformation. Today, many tasks have become mechanised and computerised, which means that it is superiority of thought and skill that counts, not muscle power; therefore, those tasks that were performed by men because they required greater physical strength, can now be performed by women too. Today scientific skill, intelligence and specialised knowledge have the final word, and in these respects women have shown that they are not inferior to men, and, indeed, at some more delicate tasks women may be superior. Consequently, the issue of men's physical superiority over women is no longer relevant, and there is no basis for excluding women from occupations or positions such as serving as judges or witnesses, being in positions of leadership, or taking on the guardianship of their small children. With the elimination of the reason for such exclusions, their legal consequences should also be eliminated.

The second point is that men's superiority leads, at most, to their assuming some responsibilities (including the protection of the family); it can never be an inherent superiority or a higher human value. There is no reason to conclude that men are innately superior and more worthy than women; and neither the Qur'an nor Islam have drawn such a conclusion. In matters of faith, the Qur'an considers men and women to be mutually responsible, and regards salvation as contingent only on faith (*imān*), piety and good deeds, and nothing more.

As for the issue of men providing for women, inevitably, if women are not part of the labour force, they are unable to earn enough income to be economically autonomous; hence, men assume their upkeep, and, in practice, such a system develops its own laws and legal order.

This economic relationship, whereby men provide maintenance, turns marriage into a transaction. If we examine some of the legal regulations and traditions among the Muslims, we can see the symbols of such a transaction. One of them is the nature and philosophy of dower (*ṣadāq*, *mahr*), evident in the formula that seals the contract. In *fiqh*, *ṣadāq* is defined as what the husband pays to the wife in return for access to her *buḍʿ*. Etymologically, *buḍʿ* derives from 'wealth', but here it denotes a woman's sexual organs, or her sexuality. Such a usage clearly reveals the transactional side of marriage. The woman offers a valuable asset, her sexuality, and, naturally, the man who can pay can acquire the asset. Hence, it is said that *al-tazwīj huwa al-tamlīk al-buḍʿ bi al-ʿiwaḍ maʿlūm* (marriage is the ownership of the vagina in return for a stated compensation), that is to say, in marriage a man buys a woman's sexual organ in return for *mahr*. The words used in the marriage formula more or less admit such a notion; in particular, words such as *tamattuʿ* (enjoyment) and *istimtāʿ* (to enjoy) refer solely to the right acquired by the husband; it is not mutual. Likewise, the terms *ījāb* (offer) and *qabūl* (acceptance) in the marriage formula speak of such a one-way transaction, in the sense that a woman offers herself to a man and man accepts this offer. Some *fiqh* idioms also use the notion of the sale of a woman to a man. The issue of the link between *nushūz* (the wife's refusal of her husband's sexual demands) and *nafaqa* (maintenance) also supports such a claim. In such a way of thinking, first, relations between men and women are reduced to the sexual side, and secondly, a woman has only a single precious asset, her sexuality, which she offers to those who want to buy; women are thus reduced to instruments for men's use and pleasure. Indeed, in current language, woman 'gives' and man 'takes' pleasure; woman is married and man marries.[11]

Yet, in early Islam, according to the Qur'anic recommendation (4:4), *ṣadāq* is merely a gift that a man gives his wife at the time of marriage, and has no commercial nature or connotation. For this reason it cannot be compulsory; *ṣadāq* is derived from *ṣadaqa* (gift) and giving. A gift cannot be obligatory.[12] The most that one can say is that in those times a woman did not enjoy economic independence, and the Qur'anic recommendation to make such a gift at the time of marriage was a useful and welcome financial help to women, and could help to make relations between spouses more congenial. The issue of *mahr* and its legal consequences among Muslims (including the link between *mahr* and the trousseau, *jehiziyeh*, and the need to pay the *mahr* upon request, given its high value and men's inability to pay) is a great problem for Muslims, apparently created over the centuries by a minor misinterpretation.

We know that the traditional family system, predicated on beliefs in men's inherent superiority and their role as sole maintainers and providers, is rapidly changing. The structure, relations and even definition of the family are now different from the past. In the past, Muslim jurists conceptualised men and women's relations, and even the family, through the prism of sexuality: apparently men's sexual pleasure and social reproduction were the core philosophy for marriage.[13] But today in most countries there is no employment that is exclusively male or female; men and women work alongside each other and share financial and other responsibilities in the family and in bringing up the children. In such conditions, the logic of men's guardianship over women as based on their role as sole provider has already lost its meaning.

It must be pointed out that the Prophet, while introducing structural reforms in Hijaz society, took several important steps in reforming the institution of the family and improving the rights and welfare of women of his time,[14] as has been mentioned by many Muslim and non-Muslim scholars.[15] But he could not bring about instant, revolutionary and radical transformations in the family system. No one could. Why? Because it would have been a fantasy, doomed to fail in practice. Law, as well as aiming to make social relations more just, is essentially the formulation of dominant social realities. Law is not written for a hypothetical dream society. The Prophet and the revelation too did not seek to devise an immutable, idyllic and perfect society. Some Muslims believe erroneously that Islam and the Qur'an wanted to establish the ultimate perfect society in their time. Certainly, Islam contains great ethical and humane ideals, but these are to be pursued gradually and in relative terms. Is it possible in the course of ten years, or even 23 years, to create the ideal, perfect society? Qur'anic and Islamic regulations relating to society and the family were based on an acceptance of existing realities; they sought to reform them by adopting some transformative measures and nothing more.

When it comes to justice we need to separate three subjects: the ideal of justice, the definition of justice and the manifestation of justice. An ideal, by definition, is not bound by time and space, but the definition and, in particular, the manifestation of justice, is also changing, to the extent that, at a certain conjunction of time and place, a ruling might be just, while being oppressive at another.

The important question is: are verse 4:34 and similar ones basically describing social reality in seventh-century Medina, or formulating a value system and an eternal law? In other words, are Islam and the Qur'an descriptive or prescriptive? Regrettably, from the earliest times, most Muslims, and even the *'ulamā'*, have not paid due attention to this point, confusing a description of reality with recommendation and evaluation; hence, they have reached incorrect and misleading conclusions. To take descriptive verses as prescriptive is an error. Of course, this is an epistemological error and has nothing to do with Islam and the Qur'an. But if we can rectify this error, we can eliminate many other misunderstandings and errors in *fiqh* and Islamic law.

From the above discussion, we can conclude that laws and concepts relating to the family and women's rights, including men's guardianship and authority over women on the grounds that men provide for women (the subject of the verse 4:34), have today lost, or are in the process of losing, their legislative rationale (*falsafa tashri'ī*). On the basis of the *fiqh* principle that 'the ruling is related to its subject matter', the jurists have no other option but to admit that some of these rulings must be abrogated (*mansūkh*). In some cases these rulings may have retained their subject matter, but when they do begin to lose it, then the jurists should be prepared to declare them abrogated. Most jurists believe that there are several occurrences of abrogation in the Qur'an itself, yet many of these abrogated verses were retained when the sacred text was compiled. It is noteworthy that such a perspective is now spreading among traditional and open-minded jurists; for instance, to justify the time-bound and place-specific nature of some of the Qur'anic verses, the late Ayatollah Mohammad Hadi Maʿrefat, the scholar and jurist in Qom, employed the concept of 'preparatory abrogation' (*naskh tamhīdī*), which he defines as the Qur'anic method for eradicating some of the Jahiliyya habits and customs. In order to abolish certain pre-Islamic customs, such as slavery and the mistreatment of women, Islam devised, he contends, either long-term or short-term measures. Certain Qur'anic verses relating to these matters were either abrogated at the time of the Prophet, or the ground was prepared through a series of measures for their abrogation. In his words, 'this is an abrogation, the grounds for which were prepared at the time of the Prophet'; the issue of men's authority over women, which included severe and painful beating, is one such matter. He goes on to say that, although beating is mentioned in the Qur'an (4:34), the Prophet interpreted it in such a way as led to its reduction at that time and its abolition in the long term. Thus, the apparent meaning of the second part of the verse was abrogated, being in clear opposition to the Prophet's command, and his and the Imams' eloquent recommendations.[16] In other words, the verse prepared the ground for the abrogation of men's authority over women in the long term.

It must be pointed out that, on the whole, Muslim jurists have not paid due attention to the sequence of revelation of verses containing legal rulings, nor to the philosophy and function of the earlier rulings (the objectives of Shariʿa); they tend to issue fatwas on the basis of a single verse, or one verse and several hadith, and, astonishingly, claim such inferences to be divine and immutable. Their traditional line of argument is that any legislation found in the Qur'an and Sunna is eternal and not open to question, but this is neither logical nor acceptable. If it were, then slavery – the sale and purchase of human beings, the taking of slaves in war – and all those rulings relating to it, including the taking as booty of women whose husbands had just died, sleeping with them and selling them and their children, are also religiously sanctioned (*mashrūʿ*) and acceptable! Is there a Muslim jurist today who dares to defend these rulings and attribute them to God, religion, revelation and the Prophet? If the answer is negative, then why and on what grounds do we introduce all these discriminations and injustices in the name of Islam, often without any basis in the Qur'an and the authentic Sunna? What is the juristic logic and rationale for such a dogmatic defence?

It can be said with certainty that if the trend of positive changes for women introduced by Islam had continued after the Prophet, not only would we not be facing such problems now, but even in those early centuries women would have occupied high positions in society and civilisation, and in the fields of economy, art and knowledge. We would not have been in this position in the twenty-first century, where we have to argue over obvious and basic issues and need to wage a great struggle (jihad) to secure minimum rights for Muslim women. Those (including 'Umar ibn al-Khattab),[17] who at the time of the Prophet constantly objected to his practice in enhancing the rights and status of women, after his death assumed the leadership and management of the newly founded Islamic society and returned to the pre-Islamic misogyny and mindset, albeit defending it this time in the name of Islam and the continuation of the Prophetic Sunna.

In conclusion, if we take *wilāya* in its original Qur'anic sense of reciprocal and faith-based responsibility, and *qiwāma* in the sense of men's protection of women, then not only is there no problem with these concepts, but their sanction in Islam in the past was very useful, and had relevance in reality, as it still has. If we do not see history as a story of ideals, we recognise that in recent millennia, for whatever reason, women were weaker than men in defending themselves and were more vulnerable when faced by threats and insecurity. In particular, in all historical eras women's sexuality was desired and controlled by men; while many wars, invasions and raids were conducted to gain access to women. Basically, in all societies, especially during war, because of their physical and sexual attributes women were subject to rape and greater harm; and this is still the case today. It was in such a milieu that concepts such as *nāmūs* (sexual honour) and its protection, *ghayra* (sexual jealousy) and manliness (*mardanegi*) emerged as ethical values and as a familial duty for the physically stronger sex. Therefore, we can see that in societies (such as Iran) where the possibility of harm was greater, these values became more pronounced, stronger and enduring. Probably this historical fact played a role in giving rise to misconceptions such as women being evil or their sexuality being a danger – an idea that has penetrated the traditions of many peoples, and has made its way even into the sayings of some great personalities in Islam. There is a great possibility that such sayings were fabricated in later centuries, as they are in stark contrast with the values, principles and teachings of Islam as a religion.

Nevertheless, the combination of old family systems and Muslim jurists' belief in men's superiority as reflected in concepts like *wilāya* and *qiwāma* gave rise to a discriminatory legal system that sanctioned women's inferiority and constrained their freedom of choice in most spheres of life, particularly marriage. In this system, a daughter inherits half as much as a son; a wife inherits only a fraction of her husband's estate; divorce is in the hands of the man, who by respecting certain conditions can marry a person of another religion, while a woman cannot; a man can be polygamous but a woman cannot; a wife must submit to her husband's sexual desires in order to receive her maintenance; a woman, in the opinion of the majority of jurists, is banned from positions of leadership and judgeship; according to most fatwas, a virgin cannot marry without the permission of her father; *mahr* is regarded as an intrinsic element of marriage and so on. The time has come for a fundamental intellectual shake-up in this system, and for building a new legal structure within the Qur'anic and tawhidic value system, with an eye, of course, to contemporary understandings of justice and notions of rights.

Notes

1 For instance, in pre-Islamic Arabia it was believed that women were possessed by an evil force during their menses; most probably the ban on sexual activity during this period, and even the obligation of *ghusl* (the complete bath) after intercourse or at the end of menses, have to do with purification after the exit of the evil spirit from body and soul.

2 This is the subject of verse 33:33; although *tabarrūj* in this verse denotes 'women offering themselves [sexually]', not simply the act of dressing up and the beautification of face and body as it is understood now.

3 In *Nahj al-Balāgha* there is a saying attributed to Imam 'Ali, that women are entitled to less inheritance than men because they are defective in reason and faith; they are defective in reason because the testimony of two women equals that of one man; they are defective in faith because they cannot pray or fast during their menses. From this it is concluded that men should avoid women who are evil and disobedient; beware of the ones who are good and obedient; and ignore their good advice so that they cannot tempt men into doing evil. Such views and arguments are unacceptable because they contradict the Qur'anic premises and Islam and are not in line with the conduct and practice of 'Ali himself.

4 In my book *Reason at the Feast of Religion* I have dealt with these in detail. Eshkevari, Hassan Yousefi, *Kherad Dar Ziyafat-e Din* (Tehran: Qasideh, 1379/2000).

5 Among such contemporary jurists are Ayatollah Ahmad Khonsari and Ayatollah Yousef Sane'i.

6 See Abdolkarim Soroush's lecture for the Erasmus Prize, 2004 (http://www.dai-heidelberg.de/content/e849/e273/e193/soroush_ger.pdf).

7 On the changeability of social rulings in Islam, see my article on 'Ahkam-e Ejtema'i-ye Islam va Hoquq-e Bashar' [Islam's social rulings and human rights], available on my website (http://yousefieshkevari.com/?p=751). It has also been translated into German and published in Amirpur, Katajun (ed.), *Unterwegs zu einem anderen Islam: Texte iranischer Denker* (Freiburg, 2009), pp. 149–80.

8 Although most Persian translators of the Qur'an render *ma'rūf* as 'proper', these verses clearly show that in employing the term the Qur'an intends more than a neutral ethical recommendation. *'Urf* and *ma'rūf* are the good customs and practices of people at any time and on any place on earth. 'Proper' as a translation for *ma'rūf* is, of course, correct, but it only conveys an element of this concept,

not its totality. This is the very meaning of *aḥkām imḍā'ī* – rulings in the Qur'an that endorse the good customs of the time. The verses (3:104, 110) that command 'enjoining good and forbidding evil' (*al-amr bi al-ma'rūf wa al-nahy 'an al-munkar*) can also be understood in this light.

9 Translator's note: see previous note; in this instance, however, the English renderings of *ma'rūf* are, variously, 'just' or 'equitable'.

10 We do not deal with the second part of the verse, which is not our concern here.

11 Cf. Mir-Hosseini, Ziba, 'Towards gender equality: Muslim family laws and the Shari'a', in Z. Anwar (ed.), Wanted: Equality and Justice in the Muslim Family (Musawah: An Initiative of Sisters in Islam, 2009), available at http://www.musawah.org/wanted-equality-and-justice-muslim-family (accessed 10 September 2012).

12 It must be noted that Morteza Motahhari, in response to the objections of those who, influenced by modern thought, questioned the economic and transactional aspect of *mahr*, defended this tradition as a gift, yet went on to say, on the basis of the fatwas of the jurists, that *ṣadāq* is obligatory.

13 In particular, a saying of the Prophet that the purpose of marriage is to multiply the Muslim population; see al-Haddad, al-Tahir, *Imra'tunā fī al-Sharī'a wa al-Mujtama'* [Our Women in the Shari'a and Society] (Cairo: Al-Madani, 1999), p. 30.

14 For example, the Prophet recognised women's human dignity; supported their rights to manage their property and to engage in all economic activities (he educated and supported 'A'isha, the Mother of the Faithful, a politically astute woman); regarded men and women as equal on all fronts including faith, salvation and individual responsibility; urged men to observe equality and justice in dealing with women; limited the number of wives a man could acquire; endorsed women's free choice in marriage; and so on. The Prophet's recurrent advice to treat women with kindness and to ensure their security and status in the family and society played a role in respecting their rights and reducing violence against them. This was reflected in his own relations with his wives, and in many of his sayings, including his last sermon, a few months before his death (known as the Farewell).

15 One such non-Muslim Western scholar is Karen Armstrong; see her small but rich book, *Muhammad: A Prophet for Our Time* (London, New York, Sydney: HarperCollins, 2006), translated into Persian by Farhad Mahdavi (Germany: Nima, 2008).

16 Ranani, Mehdi Soltani, 'Naskh az Didgah-e Ayatollah Ma'refat' [Abrogation in the Qur'an in Ayatollah Ma'refat's perspective], *Majalleh Takhassosi Elahiyat va Huquq* [Specialised Journal of Theology and Law] 46 (Winter 1386/1997), pp. 179–92.

17 The Prophet's father-in-law, who became the second caliph. In a variety of Islamic sources we come across 'Umar's frequent protests to the Prophet regarding his treatment of women and his wives, including the following

famous sarcastic remark: 'In Mecca we ruled our women and in Medina our women became our rulers.' According to many sources, when the verses of the Qur'an were being collected during the time of the first caliph (Abu Bakr), 'Umar introduced a short verse containing the stoning punishment for adultery and claimed that it was part of the revelation. But the seven-person group responsible for the collection did not accept it, as he could not produce two just witnesses. Mernissi has shown the regressive trend in status and rights that women experienced after the death of the Prophet, and examined its causes, including the perspectives and role played by 'Umar. F. Mernissi, *Women and Islam: An Historical and Theological Enquiry* (Oxford: Blackwell, 1991); Persian translation by Maliheh Moghazee, *Zanan-e Pardehneshin va Nokhbegan-e Jowshanpush* (Tehran: Nashr-e Nai, 1380/2001).

10

REVISITING WOMEN'S RIGHTS IN ISLAM*

'Egalitarian Justice' in Lieu of 'Deserts-based Justice'[1]

Mohsen Kadivar

In traditional Islamic thought women's rights have been defined on the basis of a 'deserts-based' notion of justice (*al-ʿadāla al-istiḥqāqiyya*), by which individuals are entitled to justice according to their status, abilities and potential. This notion of justice leads to proportional equality, which recognises rights for individuals in proportion to their 'deserts'. In modern times this notion of justice has encountered enormous problems. Can we reread the Qur'an and the traditions in the light of an egalitarian notion of justice that is premised on fundamental equality between men and women?

This chapter is an attempt at such a rereading. It is written from the position of an Usuli Shiʿi,[2] with the method of 'ijtihad in foundations' (*al-ijtihād fī al-uṣūl*), that is, *ijtihād* in the theoretical and philosophical foundations of Islamic law. The chapter is based on the following premises: (i) The rulings (*aḥkām*) on women in the Qur'an and the traditions (Sunna) strongly defend the principle of justice.

* Translated from Persian by Ziba Mir-Hosseini.

(ii) These rulings are explained by arguments and proofs. (iii) Justice is a prior principle to religion, and the definition of justice and justification of the different approaches to it are matters of reason and philosophy. (iv) Some Qur'anic verses and hadith relating to women are generally based on justice and non-discrimination, others appear (*ẓāhir*) to be based on a deserts-based notion of justice and proportional equality. (v) Muslim scholars, who (whether exegetists, hadith specialists, theologians, jurists, mystics or philosophers) have been predominantly men, understood and continue to understand justice as deserts-based justice, and equality as proportional equality. (vi) There are undeniable biological and psychological differences between men and women. (vii) The site of discussion is those rulings that grant women, because they are women, greater or lesser rights than men; these rulings are mainly found in the two fields of civil and penal law, so rulings that do not treat men and women differently (those pertaining to worship and commerce and the majority of those relating to matters of belief and ethics) fall outside our discussion.

There are two parts to my thesis in this chapter. First, the notions of egalitarian justice and fundamental equality accord better with the spirit of the Qur'an and Islamic standards. Secondly, the verses and the hadiths that have been invoked as justifying disparity in men's and women's rights are not an obstacle to egalitarian justice and fundamental equality.

The chapter consists of four sections. Section one is a review of the most important rational and textual arguments for legal parity and difference. Section two examines the perspective and arguments of 'deserts-based justice'. Section three describes those of 'egalitarian justice' and 'fundamental equality', and explores how they are more in line with the spirit of the Qur'an and Islamic standards. Finally, section four takes the Qur'anic verses and hadiths invoked to justify legal differences between men and women, and rereads them in the light of egalitarian justice.

1. The most important textual and rational arguments for legal equality and inequality

In the Qur'an and traditions we encounter two types of argument regarding women's rights. The first type treats men and women as equal, entitled to the same human rights without any legal difference. The second suggests that men are superior to women, thus they enjoy more rights but at the same time are charged with protecting women. There are rational arguments, independent of the texts, for the essential goodness of justice and the essential badness of injustice and discrimination. Before engaging in any kind of interpretation, let us examine the most important of these verses and hadiths, and elucidate their rational arguments.

a. Qur'anic arguments for the legal equality of men and women

The verses indicating equality can be divided into five groups, implying: (i) equality in creation; (ii) equality in the hereafter; (iii) equality in rights and duties; (iv) equality in rewards and punishments in this world and the other; and (v) equality in married life.

(i) This group presents men and women as created from the same essence, and rejects gender-based superiority. Gender does not produce human dignity and closeness to God; how can it produce superiority?

> O mankind! We created you from a single (pair) of a male and a female, And made you into nations and tribes, that ye may know each other. Verily the most honoured of you in the sight of Allah is the most righteous of you (49:13).[3]

Gender, tribe, race, colour, wealth, status and power do not produce superiority; God-consciousness (*taqwā*) is the measure of dignity and closeness to God. *All people, male or female, are descended from a single man and woman* (4:1).

(ii) In the afterlife, God treats men and women in the same way. Gender plays no role in salvation, which is determined by belief and righteous action.

> Whoever works righteousness, man or woman, and has faith, verily, to him will We give a new life and life that is good and pure, and We will bestow on such their rewards according to the best of their actions (16:97).[4]

The Qur'an names ten categories of believing men and women who will receive forgiveness and great reward:

> For believing men and women, for devout men and women, for true men and women, for men and women who are patient and constant, for men and women who humble themselves, for men and women who fast (and deny themselves), for men and women who guard their chastity, for men and women who engage in Allah's praise, for them has Allah prepared forgiveness and great reward (33:35).

Here too gender difference has no place.

(iii) Equality in rights and obligations:

> The believers, men and women, are protectors, one of another: they enjoin what is just, and forbid what is evil; they observe regular prayers, practice regular charity, and obey Allah and His messenger. On them Allah pours His mercy (9:71).

This verse recognises that believing men and women have a responsibility to protect each other. The equality of men and women in the important duties of 'enjoining good and forbidding evil' and mutual protection leaves no doubt; if women lacked the essential ability, they would never be charged with such responsibilities. This verse provides the basis for understanding the second type of verses (inequality).

(iv) Equality in rewards and punishments in this world and the other. Qur'an 48:5, 6 and 25, and 57:12–13 treat men and women equally in regard to entitlement to reward or punishment. Likewise, Qur'an 5:38 and 24:2, 26 and 31 speak of identical worldly punishments for male and female thieves, fornicators and wrongdoers.

(v) Equality in marital life. Qur'an 2:187 gives a picture of equal shares for spouses in their shared life: 'They are your garments and you are their garments.' This picture is repeated in 30:21: the creation of men and women is among the signs of God, and the presence of each is a source of tranquillity, love and mercy for the other. Should not this logical foundation be the basis for understanding other Qur'anic verses relating to the family?

b. Rational arguments for justice in the realm of women's rights

Can reason on its own (*al-'aql al-mustaqill*) give a ruling about women's rights? Let us review some preliminary points here. First, certain acts are either good or evil inherently, that is to say, without a ruling from the Lawgiver. This is the basic claim of the Muslim rationalists (People of Justice, that is, the Shi'a and the Mu'tazili). Secondly, reason has the capacity, independent of scripture, to decide whether such acts are good or evil; this is the main claim of the Shi'a Usulis as opposed to the Shi'a Akhbaris. Thirdly, most Usulis claim that if reason considers something good, religion declares it mandatory, and if reason finds it bad, religion declares it forbidden. Fourthly, *shar'ī* rulings that are based on the principle of correlation (between reason and Shari'a) are valid (*ḥujja*), in the sense that when we are absolutely sure that the Lawgiver has not forbidden it, our rational ruling (based on the principle of correlation) can be counted as a *shar'ī* ruling. This is the claim of most Usulis as opposed to those who reject the ruling of reason.

Among these four preliminary points, the first and last are important; that is to say, we can settle the question (i.e. whether reason can produce a *shar'ī* ruling independent of texts), if we can demonstrate the validity of the first point, and if the conditions for the fourth point are present. Now, we can restate the first point as follows: rulings related to women's rights are in the realm of reason. Legal justice in regard to men and women is a good thing. Reasonable people, as they are reasonable, approve of legal justice. Legal justice is one of the praised ideas and common premises (*al-ārā' al-maḥmūda wa al-qaḍāyā al-mashhūra*). Reasonable people, as they are reasonable, praise those who implement justice, and blame those who neglect it.

Practical reason rules that legal justice is good (and injustice and legal discrimination are bad), because it is consistent with the human soul, which recognises the public benefit (*naf' 'amm*) in legal justice (and the harm caused by injustice and discrimination). People seek the public good (*maṣlaḥa 'amm*) that comes from justice, and resist the corruption stemming from injustice and legal discrimination. People recognise that this is a public, not a personal matter; indeed that it is a universal matter, of interest (*maṣlaḥa*) to the whole human species. This interest is necessary for the protection of order in human society and for the survival of the human species. The basis of this recognition is the rational faculty. So all reasonable people, as they are reasonable, praise it. By the same token, legal discrimination is a great cause of corruption (*mafsada*) to humanity, therefore all reasonable people disapprove of it, finding it unwholesome and evil.

When reasonable people, as they are reasonable, collectively agree that justice is good and deserves to be praised, and that legal discrimination is evil and deserves to be blamed, on the grounds that they are, respectively, beneficial and harmful to the public interest, then Shi'i Usulis will consider it to be a rational ruling.[5] Legal justice reflects the perfection of human societies, and legal discrimination the imperfection of them. Reason perceives such perfection and imperfection in a general way: perfection is in the interest of humankind while imperfection leads to injury. People of reason, as they are reasonable, make this judgement in order to obtain beneficial consequences and to reject harmful consequences for humanity. The Lawgiver necessarily concurs with reasonable people, because it is a basic principle of the 'People of Justice'[6] that the Lawgiver is reasonable and, in fact, is the head of all reasonable people.

Legal justice is a cause of goodness, and injustice and legal discrimination are causes of evil. On this basis, justice and discrimination are essentially good and evil respectively. Reasonable people praise those who stand for justice and blame those who stand for injustice and discrimination. The goodness of justice and the evil of injustice are absolutes that transcend questions of expediency and usefulness.[7]

c. Textual arguments for the legal superiority of men over women

The most important textual arguments for men's superiority over women can be found in four verses from the Qur'an and two hadiths from the Prophet Muhammad and Imam 'Ali.

> And women shall have rights similar to men to the rights against them, according to what is equitable; but men have a degree (of advantage) over them. (2:228)

> And in no wise covet those things in which Allah has bestowed His gifts more freely on some of you than on others; to men is allocated what they earn, and to women what they earn; but ask Allah of His bounty. (4:32)

> Men are the protectors and maintainers of women because Allah has given the one more than the other, and because they support them from their means. (4:34)

> Is then one brought up among trinkets, and unable to give a clear account in a dispute (to be associated with Allah)? (43:18)

A sound hadith from the Bukhari collection:

> When I was in doubt whether the supporters of 'A'isha were in the right and whether or not I should join them in their fight, God helped me by a saying from the Prophet and saved me from falling into the trap. When the news was brought to him that the daughter of the Persian king Kasra had assumed the throne, the Prophet said: People who entrust their affairs to women will never know prosperity and find salvation.[8]

From Imam 'Ali's sermon about women's defectiveness after the Battle of the Camel:

> O people, women are inferior to men in faith, in wealth and in reason. The proof of their deficiency in faith is that they do not pray or fast during their menses, the proof of their deficiency in reason is that the testimony of two of them equals that of one man, and the proof of their deficiency in wealth is that their share in inheritance is half of that of men. So keep away from bad women and be careful with the good ones, and do not give in to them when they are good, so that they do not expect you to obey them when they are bad.[9]

2. Women's rights from the perspective of deserts-based justice

In this section I first present women's rights in the words of the chief proponents of deserts-based justice, then narrate the rational and textual arguments they put forward.

a. Deserts-based justice and women's rights in the discourse of contemporary thinkers

'Allameh Seyyed Mohammad Hossein Tabataba'i (d. 1981) clearly sets out his perspective on women's rights during his interpretation of the above verses. Given his high level of learning and his nearness to us in time, he is one of the most important exponents of deserts-based justice.

In the following paragraphs I summarise his views.

Islam upholds equality between men and women in organising their lives, but woman has been created with two distinctive traits. One is that woman is like soil for the cultivation and growth of the human species; therefore, the survival of the human species depends on women. For this reason, there are rulings for women like those for agricultural land; hence, they are distinct from men. The second trait is that, besides their physical delicacy, women have been endowed with mental weakness, which has a bearing on their social status and duties.

Men and women can have two kinds of superiority. One is specific to men (their share of inheritance) and women (their entitlement to maintenance); the other is not specific to men or women but is based on behaviour and attributes that bestow superiority, such as faith, knowledge, piety (*taqwā*), and other virtues praised by religion.

All rulings related to worship and social rights treat men and women the same, except in matters that, by nature, require difference. The most important of these are: women cannot lead in political or judicial affairs; in war, they are not required to engage in combat, though medical aid and nursing the wounded is another matter; women's inheritance share is half of that of men; for women hijab and covering the site of ornaments (*zīna*) is mandatory; women are required to submit to their husbands in sexual matters. A woman is compensated for her loss in these areas by her lifelong right to maintenance by her father or husband. The husband is obligated to protect his wife as best he can. The right to raise and care for the children rests with the woman. God has mandated these in order to protect a woman's life, her (sexual) honour and even her reputation, and she is excused prayer and fasting during her menses. Women must be treated leniently in all conditions.

A woman need not seek knowledge apart from that pertaining to major religious beliefs and practical obligations (i.e. laws regulating worship and social affairs), and she has no other duty than that of obeying her husband and meeting his sexual desires. She is not required to go out to work, to manage the family or to study, though all these activities are advantageous, and not forbidden to women.

According to Tabataba'i, equality is a natural prerequisite of social rights and duties, but equality that stems from social justice does not require that all social ranks be distributed among all members of society. The prerequisite of social justice that can be interpreted as equality is for all to have their proper rights. Thus, equality between individuals and classes means only that every person should get what they are entitled to, without conflict between these entitlements. Qur'an 2:228 stresses equality in men's and women's rights and yet admits the natural differences between them.

Women are like men in being endowed with thought, free will, authority and control in all areas of personal and social life (except those mentioned), yet in these areas they differ from men in certain respects. Biologically, the average woman is inferior to the average man in brainpower, heart, veins and nerves, let alone height and weight. For this reason, women's bodies are softer and weaker and men's rougher and physically stronger; and women have gentler feelings such as love and tenderness and a greater interest in beauty and self-adornment, while men are more rational than women. Thus, women's life is emotional and men's life is rational.

In Islam, the difference in social duties and obligations (of men and women) is due to their different emotional and rational faculties. For example, men are specialists in politics, law and warfare, where rationality plays a greater role, while women specialise in raising children and managing the household. Men are responsible for the expenses of women and children, for which God compensates them with a double share in inheritance. In reality, men possess two-thirds of the property, but women too get two-thirds (one-third by ownership and one third as beneficiary of men [i.e. their right to maintenance and dower]). Consequently, men have overall control because of their rationality, while women get more assistance because of their emotional advantages.

The above paragraphs summarise Tabataba'i's 'What did Islam innovate on the women's issue?', a section of his long 'scientific discussion' of the rights of women.[10] In the following section, entitled 'The liberty of women in the West', Tabataba'i proceeds to argue as follows.

If it is objected that such concessions to women are the cause of the women's lack of social progress, the answer is that Islamic rulings themselves are not the problem; rather, it is their incorrect application. Non-pious rulers are the main cause of women's lack of maturity and adequate upbringing. The contemporary West assumes the universal legal equality of men and women, ignoring women's immaturity compared to men; the prevalent view is that if women are inferior to men in maturity and virtue, it is because of centuries of poor upbringing, whereas by nature men and women are created equal.

We criticise such a view, Tabataba'i continues, by saying that, if women were not created inferior, their natural equality with men would, in time, have manifested itself, and women's primary and secondary faculties would have become the same as men's. In the course of history, and even in the modern times in the West, in all matters where Islam has officially recognised men's priority over women (politics, law and warfare), men are still dominant and we do not see equality.[11]

'Allameh Tabataba'i explains verse 4:34 as follows: what is meant by superiority (*faḍīla*) is the advantages that the Lawgiver has given men and women through specific rulings, such as men's advantage over women in terms of polygamy and a greater share of inheritance, and women's advantage over men in their right to claim maintenance and dower from their husbands. God has instilled these advantages in the human soul. The term *qayyim* means someone who stands *qiyām*, responsible for another. *Qawwām* and *qayyim* are intensive forms of the same *qiyām*. What is intended by *mā faḍḍala Allāh* ('Allah has given the one more') is the advantage that God has given men in creation and nature, that is, their superior reasoning power, which enables them to handle difficult tasks. Women's life is based on emotion, tenderness and gentle feelings. 'They support them' refers to maintenance and dower. The corollary of the generality of these reasons for men's authority ('Allah has given one more' and 'they support them') is that the ruling is not limited to husbands and wives, but is generalised to the authority of the class of men over the class of women, in public matters which affect the survival of both. For instance, government, judgment and military defence demand physical and intellectual strength. Anyway, the beginning of the verse, 'men are the protectors and maintainers of women', sets a general rule, and subsequent phrases in the verse are elaborations of this. A woman's duties to obey her husband when he is present and to keep chaste in his absence outweigh any rights that may conflict with them.[12]

In the commentary on the Qur'an 43:18, 'Allameh Tabataba'i states that women are naturally stronger than men in feelings and kindness, and weaker in reason. The clearest manifestations of their emotionality are their extreme partiality to bodily adornment and their weakness in argument, which is based on the rational faculty.[13]

Ayatollah Morteza Motahhari pursued his teacher's line of argument when giving the following philosophical exposition of the notion of (deserts-based) justice:

> Islam is not opposed to equal rights for men and women, but is opposed to identical rights ... Since men and women are different by nature, then different rights for them are not only more concordant with both justice and natural rights but provide more happiness in the family and progress in society. Justice and the natural and human rights of men and women require a certain disparity in rights ... Any innate aptitude is in itself the basis of, and evidence for, a natural right.[14]

In the last years of his life, Ayatollah Hossein 'Ali Montazeri Najafabadi gave a juristic exposition of (deserts-based) justice when he said, 'all rights and duties for men and women must be based on justice, and justice does not mean equality of men and women in all matters, rather it means giving rights to each according to their deserts, and duties to each according to their abilities'.[15]

b. Formulation of the arguments in the school of deserts-based justice

The textual and rational arguments of all these thinkers, who have been my teachers directly or indirectly, can, in effect, be stated as follows.

First, the textual arguments for legal equality are the starting point, in the sense of the context for discussion of legal equality between men and women, unless there are valid arguments for inequality.

Secondly, the textual arguments against legal equality are those valid arguments that allow a specific case to deviate from the context. In such a case, a specific or contingent argument is considered as definite contextual evidence (*qarīna qaṭʿiyya*) that allows the jurist to disregard the general and absolute, and there is no room to appeal to arguments for legal equality.

Thirdly, the rationale of this perspective is as follows: justice, which independent reason rules to be good, means treating people according to their natural deserts. Natural rights are revealed in innate capacities. Justice is the fulfilment of natural rights. In cases where men's and women's capacities are alike, they are entitled to the same natural and *shar'ī* rights. In cases in which their capacities differ, they are evidently entitled to different natural rights and, consequently, to unequal *shar'ī* rights. It is the essence of justice for equals to be treated equally, and for unequals to be treated unequally. It is the essence of injustice if women, who lack certain abilities and capacities, though they may possess others, are given the same rights and duties as men. This difference in rights is not discrimination; it is true justice.

In this perspective, existing juristic rulings on women are essential to justice; both text and reason support this. Correct application of these rulings will lead to happiness in this world and the next. Legal equality of men and women is rationally and religiously unacceptable.

3. Egalitarian justice and fundamental equality in the light of the Qur'anic spirit and Islamic standards

Now it is time to criticise the perspective of traditional thinkers on women's rights. In this section we shall discuss their rational arguments, and in the next section, their textual arguments. This section has three parts; first, having probed the roots of 'deserts-based justice', we shall analyse the notion of 'egalitarian justice'. We shall present the rational arguments for the superiority of egalitarian justice, and finally argue for the greater compatibility of both egalitarian justice and fundamental equality with the spirit of the Qur'an and with Islamic standards.

a. From deserts-based justice to egalitarian justice

Those in favour of deserts-based justice argue as follows: equal persons must be treated equally. They are entitled to equal rights. Those who are unequal must be treated according to their deserts. It is evident that everyone's rights are commensurate with their capacities, abilities and potentials, and equal rights for those who are unequal is injustice. In this perspective, humans are equal, but this equality is proportional, and people have rights in proportion to their abilities. This notion of justice goes with 'proportional equality'.

This, the oldest and best-known notion of justice, is close to Aristotle's 'distributive justice',[16] which Muslims have approved as the one that is acceptable in the Qur'an and Islam.[17] The definition of justice as 'putting everything in its place and giving everyone their proper rights'[18] reflects Muslim philosophers' understanding of the Aristotelian notion, which justifies slavery and gender inequality.

After the publication of the American Declaration of Independence (1776) and the Declaration of the Rights of Man and the Citizen in the French Revolution (1789), 'proportional equality' gave way to the notion, in several constitutions, of the equality of all human beings as a divine or natural right, that is, 'fundamental equality'. This view gradually brought about a new formulation of 'distributive justice':[19] although people have different abilities and potentials they are all human beings, and are therefore entitled to equal status and respect.[20] In other words, all human beings have equal rights. This too rests on two premises: first, treat unequal cases in an equal way; secondly, the foundation of distributive justice is legal equality, unless there is sufficient reason for unequal treatment.[21]

Comparison of the older and newer notions of distributive justice in the field of women's rights shows that: a) there is no doubt that there are biological and psychological differences between men and women; b) women's biological and psychological characteristics were the justification for their having fewer rights according to the older notion; c) women's humanity is the reason for their equal rights with men on the basis of fundamental equality; d) these equal rights can be overruled only when there is sufficient reason to consider unequal rights just, such as women's right to protection (positive discrimination).

In this chapter, I refer to Muslim thinkers' understanding of distributive justice and proportional equality, that is, the Aristotelian perspective,[22] as 'deserts-based justice', and to the notion of distributive justice based on fundamental equality as 'egalitarian justice'.

b. Rational arguments for the primacy of egalitarian justice over deserts-based justice

Why are egalitarian justice and fundamental equality more reasonable than deserts-based justice and proportional equality? Here I answer this question without reference to Islam, Qur'an or Sunna, but through the following propositions.

Proposition One: Justice is a pre-religious concept. Human beings understand justice through their intellect. Everyone can recognise justice and injustice, in the broadest sense. Human beings define justice on the basis of experience and collective and historical reason. For a long time, deserts-based justice and proportional equality were dominant ideas, which accorded women, slaves and blacks lower status than men, freemen and whites. This legal inferiority was, for centuries, seen as justice and was justified rationally.

But these ideas have, for some time, been seriously criticised. People today no longer find deserts-based justice and proportional equality acceptable; the understanding of humans and their rights has changed. Human beings have rights as human beings, not as members of social categories such as females, slaves or blacks. Humanity is in the human spirit and nature, which is the same in every person, and a basis for dignity and respect. Human spirit or nature has no gender, race, colour, religion, political ideology, social status or any other attribute. In other words, the meaning of 'rights-holder' has changed, and all human beings, because they are human, deserve equal rights. If proportional equality was reasonable at the time when rights were based on such social categories, now that human beings have rights by virtue of their humanity, the notion of fundamental equality is certainly valid, and proportional equality, which entails legal inequality, can no longer be justified.

Proposition Two: The conventional contemporary understanding of justice is egalitarian justice. In other words, justice means treating all human beings equally, and no human attribute is a barrier to legal equality or a cause of legal discrimination. Legal equality is the foundation, to be set aside only for a sufficient reason. Just as being black is no justification for legal inferiority, so being female is not a valid reason for legal inequality.

Proposition Three: Deserts-based justice is built on the notion of proportional equality. It can be constructed only by 'deducing ought from is', for example, that a woman must have fewer rights because she differs from a man in biology and psychology. But deducing 'ought' from 'is' is seriously problematic;[23] it requires philosophical substantiation, yet no substantiation has yet been proposed. Note that differences between men and women are not denied; rather, what is denied is that they can be the basis of unequal rights. What philosophical argument can demonstrate that 'is' justifies 'ought'? What is the rational argument for femaleness being the basis for fewer rights? How can physical weakness or emotional strength justify fewer rights or none?

Proposition Four: Legal equality is justice, and discrimination is injustice. Further, there is no doubt that justice is essentially good and injustice essentially bad. Why is equality just and discrimination unjust? Traditional thinkers neither recognise equality as essentially good nor count it a particular of justice. In their belief, justice is linked to deserts, not to equality; people's deserts do not necessarily lead to equality. Deserts means that each person gets rights to match their capacities, no more, no less: women, slaves and non-Muslims get the rights they deserve. The equality of man and woman, of slave and free, and of Muslim and non-Muslim, is opposed to justice. However, human reason today does not see such distinctions as differences of deserts, and considers justice based on them to be oppression.

For centuries, justice based on deserts served to justify slavery, gender discrimination and the like. How, in reality, were these deserts established? Whence, and on what undisputed evidence, did we establish that a woman deserves this much and a man that much? Does the kind of anthropology that, for centuries, assumed differences of deserts and accordingly made legal discriminations have any rational evidence for its claims? I will deal with textual evidence separately. The idea of deserts is based on unfounded assumptions.

Legal discrimination is, itself, injust, because human beings are similar in dignity and in human spirit, and, given similar opportunities, have a similar potential to grow and to attain perfection. The basis for equality in rights is the unitary human essence of all human beings; humans have equal rights because they share this divine essence. Human dignity derives from this shared essence, which is also the cause of equal rights. Human beings deserve the same rights because they share the same essence. The similarity is in their essential capacities, not in how they are realised.

The People of Justice believe in divine justice.[24] They believe that justice is prior to religion. Justice is not confined to dogma and theology. The Shariʿa of a just God is just. The *fiqh* of this school is justice-centred. Justice-centredness means necessarily deriving religious rulings in accordance with the principle of justice. Justice demands legal equality for men and women, and discrimination constitutes injustice. 'Justice' here means egalitarian justice, and deserts-based justice in our time is tantamount to legal discrimination and evidence of injustice.

Proposition Five: Human dignity and legal equality are mutually consistent. If human beings have dignity because of their humanity, this means that the human essence shared by men and women is dignified (*karīm*). Legal discrimination is the denial of the principle of dignity. If, in the past, the patriarchal order in practice left no space for the principle of dignity, today that principle leaves no space for patriarchy and its demands. From the perspective of contemporary rationality, dignity and justice are meaningless without legal equality; that is to say, there is a correlation between dignity and egalitarian justice.

Proposition Six: Wisdom always means choosing the superior and rejecting the inferior. Choosing the inferior when the superior is available is unwise. If yesterday's rationality saw merit and justice in legal discrimination between men and women, today's rationality considers such discrimination to be pure oppression and a denial of human rights. A review of traditional *fiqh* rulings relating to women that are premised on legal gender discrimination reveals their definite inferiority to legal gender equality. If we leave any fair person alone with their conscience, they will inevitably prefer egalitarian justice and fundamental equality to the discriminatory rulings of traditional thinkers. This rational preference is certain.

c. Why egalitarian justice and fundamental equality are more consistent with the spirit of the Qur'an and Islamic standards

Why are egalitarian justice and fundamental equality more consistent with the spirit of the Qur'an and Islamic standards?[25] Here I shall attempt to answer this question in the context of theology.

If justice is prior to religion, clearly what comes after cannot define and determine what comes before. Being prior to religion correlates with being rational; justice is defined by rational rulings; its concepts, discourses and dominant views change in accordance with rational methods and procedures. It is undeniable that justice has a central role in Islam, the Qur'an and the Sunna. In Shi'a and Mu'tazili theology, it has a key role, in the sense that people choose their religion on the basis of justice. God is just, the world is founded on justice, and divine law-making is done justly. Human beings are capable of understanding the standards of justice, even if they are only partially able to discern its manifestations.

Justice (*'adāla*), equity (*qisṭ*) and fairness (*inṣāf*) are not defined in the Qur'an and the Sunna, but they have been strongly advocated and endorsed. Clearly, God supports the kind of justice that human beings understand with their God-given reason. If God intended another meaning of justice, different from ordinary meanings, then He would have informed Muslims of this new meaning. In this way, we can attribute the existing language and logic to the Qur'an.

If egalitarian justice is the dominant paradigm of our time, then, without doubt, justice in the Qur'an and Sunna should be understood in this context, unless there is definite contextual evidence to the contrary.

Egalitarian justice and fundamental equality are more consistent with the spirit of the Qur'an and Islamic standards because, according to Islamic teaching, God is addressing the self or human spirit, which accepted the divine covenant and carries the 'trust' (*amāna*). A person's virtue and identity is in his soul, while the cells in the human body are naturally totally changed every few years. If physical resurrection is debatable, there is no doubt about spiritual resurrection or that the soul will receive its rewards and punishments.

It is this soul, a breath of the divine spirit, which makes human beings human and distinct from other animals; the angels bowed to humans because of this divine gift. Human dignity undoubtedly belongs to this divine spirit, not to the earthly body. Respect is due to this soul, for which the body is but a cover. This single soul is the origin of male and female humans; the human soul is subject to divine duties and rights. The soul has no gender. The foundation of human duties and rights is equality. Any unequal duty or right needs definite evidence; this is what the spirit of the Qur'an and Islamic standards requires.

4. Rereading the textual evidence on legal differentiation between men and women from the perspective of egalitarian justice

Some of the *shar'ī* rulings deduced on the basis of deserts-based justice weaken Islam and, at least according to today's rationality, are unjust, unethical, inferior and unacceptable; in other words, by the standards of egalitarian justice they are discriminatory and oppressive. To those who consider these rulings unproblematic,[26] we have nothing to say, but those who are aware of the problem must admit that there are drawbacks in the notion of deserts-based justice. What are they?

Scholars (i) reach their conclusions (ii) based on specific assumptions (iii) with a specific understanding (iv) of religious arguments. We have already assessed the patriarchal approach and the assumptions and rational understanding on which deserts-based justice is based; we now assess its religious arguments.

At the time of revelation, Islam took a giant step forward on the path of women's rights, and, given the condition of women then, raised their status in the world. This advance had two elements: one was complete equality of men's and women's rights; the other was advancing women's rights but not as far as full equality. Are the rulings denoting inequality the final word of Islam? In other words, are they among the unchangeable and eternal rulings, or the changeable and temporary ones? If the former, then we are compelled to interpret them as proportionate to women's innate deserts, and the result will be deserts-based justice. But if we come to believe that the world at that time, and for centuries after, was not ready to accept egalitarian justice – just as it was unprepared for the total abolition of slavery – then we see that the Lawgiver adopted a policy of gradualism to reach the desired conditions. First, in general terms, he indicated the direction towards equality of rights, and, in arenas where public acceptance was not yet possible, he took the level of rights half a step forward, until public opinion was ready for the second half-step. Deserts-based justice was the first half-step and egalitarian justice the second.

Traditional Muslim thinkers assumed that all or most laws legislated in early Islam were fixed and eternal. If this were so, then these laws should still be producing justice and ethics that are superior to other methods, and contemporary human wisdom would not reject them. But this is not the case. This is strong evidence that these laws are not of the fixed kind. A fixed and immutable ruling is always just, ethical, superior and reasonable. However, men's privilege and *qiwāma* over women, corporal punishment of a disobedient wife, permitting the marriage of an underage girl, men's right to unilateral divorce, two women's testimony being equal to one man's, a woman's blood money (*diya*) being equal to half a man's, a son's inheritance being twice that of a daughter, men's obligation to pay maintenance and dower – these rulings are all debatable. The Holy Qur'an (4:34) gave two causes for men's *qiwāma* over women: one is that 'Allah has given the one more' and the other that 'they support them from their means'. That 'men have a degree over them (women)' (2:228) was, without doubt, a function of these two causes. When God provided justification, it meant that the ruling was neither unquestioned (*taʿabbudī*) nor scripture-bound (*tawqīfī*). While the two causes remain, so does the effect, that is, men's *qiwāma*; but when the causes go, so also does the effect. Traditional thinkers, as we said, interpreted the first cause as men's innate superiority over women, and the second as mandating men's obligation to pay maintenance and dower; with the first cause, they mention men's superior mental and physical powers and women's emotional intensity and bodily weakness. But is men's pre-eminence permanent and indicative of women's lesser deserts? We must consider the following three points.

(i) In the Qur'an, God favours the children of Israel over other peoples: 'Children of Israel! Call to mind the (special) favours which I bestowed upon you, and that I preferred you to all others' (2:47, 122). Similarly, the supremacy of Israelites over the world is mentioned in 45:16 and 7:140. There is no doubt that the Israelites are not superior to the followers of Jesus Christ or the *umma* of Muhammad, and that 'other peoples' here means people before the calling of these two prophets. These verses are situational premises (*al-qaḍāyā al-khārijiyya*) not absolute premises (*al-qaḍāyā al-ḥaqīqiyya*), that is, they denote superiority in a specific time and place, not superiority innate and inherent in the children of Israel.

By exactly the same logic, men's superiority to women can relate to a specific era and is a situational premise; that is, it was relevant to a past situation when almost all women, because they were regarded as inferior, did not receive adequate upbringing and education. It does not relate to a time when, in spite of physical differences, women, like men, are counted as humans with equal rights.

(ii) The Holy Qur'an hails Blessed Mary as superior to all other women. 'Behold! The angels said: O Mary! Allah hath chosen thee and purified thee – chosen thee above the women of all nations' (3:42). Does 'women of all nations' mean women at that time, as a situational premise, or all women in the world from creation until the end of the world, even Fatima and Khadija, as an absolute premise?

The apparent meaning (*ẓuhūr*) of both verses is permanent superiority, but the superiority of Blessed Mary and the Children of Israel becomes time-bound, on the basis of 'assured disjunctive context'; and the same method limits the scope of reference of the verses discussed relating to the superiority of men over women. The context was one in which reasonable people, because they were reasonable, considered men's physical and intellectual superiority to be virtues deserving superior rights; this was the same time-bound context in which women could not live without male physical and financial protection. Naturally, in such a context women themselves accepted men's greater rights; and reasonable people (*sīra al-ʿuqalāʾ*) also considered men's superior rights to be just and fair.

But when reasonable people no longer recognise the biological, physical and psychological differences between men and women as a cause for men's superior rights; when fair-minded men and women themselves regard such a difference in rights not as justice, but as pure discrimination; and when both men and women share economic activities in the family and society, then there is no longer any doubt that such verses, like those relating to slavery, denote temporary rulings, not permanent ones.

The fact that such verses contain causes indicates that they are cause-based, and in a context when the cause is not realised, then the effect of the ruling is likewise annulled. If the issue were unquestioning imitation (*taʿabbudī*), the cause would not have been given; if the cause was stated, then the way is open for rational discussion.

(iii) The Holy Qur'an speaks of inequality in the distribution of material wealth and the superiority of some people over others as facts of social life:

> Is it they who would portion out the Mercy of thy Lord? It is We Who portion out between them their livelihood in the life of this world: And We raise some of them above others in ranks, so that some may command work for others. But the Mercy of thy Lord is better than the (wealth) which they amass. (43:32)

> Allah has bestowed His gifts of sustenance more freely on some of you than on others. (16:71)

> See how We bestowed more on some than on others; but verily the Hereafter is more in rank and gradation and more in excellence. (17:21)

There is no doubt that these verses attribute socio-economic inequalities to God. Likewise, human differences in talents and abilities cannot be denied. But the basic question is as follows: are these obvious socio-economic inequalities, which are actually rooted in the difference in human temperaments, the basis for unequal rights among these different human beings? The Qur'anic and Islamic answer is, definitely not. In that case, how can we say that gender difference is the cause of unequal *sharʿī* rights? Above all, in a time and context when women, like men, share in household expenses, and have proved their human capacities in the scientific fields. In the last few decades, women have shown that, when they enjoy the same opportunities and facilities as men, there is no noticeable difference between them in science and intellectual endeavours. At the very least, according to contemporary rationality, legal discrimination seems unjustifiable.

Given the above three points, we can conclude that, although we accept that the apparent meaning of the verses discussed is deserts-based justice and proportional equality, we must reject their invocation as immutable and eternal rulings in the form of absolute premises.

All verses and hadiths that imply legal discrimination against women are, first, situational and not absolute premises, that is, they refer to a specific time and place and do not affirm innate characteristics of men and women for all time and all places; ultimately, they refer to women's secondary and temporary dispositions in a specific era. Secondly, these rulings are mutable and temporal, not fixed and eternal. Thirdly, even if the temporality of these rulings is not accepted, the arguments for egalitarian justice and fundamental equality are strong enough to lead to their provisional abrogation, in the sense that as long as the arguments for egalitarian justice enjoy solid rational validity, rulings denoting inequality are considered abrogated on the basis that their validity has expired. We say 'provisional' out of extreme caution, but, according to contemporary rationality, we cannot imagine that past rationality will return.

In reality, of the three kinds of existing arguments in the realm of women's rights, the rational arguments for deserts-based justice have reinforced the textual arguments for equal rights as the spirit of the Qur'an and Islamic standards. These two kinds of rational and textual arguments have restricted (*taqyīd*) the textual arguments for inequality in terms of their time frame. On the basis of these two types of textual and rational arguments as the contextual evidence, the textual arguments against equality are temporal rulings that become situational premises whose validity has expired.

5. Response to two predictable objections

Some may object that the wise Lawgiver of the world could have legislated fundamental equality of rights between men and women from the outset, clearly and explicitly, as a permanent ruling, to avoid the need for complex logical arguments for abrogation. Or do equal rights, which contradict the apparent meaning of the Book and Sunna, not throw a question mark around other *sharʿī* rulings?

In response we can say: the problem is in the assumption that the *sharʿī* rulings in the Qur'an and Sunna are all fixed and permanent. Has this assumption been proven? Is it so obvious that it needs no verification? This assumption is neither obvious nor has a valid argument been offered to prove it. Rather, there are valid arguments against it. There is no question that social, cultural, economic and political conditions in human societies change greatly over time, and, consequently, the subject matter of many rulings changes. Besides, the conduct of reasonable people can change in the course of history: a revealing example of a transformation in the conduct of reasonable people took place in the dominant views of thinkers and societies, past and present, with regard to slavery. This also applies to women's rights; until a century ago, the common sense view was totally different from that of today.

Yesterday's human mindset did not have to face today's conditions. Further, until a century ago *sharʿī* rulings in the Qur'an and Sunna regarding women's rights were – according to the common sense of the time – just, ethical, rational and defensible, and capable of meeting the demands of human societies. Had the Qur'an and Sunna issued rulings according to a human mindset that was not established until centuries later, the Muslims, who were the first addressees, would not have accepted them. It cannot be denied that the Qur'an declares the licence to abrogate rulings, and that provisional and abrogated rules exist alongside permanent and abrogating ones in the text of the Qur'an and the Sunna. 'What God Revealed' (*mā anzala Allāh*) must be accepted as it was legislated; if it was legislated as permanent, it must be considered an immutable ruling, and if it was legislated as provisional, then it must be accepted as a changeable ruling. Denial of the immutability of provisional *sharʿī* rulings is not a denial of 'What God Revealed'. Likewise, anything the Prophet legislated as permitted or forbidden (*ḥalāl wa ḥarām*) remains so until the day of resurrection, provided such instructions were legislated as permanent. In other words, not all the Prophet's rulings are permanently valid; some were meant to be temporal.

The *sharʿī* rulings in the Qur'an and Sunna, which Muslims at the time of revelation saw as just, ethical, reasonable and superior, are valid as long as they fulfil these criteria. Once we discern with certainty – not conjecture – that a ruling is no longer just, ethical, reasonable and superior, this means that it was a temporary ruling whose validity has expired. This discernment is a specialist matter and must be done by a *mujtahid* who, in addition to his knowledge of jurisprudence, is also aware of the conditions of time and place. Besides slavery and women's rights, *sharʿī* penal laws are among those in need of fundamental revision.

This '*ijtihād* in foundations' allows a disciplined rethinking of such temporary rulings. By *foundation* we refer to anthropology, cosmology, linguistics, hermeneutics and the methodology of jurisprudence (*uṣūl al-fiqh*). If there were revisions in these foundations, without doubt the outcome of the jurisprudence of the *mujtahids* would have been different. We must not fear disciplined change in *sharʿī* rulings. On the contrary, we should fear presenting temporary rulings as permanent, and thereby weakening Islam. We cannot deduce *sharʿī* rulings for the people of today on the basis of the anthropology of the past.

6. Conclusion

There are two types of verses and hadiths regarding women's rights in the Qur'an and Sunna. The first type designates full human rights for women, and recognises equal rights for men and women as humans, despite bodily differences between them. The second type considers that women, because of their lesser capacities, are entitled to fewer rights than men in managing the home and in society. At the same time, reason and Shariʿa required that women be treated with justice and according to what is commonly accepted as good or right (*maʿrūf*).

Muslim scholars, following Aristotle, construed justice as deserts-based on the basis of proportional equality, and considered women as entitled to fewer rights because of what they considered to be women's inherent lesser capacity. They took the first type of verses and hadith as the basis for equal rights, and the second type as the standard for women's rights and duties, and defended patriarchy as consistent with justice and Shariʿa.

Both proportional equality and deserts-based justice are indefensible and unjustified. Contemporary rationality recognises humans, as they are humans, as rights-holders, and thus upholds fundamental equality and egalitarian justice. This notion of justice is very close to human dignity and Qur'anic anthropology. The first type of verses and hadiths, on grounds of contextual rational argument, imply fixed and permanent rulings, and, by analogy, verses that apparently imply legal inequality and greater legal rights for men are considered temporary rulings whose validity has expired.

According to egalitarian justice and fundamental equality, although women differ from men physically and psychologically, they are entitled to equal rights because they are human, and it is humanity – not gender, colour, race, class, religion, political ideology – that carries rights, duties, dignity, and trust and divine vicegerency. This position is more consistent with the Qur'anic spirit and Islamic standards; evidence for legal inequality, because of its temporariness, cannot be counted an obstacle to the realisation of legal equality.

Notes

1 This is my third article on the issue of women's rights. The previous ones are: 'Religious intellectuals and the rights of women', written in 2003, and 'Women's rights in the hereafter', written in 2005; both appeared as chapters in my book *Haqq al-Nass: Islam va Hoquq-e Bashar* [The Right of Humans: Islam and Human Rights] (Tehran: Kavir, 2008), pp. 287–314 and 315–37 respectively. I would like to thank the Oslo Coalition for inviting me to contribute this chapter, and Dr Ziba Mir-Hosseini for her comments, and, most importantly, for translating it into English.

2 The Usuli (rationalists) are the majority school of Shi'i jurisprudence, which, in contrast to the minority Akhbari (traditionalists), recognises reason (*'aql*) as a source for the derivation of law. Akhbaris gained influence in the seventeenth century but by the late eighteenth century the Usulis had crushed them.

3 Translations of the Qur'anic verses are from Yusuf 'Ali.

4 The same theme is repeated in other verses, including 40:40, 4:123, 3:195.

5 In such an analysis, justice and injustice, and the rational discernment of good and bad, are matters of dispute between the 'People of Justice' (Shi'a and Mu'tazila) and the Ash'aris, or in other words, between rationalists and voluntarists. The Mu'tazila school, which flourished in the ninth and tenth centuries, has influenced Shi'i thought, but was marginalised among Sunnis, where the Ash'ari school, in particular, became prevalent instead.

6 See previous footnote.

7 For the arguments for 'independent reason', I have drawn on the chapter on *al-mulāzamāt al-'aqliyya* (rational accompaniments) in Shaykh Mohammad Reza al-Muzaffar's valuable book *Uṣūl al-Fiqh* (Beirut: Al-'Alami, 1999), Vol. 2, pp. 261–97.

8 *Ṣaḥīḥ al-Bukhārī*, Vol. 5, book 59, no. 709.
9 *Nahj al-Balāgha*, ed. Subhi Saleh (Beirut, 1967), Sermon 80, p. 125.
10 This was written separately, after the commentary on Qur'an 2:228–42, in *Al-Mīzān fī tafsīr al-Qur'ān* (3rd edn, Beirut: al-'A'lami, 1974), Vol. 2, pp. 260–77.
11 *Ibid.*, pp. 276–7.
12 *Ibid.*, from the summary of his commentary on Qur'an 4:32–5, in Vol. 4, pp. 335–9 and his separate discussion of the meaning of *qiwāma* (guardianship) of men over women, p. 346.
13 *Ibid.*, Vol. 18, p. 90.
14 Motahhari, Morteza, *Nezam-e Huquq-e Zan dar Islam* [The System of Women's Rights in Islam] (Tehran: Sadra, 1990), pp. 144, 155 and 180.
15 Montazeri Najafabadi, Hossein 'Ali, *Hokumat-e Dini va Hoquq-e Ensan* [Religious Government and Human Rights] (Qom, 2007), pp. 119–20. This book (pp. 119–29) contains his last views on the matter; for his earlier views, see *Dirāsāt fī Wilāya al-Faqīh wa Fiqh al-Dawla al-Islāmiyya* [Lessons in the Rule of the Jurist and the Jurisprudence of an Islamic Government] (Qom, 2003), Vol. 1, pp. 335–62, where he invokes the hadith from Bukhari and *Najh al-Balāgha* that we mentioned above. Also noteworthy is Montazeri's explanation of Sermon 80 of *Nahj al-Balāgha*, which he begins with 'probably Imam 'Ali in this Sermon is referring to 'A'isha [because of her role in rebelling against him in the Battle of the Camel] and those similar to 'A'isha, not to all women in the world'. *Sharha-ye Nahj ol-Balagheh* (Tehran: Sara'i, 2003), Vol. 3, pp. 234–7.
16 In chapter 2 of *The Nicomachean Ethics*, distributive justice is one of the three kinds of specific justice that is distinct from general justice. Aristotle defines the relationship between distributive justice and proportional equality in the following two works: *Politics*, 1282b, lines 16–21; *The Nicomachean Ethics*, 1331a, lines 10–28.
17 *The Nicomachean Ethics*, translated into Arabic by Ishaq ibn Hunayn in the tenth century, was available to Muslim philosophers. I refer to the 1979 edition by Abdulrahman Badawi, published in Kuwait. Aristotle's *Politics* was not translated at that time, though some Muslim scholars were partially familiar with it, including al-Kindi, *Rasā'il al-Kindī al-Falsafiyya* (Cairo, 1956), Vol. 1, p. 384; al-Mas'udi, *al-Tanbīh wa al-Ishrāf* [The Book of Notification and Verification] (Linden, 1956), p. 118; Miskawayh, *Tartīb al-Sa'āda*, cited in the footnote of Mulla Sadra's *al-Mabda' wa al-Ma'ād* [The Origin and the Return] (Tehran, 1896), pp. 458–9; and Ibn Sina, *Risāla al-Aqṣal al-Ḥikma* [Treatise on the Divisions of Philosophy] (Tehran, 2009).
18 As an example, Mulla Hadi Sabzevari mentioned this phrase as the definition of justice in his book *Sharḥ al-Asmā' al-Husnā wa-Sharḥ du'ā' al-ṣabāḥ* [Commentary on the Beautiful Names] (Tehran: Maktabat Basirati, n.d.), p. 54.

19 John Rawls is the best-known thinker on this notion of justice; the important discussion of conceptions of, and approaches to, justice as fairness cannot be dealt with here and requires another chapter.

20 Tawney, R. H., *Equality* (New York: Capricorn, 1961), pp. 35, 37, 90.

21 Berlin, Isaiah, 'Equality', in *idem, Concepts and Categories: Philosophical Essays* (Oxford University Press, 1980), pp. 82–4.

22 It must be said that the notion of Aristotelian justice has been revised by some neo-Aristotelian philosophers, such as Martha Nussbaum and Alasdair McIntyre; in her reading, Nussbaum distances herself from Aristotle's proportional equality and comes closer to fundamental equality. For a discussion, see McKerlie, Dennis, 'Aristotle's theory of justice', *Southern Journal of Philosophy* 39 (2001), pp. 119–41.

23 Popper, Karl, *The Open Society and Its Enemies* (4th edn, London: Routledge and Kegan Paul, 1962), Vol. 1, p. 62.

24 Shiʿite Muslims and Muʿtazili Sunni Muslims.

25 Fazlur Rahman has used the phrase 'harmony with the Qur'anic spirit' in discussing women's rights; see his 'Status of women in Islam: a Modernist Interpretation', in Hanna Papanek and Gail Minault (eds), *Separate Worlds: Studies of Purdah in South Asia* (Delhi: Chanakya Publications, 1982), pp. 285–310.

26 I have referred to some of these rulings in a chapter, 'Religious intellectualism and human rights', in my *Haqq al-Nass*, pp. 94–9.

Part III
Instead of a Conclusion

11

THE PARADOX OF EQUALITY AND THE POLITICS OF DIFFERENCE

Gender Equality, Islamic Law and the Modern Muslim State[1]

Anver M. Emon

1. Introduction

The pursuit of gender equality in Islamic family law, as codified in various Muslim states, is neither a new phenomenon nor one that is lacking considerable study. Indeed, many scholarly monographs, edited collections and academic journals present thoughtful, well-researched and passionate contributions that are animated by the goal of gender justice in the Muslim world.[2] This chapter is indebted to that vast body of literature, and, indeed, is a humble offering that stands in the shadow of all that has come before. The aim of this chapter is to bring the reader's attention to a subtle irony that underlies the pursuit of justice. That irony has everything to do with what is often called the 'paradox of equality'. If equality requires *the same treatment of those who are similarly situated*, the paradox of equality reminds us that we cannot treat similarly those who are *not* similarly situated. Indeed, there are times when justice demands that we legally differentiate between people because of their differences.[3]

Legal differentiation is a common feature of the law, a *sine qua non* of justice. To take a rather mundane and perhaps indelicate example, we often find separate bathrooms for men and women.[4] Furthermore, in the interest of accommodating the needs of those who are disabled, we may create yet a third bathroom that is specially designated for them and equipped with certain devices designed to aid those who might require assistance. We may even argue (and convincingly so) that differentiation in these cases is right, good and just. In all these cases, though, we cannot deny that men and women are treated differently, and that the disabled are treated differently again. For some, this example might seem silly; it is so banal that they might think it takes us away from the hard cases of equality that find expression in the contributions to this volume. However, this example is offered to emphasise an important dynamic that underlies the paradox of equality. Arguably, this example is only banal because we consider the differences between men, women and the disabled in this specific situation so obvious, indeed *so very natural*, as to require virtually no argument or rationale to explain why differentiation occurs and is laudable. The presumption of naturalness is key to understanding the basis by which differentiation is often justified and legitimated. From a critical perspective, though, that presumption demands our greatest attention and vigilance lest it be used as post-hoc justification to discriminate. As Joan W. Scott reminds us, 'maternity was often given as the explanation for the exclusion of women from politics, race as the reason for the enslavement and/or subjugation of blacks, when in fact the causality runs the other way: processes of social differentiation produce the exclusions and enslavements that are then justified in terms of biology or race', or, in other words, in terms of presumptions of what we consider obvious, unavoidable and natural.[5] For example, the banality of the example above disappears once we consider access to bathrooms in the Jim Crow era in the twentieth-century United States, when African Americans had to use separate, and often deficient, facilities.[6] The recent novel, *The Help*, which has become a major motion picture, depicts how presumptions of natural differences could justify what would now be considered highly discriminatory allocations of access to washrooms.[7]

In this simple, if admittedly vulgar, example, we see the paradox of equality at work – sometimes people have to be treated differently in order for justice to be served.[8] They are treated differently because of some characteristic or feature that is deemed so natural as to warrant differentiation. Yet, the example also illustrates how presumptions of natural difference must be subjected to vigilant scrutiny lest differentiation become unjust because it is discriminatory. Differentiation, as used in this chapter, is distinct from discrimination. Discrimination is an evaluation that a particular differentiation constitutes disadvantages against a particular group *and* that such disadvantages render the differentiation *illegitimate*. Legal differentiation by itself is, therefore, a common and expected feature of the law. The paradox of equality offers analytic bite by asking whether the presumptions under which a particular factual difference leads to a legal differentiation may be discriminatory, and thereby illegitimate under the law.

This chapter approaches the question of gender equality from the vantage point of the paradox of equality. Instead of focusing narrowly on whether and how women are discriminated against, and challenging the role of patriarchy in animating such discrimination, this chapter will step back and instead inquire whether and why differentiation in the law is justified and legitimated, and explore how legal differentiation in one context can be discrimination in another. The chapter will, thereby, distinguish between factual difference, legal differentiation and discrimination. These distinctions are significant because they beg important questions that all too often remain unaddressed: what makes certain factual differences irrelevant as a matter of law, while others are legitimate bases for legal differentiation, and yet others are deemed discriminatory and thereby illegitimate as a basis for legal differentiation? For instance, the factual difference between a 5-year-old and a 6-year-old boy may not matter in terms of how one measures the relevant standard of care in the Common Law of Tort, where the boy is sued for negligently injuring another child. But the factual difference between a 5-year-old boy and a 17-year-old boy provides a basis for legal differentiation: the 17-year-old will be held to a higher standard of care.[9]

This chapter contributes to the existing literature on gender, equality and Islamic law by interrogating the nuances of equality from the vantage point of the paradox of equality. Part 2 examines the different strategies used by those advocating gender equality in the Muslim family. Part 3 illustrates how the paradox of equality is an ancient concept with roots in both Greek and Islamic philosophy. Part 4 shows how the vantage point of the paradox of equality allows us to critically question and explore the assumptions that animate the development of legal rules that differentiate and discriminate against people on different grounds. Parts 5 and 6 examine how Islamic law has legitimated differential treatment of men and women by reference both to the law and to extra-legal factors associated with the post-colonial condition of Muslim societies. Part 7 brings the analysis to a close by suggesting that to shift what the historical tradition represents as legal differentiation between men and women to be discriminatory, and thereby illegitimate as a matter of Islamic law, will involve both legal and extra-legal factors. Drawing upon scholarship about the women's movement in the United States, this chapter suggests that legal change in the Muslim world will require more than just attentiveness to the intricacies of legal texts and legal reasoning. It will require social movements to occupy the streets and articulate alternative legal outcomes to expand the scope of what is legally intelligible, meaningful and possible. This chapter implicitly suggests that social movements would do well to bear in mind the paradox of equality as they design their research and activist agendas. The paradox of equality helps to identify the unstated assumptions that make legal differentiation possible, thereby quietly justifying what is tantamount to discriminatory treatment against women under the law in some Muslim countries.

2. Equality in Muslim reformist writings

A review of literature concerning gender and justice in Islamic law shows that Muslim writers begin from the starting point of a patriarchy that is either considered embedded in the tradition or imposed upon it from outside. For instance, Fatima Mernissi, in her path-breaking work, writes in an autobiographical moment: 'When I finished writing this book I had come to understand one thing: if women's rights are a problem for some modern Muslim men, it is neither because of the Koran nor the Prophet, nor the Islamic tradition, but simply because those rights conflict with the interests of a male elite.'[10] Others note that patriarchy can certainly be read from the main source-texts of Islam, such as the Qur'an, but are keen to suggest that patriarchy is separable from the Qur'an's message. Asma Barlas acknowledges that describing the Qur'an as patriarchal is anachronistic at best. Rather, the aim of her book is to 'challenge oppressive readings of the Qur'an' and 'to offer a reading that confirms that Muslim women can struggle for equality from within the framework of the Qur'an's teachings'.[11] Acknowledging that patriarchal readings of the Qur'an abound, Barlas nonetheless seeks to find a way to gender equality through the sacred text. A third approach, complementary to Barlas', is the hermeneutic approach of Farid Esack. Rejecting predominant paradigms of gender relations that perpetuate existing power imbalances between men and women, Esack reads the Qur'an through the hermeneutic lens of justice, and not mere kindness, given that the former proffers modes of redress while the latter does not necessarily do so, and as such perpetuates the existence of oppression.[12] Theories of interpretation are proffered, building on hermeneutic principles of justice in light of the relationship between the reader, the text and meaning.

At the heart of these writers' concerns is the need to recognise and articulate a conception of gender equality as a character of justice in Islam. However, the meaning and implications of gender equality are not always shared between them. For Mernissi, equality is captured in the language of common and shared 'rights' at the political, social and sexual level. She correlates this rights-oriented view of equality with the historic independence of Muslim states from colonial subjugation. These new states were 'born' into an international system of equal and sovereign states, where the aspiration to democracy, constitutionalism and rule of law forced a recognition of the individual as *citizen*. As new Muslim states entered the international community and redefined themselves, 'in the eyes of their former colonizers, they were forced to grant their new citizenship to all their new nationals, men and women … The metamorphosis of the Muslim woman, from a veiled, secluded, marginalized object reduced to inertia, into a subject with *constitutional rights*, erased the lines that defined the identity hierarchy which organized politics and relations between the sexes.'[13] Mernissi's equality, arguably, is one that draws upon presumptions about the state, constitutionalism and the citizen as rights bearer. Likewise, Esack's passionate plea for gender justice perpetuates the language of rights.[14] When writing about the rights 'given' to Muslim women, he asks: 'Are human rights a gift awarded to well-behaved little children as if women … exist outside the world of Islam … in the same way that children are seemingly external to the world of adults?'[15] Esack uses the language of rights to characterise his agenda of gender justice, which is constituted by a commitment to equality: 'The right to self-respect, dignity, and equality comes with our very humanness.'[16] When Mernissi and Esack write about 'equality', they have in mind a particular substantive content that arguably echos the language of classical liberal notions of rights. Whether defined by a constitution that grants rights pursuant to general human rights norms, or even human rights treaties such as the Universal Declaration of Human Rights,[17] equality for both authors reflects a certain content (namely, a liberal one), expressed in terms of rights.

Departing from the rights-based models of equality, Barlas' approach recognises that justice may, in fact, require legal differentiation; in other words, she invokes the 'paradox of equality'. In her attempt to unread patriarchy in the Qur'an, Barlas argues that the Qur'an is egalitarian and antipatriarchal.[18] But she cautions that this does not mean that the Qur'an does not treat men and women differently. Rather, sexual equality need not mean the absence of differential treatment. She writes:

> [W]hile there is no universally shared definition of sexual equality, there is a pervasive (and oftentimes perverse) tendency to view differences as evidence of inequality. In light of this view, the Qur'an's different treatment of women and men with respect to certain issues (marriage, divorce, giving of evidence, etc.) is seen as manifest proof of its anti-equality stance and its patriarchal nature. However, I argue against this view on the grounds both that … treating women and men differently does not always amount to treating them unequally, nor does treating them identically necessarily mean treating them equally.[19]

To be anti-patriarchal does not mean that factual difference must be obscured, or that legal differentiation must be avoided at all times and places.

The examples of Mernissi, Esack and Barlas are offered to show different ways in which gender justice and equality are framed in contemporary debates on Islamic law. The specific agenda of each author is less relevant for this chapter; what is more significant are their different approaches to the notion of equality. One approach implicitly conveys a liberal-sounding rights-based approach to the content of equality. Another views equality and justice as requiring a determination of whether differences exist in fact, and whether those factual differences justify differential treatment, or whether such differential treatment might actually be discriminatory, and thereby illegitimate. This latter approach to equality is particularly important for this chapter, as it explores the analytic contribution of the 'paradox of equality' to the future of gender equality in the Muslim world.

3. The paradox of equality

The paradox of equality is that, as a principle of justice, it recognises that equality is not merely about being treated the same. Rather, the paradox reveals that equality as a matter of law is not only about treating two things equally because they are the same or share a quality of sameness. Equality as a matter of law must also treat two people differently when they are deemed to be sufficiently different, as a matter of fact, to warrant or justify such legal differentiation. Indeed, to treat different people as the same might lead to injustice or, at the very least, considerable discomfort. By bringing forward the contrasting tendencies in equality, the paradox of equality requires us to distinguish between the *fact* of sameness and difference, and the *normative implications* given to that factual sameness or difference. That distinction then begs certain fundamental and difficult questions: when and under what conditions should a certain factual difference between two people lead to and justify legal differentiation that entails different distributions of resources and different sets of rights claims? And under what circumstances does that legal differentiation become discriminatory? For instance, in various constitutional democracies, both men and women have the right to vote. In this case, gender difference is irrelevant (although that was not always the case). On the other hand, because of the factual difference of gender, public toilets are generally gender segregated – a normative *differentiation*. In contrast, a rule that prohibits abortion is discriminatory given the undue burden such a rule places upon women, while men suffer no such burden. In all three cases, the normative or legal implication of factual difference resonates differently; the paradox of equality alerts us to the different registers, and begs important questions about the conditions under which a factual difference matters or not.

This chapter interrogates the nature of equality by interrogating the dynamics of the paradox of equality. Equality, differentiation and discrimination are terms of art that alert us to the *fact of difference*. They prompt us to inquire whether and why a particular factual difference can or must imply legitimised forms of differentiation, and the conditions under which such differentiation may actually be discriminatory. This approach to equality and discrimination allows us to unpack the assumptions of justice that underlie rules which differentiate between people, and subject those assumptions of justice to critical scrutiny. In doing so, this chapter will make plain the need for multiple strategies to counter the presumptions that perpetuate the legitimacy of legal differentiations which have discriminatory features and impact.

a. Islamic philosophy, musāwa *and the paradox of equality*

Approaching the issue of equality in light of its paradoxical quality allows us to adopt a critical stance on the pre-modern Islamic legal tradition without, at the same time, uncritically reading into that critique liberal notions of equality. Furthermore, to think about equality in terms of the paradox draws upon a principle of justice that, arguably, is shared across traditions. For instance, in his *Nichomachean Ethics*, Aristotle wrote about justice as equality: 'Now since an unjust man is one who is unfair, and the unjust is the unequal, it is clear that corresponding to the unequal there is a mean, namely that which is equal; for every action admitting of more and less admits of the equal also. If then the unjust is the unequal, the just is the equal – a view that commends itself to all without proof.'[20]

This view about justice as equality finds expression centuries later in the works of Muslim philosophers writing about justice. The pre-modern Muslim philosopher al-Farabi (d. 950), for instance, held that at its foundation, justice (*'adl*) has to do with distributional equality of the goods in society, and thereafter the protection of each person's enjoyment of his or her share. He wrote:

> Justice, initially, is in [demarcating] the portion of the shared goods (*qisma al-khayrāt al-mushtaraka*) that are for all in the city. Therafter, [justice] has to do with preserving the distribution among them. Those goods (*khayrāt*) consist of security, property, dignity, rank, and all the goods that are possible for all to share in. Each person among the people of the city has an equal share (*musāwī*) of these goods based on his worth (*isti'hālihi*). To diminish or exceed his portion is unjust (*jawr*). Any diminishment is unjust toward the individual. Any increase is unjust to the people of the city. Perhaps any diminishment is also unjust to the people of the city.[21]

The later pre-modern Muslim philosopher on ethics, Miskawayh (d. 1030) addressed, in his *Tahdhīb al-Akhlāq*, the relationship between the just person, the pursuit of equality, and the way in which both result in a unity of the 'highest honour and most eminent rank'. He stated:

> The truly just man is he who harmonizes all his faculties, activities, and states in such a way that none exceeds the others. He then proceeds to pursue the same end in the transactions and the honors which are external to him, desiring in all of this the virtue of justice itself and not any other object ... And justice, being a mean between extremes and a disposition by which one is able to restore both excess and deficiency to a mean, becomes the most perfect of virtues and the one which is nearest to unity.[22]

For Miskawayh, the pursuit of justice is the pursuit of the mean between extremes, and the pursuit of the mean has to do with ensuring equal distributions among similarly situated individuals. Various terms that are derived from the Arabic word for justice point to the importance of balance and equality (*musāwa*).[23] Indeed, equality is the noblest of all proportions for '[i]n its basic meaning, it is unity or a shadow of unity', thus alluding to the oneness and unity of God at the heart of Islamic beliefs.[24]

For the three philosophers, though, equality does not prescribe that we treat each person in the polity exactly like the other. Indeed, all seem to recognise that the just portion that each enjoys will depend, in part, on how one person relates to another. There may be good reasons to differentiate between people, hence invoking the paradox of equality. Al-Farabi's reference to justice as equal distribution based on one's worth or value (*isti'hāl*) suggests that equal distribution to all is not the goal of justice. Rather, justice is about equal treatment of those who are considered equals. But factual differences between people may shift the balance of equality, requiring different allocations to different people in the interest of justice.[25] In this case, legal differentiation is not only appropriate, but a constitutive feature of justice. For instance, Aristotle wrote:

> And there will be the same equality between shares as between the persons, since the ratio between the shares will be equal to the ratio between the persons; for if the persons are not equal, they will not have equal shares; *it is when equals possess or are allotted unequal shares, or when persons not equal equal shares, that quarrels and complaints arise.*[26]

Miskawayh, referring to a shoemaker and carpenter, acknowledged that their respective products will have different worth. 'Thus when the shoemaker takes from the carpenter the latter's product and gives him his own, the exchange between them is a barter if the two articles are equal in value. But there is nothing which prevents the product of the one from being superior in value to that of the other.'[27] In other words, it may be that one product is worth more than the other, thereby requiring more than a one-to-one exchange.

The example above is embedded in the context of commerce and barter. But it nonetheless begs the question: what determines whether two people are factually different, and whether justice demands that their factual difference requires different distributions, whether of property, dignity or standing in society? The answer to this question may differ depending on the good to be distributed, but it illustrates a difficulty in the way we account for justice as equality. Justice as equality seems to presume a standard by which we judge whether people are, in fact, equally situated, as well as a standard to determine which factual differences are normatively relevant and which are not. In the case of commodities of exchange, we might use an intermediary device, such as money or the market, to offer an accepted standard by which to measure difference, and to account for which differences matter, for the purpose of setting comparative price points. However, what operates as a measure or standard of equality and justice when the goods being distributed are not commodities of exchange, but rather the freedoms and liberties we can enjoy under the law? Will the scope of freedom depend on whether we are black or white, part of the religious majority or a member of a religious minority, a man or a woman? On what basis is factual difference rendered sufficiently relevant to justify differentiation under the law?

4. From *musāwa* to *ḥusn* and *qubḥ*: legitimating differentiation in Islamic law

The philosophical approach to equality introduces the paradox of equality as an analytic vantage point from which to identify and critique the assumptions that animate rules (formal or otherwise) which legitimate differentiation. But on what bases are factual differences deemed sufficient to justify such differentiation? The philosophical approach to the paradox of equality begs the question, but does not necessarily help us answer that question. Rather, as will be suggested in this section, the move from factual difference to legal differentiation involves a variety of value judgements, which enter into the realm of law and animate and legitimate rules that differentiate between peoples. Two Arabic terms of art, *ḥusn* and *qubḥ*, offer conceptual sites through which such value judgements enter into a legal inquiry. *Ḥusn* and *qubḥ*, which literally mean 'good' and 'bad' respectively, are ethical terms of art utilised in the genre of *uṣūl al-fiqh* and, importantly for this chapter, reflect the interpretive dynamic of jurists moving from ethical determinations of the good and the bad, to legal rules of obligation and prohibition. By attending to the ways in which Muslim jurists moved from ethical norms to legal rules, we can identify the assumptions they imported into their determinations of legitimate differentiation between two people, so as to facilitate critique about the normative significance of the factual difference between them, and the discriminatory effect of any differentiation.

In Sunni *uṣūl al-fiqh* treatises, for instance, the terms *ḥusn* and *qubḥ* were invoked in debates about the ontological authority of reason as a source of law when there is an absence of guidance from foundational source-texts, such as the Qur'an (*min qabla wurūd al-shar'*). In his chapter in this volume, Mohsen Kadivar addresses a similar theoretical issue with regard to the Shi'a Usulis. For these jurists, the question was whether reason has sufficient authority to be a source of Shari'a norms, with the threat of divine sanction or promise of divine reward. Some allowed such a possibility, while others suggested that claims about the good and bad are certainly morally relevant, but have no bearing on legal obligations and prohibitions. Exploring the intricacies of these terms and their implications for law and philosophy is beyond the scope of this chapter.[28]

One issue of that debate, though, is particularly relevant here, namely, the issue of determinacy. When ascertaining the substantive content of the good and the bad, jurists were concerned with the extent to which their reasoned deliberations about the good and the bad reflected a determinable divine will, or whether they were historically contingent attitudes that had less to do with God and more to do with the human condition prevailing at a given moment. For instance, the pre-modern Shafiʿi jurist al-Juwayni (d. 1085) exercised considerable caution when attributing a particular rule of decision to God, since the justifications for any particular legal rule are vulnerable to human contingency and fallibility. Al-Juwayni did not deny that reason enables us to judge if something is dangerous (*ijtināb al-mahālik*) or offers certain benefits (*ibtidār al-manāfiʿ*). To deny this, he held, would be unreasonable (*khurūj ʿan al-maʿqūl*).[29] Such moral reasoning falls within the normal capacity of human activity, or what al-Juwayni called the *ḥaqq al-ādamiyyīn*. But this is different from asking what is good or bad in terms of God's judgement (*ḥukm Allāh*).[30] For al-Juwayni, God's determination of an act's Shariʿa-value has an authority that human reason cannot enjoy. In Shariʿa, whether something is obligatory or prohibited depends on whether God has provided punishment or reward for the relevant acts.[31] Unless we have indicators from God, such matters are unknowable by humans (*wa dhālika ghayb*).[32] We cannot make Shariʿa judgements, based purely on a rational analysis, into harms and benefits, since any such conclusion offers no authority to justify divine sanction, whether in this life only or in the hereafter. This does not mean that we cannot make moral determinations of good and bad. Indeed, it is natural that we would do so. But we can do so only on issues not already addressed by God, and we cannot claim divine authority for them since God has made no decision on them. As al-Juwayni said, 'it is not prohibited to investigate these two characteristics [i.e. *ḥusn* and *qubḥ*] where harm may arise or where benefit is possible, on condition that [any determination] not be attributed to God, or obligate God to punish or reward'.[33]

In this passage, al-Juwayni predominantly worried about the authority of reason and the omnipotence of God. But his concern was, no doubt, animated by an anxiety about whether we presume too much when we legislate in the name of God, based on the contingencies of our moral vision. We cannot be certain that our analysis of God's position is objectively true or right. We may only have an approximation of God's will, or we might have a strong conviction short of certainty that our position is right. In other words, far from being true or right, any legal conclusion bears the authority that arises from the jurist's most compelling opinion, or what al-Juwayni called *ghalabat al-ẓann*. It is something less than certainty, but is sufficient for the purpose of decreeing a rule of law, as long as we understand that the authority of the rule is thereby limited.[34]

Consequently, the concern about the authority of reason is tied to the authority of the law in light of the epistemic frailty of the human agent, who must, at times, interpret the law without any express evidence of God's will.[35] This anxiety about truth and objectivity allows us to appreciate that, at a certain level, jurists were aware that *fiqh* pronouncements are built upon a certain degree of human subjectivity, thereby rendering any *fiqh* rule vulnerable to a subjectivist critique. We cannot ignore this fact when considering how factual differences are deemed sufficiently relevant to justify legal differentiation. When jurists used terms like *ḥusn* and *qubḥ*, they utilised these general, technical terms to give an objective frame to their own historically conditioned attitudes and predispositions about when factual differences should lead to legal differentiation.

For instance, the pre-modern Ashʿarite theologian al-Baqillani (d. 1013) argued that one can rationally know the good (*ḥusn al-fiʿl*) or the bad (*qubḥ*) of an act, where such notions are general and abstract. One can make determinations of the bad, for example, on the basis of what one finds distasteful (*tanfuru ʿanhu al-nufūs*).[36] To illustrate his point, al-Baqillani argued that one can know, without reference to scripture, the goodness of the believer striking the unbeliever, and the badness of the unbeliever striking the believer.[37] For al-Baqillani this distinction seemed obvious and apparent (a differentiation), whereas to modern readers it may seem abhorrent and unjustifiable (discriminatory). How might we understand al-Baqillani's normative claims regarding the factual difference of religious diversity? The paradox of equality immediately alerts us to consider al-Baqillani's underlying assumptions, which rendered the factual difference between the believer and non-believer sufficiently relevant to justify differentiation.

If we view al-Baqillani's conclusion in the light of the more general set of rules governing the unbeliever, in particular the *dhimmī*, we find a complex legal, historical and political dynamic at work. The *dhimmī* was the non-Muslim permanent resident in Islamic lands. Jurists erected various rules governing and restricting the freedoms and liberties of *dhimmī*s in the Muslim polity; they did so in part because they deemed the factual difference in religious commitment between the Muslim and the *dhimmī* relevant to justifying differential treatment under the law. To understand why the factual difference of religious diversity occasioned a differential legal regime requires understanding the socio-political and cultural context that gave intelligibility to the *dhimmī* rules.

The *dhimmī* rules arose amidst a historical backdrop of Muslim conquest of lands, reaching from Spain to India by the eighth century CE. In this context of conquest and colonial rule arose the Pact of ʿUmar, as an initial statement of the rules regulating non-Muslims living in the Muslim polity.[38] This initial statement was supplemented by later developed rules, whose legitimacy relied on an ethos of Islamic universalism, even as the Islamic empire gave way to multiple polities of regional and local power. A universalist ethos, and the memory of imperial conquest, offered a normative framework to render the *dhimmī* rules meaningful and legitimate. That framework was, arguably, a lens through which Muslim scholars such as al-Baqillani understood and ordered their world. Conquest initially presented itself as an economic and political phenomenon, but soon became part of a collective memory that informed the way Muslim scholars understood their past and its implications with regard to the aims, purposes and aspirations of governance and law.

As part of the historical memory of a community, the conquest period became aspirational, especially as later centuries witnessed the demise of the Islamic empire into fractionalised polities. As the contemporary historian of Islam Marshall Hodgson states, the period of the early caliphates 'tends to be seen through the image formed of it in the Middle Periods; those elements of its culture are regarded as normative that were warranted sound by later writers'.[39] For Hodgson, in the Middle Period (roughly the mid-tenth century to 1500), the challenges of 'political legitimation, of aesthetic creativity, of transcendence and immanence in religious understanding, of the social role of natural sciences and philosophy – these become fully focused only in the Middle Periods',[40] in part by nostalgic reference to an imperial past. The memory of a glorious, righteous imperial past offered a lens for Muslim jurists to understand how a Muslim polity *should* regulate interactions with non-Muslims, given the fact of diversity, and despite imperial fragmentation.

Consequently, when al-Baqillani remarked about the goodness of the believer beating the non-believer, and the evil of the non-believer beating the believer, we cannot ignore the fact that his substantive valuation was dependent upon a particular vision of the Islamic past, which informed certain aspects of his present. The horizon of the past and his present were fused to create a norm that depended, for its very intelligibility, upon the ethics of universalism, imperialism and the subordination of the other.

5. Legitimating gender differentiation

Heeding the distinction between justice as equality, and justice as the good and the bad, though, is not meant to suggest that this study prefers the philosopher's justice over the jurist's. Rather, the philosophical principle of equality provides a vantage point from which we can appreciate the underlying (and often unstated) assumptions that make legal determinations not only possible, but intelligible. By distinguishing between the fact of difference and the normative implications of that factual difference, we can better identify the assumptions that allow jurists to justify differentiation as a matter of law, and thereby appreciate the scope of critique required to render those assumptions as inherently discriminatory.

This brings us to the issue of gender difference, and global calls for equality in Muslim family law. The existing literature on gender discrimination, in both

Islamic legal doctrine and Muslim-majority state family law regimes, is vast and need not be reviewed here.[41] Indeed, other contributions to this volume outline the doctrines that pose difficulties to gender equality advocates. For the purpose of understanding the doctrines in terms of the paradox of equality, of central interest is the rationale used to justify discriminatory treatment between men and women under Islamic law. This rationale uses the fact of gender difference to justify differentiation.

For instance, Murtaza Mutahhari (d. 1979), a student of Ayatollah Khomeini, argued that legal gender differentiation reflects the very conditions of justice that are captured in the paradox of equality. He took aim at critics who held that gender differentiation in matters of divorce and inheritance law is 'contemptuous of, and insulting to, the female sex' – or, in other words, discriminatory.[42] Instead, he implicitly acknowledged that the justification of gender differentiation accounts for the considerations that lie at the heart of the paradox of equality:

> [W]oman and man, on the basis of the very fact that one is a woman and the other is a man, are not identical with each other in many respects. The world is not exactly alike for both of them, and their natures and dispositions were not intended to be the same. Eventually, this requires that in very many rights, duties, and punishments they should not have an identical placing.[43]

For him, the undeniable naturalness of the fact of biological difference was suitably significant to justify legal differentiation between men and women.

In other cases, the fact of gender difference is deemed significant by recasting the difference as shorthand for complex social dynamics that require differentiation. For instance, the Qur'an asserts that a son will inherit twice the amount of his sister(s).[44] The verse itself does not explain the rationale behind the discriminatory distribution. Pre-modern Muslim jurists identified this verse as representing a departure from pre-Islamic practices, which often denied daughters any inheritance share.[45] Contemporary writers explain and justify the verse's distribution by reading the fact of gender difference as an efficient way to capture the heart of the matter – socio-economic factors concerning the distribution of economic responsibility for the family. Acknowledging the change from pre-Islamic practice, they recognise that personal status laws, such as inheritance rules,

> were formulated to meet a woman's needs in a society where her largely domestic, childbearing roles rendered her sheltered and dependent upon her father, her husband, and her close male relations … Because men had more independence, wider social contacts, and higher status in the world, their social position was translated into greater legal responsibilities … as well as more extensive legal privileges in proportion to those responsibilities.[46]

In the case of inheritance rules, the fact of gender difference in the Qur'an is made to encompass a historically contingent social hierarchy. That economic and social hierarchy is read into the original Qur'anic verse, which makes no reference to such social conditions. The verse only references the fact of gender difference. The legitimacy of the verse's inheritance rule, therefore, is explained after the fact, and is intelligible once we appreciate the paradox of equality as a feature of justice. But attention to the paradox of equality also illuminates the poverty of the after-the-fact justification to account for changed historical contexts. Despite changes in lived economic realities, and calls to reform Islamic family law, such as the laws of inheritance, little change has been forthcoming.

6. Post-coloniality and the paradox of equality

The failure of reformist attempts is not simply a function of the power of the Qur'anic or other source-text to subvert the claims of history. Rather, the imperatives of a post-colonial history more often than not subvert the demands of changing socio-economic conditions, and thereby undermine calls for reform in Islamic family law. Gender-based legal reform is not a new issue, whether one looks to the Muslim world or elsewhere. Gender difference, as a site of legal debate, has been, and continues to be, an ongoing issue of contention in countries spanning the globe. As such, the Muslim world is hardly unique in being a site of gender-equality debates. Rather, what makes the Muslim world appear unique and distinct is the historical moment in which demands for gender-based reform are made: a post-colonial context of newly independent Muslim states embedded in informal modes of hegemony exercised by the global North over the South. In the twentieth century, the elites of these relatively newly minted Muslim states participated in the international scene, but did not (and presumably could not) go so far as to ignore the traditional modes of identity that animated segments of their domestic society. The traditional models of identity, arguably, gave content to the national identity and political authenticity of new Muslim-majority states, in an international arena beset by pre-existing and ongoing asymmetries of power.[47] In this context, calls for gender reform inflamed (and still do) conservative segments in Muslim polities that viewed claims for gender equality as yet another colonial imposition, or as premature given the fragile state of the nation. Ann McClintock, writing about the importance of viewing nationalism in gendered terms, notes that

> *gender* difference between women and men serves to symbolically define the limits of *national* difference and power between *men*. Excluded from direct action as national citizens, women are subsumed symbolically into the national body politic as its boundary and metaphoric limit ... Women are typically construed as the symbolic bearers of the nation, but are denied any direct relation to national agency.[48]

The nationality of a new state could not avoid being framed, in a post-colonial setting, by the asymmetry between it and its former colonial powers. In these contexts, women contributed to the notion of nationhood, but only passively so. Women were made to represent the nation's ideals, but had no power to determine the content of those ideals. Those ideals drew upon a historical tradition whose continuity had as much to do with the post-colonial condition as with religious adherence.

Attentiveness to the post-colonial context reminds us that, since the twentieth century, the debates on gender reform have been embedded in a larger contest about post-colonial identity formation, in which the content of national authenticity was defined (and often still is) in religious doctrinal terms. Furthermore, the burden of that content has been placed squarely on the shoulders of those who, more often than not, have had too little power to assert their voice. These political circumstances allow us to appreciate why the factual difference between men and women may seem significant enough to justify legal differentiation in the Muslim world today. To recast that differentiation as discrimination, therefore, requires more than arguments over competing Qur'anic verses, hadith texts or methodologies of interpretation.

7. (En)countering difference: social movements and the rereading of equality

Those who read this chapter may be disappointed with the absence of any slam-dunk legal argument for gender equality in Islamic law. But such disappointment is premised on unfair expectations of what is possible within the law. Yes, it is true that there are possible readings of Qur'anic verses that can lead to a principle of gender equality.[49] Yes, certain hadith texts that justify gender-based discrimination can be challenged as lacking sufficient authenticity to justify the rule for which they are invoked.[50] And, yes, some scholars recognise the need to offer a more general theory of gender relations in Islam to animate new interpretations of Islamic law.[51] Looking for solace in technical legal arguments is quite reasonable, and, most importantly, quite efficient. It allows the proponent of gender equality to make an argument on the assumption that the reader is a reasonable one, open to new readings of the Islamic legal sources, and thereby willing and able to change his or her mind.

However, the dilemma is that changing minds on what might seem to be a minor, technical, legal issue actually involves significant reformulations of socially and culturally embedded ideas about the right and the wrong, the good and the bad – all of which transcend the merely legal. For instance, reasonable arguments can be made to justify the equal treatment of men and women under Islamic inheritance rules. Those arguments can be, and are, based on historical changes in the economic reality of men and women, and the increasing need for families to have multiple wage earners to ensure adequate financial well-being. But to make a modification to that particular legal rule has implications not only on estate distribution upon death, but on the social and cultural imagination of the nature of the workplace and the well-being of the family. Indeed, any modification to a specific legal rule may bring with it considerable socio-cultural concerns that exist outside the province of the law, but are no less relevant to consider.

As such, we cannot exclude the importance of harnessing extra-legal factors in the pursuit of gender equality in Islamic law. The role of social movements is particularly crucial in affecting the way in which judges and jurists engage in the ongoing enterprise of legal interpretation.[52] For instance, Professor Riva Siegel of Yale Law School has written about the Equal Rights Amendment in the United States, which sought to ensure gender equality as a constitutional principle. That amendment was never formally passed, pursuant to the procedures outlined in Article V of the US Constitution. But, as Siegel shows, the failure to amend the Constitution does not mean the social movement failed to change US constitutional law concerning gender equality. Rather, she adopts a different view of legal development, which recognises that judges interpret the Constitution 'in the midst of a popular debate about the Constitution'.[53] She further elaborates:

> Americans on both sides of the courthouse door are making claims about the Constitution. Outside the courthouse, the Constitution's text plays a significant role in eliciting and focusing normative disputes among Americans about women's rights under the Constitution – a dynamic that serves to communicate these newly crystallizing understandings and expectations about women's rights to judges interpreting the Constitution inside the courthouse door. Such communication occurs whether or not the activities in question satisfy Article V … for constitutional lawmaking.[54]

For Siegel, the meaning of the Constitution can change as long our appreciation of judicial interpretation recognises the agency of the jurist who interprets the law in light of ongoing contests about its meaning. Consequently, whether or not social mobilisations lead to formal legal change, such movements affect the climate within which judges appreciate the nature of the legal conflict before them. In a context of social movements around legal change, participants make claims about the law's meaning. 'Sometimes such mobilisations result in constitutional amendments; most often they do not. But even when no formal act of law making occurs, constitutional contestation nonetheless plays an important role in transforming understandings about the Constitution's meaning inside and outside the courts.'[55] Importantly, Siegel is writing about the judicial process, and not the legislative one. Her theory of legal change assumes a constitutional legal order, and a sufficiently democratic political order that permits expressions of dissent openly and publicly.

Those politico-legal characteristics do not necessarily obtain in the Muslim world. Nonetheless, her thesis about social movements is important, if only to illustrate the scope of intervention required for effective legal reform.

If we accept the relationship between social movements and legal change, then we cannot ignore the effect of gender-equality social movements on the possibility of legal change in the Muslim world. For instance, Amina Wadud writes about waging a gender jihad, and offers numerous stories from 'the trenches'.[56] More often than not, the stories show that the effort to make changes on the ground have led to limited, if any, success in legislative reform or changes to mosque culture around the world. Nonetheless, her personal dedication to the cause of gender equality has resulted in considerable public engagement with the status and role of women in Islam generally, and the Muslim world specifically. Sisters in Islam, a Malaysian civil society organisation committed to gender equality, has been at the forefront of challenging the patriarchal tradition still affecting Muslim women in Malaysia. While Sisters in Islam has made serious gains in the domestic Malaysian sphere, those gains have not come without cost. In 2005, Sisters in Islam published the book *Muslim Women and the Challenges of Islamic Extremism*, edited by Norani Othman, a professor at the National University of Malaysia. In July 2008, Malaysia's Ministry of Home Affairs banned the book, claiming that it undermined public order. Sisters in Islam petitioned a court for judicial review of the ministerial order, and the presiding judge reversed the ban.[57] The ban illustrates the challenges facing social movements that operate within a political climate that is less than open. In fact, the ban is a reminder that the effectiveness of social movements (and thereby the possibility of legal reform) is directly connected to the openness of a society. Nonetheless, the success in overturning the ban illustrates the power of social movements to change the discursive context in societies that may not be as open as most would prefer. The Malaysian example shows that, in less than fully open societies, social movements have the potential to expand the scope of legal arguments that are intelligible, meaningful and possible.

8. Conclusion

The beginning of this chapter paid tribute to the many voices that have come before to advocate for gender equality in Islamic family law. Those voices, while differing from each other in method, approach and aim, nonetheless speak in unison about the need to reflect on the ongoing existence of gender discrimination in the Muslim world. For some, that reflection requires an analysis of pre-modern source-texts and their authenticity. For others, it requires unpacking the Qur'anic and legal discourses of the patriarchal attitudes that have, for so long, animated them. And yet others would suggest that there is no chance of reforming Islamic law, and that, instead, recourse must be made to a tradition of human rights, whose content is informed by contemporary treaties, such as CEDAW. All of these approaches have their merits, and all can be criticised; but, in the aggregate, they constitute the voices of a social movement advocating for change. In some cases that change will come by reference to human rights standards. In others, it will come by reference to new, authoritative interpretations of source-texts within the Islamic legal tradition. And yet other cases will require a blending of international law, domestic constitutional law and aspects of Islamic law. This fusion will create a legal outcome which reflects the legal pluralism that has become so characteristic of the modern state in an increasingly globalised world.

The strategies may differ, and the outcomes will be inspired by different animating impulses, but in all cases the effectiveness of any particular strategy requires acknowledgement that the paradox of equality operates in the background and may limit the effectiveness of those advocating for gender equality in the Muslim world. Attentiveness to the paradox of equality will beg important questions about what factual differences are legally relevant and why. The paradox of equality reminds us that, while differently situated people should be treated differently to satisfy the demands of justice, what constitutes a legally relevant factual difference is often a naturalised construct that is waiting to be denaturalised and deconstructed. But, as gender activists around the world already know, the threat of such deconstruction has the potential to create considerable instability, whether politically, socially, culturally or legally. This does not mean that gender equality is not possible in the Muslim world. Rather, it suggests that we do not exist in a vacuum or make normative claims from a position *ex nihilo*. Our claims about and for justice are necessarily embedded in a set of predispositions from which it is difficult to escape. These predispositions influence how we decide which factual differences are appropriate for legal differentiation, and which are not. To view the idea of equality from the perspective of the paradox of equality helps to illuminate the scale and scope of any intervention that seeks to undo and reverse a legal differentiation, on the grounds that it is discriminatory.

Notes

1 The author wishes to thank Zainah Anwar, Lynn Welchman and the editors for their encouragement and support of this research. My colleague, Sophia Reibetanz-Moreau, was generous with advice and insight on contemporary philosophical debates on equality. Special thanks go to my friend and colleague, Robert Gibbs (University of Toronto) for our engaging debate and discussion on Aristotle's *Nichomachean Ethics*. Although he may not realise it, Akhil Amar of Yale Law School deserves special thanks for introducing me to the diversity of scholarship on constitutional interpretation in the United States. Rumee Ahmed and Ayesha Chaudhry read an earlier draft of this chapter and helped make it

better. My very able research assistant, Kate Southwell, provided helpful copy-editing and improved the readability of the chapter. Lastly, I thank the Oslo Coalition for its hospitality in early January 2010 in Cairo, Egypt, where I had an opportunity to share some of the ideas that are presented herein at a workshop featuring other authors in this volume.

2 Examples of such works include: Wadud, Amina, *Qur'ān and Woman: Rereading the Sacred Text from a Woman's Perspective* (Oxford: Oxford University Press, 1999); Mernissi, Fatima, *The Veil and the Male Elite: A Feminist Interpretation of Women's Rights in Islam* (Reading, MA: Addison-Wesley, 1991); Ahmed, Leila, *Women and Gender in Islam: Historical Roots of a Modern Debate* (New Haven: Yale University Press 1993); Mir-Hosseini, Ziba, *Islam and Gender* (Princeton: Princeton University Press, 1999). For a journal devoted to such issues, see *Hawwa: Journal of Women of the Middle East and the Islamic World* (Brill).

3 Joan W. Scott has made similar remarks about equality. See Scott, Joan W., 'The conundrum of equality', *Institute for Advanced Studies, Occasional Paper Series* (March 1999), available at http://www.sss.ias.edu/files/papers/papertwo.pdf (accessed 13 September 2012).

4 While examples in lieu of the loo might be less crude, the example of the bathroom offers an important arena for exploring fundamental concerns about equality. See, for instance, Molotch, Harvey, 'The rest room and equal opportunity', *Sociological Forum* 3/1 (1988), pp. 128–32.

5 Scott, 'The conundrum of equality', p. 5.

6 For more extensive analysis of Jim Crow and racial discrimination, see Wynes, Charles E., 'The evolution of Jim Crow laws in twentieth century Virginia', *Phylon* 24/4 (1967), pp. 416–25; Weyeneth, Robert R., 'The architecture of racial segregation: the challenges of preserving the problematical past', *The Public Historian* 27/4 (Autumn2005), pp. 11–44; Abel, Elizabeth, 'Bathroom doors and drinking fountains: Jim Crow's racial symbolic', *Critical Inquiry* 25/3 (Spring 1999), pp. 435–81.

7 Stockett, Kathryn, *The Help: A Novel* (New York: Penguin, 2009).

8 The banality of this example is also rendered complicated when considering how the neat dichotomy between male and female bathrooms does not account for the transgendered, or those in varying phases of gender-reassignment.

9 *McHale* v *Watson* (1966), 115 CLR 199 (Aust. HC); see also Moran, Mayo, *Rethinking the Reasonable Person* (Oxford: Oxford University Press, 2003) for a discussion of this case and others addressing the reasonable person standard of care.

10 Mernissi, *The Veil and the Male Elite*, p. ix.

11 Barlas, Asma, *'Believing Women' in Islam: Unreading Patriarchal Interpretations of the Qur'ān (Austin: University of Texas Press, 2002)*, p. xi.

12 Esack, Farid, *On Being a Muslim: Finding a Religious Path in the World Today* (1999; repr, Oxford: Oneworld, 2002), pp. 111–36.

13 Mernissi, *The Veil and the Male Elite*, p. 22.
14 Esack, *On Being a Muslim*, p. 114.
15 *Ibid.*, p. 115.
16 *Ibid.*
17 See, for example, Mernissi, *The Veil and the Male Elite*, pp. 2, 23.
18 Barlas, *'Believing Women' in Islam*, p. 5.
19 *Ibid.*, p. 5.
20 Aristotle, *Nichomachean Ethics*, trans. Harris Rackham (Hertfordshire: Wordsworth, 1996), p. 118.
21 Al-Farabi, Abu Nasr, *Fuṣūl Muntaẓa'a*, ed. Fawzi Najjar (Beirut: Dar al-Mashraq, 1971), p. 71.
22 Miskawayh, Ahmad b. Muhammad, *The Refinement of Character*, trans. Constantine K. Zurayk (Beirut: American University of Beirut, 1968), pp. 100–1. For the original Arabic, see Miskawayh, *Tahdhīb al-Akhlāq wa Taṭhīr al-A'rāq*, ed. Ibn al-Khaṭīb (n.p.: Maktabat al-Thaqafa al-Diniyya, n.d.), p. 123.
23 Miskawayh, *Refinement*, p. 101; Miskawayh, *Tahdhīb al-Akhlāq*, p. 124.
24 Miskawayh, *Refinement*, p. 101; Miskawayh, *Tahdhīb al-Akhlāq*, p. 123.
25 See also, Mohsen Kadivar's contribution to this volume and his discussion of 'deserts-based' justice, which speaks of the same ideas about factual difference and legal differentiation.
26 Aristotle, *Nichomachean Ethics*, p. 118 (emphasis added).
27 Miskawayh, *Refinement*, p. 103; Miskawayh, *Tahdhīb al-Akhlāq*, p. 127.
28 For an introduction to this debate, see Emon, Anver M., *Islamic Natural Law Theories* (Oxford: Oxford University Press, 2010); *idem*, 'Natural law and natural rights in Islamic law', *Journal of Law and Religion* 20/2 (2004–5), pp. 351–95.
29 Al-Juwayni, *Al-Burhān fī Uṣūl al-Fiqh* (Beirut: Dar al-Kutub al-'Ilmiyya, 1997), Vol. 1, p. 10.
30 *Ibid.*
31 *Ibid.*
32 *Ibid.*
33 *Ibid.* (*lam yamtani' ijrā' hādhayn al-waṣfayn fīnā idhā tanajjaza ḍarrarun aw amkana naf'un bi sharṭ an lā yu'zā ilā Allāh wa lā yūjibu 'alayhi an yu'āqibu aw yuthābu*). As such, a ruler can make laws in areas not addressed by God. But he cannot claim they have the authority of Shari'a, as if they reflect the divine will.
34 Emon, Anver M., '*To most likely know the law:* objectivity, authority and interpretation in Islamic law', *Hebraic Political Studies* 4/4 (2009), pp. 415–40.
35 The link between authority and epistemic limitations lies at the heart of much scholarship on the licence to interpret and the authority of the interpretive product. See, for example, Abou El Fadl, Khaled, *Speaking in God's Name: Authority, Islamic Law, and Women* (Oxford: Oneworld Publications, 2001).

36 Al-Baqillani, Abu Bakr Muhammad b. al-Tayyib, *al-Taqrīb wa al-Irshād al-Ṣaghīr*, ed. 'Abd al-Hamid b. 'Ali Zunayd (Beirut: Mu'assasat al-Risala, 1998), Vol. 1, p. 284.

37 Al-Baqillani, *Al-Taqrīb wa al-Irshād*, Vol. 1, p. 284.

38 For competing views on the Pact's historical authenticity, see Tritton, A. S., *The Caliphs and their Non-Muslim Subjects: A Critical Study of the Covenant of 'Umar* (London: Frank Cass and Co., 1970); Dennett, Daniel C., *Conversion and the Poll Tax in Early Islam* (Cambridge, MA: Harvard University Press, 1950), pp. 63–4.

39 Hodgson, Marshall, *The Venture of Islam*, Vol 2: *The Expansion of Islam in the Middle Periods* (Chicago: Chicago University Press, 1974), p. 3.

40 *Ibid.*, p. 3.

41 For an introduction to the field of gender and Islamic law, see Tucker, Judith, *Women, Family and Gender in Islamic Law* (Cambridge: Cambridge University Press, 2008). For an outline of contemporary family law regimes in Muslim states, see An-Na'im, Abdullahi Ahmed, *Islamic Family Law in a Changing World: A Global Resource Book* (London: Zed Books, 2002). For critical analyses of Islamic legal doctrines concerning women and gender, see Abou El Fadl, *Speaking in God's Name*; Mir-Hosseini, Ziba, *Islam and Gender: The Religious Debate in Contemporary Iran* (London: I.B.Tauris, 2000); Welchman, Lynn, *Women and Muslim Family Laws in Arab States: A Comparative Overview of Textual Development and Advocacy* (Amsterdam: Amsterdam University Press, 2007); Sonbol, Amira El-Azhary, *Women, the Family, and Divorce Laws in Islamic History* (Syracuse: Syracuse University Press, 1996).

42 Muttahari, Murtaza, 'The human status of woman in the Qur'ān', in Roxanne L. Euben and Muhammad Qasim Zaman (eds), *Princeton Readings in Islamist Thought: Texts and Contexts from al-Banna to Bin Laden* (Princeton: Princeton University Press, 2009), p. 254.

43 Muttahari, 'The human status of woman', p. 261.

44 Qur'an, 4:11.

45 See, for instance, al-Qurtubi, Abu 'Abd Allah Muhammad, *Al-Jāmi' li Aḥkām al-Qur'ān* (Beirut: Dar al-Kutub al-'Ilmiyya, 1993), Vol. 5, pp. 39–40.

46 Esposito, John L. and Natana J. Delong-Bas, *Women in Muslim Family Law* (2nd edn, Syracuse: Syracuse University Press, 2001), p. 46.

47 Indeed, Anghie, Antony, *Imperialism, Sovereignty and the Making of International Law* (Cambridge: Cambridge University Press, 2004), argues that international law continues to perpetuate the dynamic of colonialism and asymmetries of power between the global North and South.

48 McClintock, Ann, 'Family feuds: gender, nationalism and the family', *Feminist Review* 44 (1993), pp. 61–80 at p. 62.

49 See the works of Amina Wadud, Asma Barlas and Fatima Mernissi, all of which are cited in this chapter.

50 See, for instance, Abou El Fadl, *Speaking in God's Name*.

51 See, for instance, Ali, Kecia, *Sexual Ethics in Islam: Feminist Reflections on Qur'ān, Hadith and Jurisprudence* (Oxford: Oneworld Publications, 2006).

52 For a recent contribution to the study of women's social movements and the significance of hybridity, see Goss, Kristin A. and Michael T. Heaney, 'Organizing women *as women*: hybridity and grassroots collective action in the 21st century', *Perspectives on Politics* 8/1 (March 2010), pp. 27–52.

53 Siegel, Riva B., 'Text in contest: gender and the constitution from a social movement perspective', *University of Pennsylvania Law Review* 150 (2001), pp. 297–351 at p. 314.

54 *Ibid.*, p. 314.

55 Siegel, 'Text in contest', p. 303.

56 Wadud, Amina, *Inside the Gender Jihad: Women's Reform in Islam* (Oxford: Oneworld Publications, 2006).

57 Gooch, Liz, 'Ban on book is overturned by court in Malaysia; government had said the publication might confuse Muslim women', *International Herald Tribune*, 26 January 2010, p. 3.

ABOUT THE CONTRIBUTORS

Faqihuddin Abdul Kodir is founder of the Fahmina Foundation, an Indonesian NGO working on gender and democracy for Muslim communities. He is lecturer on the hadiths of legal injunctions (*aḥkām*) in the State Institute for Islamic Studies (IAIN) Syekh Nurjati and the Fahmina Institute for Islamic Studies (ISIF) Cirebon-Indonesia, and a student of the PhD programme in the Indonesian Consortium for Religious Studies (ICRS) at Gajah Mada University in Yogyakarta. He is the author of *Hadith and Gender Justice: Understanding the Prophetic Traditions* (2007).

Nasr Hamid Abu-Zayd (1943–2010) was a leading scholar and intellectual engaging with the hermeneutics of the Qur'an from a liberal Islamic perspective informed by the modern humanities. After obtaining his PhD in Arabic and Islamic Studies in 1981, he joined the Department of Arabic at Cairo University, and spent 1985–89 as a visiting professor at Osaka University. His writings provoked religious controversy over his elevation to full professor. In 1995, the Cairo Appeals Court declared him an apostate and dissolved his marriage. Abu-Zayd and his wife went into exile in Europe, their lives at risk from radicals. After 1995, Abu-Zayd taught as a professor of Islamic studies at Leiden University, served as the Ibn Rushd Chair at the University for Humanistics in Utrecht, and held a fellowship at the Wissenschaftskolleg in Berlin. His voluminous publications include three books in English, *Voice of an Exile: Reflections on Islam* (with Esther R. Nelson, 2004), *Rethinking the Qur'an: Towards a Humanistic Hermeneutics* (2004), and *Reformation of Islamic Thought: A Critical Historical Analysis* (2006).

Zainah Anwar is a founding member of Sisters in Islam (SIS) and is currently the Director of Musawah, the global movement for equality and justice in the Muslim family. She is at the forefront of the women's movement pushing for an end to the use of Islam to justify discrimination against women. The pioneering work of SIS in understanding Islam from a rights perspective and creating an alternative public voice of Muslim women demanding equality and justice led it to initiate Musawah in 2009. This movement brings together activists and scholars to create new feminist knowledge in Islam to overcome the tension between Islam and human rights and the disconnect between law and reality. Anwar also writes a monthly newspaper column on politics, religion and women's rights, called *Sharing the Nation*. She is a former member of the Human Rights Commission of Malaysia. Her book *Islamic Revivalism in Malaysia: Dakwah among the Students* has become a standard reference in the study of Islam in Malaysia.

Aïcha El Hajjami holds a doctorate in Public Law (*doctorat de troisième cycle*) from the Paris II Faculty of Law. She has taught at the Public Law departments of the Law faculties of Fès and Marrakech (1978–2005), and is the author of numerous studies in the field of women's political and legal rights. She is a founding member of the Centre d'Etudes et de Recherche sur la Femme et la Famille at the Faculty of Law in Marrakech, and a consultant to various national and international bodies.

Anver M. Emon is Professor and Canada Research Chair in Religion, Pluralism, and the Rule of Law at the University of Toronto Faculty of Law. Emon's research focuses on premodern and modern Islamic legal history and theory; premodern modes of governance and adjudication; and the role of Shari'a both inside and outside the Muslim world today. The author of *Islamic Natural Law Theories* (2010) and *Religious Pluralism and Islamic Law: Dhimmis and Others in the Empire of Law* (2012), Professor Emon is the founding editor of *Middle East Law and Governance: An Interdisciplinary Journal*, and is the series editor of the *Oxford Islamic Legal Studies Series*.

Hasan Yousefi Eshkevari is one of the leading religious reform thinkers of Iran and was trained as a cleric in the Qom seminaries. He was elected to the first parliament after the 1979 Revolution, where he aligned himself with the liberal forces. Becoming disillusioned with the direction that Islamic Republic was taking, he left politics to devote himself to academic research and writing. He established the Ali Shariati Research Centre, and was contributing editor of the now-banned newspaper *Iran-e Farda*. In 1997, with the election of President Khatami, he became a regular contributor to reformist media, and a key figure in the reform movement. In 2000, the Special Court for Clergy condemned him to death for 'apostasy' and 'war against Islam' for his liberal views on women and his critique of theocracy; the sentence was later commuted to five years' imprisonment. He was released in 2005, and since 2008 he has lived in exile. Eshkevari was editor of the Iran-based *Shi'a Encyclopedia* and an acclaimed contributor to the *Great Encyclopedia of Islam*; he has published 15 books and over 100 articles in Persian academic journals and periodicals. Some of his writings have been translated into English in Mir-Hosseini and Tapper (eds), *Islam and Democracy in Iran: Eshkevari and the Quest for Reform* (2006).

Mohsen Kadivar is a philosopher and a research professor of Islamic Studies in the department of religious studies at Duke University. He has been a visiting professor at Harvard Law School (2002), University of Virginia (2008–2009), Duke University (2009–2015), and Keohane Distinguished Visiting Professor at UNC and Duke (fall 2014). Kadivar studied at the Islamic Seminary at Qom, finishing with a certificate of *Ijtihad*, and earned a PhD in Islamic Philosophy and theology from Tarbiate Modarress University in Tehran. He taught for three decades in Iran. Specializing in classical Islam and contemporary Islamic thought, his main intellectual interests and topics of publications include: classical Islamic philosophy, classical and modern Shiʿi theology and legal theories, and human rights and democracy in Islam. Kadivar has published 23 books in Persian and Arabic, and several articles in English. Two of his books are forthcoming in English translation, *Human Rights in Islam* (in the UK, from the Institute for the Study of Muslim Civilisations) and *Apostasy, Blasphemy, & Religious Freedom in Islam*: *A Critique Based on Demonstrative Jurisprudence* (in the US). His book *Islamic Theocracy in a Secular Age: Revisiting Shiʿite Political Theology & Ideology of Islamic Republic of Iran* is forthcoming from UNC Press.

Lena Larsen is the director of the Oslo Coalition on Freedom of Religion or Belief at the Norwegian Centre for Human Rights, University of Oslo (since 1999). She obtained her PhD with the dissertation *Fiqh Facing Everyday Challenges: Fatwas as Solutions for Muslim Women in Western Europe* (2011). She has co-chaired the Oslo Coalition project New Directions in Islamic Thought since 2003, and is co-editor of *New Directions in Islamic Thought and Practice: Exploring Muslim Reform and Tradition* (2009, with Kari Vogt and Christian Moe). She is Assistant Editor of *Facilitating Freedom of Religion or Belief: A Deskbook* (2004), and contributed a chapter on economy and gender roles in marriage to Mir-Hosseini et al. (eds.), *Men in Charge? Rethinking Authority in Muslim Legal Tradition* (2015). She is a member of the advisory committee at the Faculty of Theology, University of Oslo, for a continuing education program for religious leaders with a foreign background. She was awarded a Science and Arts Medal by Egypt in 2008.

Muhammad Khalid Masud (PhD, McGill University, 1973) is Judge of the Shariat Appellate Bench, Supreme Court of Pakistan. Formerly Director General, Islamic Research Institute, International Islamic University, Islamabad, Chairman of the Council of Islamic Ideology, Islamabad, and Professor and Academic Director of the International Institute for the Study of Islam in the Modern World (ISIM), Leiden, the Netherlands, he has published extensively on Islamic law, contemporary issues and trends in Muslim societies. His publications include *Shatibi's Philosophy of Islamic Law* (1995), *Iqbal's Reconstruction of Ijtihad* (1995), *Shari'a Today: Essays on Contemporary Issues and Debates in Muslim Societies* (2013) and *Ummat Muslima dahshatgardi ke gradab men* (Narrative, 2015). He has edited *Travelers in Faith: Studies on Tablighi Jama'at* (2000) and *Atharhwin sadi men Islami fikr ke rahnuma* (2008); translated into Urdu T. Izutsu's *Ethical Terms in the Qur'an* as *Mafahim-i Qur'an* (2005) and Rabindra Nath Tagore's *Fire Flies* as *Nuqush Tagore* (2012); and co-edited *Islamic Legal Interpretations: Muftis and their Fatwas* with Brinkley Messick and David Powers (1996), *Dispensing Justice in Islam: Qadis and their Judgments* with David S. Powers and Ruud Peters (2006), and *Islam and Modernity, An Introduction to Key Issues and Debates*, with Armando Salvatore and Martin van Bruinessen (2009).

Ziba Mir-Hosseini (www.zibamirhosseini.com) is a legal anthropologist, specializing in Islamic law and gender, and a founding member of the Musawah Global Movement for Equality and Justice in the Muslim Family (www.musawah.org). She is the 2015 recipient of the American Academy of Religion's Martin E. Marty Award for the Public Understanding of Religion. Currently Professorial Research Associate at the Centre for Islamic and Middle Eastern Law, University of London, she has held numerous research fellowships and visiting professorships. She has published books on Islamic family law in Iran and Morocco, Iranian clerical discourses on gender, Islamic reformist thinkers, and the revival of *zina* laws. She has also co-directed two award-winning feature-length documentary films on Iran: *Divorce Iranian Style* (1998) and *Runaway* (2001). Her latest book is *Men in charge? Rethinking Authority in Muslim Legal Tradition*, edited with Mulki Al-Sharmani and Jana Rumminger (2015).

Christian Moe is an independent writer and researcher based in Slovenia. He has written on Islam, human rights, and religious affairs in the Balkans.

Marwa Sharafeldin holds a PhD from Oxford University's Centre for Socio-Legal Studies in the Law Faculty, on *Personal Status Law Reform in Egypt: Women's Rights NGOs Navigating Between Islamic Law and Human Rights*. She is a scholar-activist based in Egypt, working on women's rights. Her research lies in the intersection between Islamic law, international human rights law and feminist civil society activism in the Muslim world. Her publications include "Islamic Law Meets Human Rights: Reformulating *Qiwama* and *Wilaya* for Personal Status Law Reform Advocacy in Egypt", in Mir-Hosseini et al., *Men in Charge? Rethinking Authority in Muslim Legal Tradition* (2015); "Gender and Equality in Muslim Family

Law" (UNDESA, 2015); and "Challenges of Islamic Feminism in Personal Status Law Reform: Women's NGOs in Egypt between Islamic Law and International Human Rights Law", in Abou-Bakr (ed.), *Feminist and Islamic Perspectives: New Horizons of Knowledge and Reform* (2013). Sharafeldin is also the co-founder of several women's rights NGOs and networks in Egypt and the Arab world. She has been a Board Member in the Musawah global Movement for Equality and Justice in the Muslim Family, as well as an Advisor for several international women's rights organizations. She is a member of the UN Women's Expert Advisory Group for the Progress of the World's Women Report on the Family.

Mulki Al-Sharmani is a Docent and Academy of Finland research fellow, Faculty of Theology, University of Helsinki. She holds a doctorate degree in cultural anthropology from the Johns Hopkins University, Baltimore, USA. She is the editor of *Feminist Activism, Women's Rights and Legal Reform* (2013), and the co-editor (with Ziba Mir-Hosseini and Jana Rumminger) of *Men in Charge? Rethinking Authority in Muslim Legal Tradition* (2015).

Kari Vogt is Associate Professor (Emerita) at the Department of Cultural Studies and Oriental Languages at the University of Oslo, Norway. She has published widely on Islamic and Middle East issues.

INDEX

The order follows the English alphabet. A selection of Qur'anic verses and hadith are included.

maqāṣid 62, 66, 68, 93, 105 n.58, 132, 141–2, 146, 156, 159, 171, 207
as approach to reform 2–3, 26, 70–1, 99, 160, 164
equality and justice as 63, 164
Ma'qil Ibn Yasar 89–90
Ma'refat, Mohammad Hadi 207
ma'rifat-e dini 25
see also knowledge
marji'iyāt
see reference frames
marriage 23, 58, 143, 156
annulling 87
assets acquired in 84, 97–100, 104 n.58
based on free choice 16
as based on love and mercy 13, 16, 52, 183, 185, 216
classical law of 10
discord in 17, 43, 79 n.39, 95
economic roles in 39, 43, 48, 51, 67
fiqh conceptions of 8, 11, 29 n.15, 38, 48, 153
forced 88, 103 n.26, 128, 130
informal 105 n.65
in legal models and real life 48, 51
mutual consultation in 183
as ownership of vagina (*buḍ'*) 137, 153, 205
as partnership or shared responsibility 16, 71, 84–5, 116–7, 184
patriarchal model of 37, 49
in the Qur'an 52
rights and duties in 10, 199
as transaction 91, 139, 204–5
in tribal system 129
by the woman's consent 86–8, 183
women contracting 89–91, 103 n.26, 133, 135, 138, 140
marriage age 11, 82, 84–5, 100, 102 n.20, 102 n.22, 144
see also child marriage
marriage contract 10, 153
civil or sacred 139
stipulations in 40, 91
see also nikāḥ
marriage guardian
see walī
marriage guardianship
see wilāya
ma'rūf 90, 137, 156, 195–6, 201–2, 209 n.8, 210 n.9
Mary (Maryam) 228
al-masā'il al-khilāfiyya 83
masā'il mustaḥdatha 1
maṣlaḥa 93, 142, 157, 159–60, 166 n.7, 217
of the girl 85
three zones of 142–4, 146
maṣlaḥa mursala 142
Masud, Muhammad Khalid 123 n.16
maternity 238
matn 173–4, 176, 185, 189 n.52
matrimonial house 39–44, 51, 54 n.19, 55
El Mawahibi, Mohammed El Habti 83, 101 n.10
Mdaghri, AbdelKabir Alaoui Mdaghri 83, 102 n.14
mediation 40
Medina 206
menstruation 11, 87, 192, 209 n.1
Mernissi, Fatima 25, 33 n.50, 240–1
methodology 251
of Islamic sciences 63, 71, 173, 231
of reform 3, 9, 57, 109, 127
minorities 115, 118
minors 130, 133
Mir-Hosseini, Ziba 123 n.16
Miskawayh (d. 1030) 243–4
modernism 21, 24, 127
Fazlur Rahman on 33 n.47
modernity 82, 99, 109, 127
Mohammed V (1909–1961) 81
Mohammed VI (b. 1963) 83
monogamy clause 91
Montazeri (Najafabadi), Hossein 'Ali (d. 2009) 221, 233 n.15
Morocco 2–3, 81–100, 116–7
court practice in 48
king of
see Hassan II, Mohammed V, Mohammed VI
political opening in 82
women's groups 31 n.26
Motahhari, Morteza (d. 1979) 199, 210 n.12, 221, 249
mubāḥ 93, 167 n.15, 199